INDIVIDUAL DIFFERENCES IN CONSCIOUS EXPERIENCE

ADVANCES IN CONSCIOUSNESS RESEARCH

ADVANCES IN CONSCIOUSNESS RESEARCH provides a forum for scholars from different scientific disciplines and fields of knowledge who study consciousness in its multifaceted aspects. Thus the Series will include (but not be limited to) the various areas of cognitive science, including cognitive psychology, linguistics, brain science and philosophy. The orientation of the Series is toward developing new interdisciplinary and integrative approaches for the investigation, description and theory of consciousness, as well as the practical consequences of this research for the individual and society.

Series B: Research in Progress. Experimental, descriptive and clinical research in consciousness.

Volume 20

Robert G. Kunzendorf and Benjamin Wallace

Individual Differences in Conscious Experience

INDIVIDUAL DIFFERENCES IN CONSCIOUS EXPERIENCE

Edited by

ROBERT G. KUNZENDORF
University of Massachusetts at Lowell

BENJAMIN WALLACE
Cleveland State University

JOHN BENJAMINS PUBLISHING COMPANY
AMSTERDAM/PHILADELPHIA

The paper used in this publication meets the minimum requirements of American National Standard for Information Sciences — Permanence of Paper for Printed Library Materials, ANSI Z39.48–1984.

Library of Congress Cataloging-in-Publication Data

Individual differences in conscious experience / edited by Robert G. Kunzendorf, Benjamin Wallace.

p. cm. -- (Advances in consciousness research, ISSN 1381-589X ; v. 20)

Includes bibliographical references and indexes.

1. Consciousness. 2. Subconsciousness. 3. Altered states of consciousness. I. Kunzendorf, Robert G. II. Wallace, Benjamin. III. Series.

BF311.I48 1999

155.2'2--dc21 99-41414

ISBN 90 272 5140 1 (Eur.) / 1 55619 436 6 (US) (Pb; alk. paper) CIP

John Benjamins Publishing Co. • P.O.Box 75577 • 1070 AN Amsterdam • The Netherlands

John Benjamins North America • P.O.Box 27519 • Philadelphia PA 19118-0519 • USA

Dedicated to our in-laws:
To Zelma and Martin Ritvo,
To Sylvia Cohen,
and
In memory of Homer Cohen

Table of Contents

Preface

As editors, we are grateful to the John Benjamins Publishing Company and its *Advances in Consciousness Research* series editor, Max Stamenov, for encouraging us to put together this book on the problematic but important topic of individual differences in conscious experience. Historically, nomothetic approaches to the study of mind have been adopted by most theoreticians and researchers, and problematic individual differences in consciousness, subconsciousness, and self-consciousness have been ignored or dismissed. In the first chapter of this book, Robert Kunzendorf and Benjamin Wallace analyze historic examples of some of these individual differences that have been prematurely dismissed — examples from experimental, physiological, and clinical psychology. Kunzendorf and Wallace conclude that theories embodying the constraints of individual differences in subjective experience should be given greater credence than approaches ignoring those constraints. From the historical analyses and conclusions in this first chapter emerges a framework for appreciating the many individual differences discussed in this book and their constraints on future theorizing.

The remainder of the book is divided into three parts. The chapters in Part I focus on individual differences in *consciousness*, by which we mean *conscious qualia* or *conscious sensations*. The chapters in Part II deal with differences in *subconsciousness*, and those in Part III deal with differences in *self-consciousness*.

Individual Differences in Consciousness

Chapters 2 and 3 deal with a crucial phenomenon in consciousness research — pain — from the perspective of individual differences. In Chapter 2, Richard Chapman, Yoshio Nakamura, and Leticia Flores take issue with the classic Cartesian model for understanding and treating pain, and develop an alternative model that defines pain as a conscious construction integrating the individual's "past experience, present expectations and...emotional status...with the immediate sensory signaling of tissue trauma". In Chapter 3, Joel Katz extends the study of pain to another crucial phenomenon — the phantom limb — and notes how individual differences in phantom-limb pain can be attributed to both peripheral and central factors.

Whereas interest in painful sensations derives from their causal effects on evolution, development, and behavior, interest in visual, auditory, and gustatory sensations derives from their lack of causal efficacy and the consequent arbitrariness of their subjective qualities.[1] Individual differences in gustatory sensations or "tastes", the very name of which connotes this arbitrariness, are addressed in Chapter 4 by Richard Mattes and Gary Beauchamp.

Two chapters on visual sensations — in particular, "centrally excited sensations" (Külpe 1983/1895, p. 169) or visual images — follow. Chapter 5 by Alan Richardson is a review of individual differences in the phenomenology of imaginative visual sensations and the conditions of their occurrence. In demonstrating that both the phenomenological and the physiological effects of imaging are more pronounced in young children, Kunzendorf (1989) and Kunzendorf, Justice, and Capone (1997) have suggested that individual differences in visual imagery are largely developmental differences. Chapter 6 by Leonard Giambra confirms that various phenomenal features of imagery — its vividness, its frequency of occurrence, etc. — continue to decline across the adult lifespan.

Individual Differences in Subconsciousness

Moving beyond individual differences in consciousness, the book continues with chapters emphasizing individual differences in subconsciousness. Initiating this change in emphasis, Chapter 7 by Gary Schwartz shows that subconscious olfactory phenomena are actually conscious sensations which are unaccompanied by any awareness or self-consciousness. Then, in the succeeding chapter, Arthur Reber and Rhianon Allen argue that implicit learning and other subconscious operations, because they constitute the evolutionary foundation for later self-conscious processes, should exhibit fewer individual differences than self-conscious processes.

Individual Differences in Self-Consciousness

The next two chapters call attention to individual differences in dreams, and take issue with the nomothetic tendency to equate dreaming with subconsciousness and wakefulness with self-consciousness. Chapter 9 by Ernest Hartmann demonstrates that the wakeful daydreams of certain individuals — those with "thin boundaries" between sleep and wakefulness, cognition and emotion, etc. — are as bizarre and seemingly subconscious as the nocturnal dreams of individuals with "thick boundaries". Conversely, the subsequent chapter by Stephen LaBerge and Donald DeGracia shows that the nocturnal dreams of certain other individuals are sometimes accompanied by self-awareness or "lucidity."

The two ensuing chapters offer new perspectives on hypnosis, the classic example of an altered state of self-consciousness. In Chapter 11, Ronald Pekala and V. K. Kumar characterize hypnosis as a state in which the mind's subsystems become dissociated from each other and from self-consciousness, and hypnotizability as a trait in which the individual's subsystems are partially dissociated already and are susceptible to further dissociation. Thereafter, Chapter 12 by Benjamin Wallace and Leslie Fisher identifies hypnotic subconsciousness and self-conscious vigilance with the troughs and peaks of various biorhythms, and pinpoints individual differences in the timing of these rhythmic phases.

The final two chapters explore some of the clinical implications of individual differences in self-awareness. Focusing on mental images that define one's self-concept from a first-person perspective and one's personality from a third-person perspective, Chapter 13 by Jefferson Singer, Jerome L. Singer, and Carolyn Zittel shows how someone with a large discrepancy between conscious images of one's real self and conscious images of one's ideal self is likely to manifest a neurotic personality. Then, the concluding chapter by Robert Kunzendorf presents both a philosophical framework for understanding self-consciousness in non-Cartesian terms and an experimental paradigm for exploring individual differences in self-conscious phenomena. The theory and the paradigm are applied to the clinical phenomena of psychotic hallucinating, dissociative perceiving and forgetting, and phobic imaging.

The above chapters have been contributed by scholars who, collectively, have published more than 50 books and more than 1000 articles. As editors, we are grateful to the authors for these fine contributions, and we recommend them to all readers with philosophical, psychological, physiological, or clinical interests in subjective experience.

Robert Kunzendorf and Benjamin Wallace

Notes

1. In a footnote addressing this issue, Kunzendorf and Wallace's introductory chapter speculates that heat nociceptors and their painful sensations might have evolved into heat-at-a-distance (light) receptors and visual sensations, that pressure nociceptors and their painful sensations might have evolved into pressure-at-a-distance (sound) receptors and auditory sensations, and that intestinal nociceptors and their painful sensations might have evolved into poison-at-a-distance receptors and gustatory (then olfactory) sensations.

References

Külpe, O. 1895. *Outlines of Psychology* (E. Titchener, trans.). London: Sonnenschein. (Originally published 1893)

Kunzendorf, R. G. 1989. "Afterimages of eidetic images: A developmental study". *Journal of Mental Imagery* 13(1): 55–62.

Kunzendorf, R. G., Justice, M. and Capone, D. 1997. "Conscious images as 'centrally excited sensations': A developmental study of imaginal influences on the ERG". *Journal of Mental Imagery* 21(1/2): 155–166.

Individual Differences in Subjective Experience

First-Person Constraints on Theories of Consciousness, Subconsciousness, and Self-Consciousness

Robert G. Kunzendorf
University of Massachusetts Lowell

Benjamin Wallace
Cleveland State University

Students of consciousness frequently overlook individual differences in first-person data. But in doing so, they implicitly undercut theories that reflect the constraints imposed by such data. In this introductory chapter, we call attention to three historic examples of this unfortunate tendency. First, we examine the historic "imageless thought" debate, as it relates to Külpe's (1895) theory of individual differences in consciously-imaged sensation. Second, we discuss the Freudian theory of universal subconsciousness as it contrasts with Prince's (1910, 1921, 1925) notion of individual differences in subconscious dissociation. Third, we consider the "depressive realism" debate as it pertains to Becker's (1973) theory of individual differences in self-consciousness. We hope that, through these historical examples, both the necessity and the merit of taking individual differences into theoretical account will become apparent.

Külpe on Individual Differences in Consciousness

Too many histories of psychology would have us believe that Külpe's arguments for imageless thought are arguments against the theoretical importance of individual differences in conscious imagery. Let us consider, however, the arguments that Külpe (1895) actually made:

> Anatomical investigations show that the sensory centres [of the cortex] are very uniform in structure; whereas the peripheral sense organs present obvious differences, which are plainly of importance for the differences in the conscious processes which they mediate…The specific cortical areas with

> which the sensations of the various senses and the different motor impulses are correlated [are] not to be regarded as the inevitable substrate of a class of sensations or of a sensation quality, on the same plane with the peripheral organ, but only as a condition of its appearance which has acquired importance...There is, however, one recent discovery of which mention must be made, as it seems to throw light upon many points of difficulty in the theory of sensation, — the discovery of sensory nerve fibres with centrifugal conduction...sensory fibres, originating in the brain and ending in the sense-organ.[1] This fact helps to explain [why] 'centrally excited' sensations, — memorial images, as they have also been very inappropriately named — are at least in many instances correlated with a co-excitation of the peripheral organs. (pp. 84–85)

In essence, Külpe argued that memories and thoughts are uniformly "imageless" phenomena which parallel the cortical activities of structurally uniform neurons. In addition, he argued that imaged or "centrally excited" sensations paralleling unique retinal structures are constructed from the memories and thoughts of vivid imagers, but not from the memories and thoughts of imageless thinkers.

These historically disregarded arguments are potentially very important for three reasons. First, they explain why, in Külpe's times as in present times, individual differences in the subjective vividness of imagery tend not to be correlated with individual differences in cognition. Second, they explain where to look for the physiological underpinnings and the behavioral effects of consciously imaged sensations. Third, they explain away the conundrum of the "inverted spectrum", a conundrum which has led theorists to conclude that all conscious sensations are epiphenomena without any causal effects on behavior.

Külpe's (1895) notion regarding "imageless" thought and memory was, in part, a response to Galton's (1883) finding that many scientific thinkers do not have vivid imagery, as well as his own observation (p. 176) that some individuals with normal memory have no conscious imagery. Since Külpe's time, numerous studies have confirmed that individual differences in the subjective vividness of visual imagery are correlated neither with *spatial-thinking abilities* (Bethel-Fox, Lohman & Snow 1984; Durndell & Wetherick 1976; Katz 1983; Lorenz & Neisser 1985; Paivio 1971; Parrott 1986; A. Richardson 1977), *mental-rotation abilities* included (Ashton, McFarland, Walsh, & White 1978; Dean & Morris 1991; Divesta, Ingersoll, & Sunshine 1971; Hatakeyama 1984; Kosslyn, Brunn, Cave, & Wallach 1984; McKelvie & Rohrberg 1978), nor with *visual-memory abilities* (Bartlett 1921; Berger & Gaunitz 1977; Betts 1909; Chaguiboff & Denis 1981; Chara & Hamm 1989; Chara & Verplanck 1986; Cohen & Saslona 1990; Danaher & Thoresen 1972; Ernest & Paivio 1971; Fernald 1912; Hall, Talukder, & Esposito 1989; Heuer, Fischman, & Reisberg 1986; Hunter, Moore, &

Wildman 1982; Kosslyn & Alper 1977; McKelvie 1992; McKelvie & Demers 1979; Mou, Anderson, Vaughan, & Rouse 1989; Phillips 1978; Rehm 1973; Reisberg, Culver, Heuer, & Fischman 1986; Reisberg & Leak 1987; A. Richardson 1977; J. T. E. Richardson 1980; Rimm & Bottrell 1969; Sheehan & Neisser 1969; Thorndike 1907; Wagman & Stewart 1974; Walczyk 1995; Walczyk & Hall 1988).

Unfortunately, most contemporary psychologists have not even considered Külpe's explanation for the statistical independence of individual differences in subjective imagery and individual differences in objective remembering and thinking. Instead, most contemporary students of cognition have followed the lead of Kosslyn (1994 p. 3) and have redefined the image as an objectified "internal representation that is used in information processing, not [as] the experience itself."

Accordingly, when Kosslyn, Thompson, Kim, Rauch, and Alpert (1996) obtained individual differences in PET scans of the visual striate cortex during visual imaging, they correlated these cortical differences with geometrical judgment times (rather than subjective vividness ratings).[2] Perhaps, the resulting correlation tells us something about the cortical underpinnings of subjectively "imageless" geometrical thought but, certainly, it tells us nothing about the neural underpinnings of conscious imagery.

Unlike the correlational study by Kosslyn et al., however, two studies by Kunzendorf have tested Külpe's hypothesis — that conscious visual images are centrifugally innervated, retinally localized sensations — and have yielded promising results. In Kunzendorf's (1984) study, the electroretinograms (ERGs) of 4 college students with extremely vivid "eidetic" imagery tended to be *uni*modal not only when the students looked at green light flashes, but also when they looked at red flashes and vividly imaged green flashes instead. Conversely, the ERGs of these 4 eidetikers tended to be *bi*modal not only when they looked at red flashes, but also when they looked at green flashes and vividly imaged red flashes instead. In Kunzendorf and Hall's (1999) study, 66 randomly-sampled students imaged whiteness for 15 secs or 60 secs, then stopped imaging and observed a white ERG-inducing flash; the ERGs of students with more vivid imagery exhibited lower amplitudes (i.e., greater retinal fatigue) after 60 secs of imaging.

Consistent with Külpe's argument and Kunzendorf's evidence for the peripheral localization of imagery, research indicates that people with subjectively vivid images have better control over peripheral-nervous-system functions in general. Accordingly, the subjective vividness of mental imagery is positively correlated not with central-nervous-system abilities like thinking and remembering, but with sensory phenomena like *faster visual discrimination* (Berger & Gaunitz 1977, 1979; Gur & Hilgard 1975), *more accurate visual searching* (Powell 1986; Wallace 1988; 1991), *greater aesthetic sensitivity* (Bilotta & Lindauer 1980; Kunzendorf 1982; Lindauer 1977), and *better Gestalt closure* (Wallace 1990). Indeed, the subjective vividness of imagery is positively correlated with other peripherally mediated phenomena as well, like the voluntary control of *electrodermal activity* (Drummond, White, & Ashton 1978; Ikeda & Hirai 1976; Kunzendorf & Bradbury 1983), *local skin temperature* (Kunzendorf 1981), *heart rate* (Carroll, Baker, & Preston 1979; Grossberg & Wilson 1968; Hirschman & Favaro 1980; Kunzendorf 1984; Kunzendorf, Francis, Ward, Cohen, Cutler, Walsh, & Berenson 1996–1997; Lang 1984; Lang, Kozak, Miller, Levin, & McLean 1980), *blood pressure* (Kunzendorf, Francis, Ward, Cohen, Cutler, Walsh, & Berenson 1996–1997); *penile and vaginal engorgement* (Smith & Over 1987; Stock & Geer 1982), and *salivary flow* (White 1978).

By positing that sensations or qualia are the subjective aspects of sensory transmitters, Külpe not only can explain why individual differences in imaged sensations have causal effects on peripheral phenomena, but also can explain why sensations are not interchangeable epiphenomena with no causal efficacy. If it were the case that red and green sensations could be interchanged or "inverted" by rewiring the brain, then everyone with an "inverted spectrum" would subjectively experience red broccoli, but would still call broccoli "green" and would still insist on broccoli and cucumbers being more similar in color than broccoli and radishes. If this were the case, then sensations of color would truly be epiphenomenal. But according to Külpe, it cannot be the case because red sensations are subjective aspects of those cone-shaped retinal structures that are innervated either by 650-nanometer light waves or by centrifugal nerve impulses. An adult's centrifugal nerves might be wired to produce anticipatory images of red broccoli on the retina, or a child's centrifugal nerves might temporarily develop in this direction, but their perceptual sensations of broccoli would always be green and would always provide corrective feedback enabling them to learn green imaging (Kunzendorf 1990; Kunzendorf, Justice, and Capone 1997). By implication, subjective redness is a *necessary* aspect of the retinal material that first responds to 650-nanometer light waves, and subjective greenness is a *necessary* aspect of the retinal material that causally responds to 500-nanometer light waves.[3]

Prince on Individual Differences in Subconsciousness

Prince (1910, 1921, 1925) developed an historically important theory of the subconscious which, albeit less sexy than Freud's theory of the unconscious, is more compatible with modern materialism. Let us first consider Freud's (1924) theory:

> The unconscious system may therefore be compared to a large ante-room, in which the various mental excitations are crowding upon one another, like individual beings. Adjoining this is a second, smaller apartment, a sort of reception-room, in which consciousness resides. But on the threshold between the two there stands a personage with the office of door-keeper, who examines the various mental excitations, censors them, and denies them admittance to the reception-room when he disapproves of them...The excitations in the unconscious, in the ante-chamber, are not visible to consciousness which is of course in the other room, so to begin with they remain unconscious. When they have pressed forward to the threshold and been turned back by the door-keeper, they are *'incapable of becoming conscious'*; we call them then *repressed*....I should like to assure you that these crude hypotheses, the two chambers, the door-keeper on the threshold between the two, and consciousness as a spectator at the end of the second room, must indicate an extensive approximation to the actual reality. (pp. 305–306)

Naively adopting a dualistic subject-object dichotomy, Freud posited a "spectator", homunculus, or 'subject of consciousness' which somehow becomes 'conscious of' excitatory objects coming out of an unconscious realm. In addition, he projected this unconscious realm onto all minds, once he convinced himself that his own recollection of incest reflected the psychoanalytic uncovering of a universal Oedipal fantasy.

Unlike Freud's theory of the *un*conscious, Prince's theory incorporated Leibniz's (1765/1896) argument against subject-object dualism and for *sub*conscious sensation. Leibniz argued that no entity, physical or spiritual, could be 'conscious of' physical objects outside itself. Accordingly, Leibniz defined the mind not as a 'subject of consciousness', but as an 'assemblage of conscious sensations' paralleling an assemblage of neural events. Furthermore, he realized that such an assemblage of conscious sensations could exist with or without self-consciousness *that one is having the sensations*, because self-consciousness parallels unique neural events that are sometimes active and other times inactive. Prince (1910) recast Leibniz's argument into more materialistic terms and used it to interpret individual differences in psychopathology:

> If it is true that dissociated brain systems can functionate (as in other parts of the nervous system), and if it is true that they have psychical equivalents, then whether we are self-conscious of any given state of consciousness must depend, it would seem, upon whether the brain process, correlated with it, is synthesized in a particular way with the larger system of brain processes which is correlated at a given moment with the self-conscious personality. And in so far as a brain process can occur detached from the main system of brain processes, so far can consciousness occur without self-consciousness. (p. 94)

Thus, according to Prince (1925), when potentially traumatic sensations become *sub*conscious in an hysteric, they remain conscious but become dissociated from any self-conscious awareness *that one is perceiving them*:

> Now, given an hysteric of a certain type with absolute anesthesia of the skin, no tactile stimulus is felt, much less perceived, *no matter how intensely the attention is concentrated* on the stimulated area. The lack of awareness of the tactile stimulus is not due, therefore, to lack of focusing attention...Now put that hysteric into another state of mind, or personality, that is to say hypnosis, and he recalls, first, that there did actually occur the sensation of a "prick" or "touch"; and, second, that when it occurred he was unaware of it. He further insists that it was a veritable sensation-in-being. (p. 177).

Here, no *unconscious realm* of Oedipal ideation is deemed to be operative in the hysteric, much less deemed to be universal. Rather, a *subconscious mode* of information processing is deemed to be operative in the hysteric, and a self-conscious mode of information processing is deemed to be operative across the normal range of individual differences.

Consistent with Prince's position on individual differences in subconsciousness, laboratory research by Kunzendorf and Karpen (1996–1997) shows that the person who scores high on dissociation/hysteria scales is more likely to experience subconscious sensations — i.e., conscious sensations without self-consciousness *that one is perceiving the sensations*. Moreover, research by Kunzendorf, Jesses, Dupille, and Butler (1990–1991) and Kunzendorf and Moran (1993–1994) shows that Silverman's (1976) and Rosenzweig's (1943) paradigms for measuring laboratory-induced Freudian repression are actually measuring the dissociation of conscious sensation from self-consciousness.

Indeed, psychodynamic psychologists might benefit from further consideration of Prince's approach to the subconscious, in lieu of Freud's approach to the unconsciousness. At the same time, experimental psychologists who eschew both the unconscious and the subconscious might benefit from further consideration of individual differences in subconsciousness.

Becker on Individual Differences in Self-Consciousness

Becker espoused the clinically unorthodox view that people with nonpsychotic depression are overly self-conscious and, thus, more in touch with reality than normal people. According to Becker (1973 p. 188–189), the person with nonpsychotic depression

> ...opts out of life because he is having trouble maintaining his illusions about it, which proves nothing less than that life is possible only with illusions... Reality [is] unbearable, because with him the mechanisms of illusion are known and destroyed by self-consciousness. He can no longer deceive himself...[4]

This depressive "hyper-self-consciousness", as Becker (1973 p. 191) calls it, has been experimentally confirmed in two studies by Kunzendorf and McLaughlin (1988–1989).

Building on the "depressive realism" literature (reviewed by Alloy & Abramson 1988), Kunzendorf and McLaughlin's first study demonstrated that the depressed student liminally perceives death-related words just as accurately as neutral words, whereas the normal student liminally perceives death-related words less accurately than neutral words. Kunzendorf and McLaughlin's second study further demonstrated that the depressed student self-consciously perceives death-related words, whereas the normal student experiences death-related words without self-consciousness *that one is perceiving them (rather than imaging them).*

Clinically, this implies that the depressed patient is unable to ignore distressing percepts, because he or she is acutely self-conscious that such percepts are real. In addition, it implies that the depressed patient is unable to entertain normal hopes, because he or she is acutely self-conscious that such hopes are imaginary.

Within the broader context of this chapter, the important point here is that our understanding of individual differences in self-consciousness greatly influences our understanding of the difference between abnormality and normality. The psychodynamic approach of Prince equates abnormality with subconsciousness, at one extreme, and normality with self-consciousness, at the other extreme. In contrast, the existential approach of Becker equates abnormality with both too little and too much self-consciousness, and views normality as the "golden mean" between these two extremes of self-consciousness.

We conclude, therefore, that individual differences in subjective experience — and their implications for theories of consciousness, subconsciousness, and self-consciousness — deserve far greater attention than they have been afforded in the past. We hope that his book will generate some of the deserved attention.

Notes

1. Presumably, Külpe was referring to Ramón y Cajál's (1888) discovery of centrifugal nerve fibers in the retina of birds. More recent research not only confirms the existence of centrifugal fibers to the human retina, but also reveals individual differences ranging from 8 to 100,000 such fibers per human (Labandeira-Garcia, Guerra-Seijas, Gonzalez, Perez, & Acuña 1990; Repérant, Miceli, Vesselkin, & Molotchnikoff 1989; Wolter 1979).
2. Farah and Peronnet (1989) did obtain, in vivid imagers, a larger difference between the Visual Evoked Potential 400–800 msecs after an *unimaged* abstract word and the VEP 400–800 msecs after an *imaged* concrete word. However, contemporaneous research by Kunzendorf and Hoyle (1984) indicates that this cortical potential actually registers the greater amounts of centrifugal 'neural effort' behind more vividly imaged sensations *except during hypnoidal states*, and thus distinguishes perceptual sensations from vividly imaged sensations *but not from hypnotically hallucinated sensations*. Moreover, early research by Armington (1964) indicates that, when brighter or more vivid sensations are visually perceived, there are corresponding increases in the retinal potential within 55–75 msecs of stimulus onset, and in the occipital VEP within 150–200 msecs *not 400–800 msecs*.
3. Kunzendorf (1999) presumes that retinal receptors and their *causally necessary* sensations of color have evolved from heat nociceptors and their *causally sufficient* qualia of pain. Consider an evolutionary scenario wherein two primitive organisms evolved damage-detecting systems, but only one of these systems was embodied in hardware which, when damaged by heat or by pressure, manifested the subjective aspect of pain. Whenever both organisms were tempted to do something that could aggravate pre-existing damage, rather than heal it, only the organism with conscious pain had a causally sufficient "subjective reinforcement" for avoiding the temptation and surviving the damage. Kunzendorf (1999) further presumes that, in subsequent organisms, damage-detecting systems with subjectively painful aspects began to evolve into danger-detecting systems with subjectively necessary aspects other than pain. Accordingly, some heat nociceptors began to evolve into thermal receptors with subjective "degrees of hotness" mapping "degrees of danger" across the skin, while other heat nociceptors — those attuned to painful damage from visible heat (light greater than 1,000,000,000 millilamberts) — began to evolve into light-dark receptors with subjective "degrees of brightness" mapping "degrees of danger" across visible space far away from the skin. Similarly, some pressure nociceptors began to mutate into mechanoreceptors with subject "degrees of pressure" mapping "degrees of danger" across the skin, while other pressure nociceptors — those attuned to painful damage from audible pressure (sound greater than 130 dB SPL) — began to mutate into auditory receptors with subjective "degrees of loudness" mapping "degrees of danger" across audible space far away from the skin. The physical and subjective aspects of visual and auditory receptors have continued to evolve, to the point where far more than danger is detected for a variety of adaptive purposes.
4. Here Becker (1973 p. 188) quotes Rank (1945 p. 93).

References

Alloy, L. B. and Abramson, L. Y. 1988. "Depressive realism: Four theoretical perspectives". In L. B. Alloy (ed.), *Cognitive Processes in Depression*. New York: Guilford, 223–265.

Armington, J. C. 1964. "Relations between electroretinograms and occipital potentials elicited by flickering stimuli". *Documenta Ophthalmologica* 18: 194–206.

Ashton, R., McFarland, K., Walsh, F. and White, K. 1978. "Imagery ability and the identification of hands: A chronometric analysis". *Acta Psychologica* 42: 253–262.

Bartlett, F. C. 1921. "The function of images". *British Journal of Psychology* 11: 320–337.

Becker, E. 1973. *The Denial of Death*. New York: Free Press.

Berger, G. H. and Gaunitz, S. C. B. 1977. "Self-rated imagery and vividness of task pictures in relation to visual memory". *British Journal of Psychology* 68: 283–288.

Berger, G. H. and Gaunitz, S. C. B. 1979. "Self-rated imagery and encoding strategies in visual memory". *British Journal of Psychology* 70: 321–324.

Bethel-Fox, C. E., Lohman, D. F. and Snow, R. E. 1984. "Adaptive reasoning: componential and eye movement analysis of geometric analogy performance". *Intelligence* 8: 205–238.

Betts, G. H. 1909. *The Distribution and Functions of Mental Imagery*. New York: Teachers College, Columbia University.

Bilotta, J. and Lindauer, M. S. 1980. "Artistic and nonartistic backgrounds as determinants of the cognitive response to the arts". *Bulletin of the Psychonomic Society* 15: 354–356.

Carroll, D., Baker, J. and Preston, M. 1979. "Individual differences in visual imaging and the voluntary control of heart rate". *British Journal of Psychology* 70: 39–49.

Chaguiboff, J. and Denis, M. 1981. "Imaging activity and recognition of names originating in a narrative test". *Annee Psychologique* 81: 69–86.

Chara, P. J. and Hamm, D. A. 1988. "A semantic analysis of the imagery questionnaire". *Perceptual and Motor Skills* 66: 113–114.

Chara, P. J. and Verplanck, W. S. 1986. "The imagery questionnaire: An investigation of its validity". *Perceptual and Motor Skills* 63: 915–920.

Cohen, B. H. and Saslona, M. 1990. "The advantage of being an habitual visualizer". *Journal of Mental Imagery* 14(3/4): 101–112.

Danaher, B. B. and Thoresen, C. E. 1972. "Imagery assessment by self-report and behavioral measures". *Behaviour Research and Therapy* 10: 131–138.

Dean, G. and Morris, P. E. 1991. "Imagery and spatial ability: When introspective reports predict performance". In R. H. Logie and M. Denis (eds.), *Mental Images in Human Cognition*. Amsterdam: Elsevier, 331–347.

DiVesta, F. J., Ingersoll, G. and Sunshine, P. 1971. "A factor analysis of imagery tests". *Journal of Verbal Learning and Verbal Behavior* 10: 471–479.

Drummond, P., White, K. and Ashton, R. 1978. "Imagery vividness affects habituation rate". *Psychophysiology* 15: 193–195.

Durndell, A. J. and Wetherick, N. E. 1976. "Reported imagery and two spatial tests". *Perceptual and Motor Skills* 43: 1050.

Ernest, C. H. and Paivio, A. 1971. "Imagery and sex differences in incidental recall". *British Journal of Psychology* 62: 67–72.

Farah, M. J. and Peronnet, F. 1989. "Event-related potentials in the study of mental imagery". *Journal of Psychophysiology* 3: 99–109.

Fernald, M. R. 1912. "The diagnosis of mental imagery". *Psychological Monographs* 14(58): 1–169.

Freud, S. 1924. *A General Introduction to Psychoanalysis* (J. Riviere, trans.). New York: Boni and Liveright.

Galton, F. 1883. *Inquiries into Human Faculty and Its Development*. London: MacMillan.

Grossberg, J. M. and Wilson, K. M. 1968. "Physiological changes accompanying the visualization of fearful and neutral situations". *Journal of Personality and Social Psychology* 10: 124–133.

Gur, R. C. and Hilgard, E. R. 1975. "Visual imagery and the discrimination of differences between altered pictures simultaneously and successively presented". *British Journal of Psychology* 66: 341–343.

Hall, V. C., Talukder, A. B. M. A. and Esposito, M. 1989. "Individual differences in the ability to learn and recall with or without imagery mnemonics". *Journal of Mental Imagery* 13(1): 43–54.

Hatakeyama, T. 1984. "Individual differences in imagery ability and mental size comparison". *Tohoku Psychologica Folia* 43: 112–126.

Heuer, F., Fischman, D. and Reisberg, D. 1986. "Why does vivid imagery hurt color memory?". *Canadian Journal of Psychology* 40: 161–175.

Hirschman, R. and Favaro, L. 1980. "Individual differences in imagery vividness and voluntary heart rate control". *Personality and Individual Differences* 1: 129–133.

Hunter, P. A., Moore, D. M. and Wildman, T. M. 1982. "The effects of presentation mode, imagery ability and type of stimulus material on learning". *Journal of Mental Imagery* 6(1): 175–182.

Ikeda, Y. and Hirai, H. 1976. "Voluntary control of electrodermal activity in relation to imagery and internal perception scores". *Psychophysiology* 13: 330–333.

Katz, A. N. 1983. "What does it mean to be a high imager?". In J. C. Yuille (ed.), *Imagery, Memory and Cognition: Essays in Honor of Allan Paivio*. Hillsdale, NJ: Lawrence Erlbaum, 39–63.

Kosslyn, S. M. 1994. *Image and Brain*. Cambridge, MA: MIT Press.

Kosslyn, S. M. and Alper, S. N. 1977. "On the pictorial properties of visual images: Effects of image size on memory for words". *Canadian Journal of Psychology* 31: 32–40.

Kosslyn, S. M., Brunn, J., Cave, K. and Wallach, R. 1984. "Individual differences in mental imagery ability: A componential analysis". *Cognition* 18: 195–243.

Kosslyn, S. M., Thompson, W. L., Kim, I. J., Rauch, S. L. and Alpert, N. M. 1996. "Individual differences in cerebral blood flow in area 17 predict the time to evaluate visualized letters". *Journal of Cognitive Neuroscience* 8: 78–82.

Külpe, O. 1895. *Outlines of Psychology* (E. Titchener, trans.). London: Sonnenschein.

Kunzendorf, R. G. 1981. "Individual differences in imagery and autonomic control". *Journal of Mental Imagery* 5(2): 47–60.

Kunzendorf, R. G. 1982. "Mental images, appreciation of grammatical patterns, and creativity". *Journal of Mental Imagery* 6(1): 183–201.

Kunzendorf, R. G. 1984. "Centrifugal effects of eidetic imaging on flash electroretinograms and autonomic responses". *Journal of Mental Imagery* 8(4): 67–75.

Kunzendorf, R. G. 1990. "Mind-brain identity theory: A materialistic foundation for the psychophysiology of mental imagery". In R. G. Kunzendorf and A. A. Sheikh (eds.), *The Psychophysiology of Mental Imagery*. Amityville, NY: Baywood, 9–36.

Kunzendorf, R. G. 1999. *Consciousness, Self-consciousness, Subconsciousness: Theoretical, Experimental, and Clinical Implications of Psychological Materialism*. Monograph in preparation, University of Massachusetts Lowell.

Kunzendorf, R. G. and Bradbury, J. L. 1983. "Better liars have better imaginations". *Psychological Reports* 53: 634.

Kunzendorf, R. G., Francis, L., Ward, J., Cohen, R. Cutler, J., Walsh, J. and Berenson, S. 1996–1997. "Effect of negative imaging on heart rate and blood pressure, as a function of image vividness and image 'realness'". *Imagination, Cognition, and Personality* 16: 139–159.

Kunzendorf, R. G. and Hall, S. 1999. "The aftereffects of visual imaging on flash electroretinograms: Individual differences in image vividness and retinal fatigue". Manuscript in preparation, University of Massachusetts Lowell.

Kunzendorf, R. G. and Hoyle, D. 1989. "Auditory percepts, mental images, and hypnotic hallucinations: Similarities and differences in auditory evoked potentials". In J. Shorr, P. Robin, J. A. Connella, and M. Wolpin (eds.), *Imagery: Current Perspectives*. New York: Plenum, 1–12.

Kunzendorf, R. G., Jesses, M., Dupille, L. and Butler, W. 1990–1991. "Subliminal activation of intrapsychic conflicts: Subconscious realms of mind versus subconscious processes of mentation". *Imagination, Cognition, and Personality* 10: 117–128.

Kunzendorf, R. G., Justice, M. and Capone, D. 1997. "Conscious images as "centrally excited sensations: A developmental study of imaginal influences on the ERG". *Journal of Mental Imagery* 21(1/2): 155–166.

Kunzendorf, R. G. and Karpen, J. 1996–1997. "Dissociative experiences and reality-testing deficits in college Students". *Imagination, Cognition, and Personality* 16: 227–238.

Kunzendorf, R. G. and McLaughlin, S. 1988–1989. "Depression: A failure to suppress the self-conscious 'monitoring' of dismal cognitions". *Imagination, Cognition, and Personality* 8: 3–17.

Kunzendorf, R. G. and Moran, C. 1993–1994. "Repression: Active censorship of stressful memories versus source amnesia for self-consciously dissociated memories". *Imagination, Cognition, and Personality* 13: 291–302.

Labandeira-Garcia, J., Guerra-Seijas, M., Gonzalez, F., Perez, R. and Acuña, C. 1990. "Location of neurons projecting to the retina in mammals". *Neuroscience Research* 8: 291–302.

Lang, P. J. 1984. "Cognition in emotion: Concept and action". In C. E. Izard, J. Kagan, and R. B. Zajonc (eds.), *Emotions, Cognitions, and Behavior*. Cambridge: Cambridge University Press, 192–226.

Lang, P. J., Kozak, J. M., Miller, G. A., Levin, D. N. and McLean, A. 1980. "Emotional imagery: Conceptual structure and pattern of somato-visceral response". *Psychophysiology* 17: 179–192.

Leibniz, G. W. 1896. *NewEessays Concerning the Understanding* (A. G. Langley, trans.). New York: Macmillan. (Original work published 1765)

Lindauer, M. S. 1977. "Imagery from the point of view of psychological aesthetics, the arts, and creativity". *Journal of Mental Imagery* 1(2): 343–362.

Lorenz, C. and Neisser, U. 1985. "Factors of imagery and event recall". *Memory and Cognition* 13: 494–500.

McKelvie, S. J. 1992. "Does memory contaminate test-retest reliability?". *Journal of General Psychology* 119: 59–72.

McKelvie, S. J. and Demers, E. G. 1979. "Individual differences in reported visual imagery and memory performance". *British Journal of Psychology* 70: 51–57.

McKelvie, S. J. and Rohrberg, M. M. 1978. "Individual differences in reported visual imagery and cognitive performance". *Perceptual and Motor Skills* 46: 451–458.

Mou, L.-C., Anderson,N. S., Vaughan, W. S. and Rouse, R. O. 1989. "Recognition memory for nonobject drawings". *Bulletin of the Psychonomic Society* 27: 399–401.

Paivio, A. 1971. *Imagery and Verbal Processes*. New York: Holt, Rinehart and Winston.

Parrott, C. A. 1986. "Visual imagery training: Stimulating utilization of imaginal processes". *Journal of Mental Imagery* 10(1): 47–64.

Phillips. R. J. 1978. "Recognition, recall and imagery of faces". In M. M. Gruneberg, P. E. Morris, and R. N. Sykes (eds.), *Practical Aspects of Memory*. London: Academic Press, 270–277.

Powell, N. J. 1986. "Imagery into action: Visual imagery and occupational therapy education". *Occupational Therapy Journal of Research* 6: 171–182.

Prince, M. 1910. "Chapter five". In H. Münsterberg, T. Ribot, P. Janet, J. Jastrow, B. Hart, and M. Prince (eds.), *Subconscious Phenomena*. Boston: Gorham Press, 71–101.

Prince, M. 1921. *The Unconscious: The Fundamentals of Human Personality Normal and Abnormal* (2nd ed.). New York: Macmillan.

Prince, M. 1925. "Awareness, consciousness, co-consciousness and animal intelligence from the point of View of the data of abnormal psychology: A biological theory of consciousness". *Pedagogical Seminary* 32: 166–188.

Ramón y Cajál, S. 1888. "Sur la morphologie et les connexions des éléments de la rétine des oiseaux". *Anatomischer Anzeiger* 4: 111–121.

Rank, O. 1936. *Will Therapy and Truth and Reality*. New York: Knopf.

Rehm, L.P. 1973. "Relationships among measures of visual imagery". *Behaviour Research and Therapy* 11: 265–270.

Reisberg, D., Culver, L.C., Heuer, F. and Fischman, D. 1986. "Visual memory: When imagery vividness makes a difference". *Journal of Mental Imagery* 10(4): 51–74.

Reisberg, D. and Leak, S. 1987. "Visual imagery and memory appearances: Does Clark Gable or George C. Scott have bushier eyebrows?". *Canadian Journal of Psychology* 41: 521–526.

Repérant, J., Miceli, D., Vesselkin, N.P. and Molotchnikoff, S. 1989. "The centrifugal visual system of vertebrates: A century-old search reviewed". *International Review of Cytology* 118: 115–171.

Richardson, A. 1977. "The meaning and measurement of mental imagery". *British Journal of Psychology* 68: 29–43.

Richardson, J.T.E. 1980. *Mental Imagery and Human Memory*. London: Macmillan.

Rimm, R.C. and Bottrell, J. 1969. "Four measures of visual imagination". *Behaviour Research and Therapy* 7: 63–69.

Rosenzweig, S. 1943. "An experimental study of 'repression' with special reference to need-persistive and ego-defensive reactions to frustration". *Journal of Experimental Psychology* 32: 64–74.

Sheehan, P.W. and Neisser, U. 1969. "Some variables affecting the vividness of imagery in recall". *British Journal of Psychology* 60: 71–80.

Silverman, L.H. 1976. "Psychoanalytic theory: The reports of my death are greatly exaggerated". *American Psychologist* 31: 621–637.

Smith, D. and Over, R. 1987. "Does fantasy-induced sexual arousal habituate?". *Behaviour Research and Therapy* 25: 477–485.

Stock, W.E. and Geer, J.H. 1982. "A study of fantasy-based sexual arousal in women". *Archives of Sexual Behavior* 11: 33–47.

Thorndike, E.L. 1907. "On the function of visual images". *Journal of Philosophy, Psychology, and Scientific Methods* 4: 324–327.

Wagman, R. and Stewart, C.G. 1974. "Visual imagery and hypnotic susceptibility". *Perceptual and Motor Skills* 38: 815–822.

Walczyk, J.J. 1995. "Between- versus within-subjects assessments of image vividness". *Journal of Mental Imagery* 19(1/2): 161–175.

Walczyk, J.J. and Hall, V.C. 1988. "The relationship between imagery vividness ratings and imagery accuracy". *Journal of Mental Imagery* 12(3/4): 163–172.

Wallace, B. 1988. "Imaging ability, visual search strategies, and the unvividness paradox". *Journal of Mental Imagery* 12(3/4): 173–184.

Wallace, B. 1990. "Imagery vividness, hypnotic susceptibility, and the perception of fragmented stimuli". *Journal of Personality and Social Psychology* 58: 354–359.

Wallace, B. 1991. "Imaging ability and performance in a proofreading task". *Journal of Mental Imagery* 15(3/4): 177–188.

White, K. D. 1978. "Salivation: The significance of imagery in its voluntary control". *Psychophysiology* 15: 196–203.

Wolter, J. R. 1979. "Electron microscope demonstration of centrifugal nerve fibers in the human optic nerve". *Gräfes Archiv fur klinische und experimentelle Ophthalmologie* 210: 31–41.

Part I

Individual Differences in Consciousness

How We Hurt

A Constructivist Framework for Understanding Individual Differences in Pain

C. Richard Chapman, Yoshio Nakamura and Leticia Y. Flores
University of Washington

1. Introduction

Pain is one of the most perplexing aspects of subjective experience, and yet it is among the least studied areas of consciousness research. Pain depends on consciousness for its existence and therefore it is inherently a phenomenon of consciousness. In everyday life, pain is the awareness of tissue damage or disease. It provides us with information about the location and nature of an injurious event (sensory information) and also information about the biological significance of that event (negative emotional awareness). Thus, pain is a somatic awareness with both sensory and negative emotional qualities. It is intrinsically unpleasant, threatening, and curiously individual.

Because uncontrolled pain is a major cause of human suffering, understanding the nature of pain and building a medical armamentarium of interventions to prevent or relieve it are of great importance. One of the barriers to progress on both of these fronts is the puzzle of individual differences in pain. If we were all very similar in our experience of pain, and in our responses to treatments intended to relieve pain, the prevention of suffering from sickness and injury would be straightforward. Unfortunately, the relationship between objectively defined tissue trauma and the highly individual unpleasant phenomenon of consciousness that we call pain is complex and ill-defined.

In this chapter we consider the relationship between tissue trauma and pain, highlighting the range of individual differences. We next review and contrast two approaches that purport to explain these differences: classical thinking and our own constructivist perspective that views pain within a consciousness framework. Finally, we discuss the implications of these two approaches for improving pain management.

2. Pain and Tissue Damage

Some of the puzzles confronting pain researchers challenge consciousness research as well. One such puzzle is the astonishingly poor fit of tissue trauma measures to the pain intensity reports that injured patients provide. Acute pain, that associated with recent unhealed injury, provides ready examples. The size of a surgical wound is a poor predictor of the amount of pain a postoperative patient experiences (Bonica 1990). Bigger wounds do not necessarily cause greater pain. Moreover, measures of the area or depth of a burn wound are weak predictors of pain in the burn trauma patient (Everett et al. 1994). Pain intensity does not increase with size of lesion or threat to survival.

Progressing disease (any painful disease condition that does not heal) tells a similar story. The observable deformities of arthritis do not gauge the severity of the patient's pain. The number of sites of bone metastasis in a cancer patient does not predict the amount of pain experienced. A trauma victim with multiple fractures does not necessarily have more pain than another who has a single fracture.

In many chronic pain conditions such as fibromyalgia (Baumstark and Buckelew 1992), a musculoskeletal disorder characterized by reported psychological dysfunction, fatigue, and a host of physical complaints such as headaches and feelings of stiffness, pain appears and persists in the absence of identifiable tissue damage. There are many chronically painful conditions in which either (a) pain exists in the absence of identifiable tissue pathology or (b) the pain severity greatly exceeds what one would expect, given the patient's condition (Magora and Schwartz 1980; Waddell and Main 1984).

Collectively, these observations suggest that the presence or absence of pain depends on tissue trauma, but other factors appear to determine the magnitude of the pain report. This paradox may stem partly from unrefined measurement technology: investigators do not always know which features of a pathological lesion to measure. Inflammation in the margin of a burn wound, for example, might be a more important determinant of pain intensity than the surface area of the wound. In this case, the trauma itself has destroyed many of the nerve endings that signal tissue trauma.

Recently, we examined pain in bone marrow transplantation patients who suffer from severe oral mucositis (Schubert et al. 1992). The preparative regimen for bone marrow transplantation typically involves supralethal doses of cytotoxic chemotherapy combined with normally supralethal doses of total body irradiation. This regimen kills neoplastic cells, but it also destroys bone marrow. Oncologists rescue their patients from these aggressive treatments by transplanting bone marrow from a genetically matched donor, but the toxicity of the preparative regimen damages organs throughout the body. Cells in the oral cavity cannot divide normally for a few weeks following the regimen, and this prevents the oral cavity from repairing itself. Consequently, tissue sloughs and large lesions appear in the mouth and pharynx. Many patients are unable to speak, and for much of the course of oral mucositis, they cannot ingest anything by mouth. Instead, they depend upon an intravenous line for hyperalimentation and blood products.

Schubert and colleagues (1992) have developed a measurement tool for quantifying the severity of oral mucositis, based on the coloration, texture and extent of visible lesions. This tool, the Oral Mucositis Index, can score the severity of oral tissue trauma. An oral medicine specialist examines a patient's oral cavity visually and assigns numbers to various features of the pathology. Repeated measurement with this tool can track the development and healing process of oral mucositis.

Measurement of both pain report and oral tissue trauma in the bone marrow transplantation patient demonstrates for the first time that a reasonable relationship exists between tissue trauma and pain (Chapman et al. 1997). However, while one can demonstrate a reasonable relationship between mean scores for tissue trauma and the mean scores for pain in this patient population, fascinating patterns of individual differences emerge. As Figure 1 indicates, some patients demonstrate a tight relationship between measures of oral mucositis severity and reported pain while others show little or no relationship. For the student of consciousness, the most fascinating aspect of individual differences issues in pain research is just this: patients vary widely in the fit of pain and suffering to tissue trauma and disease.

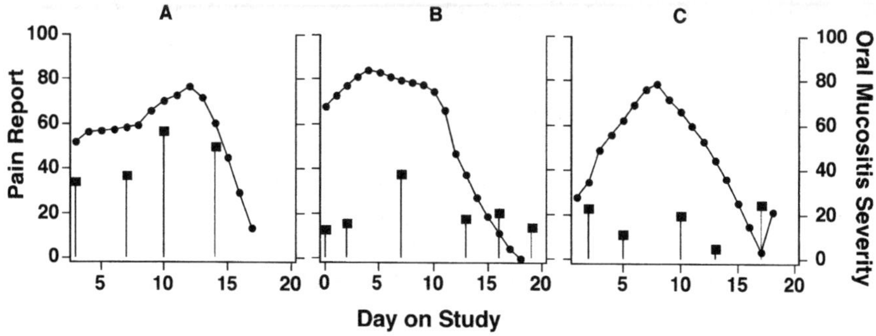

Figure 1. *Relationship between infrequent measures of oral mucositis severity (stem and box) and daily reported pain (line and circle) in three bone marrow transplantation patients. Part A illustrates data from a patient whose pain scores correspond closely to the measured oral mucositis severity. For the patient in Part B, there is clearly a relationship between oral mucositis severity and pain, but the level of pain seems exaggerated. Part C illustrates data from a patient for whom there is little relationship between the two measures.*

In a medically ideal world, the relationship between pain and tissue trauma would be tight, and very few individual differences would exist. Pain could be a major diagnostic tool for the physician, reliably indicating a need for medical intervention. Unfortunately, people can experience severe pain that reflects neither disease nor evident injury. Emergency room specialists regularly deal with chest pains that do not reflect heart attacks (Roll and Zetterquist 1990), or headaches of ill-defined origin (Thomas and Stone 1994). Moreover, many people, like fibromyalgia patients (Baumstark and Buckelew 1992), develop chronic pain conditions sufficiently debilitating to prevent normal work and productive living, despite no evidence of significant organic pathology. In some cases, seemingly modest tissue pathology can produce severe and debilitating pain states that persist indefinitely and resist surgery or other interventions. For example, about 90% of persons who suffer low back injuries heal within 4 weeks and return to work or normal life. The remaining 10%, who mostly have little or no evidence of tissue pathology, complain of debilitating pain and suffer indefinitely despite surgeries and other normally curative or palliative interventions (Krause and Ragland 1994). That patients can vary so much in recovery from trauma is a great source of perplexity to both physicians and employers.

The advent of magnetic resonance imaging has revealed that the opposite puzzle also exists. Although the literature has no reason to document it, physicians looking for pathology in persons with no pain often notice marked degeneration in their spinal processes, joints, or other areas. Naturally, they wonder why such patients fail to complain of pain. Because such inconsistencies are common, the use of pain as a diagnostic sign is fraught with difficulty. The presence of pain may or may not signal tissue pathology; the absence of pain does not guarantee that a patient is healthy.

Why people differ so much in the subjective experience of tissue trauma remains a challenge. Conventional medical understanding has progressed substantially in recent years and can begin to account for individual differences. Consciousness research, represented here as a constructivist approach, offers a strikingly different explanation. Below, we describe and contrast these approaches.

3. Accounting for Individual Differences: Two Contrasting Models

There are basically two approaches to the puzzle of individual differences in pain. The first derives from the classical viewpoint: pain is a predominantly sensory experience that signals tissue damage. This neurophysiological model, created largely from inductive reasoning, focuses on the transmission and modulation of signals that originate in damaged tissue. The model also addresses pain states that originate with injury to neurological pathways — neuropathic pain. Pain is neuropathic when the brain interprets signals originating from the abnormal firing of damaged nerves as true sensory experience. A second model accounting for individual differences is one that we have introduced elsewhere (Chapman and Nakamura 1998) under the heading of constructivism. This model holds that pain is the end product of complex central processing of sensory input — processing that generates subjective awareness from preconscious afferent signaling, memory, elements of the immediate situation, and aspects of personal motivation. It assumes that decentralized self-organization is a key mechanism in both pain and the construction of consciousness as a whole. It emphasizes the integration of multiple sources of input, the competition of many possible representations of reality for entry into the contents of consciousness, and the dynamic nature of subjective experience.

3.1 *The Classical Perspective*

The classical concept of pain holds that pain is a sensory experience best characterized in terms of (a) transduction of tissue trauma into neural signals, (b) transmission of the signals to the brain, and (c) central registration of the sensory information in somatosensory cortex. The modulation of the signals along the way is an important feature of pain. This is a centralized, linear, reductionistic perspective rooted in classical neurophysiology.

Basic Assumptions
Duthie (1994) provides a succinct statement of the classical view of pain: "The appreciation of pain requires that the energy of a painful stimulus be transformed by peripheral receptors into impulses which are conducted along sensory neurones to the CNS. Onward transmission to higher centres triggers the appreciation of pain. Pain may be alleviated either by impeding the transmission of impulses or by enhancing the mechanisms which modulate onward transmission" (p. 120). Duthie further notes (pp. 125) that "pain appreciation has never been localized to a particular region of the brain. The post-central gyrus and parietal operculum are both possibilities." These statements reveal some important assumptions: a neural message signals pain from the moment the sensory end organ is activated (indeed, this particular statement suggests that pain is a property of the stimulus), and the awareness of pain depends on the activation of specific regions in the brain.

Classical thinking holds that pain is the sensory message of peripheral tissue trauma: specifically and accurately coded in peripheral nerves as well as in pathways of central neural transmission and in the brain.

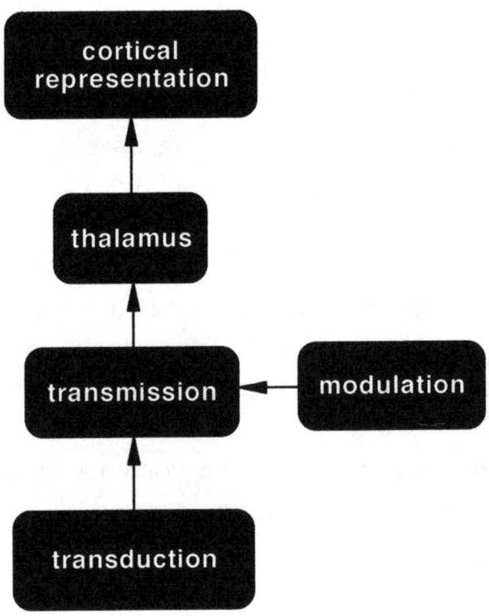

Figure 2. *The classical concept of pain. In this framework, pain is a sensory process characterized by transduction of tissue trauma via nociceptors, transmission of noxious sensory information to the thalamus, and representation of the sensation of pain in somatosensory cortex. Activation of descending inhibitory circuits located in the brain stem has a gating or dampening effect on transmission of nociception at the dorsal horn of the spinal cord.*

Figure 2 illustrates the classical concept indicating that pain is predominantly a product of rigid, unidirectional, straight-through information transmission. While almost no one today argues that mind exists apart from brain, most tacitly assume that a conscious self receives and interprets pain alarm signals, like a person attending to shouts of "fire" while watching a film in a motion picture theater. From where does this notion come?

Contemporary understanding of pain reflects the strong influence of Descartes, who in the 17th Century construed bodily processes as "clockwork mechanics" (Damasio 1994). Descartes held that body and mind were separate entities. For Descartes, pain was a specific modality — a straight-through sensory projection system that moved injury signals from damaged tissue to the brain where the mind could appreciate them. This perspective went unchallenged for two centuries, and it still exerts considerable subtle influence, even though most scientists would reject the mind — body dichotomy. Scientists and physicians alike assumed, until about 1960, that tissue trauma activates specific receptors and that signals of tissue trauma follow specific pain pathways through the spinal cord to a pain center in the brain. In classical thinking, pain is the sensory end product of an essentially passive information transmission process that operates as a biologically adaptive mechanism.

Basic Mechanisms

The transduction of tissue trauma into neural signals depends upon sensory end organs known as nociceptors (Besson and Chaouch 1987; Heppelmann et al. 1991; Willis 1993). The free nerve endings of thinly myelinated Aδ fibers function as thermal and/or mechanical nociceptors, conducting impulses at 4–44 m/s. In addition, certain unmyelinated C fibers that conduct slowly (roughly .5–1 m/s) act as polymodal nociceptors, responding to various high intensity mechanical, chemical and thermal stimuli. Both types of fibers distribute widely in skin and in deep tissue. In addition, some primary afferents act as "silent nociceptors". Normally these end organs will not respond to harmless sensory stimuli, but noxious events or chemical changes can sensitize them so that they function thereafter as nociceptors (McMahon and Koltzenburg 1990; Willis 1993).

Nociceptors innervate skin, muscle, fascia, joints, tendons, blood vessels and visceral organs. From a sensory perspective, these tissues group into cutaneous, deep and visceral types. Nociception appears to serve somewhat different functions in the three types of tissues, and the qualities of the pain that ensues from their activation varies across types. Cutaneous pain tends to be well localized, sharp, pricking or burning. Aδ fibers produce sharp, pricking pain sensations of discreet, brief duration while C fibers tend to generate burning sensations. Deep tissue pain usually seems diffuse and dull or aching in quality, although deep tissues can produce bright, sharp pains under certain conditions (e.g., muscle rupture). Visceral pain is very diffuse, often referred to the body surface, perseverating, and frequently associated with queasiness so that patients tend to describe it as “sickening”. Severe visceral pain typically produces an accompaniment of profuse sweating, nausea and vomiting.

The adequate stimuli for nociception differ across tissue types. Cutaneous receptors detect injurious stimuli from the surrounding environment, and so they respond to severe mechanical and thermal events such as cutting, burning or freezing. Nociceptors in deep tissue such as muscle detect overuse strain, deep mechanical injury like tearing and contusion, spasm or cramping, and ischemia. Their function resembles that of nociceptors in cutaneous tissue, but their responses may be more intimately linked to flexor reflexes than are those of their counterparts in skin. Muscle pain tends to foster muscle stiffness and splinting, which serves a protective function by bracing or supporting injured muscle. Visceral nociceptors do not respond to cutting or burning injury like their counterparts in cutaneous tissue but instead fire in response to pathological change. A hollow viscus needs to identify and transduce distention, stretch, and isometric contraction. A solid organ needs signal distention of the capsule that contains it and inflammation. Gebhart and Ness (1991) listed the following as naturally occurring visceral stimuli: distention of hollow organs, ischemia, inflammation, muscle spasm, and traction. The peripheral origins of pain vary markedly, depending on whether the nociceptors involved lie in superficial or deep tissues.

The centripetal *transmission* of noxious signals takes place in the spinal cord. Nociceptive afferents enter the spinal cord primarily through the dorsal route, terminating principally in lamina I (the marginal zone) but also in laminae II (the substantia gelatinosa) and V of the dorsal horn (Craig 1991). The spinal and medullary dorsal horns are much more than simple relay stations; these complex structures participate directly in sensory processing, performing local abstraction, integration, selection and appropriate dispersion of sensory impulses (Bonica 1990; Dubner 1991; Jänig 1987; Perl 1984; Willis 1988). Upon entry, nociceptive afferents synapse with projection neurons that convey information to higher centers, facilitory interneurons that relay input to projection neurons, and inhibitory interneurons that modulate the flow of nociceptive signals to higher centers (Jessell and Kelly 1991). Similar neural processing occurs in the spinal cord and the medullary dorsal horn.

There are two principal types of projection neurons: nociceptive specific and multireceptive or wide dynamic range (WDR) neurons (Jänig 1987). The former convey only tissue trauma signals; the latter respond to stimuli of increasing intensity. Ascending tracts include spinothalamic, spinoreticular, spinomesencephalic, spinocervical, and postsynaptic dorsal cord tracts. Willis (1988) and Besson and Chaouch (1987) provide useful reviews of nociceptive transmission mechanisms. In classical thinking, the spinothalamic tract is clearly the most important. Lesions of the anterolateral quadrant of the spinal cord result in a loss of pain sensation below the segmental level of the lesion on the contralateral side of the body (Bonica 1990).

The thalamus is a gateway and relay center for afferent input coming to the brain; it is the key structure in *central registration*. It consists of several functionally distinct nuclei that are reciprocally connected to many parts of the limbic system and the cortex (Bonica 1990). Medial and ventrobasal thalamic nuclei relay noxious signals to the primary and secondary somatosensory cortices (SI, SII) where refined localization and discrimination occur. In classical thinking, the appreciation of pain occurs here in these cortical areas.

Of course, pain involves modulation in addition to transmission. A revolutionary advance in classical thinking came with the integration of the concept of modulation. Gate Control Theory (Melzack and Wall 1965) is the flagship of many important statements about modulation. What had been a rigid, bottom-up information transmission system took on a top-down influence when the gate control concept came on to the scene. Figure 2 illustrates the role of modulation in pain. Gate Control Theory postulated a gating mechanism at the dorsal horn of the spinal cord that could modulate the transmission of noxious signaling. The signal dampening action of the gate depends upon the relative amount of activity in large versus small diameter fibers in the periphery.

Later incarnations of the theory took on stronger top-down features. For example, Melzack and Casey (1968) hypothesized that selective cognitive processes can activate descending fibers and thus modulate properties of the spinal cord gating mechanism. Perhaps the most important feature of the gate is that it responds to nerve impulses that descend from the brain. Although this model maintains some of the Cartesian concepts of clockwork mechanics such as information transmission mechanisms (and presumably the Cartesian Theater), it substantially expanded earlier concepts.

Returning to our analogy, the movie viewer hearing alarming sounds now finds that the shouting varies in clarity as a function of the sound and activity level of the ongoing movie. Furthermore, the clarity of the shouted message may increase or diminish as a function of how much interest the viewer has in receiving alarming news messages. An unexpected shout of "fire!" must command attention because it is important for survival. If the shout becomes familiar and repetitious, and if in the experience of the moviegoer it does not really signal an impending inferno, it simply annoys and interferes with viewing the movie. In this way chronic pain may exert a different effect on consciousness than does a sudden, novel and acute pain. In considering modulation, we begin to glimpse possibilities for explaining individual differences in pain.

Mechanism and Mind

The mechanistic assumptions of classical neurology, which hold that pain is a purely sensory phenomenon, have survived over the centuries because they have proven useful as simple working models of pain and symptom perception. However, this viewpoint becomes ever more tenuous as consciousness research and theory progress. It is not so much the clockwork mechanics of Cartesian thinking that creates the problem for contemporary science as the assumption of duality. Descartes held that the awareness of pain, like awareness of other bodily sensations, must occur in a special location where the mind observes the mechanistic body. Dennett (1991) and others concerned with consciousness characterize this concept as the Cartesian Theater. The mind observes and interprets the array of multimodality signals that the body produces. Contemporary neurophysiology, of course, rejects the existence of such a theater out-of-hand (Damasio 1994), but the notion is endemic in Western culture and intransigent.

One of the intriguing aspects of implicit Cartesian dualism is the double transduction dilemma (Dennett 1996). The classical thinker first postulates a transduction of stimulus energy into neural impulses (see Duthie's quote above). In order to account for the entry of a sensory message into awareness, he or she must postulate a second transduction from neural messaging into the "mind stuff" of awareness. Although Dennett did not address pain specifically, his challenge applies to pain theorists. None has as yet attempted to explain how objective nociceptive signaling becomes subjective pain. Postulating a second transduction reifies the concept of a mind separate from the body and is, in essence, the very dualism that everyone rejects.

Contributions of Classical Thinking

Classical thinking has generated numerous useful contributions to science and medicine. Psychophysics, for example, provides a way to quantify laboratory pain. Various intensity rating scales are ways to measure clinical pain. Classical thinking leads to three important strategies for pain relief: remove the cause of the pain (whether it is direct nociception or sensitization), block the rostral transmission of noxious signals, or enhance modulation, thereby gating or dampening rostral transmission of injury signals. The use of nonsteroidal anti-inflammatory drugs such as ibuprofen, anesthetic blocks of peripheral nerves and surgical resections of neural structures for pain relief, and opioid drugs are all legacies of classical Cartesian assumptions.

The Classical View of Individual Differences

How can patients with almost identical lesions have very different pain? Why do some feel pain with little or no disease while others fail to complain of obvious, seemingly painful pathology? Why is it that, in many cases, there is a rather poor fit between tissue trauma and pain report? These questions have fairly straightforward, albeit incomplete, answers in classical thinking.

The first answer is that not all pain, and perhaps very little clinical pain, reflects simple mechanical injury to tissue. Sensitization of nociceptors plays a major role (Alexander and Black 1992). As nociceptors become sensitized, pain thresholds diminish (allodynia) and painful responses to subsequent noxious stimuli increase (hyperalgesia). Such alterations may reflect changes in the transduction process, central changes that facilitate the transmission of noxious messages, or both. Sensitization of nociceptors can result from either repetitive stimulation or inflammation. Enhanced sensitivity is usually adaptive since it promotes recuperation and repair, minimizing further injury by discouraging all contact rather than just contact with noxious stimuli.

Once traumatized, tissue normally becomes inflamed. It is now clear that the process of inflammation sensitizes nociceptors and thereby increases their signal generating capability (Woolf 1989). Chemical by-products of inflammation, such as the prostaglandins, alter the chemical environment of nociceptors, lowering their thresholds for firing and in some cases recruiting other fibers to function as nociceptors. Thus, injured peripheral tissues can become extraordinarily sensitive because of local chemical changes. In cases where a painful focus has created intense activity in nociceptors, dorsal horn cells in the central nervous system can become sensitive to normal inputs and also excessively responsive to those inputs (Woolf and King 1990). The exaggerated response of transmission cells in the spinal cord is central sensitization.

Moreover, damage to neural tissue may disturb a central regulating mechanism and thereby produce a condition in which the sympathetic nervous system plays a role in nociception (Roberts 1986). This is called Sympathetically Maintained Pain or sometimes Complex Regional Pain Syndrome. Such conditions are rare, but excruciatingly painful, conditions in which altered function of the sympathetic nervous system contributes to a painful hypersensitivity in an affected area of the body. The classical syndrome, called causalgia, illustrates that pathological pain represents multiple physiologically complex phenomena.

Causalgia typically appears after a high velocity wound (a bullet, shrapnel or knife injury) has damaged a major nerve in a limb (Bonica 1990). Most patients experience surface pain of a burning quality immediately in the periphery of the injured extremity, and they develop shiny skin and edema in the affected area. The pain worsens and evolves into a constant hyperesthesia and allodynia (everything touching the area causes pain). With time, the pain spreads and eventually involves the entire limb. Temperature changes, light touch, friction from clothing, blowing air, movement of the limb, and any stimulus that affects the patient's emotional state can exacerbate the pain. Minor events like the cry of a child, the rattling of a newspaper, or watching a television program can provoke intense pain. Consequently, patients suffer greatly, becoming reclusive, withdrawn, and tragically incapacitated by the pain.

These examples suggest that a number of possible mechanisms accounts for some of the individual differences. Other factors contributing to individual differences in a classical model include genetic variation (presumably some people are more sensitive to tissue trauma than others), age (elderly persons are more reticent in expressing pain than their younger counterparts), sex (overall, females appear to be more sensitive to noxious stimulation and to tolerate less noxious stimulation than males), and presumably individual learning history counts for some of the differences.

Summary of the Classical Position

The classical sensory neurophysiological model of pain holds that nociception, transmission of noxious signaling, modulation and sensory registration of pain are biologically predetermined processes. This is a predominantly bottom-up, unidirectional, sequential processing model. Although mechanisms of modulation exist, pain is something that happens in the awareness of an injured or sick person such as a message that arrives. It is not something that the person produces or does. This position has major problems in explaining how a sensory experience can contribute so powerfully to suffering: why pain "hurts" is still unclear . Also, this approach cannot address the knotty problem that challenges consciousness researchers — how do signals of tissue trauma make their way into consciousness?

3.2 *The Constructivist Framework*

For the constructivist, pain is a complex, emotionally negative awareness characterized by sensory qualities and normally consequent to tissue trauma (Chapman 1995; Chapman and Nakamura 1998). The transduction, transmission and modulation aspects of classical thinking are basic mechanisms for the constructivist framework. However, while the classical model focuses on the transmission of nociceptive impulses as specific sensory signals, ours emphasizes the central processing of such signals and the construction of the contents of consciousness. Our model does not include a simple sensory registration of pain as a message. We suggest instead that pain emerges from complex patterns of massive, parallel distributed processing. It is the emergent product of a self-organizing process in a distributed neural system in the brain.

Our approach provides a framework that can help to further develop and refine a smaller-scale theory or model that attempts to account for a particular type of pain experience. We envision that when specific models appear, they need to be falsifiable in the traditional sense of philosophy of science.

Features of Human Consciousness

Consciousness develops from birth through differentiation. In the newborn, awareness is largely incoherent, but over time a unity emerges and creates the sense of self. Learning, memory, expectation and beliefs become parts of the self, and partly through the self's executive functions, shape consciousness.

Coherence. A cardinal feature of consciousness in the mature individual is its ongoing tendency to achieve coherence: consciousness is self-organizing. Fundamentally, consciousness is inherently fragmented, a cacophony of inner voices and visions. Such fragments may well arise from multiple origins. However, consciousness tends to form meaningful wholes from elements of awareness and to create a working model of both the external world and the body. It also organizes experience across time. We perceive a connectedness in moving from one thing to another. Moreover, consciousness is situated: mental events have a time and place reference.

Sense of self. What organizes awareness and insures coherence across place and time? One could describe the sense of self as an epiphenomenon of the brain's tendency to achieve coherence. The concept of self is particularly important for pain research for two reasons. First, individuals have a strong sense of the body self. A mental map of the body exists in human consciousness that Melzack calls the body matrix (Melzack 1996). When a person loses a limb or other body part, the persistence of the mental image of the body creates the experience of a phantom. That is, the sense of "whole" remains even when a part is lost. A twisted or distorted phantom limb represents an injury to the body self within the realm of consciousness and can be a cause of great distress to the patient.

Second, people have social selves: names and roles in family and society define individuals. Chronic pain syndromes, in particular, demonstrate the ways in which the persistence of pain can become a part of the social self. The representation of self is complex and multidimensional.

Purposiveness. Adaptation and survival, along with the goals and purposes of an individual, direct consciousness. Because "we use" limited mental resources, consciousness requires resource allocation. Consciousness seems therefore to involve a "searchlight" of attention. This searchlight ensures that consciousness has a center and a periphery. In addition, consciousness involves intentionality. That is, it is always about something. Our biological, psychological and social motivations drive the focus of attention. Except perhaps in certain meditation states, we are never simply "aware" in a vacuum.

Personal nature and affect. The personal nature of consciousness is so obvious that we risk overlooking it. We cannot share our thinking or feelings with one another, other than by verbal or gestural communication. My headache is something that is mine alone; you cannot share it or even know quite what it is like for me. This feature sets the phenomena of consciousness apart from those that neuroscience addresses. The objective features of a neuroscience phenomenon are the same for all observers, but the stuff in my awareness at this moment is mine alone and cannot be yours.

In addition consciousness often involves an *affective tone*: emotion colors everything we experience. That is, things seem good or bad to us to varying degrees, and this serves an important biological function in protecting us from harm and helping to ensure that we sustain those resources that we need for survival. The emotional quality of pain represents in consciousness the meaning or importance of a tissue trauma event, whereas the sensory aspect of pain provides information about what has happened and where (Chapman 1995).

A Constructivism Model for Pain

Figure 3 offers an overview of our model. Like classical thinking, this approach has a strong bottom up element, and the mechanisms of neural transmission are the same. Classical models, however, like that described by Duthie (1994), limit pain mechanisms to the transmission of signals to the thalamus and from there to the somatosensory cortices I and II, as Figure 1 indicates. In contrast, we build on the observations of several studies of regional cerebral blood flow associated with pain — observations that indicate massive, parallel distributed processing. Figure 3 indicates that we ascribe such processing to self organization. It produces coherence and sets the stage for the individual's construction of immediate experience and meaning.

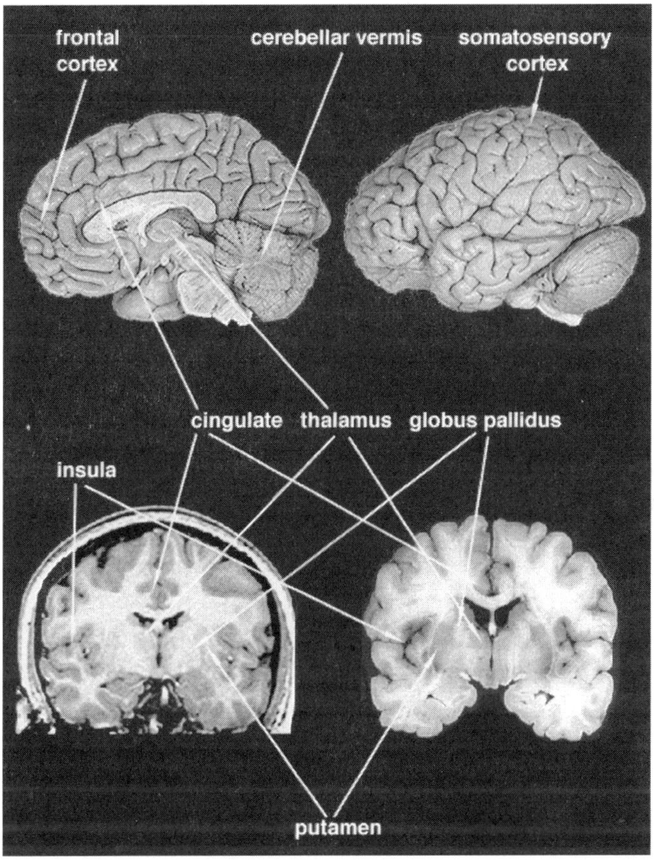

Figure 3. *A constructivist model for pain. The lowest three elements of this figure correspond to the classical model: transduction, transmission and modulation. At higher levels of the central nervous system, however, parallel distributed processing takes place. This processing integrates multimodal sensory, affective, and cognitive information, resolves competition among many elements for further processing and produces a coherent set of sensory and emotional associations. Schemata emerge from this and compete with one another for entry into the contents of consciousness. To qualify for emergence, a schema must fit memory associations and the individual's immediate model of the self and the world to incoming noxious signaling. Consciousness is not an on-off state, but rather a gradient. It has a feedback relationship to memory networks and the immediate model of the self and world. This figure represents a snapshot of a complex adaptive system evolving over time.*

A number of recent Positron Emission Tomography (PET) studies of brain metabolic activity during pain indicate that central processing is far more complex than a sensory registration model allows (Casey et al. 1994; Casey et al. 1996; Coghill et al. 1994; Jones et al. 1991; Jones et al. 1994; Talbot et al. 1991; Vogt et al. 1996). Although the time resolution of PET studies does not permit investigators to specify strictly which aspects of distributed processing are serial and which are parallel, these studies demonstrate unequivocally that extensive distributed processing occurs in many different areas of the brain.

The complexity of central processing of painful events is striking. In people experiencing pain, distributed processing involves the internal capsule (lenticular nucleus), the anterior cingulate, the insular cortex, frontal areas, the thalamus, the somatosensory cortices, the superior and inferior frontal cortex, the straight gyrus, and the cerebellar vermis (Casey et al. 1994; Casey et al. 1996; Coghill et al. 1994; Jones et al. 1991; Jones et al. 1994; Talbot et al. 1991; Vogt et al. 1996). Figure 4 illustrates the location of some of the areas. These studies reveal that the limbic brain, the seat of emotion, undertakes a major part of the processing that builds the experience of pain. The emotional aspects of pain are invariably negative, and the noradrenergic pathways may play a central role in building the disturbing emotional quality of pain (Chapman 1995).

The top figure shows (left) a saggital section of a right hemisphere and also (right) the corresponding left hemisphere of the same specimen. The low left figure is a magnetic resonance image of a brain in coronal perspective. The panel on the right shows a specimen cut at the identical plane.

As reflected in the recent PET studies cited above, the brain displays multifocal, parallel and complex central processing (Mesulam 1994; Mesulam 1990). Therefore, we propose that dynamically distributed processing in large-scale networks, operating in parallel, integrates and synthesizes noxious signaling and other products of central processing to construct the contents of consciousness. Pain is but one aspect of this complex, constantly self-organizing process, but it is a prominent aspect because of its strong emotional component.

How parallel, distributed processing in various brain regions constructs the awareness of pain and the associated suffering is still uncertain. We suggest that parallel distributed processing initiated by tissue trauma involves self-organized response patterns and that dynamically emerging response patterns, rather than pathways, are the proper focus for interpreting PET observations of people experiencing pain. The following processes characterize central processing: (1) multiple central response patterns compete for dominance (this is a fundamentally Darwinian concept of cell assemblies, articulated well by Calvin (1987); see Taylor (1996) for similar ideas about neural networks); (2) sensory signaling

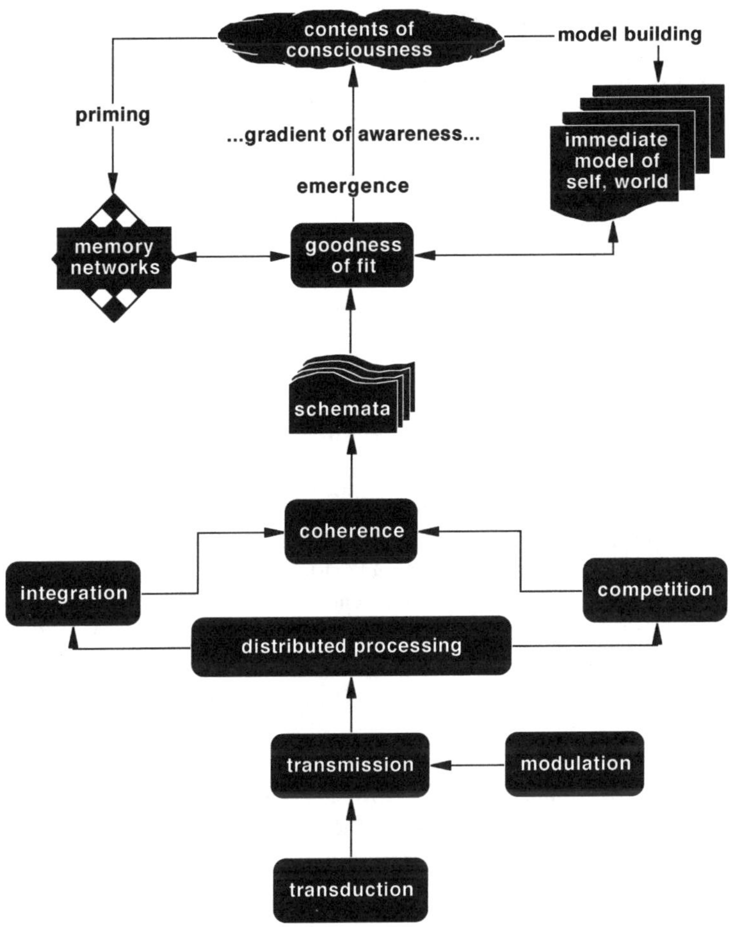

Figure 4. *Brain areas activated during the experience of pain. Emerging literature on positron emission tomography (PET) studies of pain (see text) indicates that marked regional cerebral blood flow, and therefore brain metabolism, occurs in the labeled brain areas in persons experiencing pain. This demonstrates massive, parallel processing during pain, and it indicates that multiple limbic structures, the frontal lobe, and the cerebellum are active in addition to thalamus and somatosensory cortex.*

integrates with expectation and other components of memory networks, various associations and motives appropriate to the immediate situation, and the long range goals of the person; and, (3) self-organization forms a coherent whole from the sum of the many parts of the distributed processing. This coherent whole is dynamical by nature: the contents of consciousness evolve constantly, but (with the exception of dreaming) they maintain coherence. Pain never exists in isolation. It is embedded in contextual experience, and the brain constantly works toward reconciling the disharmony that it causes. The experience of pain, ordinarily a signal of injury or disease, typically triggers various high level responses directed at escaping from or stopping the threat to biological integrity.

Pain as Consciousness

Pain is the representation of tissue trauma in consciousness. Currently, the field of consciousness research lacks a single definition for consciousness that suits all applications. We agree broadly with Greenfield's (1995) description of consciousness as "… spatially multiple yet effectively single at any one time. It is an emergent property of non-specialized, divergent groups of neurons (Gestalt) that is continuously variable with respect to, and always entailing, a stimulus epicenter. The size of the Gestalt, and hence the depth of prevailing consciousness, is a product of the interaction between the recurring strength of the epicenter and the degree of arousal …" (p. 104). Like an electron that has at a given instant both a position and velocity, consciousness has a stimulus-defined focus and a degree of arousal.

We view consciousness as an emergent property of a self-organizing process operating in a distributed neural network. Consciousness evolved because it increases the repertoire of behaviors and the functional capability of the individual. Viewed neurologically, consciousness has certain "on-off" features (coma, sleep, anesthesia), but it is useful for psychological purposes to think of it as a gradation, varying in degree of arousal, as Figure 4 indicates. This gradation is like the degree of illumination of a stage, upon which various characters appear. Specific subjects emerge into the spotlight of consciousness and then fade into the background. Constant ebb and flow in focus is a cardinal feature of consciousness.

How can the pain of, say, a migraine headache intrude into consciousness, amidst a mingled and ever changing scenario of other experiences? Such a pain would typically originate in the excitation of stretch-sensitive nociceptors in cranial blood vessels. Clearly a complex array of multisensory information arrives at the brain constantly, and this array changes over time. The signals from the nociceptors are but minor feature in the stream of neural signals that reach the brain. We propose that the brain constantly forms and reforms short-lived perceptual wholes from the constantly changing arrays of information. Immediately after a noxious stimulus (in this case, distention of a central blood vessel), non-conscious and parallel distributed processing integrates the signals from nociceptors with other representations in the brain and various memories and associations. Such processing forms a stable pattern of primary activations and associations which we identify as a *schema.*[1]

The general notion of a schema as a pattern of activation and association is familiar in cognitive psychology, clinical psychology, artificial intelligence and neural network modeling (Rumelhart et al. 1986; Williams et al. 1988). Although applications and specific definitions of the word schema vary markedly, the term refers to a normally non-conscious pattern of concepts or affects and associations that reflects a person's past experience and influence as well as expectations for the present and future. We emphasize that schemata are fuzzy, preconscious and dynamical. Rumelhart and colleagues usefully described schemata as follows: "Schemata are not single 'things.' There is no representational object which is a schema. Rather schemata emerge at the moment they are needed from the interaction of large numbers of much simpler elements, all working in concert with one another. Schemata are not explicit entities, but rather are implicit in our knowledge and are created by the very environment that they are trying to interpret as it is interpreting them ..." (p. 20).

A schema may emerge as a new network of associations, or it may be a partly preformed pattern of imagery that emerges from memory (e.g., a visual image or a tune). It is not a simple memory trace. Alternatively, a schema could be a pattern of motor skills formed from learning processes that involved extensive practice (e.g., riding a bicycle). We presume that the brain stores certain images and motor patterns associated with somatosensory and visceral sensory awareness. As it periodically retrieves, uses, and restores this information, it alters it. In other words, retrieving and using memory contents (which are more akin to networks of association than stored computer records), alters those contents to some degree.

The process of constructing consciousness is dynamical and complex. The available "construction materials" include schemata associated with immediate sources of physiological stimulation (sensory experience), immediate cognitive and affective schemata, schemata produced in imagination, and schemata stored in memory. Most schemata are short lived because the constant changes of perception over — write the neural circuitry before they have a chance to consolidate. However, some are "learned"; that is, they survive indefinitely in memory. Learned schemata are readily available for recall, and certain sensory events or other schemata can act as triggers for a particular schema.

The schema concept helps explain a painful, trigger-sensitive condition known as phantom limb pain that exists across individuals and cultures. Phantom body parts tend to appear in consciousness after a person has lost a limb. They are kinesthetically-vivid realizations of a body part that is physically absent. Sometimes a phantom limb will hurt, and no treatment directed at the stump or administered systemically can relieve it (Melzack 1990).

In a study of 68 patients with phantom limb pain, Katz and Melzack (1990) found that patients had experienced various post-amputation pains, all localized to the missing limbs. The patients described these pains as immediate and real, quite unlike recollection of a past pain state. In constructivist terms, the patients were reproducing or re-constructing pain and not simply recalling a past event. Interestingly, some of the phantom experiences involved painless experience (e.g., feeling a shoe on a missing foot) and some had multimodal sensory qualities. Katz and Melzack speculated that "a higher order somatosensory memory component," once formed, "can be activated when only some of its elements are present in the sensory input ..." (p. 333).

For the constructivist, this means that simple somatosensory stimuli can serve as *triggers*, activating preformed schemata that become part of the contents of consciousness. This leads to the principle that one schema can trigger another. Triggers for phantom limb pain are not invariably sensory. Sometimes they are cognitive or emotional in nature (Hill et al. 1996). This suggests that cognitive and affective schemata may function as triggers for chronic pain states, when tissue trauma is no longer the predominant cause of noxious signaling.

Our model also assumes that some schemata dominate others for a place in the content of consciousness at a given moment. Why some emerge and others recede begs explanation. Marcel, as Williams et al. (1988) interpret him, proposes that multiple schemata (in Marcel's terms, "perceptual hypotheses") become activated simultaneously, and each is tested automatically against the records of non-conscious processing for goodness of fit. The prevailing schema is the one that best accounts for the most data in the records (i.e., noxious signaling from tissue trauma). Figure 4 illustrates this dynamical nature of the construction of consciousness. Pain researchers often refer to the multidimensional nature of pain as a complex theoretical construct (Chapman 1995). In our view, the multidimensionality of schemata and consciousness is the underlying system-level mechanism that gives rise to pain.

Evidence for Schemata

The classical neurophysiologist may be tempted to dismiss the notion of schemata as a fanciful construct of psychologists, unrelated to demonstrable neurophysiological function. However, organized patterns of neural action resembling schemata must exist. Neurosurgical studies of patients with epilepsy indicate that complex and highly coherent patterns of multisensory experience reside in the brain, as do rather complicated patterns of motor experience. Focal electrical stimulation of the brain of an awake patient during surgery can cause chronologically distant memory fragments to suddenly emerge into consciousness. Penfield (1975) described a single case in which he repeatedly stimulated "the interpretive cortex." On one trial, the patient said, "I had a little memory — a scene in a play — they were talking and I could see it — I was just seeing it in my memory ..." (p. 27). This and other examples indicate that the activated memory patterns are multimodal and dynamic (that is, they are more like multimedia movie clips of events than simple snapshots). On another trial, the same patient said, "Just a tiny flash of feeling of familiarity and a feeling that I knew everything that was going to happen in the near future ..." (p. 25). This example indicates that (a) some patterns are emotional rather than sensory in quality and (b) the emotional schemata seem to be present and real as compared to the "memory" quality of predominantly visual or auditory events. Penfield also described eliciting involuntary motor movements from patients by stimulating motor cortex regions. These observations suggest that the brain not only forms multimodal sensory, motor, emotional and cognitive schemata, but it also stores them in memory. It is reasonable to suppose that the brain may form schemata on its own, drawing upon intrinsic memories, associations and ratiocination.

How many schemata can the contents of consciousness sustain at a given moment? In principle, consciousness can reflect several schemata simultaneously, but the contents of consciousness are limited. Normally, there is only a single focus of consciousness at a given moment in time. That exceptions can occur is quite clear. During neurosurgical brain electrical stimulation, patients appear to be fully aware of the surgical setting and an elicited experience simultaneously (Penfield 1975), and persons with agenesis or surgical transsection of the corpus callosum appear to have two simultaneous arenas of consciousness under certain experimental conditions (Gazzinaga and LeDoux 1978).

Self-Organization

Unlike the classical theorist, the constructivist does not need to assume that the brain is a passive arena through which information passes. Indeed, neural networks exist not simply to convey information throughout the brain; their major purpose is construction. Clearly, the human brain can generate its own patterns of awareness and imagery in the absence of extrinsic signaling. Moreover, it can store these patterns in memory, retrieve them selectively, modify them, and put them back into storage. Perception is more an act of constantly building and remodeling one's view of the world than it is of receiving and registering information.

Consciousness, always self-organizing, forms a representation or model of reality, and it is with this representation rather than reality itself that the brain copes. We cannot know the world as it truly is; we can only approximate it by forming dynamic, multimodal simulations. If we wish to refer to the "mind," then the ever-changing product of the process of simulation is it. The model with which the mind works is constantly changing because the environment and the needs of the individual change constantly.

How does the "mind" handle changes in information across time? Dennett and Kinsborne (1992) assert that mental representation of reality changes constantly in a non-linear way, relatively independent of time. That is, instead of generating conscious representation of stimulus events in a chronologically serial fashion, the brain constantly produces revised drafts of awareness, mixing old and newer sensory, affective and cognitive representations without particular regard for time. Put another way, elements of memory and expectation compete and eventually integrate with recent sensory messages from the environment for a place in the representation of reality. If this is the case, then schemata emerging from non-conscious processing into the contents of consciousness need not carry the most recent information that the brain has processed. A part of our immediate representation of reality comes from the past.

The multiple drafts concept of consciousness suggests that the most remarkable feature of consciousness formation is its extraordinary plasticity. The brain creates a representation of immediate reality by interweaving records of the past with sensory input from the immediate present, and it forecasts images of the future. Far from being a passive entity that merely registers information that comes in from various sensory channels, the brain is an active, adaptive system that constantly simulates the world and the body in which it dwells. Nociceptive signals may trigger complex responses and schemata, leading to elaborate experiences of pain with sensory, affective, cognitive and motor dimensions. They do not simply ring a carillon of bells attached to a rope that leads to a high place in the nervous system.

Pain and Survival

The broader framework behind our constructivist position is the theory of evolution. Pain is not an accident of human development, but rather a protective mechanism that fosters adaptation and survival in a primitive world. From a Darwinian perspective, one must ask why we would evolve the capability for complex pain schemata when a simple sensory warning signal might suffice. The answer may that high plasticity in modeling the world increases survival value, by increasing the adaptation of an individual to a changing environment.

In normal life, a pain schema merits high priority in the contents of consciousness because it represents a violation of biological tissue integrity. However, under conditions of emergency such as combat, pain can have a maladaptive value. It can interfere with the very functions upon which survival depends. In such situations, observers typically note that wounded combatants do not experience pain despite visually startling tissue trauma. For the soldier under fire, victory or escape is a more important goal than recognizing and tending to injury. Therefore, we suggest that those schemata that serve the individual's goals for the immediate situation are the most likely ones to prevail in competition for a place in consciousness. Protection and survival are high on the list of goals in most situations, and pain is normally relevant to these goals.

Constructivism and Individual Differences

The classical view of individual differences identifies a number of fundamental factors or processes that clearly contribute to the differences among persons in the perception and modulation of nociception. Importantly, it acknowledges the influence of learning on the nervous system via both classical conditioning and operant mechanisms. We do not gainsay this position but rather extend it by contending that people differ not only in how they respond biologically to tissue trauma but in how they construct the mental reality of tissue trauma. Put another way, to experience pain is to create the personal reality of pain from elements of sensory signaling. People differ in how well their pain fits their objectively measured tissue trauma, in part because each uniquely creates pain through the self-organizing processes of perception. This act of creation integrates past experience, present expectations and beliefs, immediate personal motives, emotional status, and social context with the immediate sensory signaling of tissue trauma.

Advantages of this Approach

This position, unlike its classical counterpart, can account for emerging observations of widespread, parallel, distributed processing in the brain during the pain experience. Such processes are the preconscious workings of the construction process. In addition, constructivism offers several advantages for understanding pain and its treatment. For one, this position can help explain the vast differences in response to painful events that one sees in clinical settings. People differ because they create and live with unique models of reality.

For another, we can account for the effects of various psychological interventions such as hypnosis on pain (Chapman and Nakamura 1998). These are interventions that recognize and address the uniqueness of the individual. Hypnotic suggestion alters the construction of the pain experience. This suggests that the processes of competition and integration are as much targets for pain intervention as the neural structures and synapses that transmit nociception.

In preventing or relieving pain, it is important to fit the intervention to the person. The assumptions behind classical thinking do not permit this type of accommodation. One assumes that human sensory mechanisms are basically all alike. In the constructivist model, everyone is unique in experiencing pain, and it is necessary to understand something of each person's model of reality in order to alter it. Because of this feature, constructivist thinking may ultimately provide a rationale for the development and refinement of cognitive-behavioral interventions for pain.

Finally, the link of pain to suffering, which forever eludes the classical theorist, is readily evident in this framework. We suffer with pain because we bundle awareness of tissue trauma with complex schemata that have negative cognitive and affective features.

4. Conclusion

The classical approach, despite the severe constraints of Cartesian thinking, has served medicine well. There is a need for more basic fact-gathering on nociceptive transmission and its modulation within this framework, but this approach maintains an impoverished vision of the brain processes associated with pain and it now must confront challenging brain imaging data. Neurophysiologists cannot fully interpret the findings emerging from PET studies of brain metabolism during pain, and future development in the neuroimaging field is likely to widen the gap between classical assumptions and brain imaging observations.

The pain field will soon need to acknowledge and address the issues that consciousness researchers are currently approaching in vision and other areas: What is the nature of massive, parallel distributed processing? What, if any, role does binding play in consciousness? How do complex patterns of electrical and metabolic activity in the brain produce the phenomenon of awareness? These and related questions may prove inescapable in pain research.

The classical approach also has problems in coming to grips with individual differences, having treated them historically as nuisance variables. Individual differences in pain are more than a curiosity for the researcher and a nuisance for the clinician. Medically, they are major barriers to the diagnosis of disease and impediments to optimizing analgesic interventions for injured or sick persons. Development of a framework that would allow individually tailored diagnosis and intervention for pain would be a major advance. We suggest that a constructivist perspective can provide a first step in this direction.

Constructivist thinking escapes the constraints of clockwork mechanics. Pain, in this framework, is the end product of a self-organizing process; it is not sensory registration of tissue damage in consciousness. It also avoids the conundrum of presupposing, tacitly or otherwise, that a mind separate from the brain reads the sensory messages that arrive from the periphery and acts on the new information. The constructivist's alternative holds that the brain actively constructs a simulation or model of the world and body and constantly revises it over time. This model is a mix of old and new information. Pain occurs when nociceptive messages become integrated with other patterns of brain activity and are then represented in the contents of consciousness.

Individual differences, in the long run, are only unexplained variance in a scientific model. In the field of pain, these loom large. Their persistence and their negative impact on patient care point to a need for revolutionary changes in theory. A constructivist approach offers a viable alternative in facilitating necessary changes. In so doing, this approach will bridge the pain and consciousness research communities. Each field has much to learn from the other.

Notes

1. The source of the word is Greek and its plural is schemata.

References

Alexander, J. and Black, A. 1992. Pain mechanisms and the management of neuropathic pain. *Current Opinion in Neurology and Neurosurgery* 5(2): 228–234.

Baumstark, K.E. and Buckelew, S.P. 1992. Fibromyalgia: clinical signs, research findings, treatment implications, and future directions. *Annals of Behavioral Medicine* 14: 282–291.

Besson, J.M. and Chaouch, A. 1987. Peripheral and spinal mechanisms of nociception. *Psycholgical Review* 67(1): 67–185.

Bonica, J.J. 1990. *The Management of Pain*. 2nd ed. Philadelphia: Lea and Febiger.

Calvin, W.H. 1987. The Brain as a Darwin Machine. *Nature* 330: 33–34.

Casey, K.L., Minoshima, S., Berger, K.L., Koeppe, R.A., Morrow, T.J. and Frey, K.A. 1994. Positron emission tomographic analysis of cerebral structures activated specifically by repetitive noxious heat stimuli. *Journal of Neurophysiology* 71(2): 802–807.

Casey, K.L., Minoshima, S., Morrow, T.J. and Koeppe, R.A. 1996. Comparison of human cerebral activation pattern during cutaneous warmth, heat pain, and deep cold pain. *Journal of Neurophysiology* 76(1): 571–581.

Chapman, C.R. 1995. Affective dimension of pain: A model. In B.B. Bromm and J.E. Desmedt (eds.), *Pain and the Brain: From Nociception to Cognition* 283–302. New York: Raven Press.

Chapman, C.R., Donaldson, G.W., Jacobson, R.C. and Hautman, B. 1997. Differences among patients in opioid self-administration during bone marrow transplantation. *Pain* 71(3): 213–223.

Chapman, C.R. and Nakamura, Y. 1998. Hypnotic analgesia: A constructivist framework. *International Journal of Clinical and Experimental Hypnosis* XLVI (1): 6–27.

Coghill, R.C., Talbot, J.D., Evans, A.C., Meyer, E., Gjedde, A., Bushnell, M.C. and Duncan, G.H. 1994. Distributed processing of pain and vibration by the human brain. *Journal of Neuroscience* 14(7): 4095–5108.

Craig, A.D. 1991. Supraspinal pathways and mechanisms relevant to central pain. In K.L. Case (ed.), *Pain and Central Nervous System Disease: The Central Pain Syndromes*, 157–170. New York: Raven Press.

Damasio, A.R. 1994. *Descartes' Error: Emotion and Reason in the Human Brain*. New York: Grosset/Putnam.

Dennett, D.C. 1991. *Consciousness Explained*. Boston: Little, Brown.

Dennett, D.C. 1996. *The myth of double transduction* (Paper presented at "Toward a Science of Consciousness 1996: Tucson II." Tucson, Arizona).

Dennett, D.C. and Kinsbourne, M. 1992. Time and the observer: The where and when of consciousness in the brain. *Behavioral and Brain Sciences* 15(2): 183–247.

Dubner, R. 1991. Neuronal plasticity and pain following peripheral tissue inflammation of nerve injury. In M.R. Bond, C.J. Woolf and J.E. Charlton (eds.), *Proceedings of the VIth World Congress on Pain*, 263–276. Amsterdam: Elsevier.

Duthie, D.J.R. 1994. The physiology and pharmacology of pain. In W.S. Nimmo, D.J. Rowbotham and G. Smith (eds.), *Anaesthesia*. Vol. 1: 119–31. Oxford: Blackwell Scientific Publications.

Everett, J.J., Patterson, D.R., Marvin, J.A., Montgomery, B., Ordonez, N. and Campbell, K. 1994. Pain assessment from patients with burns and their nurses. *Journal of Burn Care and Rehabilitation* 15(2): 194–198.

Gazzaniga, M.S. and LeDoux, J.E. 1978. *The Integrated Mind*. New York: Plenum Press.

Gebhart, G.F. and Ness, T.J. 1991. Central mechanisms of visceral pain. *Canadian Journal of Physiology and Pharmacology* 69(5): 627–634.

Greenfield, S. A. 1995. *Journey to the Centers of the Mind: Toward a science of Consciousness*. New York: W. H. Freeman and Company.

Heppelmann, B., Messlinger, K., Schaible, H. G. and Schmidt, R. F. 1991. Nociception and pain. *Current Opinion in Neurobiology* 1(2): 192–197.

Hill, A., Niven, C. A. and Knussen, C. 1996. Pain memories in phantom limbs: A case study. *Pain* 66(2/3): 381–384.

Jänig, W. 1987. Neuronal mechanisms of pain with special emphasis on visceral and deep somatic pain. *Acta Neurochirurgica (Wien)* 38 (Supplement), 16–32.

Jessell, T. M. and Kelly, D. D. 1991. Pain and analgesia. In E. R. Kandel, J. H. Schwartz and T. M. Jessell (eds.), *Principles of Neural Science*, 385–398. 3rd ed. New York: Elsevier.

Jones, A. K., Brown, W. D., Friston, K. J., Qi, L. Y. and Frackowiak, R. S. 1991. Cortical and subcortical localization of response to pain in man using positron emission tomography. *Proceedings of the Royal Society of London, Series B Biological Sciences*, 244(1309): 39–44.

Jones, A. K., Cunningham, V. J., Hakawa, S., Fujiwara, T., Luthra, S. K., Silva, S., Derbyshire, S. and Jones, T. 1994. Changes in central opioid receptor binding in relation to inflammation and pain in patients with rheumatoid arthritis. *British Journal of Rheumatology* 33(10): 909–916.

Katz, J. and Melzack, R. 1990. Pain 'memories' in phantom limbs: review and clinical observations. *Pain* 43(3): 319–336.

Krause, N. and Ragland, D. R. 1994. Occupational disability due to low back pain: a new interdisciplinary classification based on a phase model of disability. *Spine* 19: 1011–1020.

Magora, A. and Schwartz, A. 1980. Relation between the low back pain syndrome and x-ray findings. 3. Spina bifida occulta. *Scandinavian Journal of Rehabilitation Medicine* 12(1): 9–15.

McMahon, S. and Koltzenburg, M. 1990. The changing role of primary afferent neurones in pain. *Pain* 43: 269–272.

Melzack, R. 1990. Phantom limbs and the concept of a neuromatrix. *Trends in Neuroscience* 13: 88–92.

Melzack, R. 1996. Gate Control Theory: On the evolution of pain concepts. *Pain Forum* 5(1): 128–138.

Melzack, R. and Casey, K. L. 1968. Sensory, motivational, and central control determinants of pain. In D. R. Kenshalo (ed.), *The Skin Senses*, 423–443. Springfield: Thomas Books.

Melzack, R. and Wall, P. D. 1965. Pain mechanisms: A new theory. *Science* 150: 971–979.

Mesulam, M. 1994. Neurocognitive networks and selectively distributed processing. *Revue Neurologie Paris* 150(8–9): 564–569.

Mesulam, M. M. 1990. Large-scale neurocognitive networks and distributed processing for attention, language, and memory. *Annals of Neurology* 28(5): 597–613.

Penfield, W. 1975. *The Mystery of the Mind.* Princeton, NJ: Princeton University Press.

Perl, E. R. 1984. Characterization of nociception and their activation of neurons in the superficial dorsal horn: First steps for the sensation of pain. In L. Kruger and J. C. Liebeskind (eds.), *Advances in Pain Research and Therapy* 23–52. Vol. 6. New York: Raven Press.

Roberts, W. J. 1986. A hypothesis on the physiological basis for causalgia and related pains. *Pain* 24(3): 297–311.

Roll, M. and Zetterquist, S. 1990. Acute chest pain without obvious organic cause before the age of 40 years: response to forced hyperventilation [see comments]. *Journal of Internal Medicine* 228(3): 223–227.

Rumelhart, D. E., Smolensky, P., McClelland, J. L. and Hinton, G. E. 1986. Schemata and sequential thought processes in PDP models. In J. L. McCleeland and D. E. Rumelhart (eds.), *Parallel Distributed Processing: Explorations in the Microstructure of Cognition: Psychological and Biological Models*, 7–57. Vol. 2. Cambridge, MA: MIT press.

Schubert, M. M., Williams, B. E., Lloid, M. E., Donaldson, G. and Chapko, M. K. 1992. Clinical assessment scale for the rating of oral mucosal changes associated with bone marrow transplantation. Development of an oral mucositis index. *Cancer* 69(10): 2469–2477.

Talbot, J. D., Marrett, S., Evans, A. C., Meyer, E., Bushnell, M. C. and Duncan, G. H. 1991. Multiple representations of pain in human cerebral cortex. *Science* 251(4999): 1355–1358.

Taylor, J. G. 1996. A competition for consciousness. *Neurocomputing* 11(2–4): 271–296.

Thomas, S. H. and Stone, C. K. 1994. Emergency department treatment of migraine, tension, and mixed-type headache. *Journal of Emergency Medicine* 12(5): 657–664.

Vogt, B. A., Derbyshire, S. and Jones, A. K. 1996. Pain processing in four regions of human cingulate cortex localized with co-registered PET and MR imaging. *European Journal of Neuroscience* 8(7): 1461–1473.

Waddell, G. and Main, C. J. 1984. Assessment of severity in low-back disorders. *Spine* 9(2): 204–208.

Williams, J. M. G., Watts, F. N., MacLeod, C. and Mathews, A. 1988. *Cognitive Psychology and Emotional Disorders*. Chichester, England: John Wiley & Sons Ltd.

Willis, W. D. 1993. Mechanisms of somatic pain. In C. R. Chapman and K. M. Foley (eds.), *Current and Emerging Issues in Cancer Pain*, 67–81. New York: Raven Press.

Willis, W. D. J. 1988. Dorsal horn neurophysiology of pain. *Annals of the New York Academy of Sciences* 531: 76–89.

Woolf, C. J. 1989. Recent advances in the pathophysiology of acute pain. *British Journal of Anaesthesia* 63(2): 139–146.

Woolf, C. J. and King, A. E. 1990. Dynamic alterations in the cutaneous mechanoreceptive fields of dorsal horn neurons in the rat spinal cord. *Journal of Neuroscience* 10(8): 2717–2726.

Individual Differences in the Consciousness of Phantom Limbs

Joel Katz
University of Toronto

Many patients awake from the anesthetic after an amputation feeling certain that the operation has not been performed. They feel the lost limb so vividly and clearly that only when they reach out to touch it do they realize it has been cut off. This startling realization does nothing to subdue the reality of the limb they experience, and may even intensify the sensations which define it. This phenomenon was first reported in 1545 by the French surgeon Ambroise Paré (Keynes 1952) and later by Descartes (Lott 1986). But it was Weir Mitchell (1871) in 1871, who coined the term "phantom limb". One year later, as part of his seminal book on nerve injuries, Mitchell (1872) devoted a chapter to the study of painful and non-painful phantom limbs. The term *phantom limb* so accurately captures the nature and subjective experience of the phenomenon that it has been universally adopted by researchers, clinicians, amputees, and the public at large.

This chapter reviews the phenomenology of the painless and painful phantom limb with particular emphasis on individual differences in the conscious experience of these phenomena. The joint influence of peripheral neurophysiological factors and higher-order cognitive and affective processes are evaluated in terms of their capacity to trigger or modulate awareness of phantom limb sensations and pain. In part one the prevalence, course and qualities of painful and non-painful phantom limbs are presented. Part two documents a number of predictable changes that occur in the phantom limb over time, including fading, telescoping, and shrinking. It is suggested that the length and size of the phantom may be a perceptual marker of the extent to which sensory inputs from the amputation stump have re-occupied deprived cortical regions originally subserving the amputated limb. Part three outlines one way in which the sympathetic nervous system may influence phantom limb pain. A model involving a sympathetic-efferent somatic-afferent cycle is presented to explain fluctuations in the intensity of sensations referred to the phantom limb. The model is extended to explain the puzzling finding that only *after* amputation are thoughts and feelings capable of evoking referred sensations to the (phantom) limb. While phantom pains and other sensations frequently are triggered by thoughts and feelings, there is no evidence that the painful or painless phantom limb is a symptom of a psychological disorder. In part four, the concept of a pain "memory" is introduced and described with examples. The data show that pain experienced prior to amputation may persist in the form of a memory referred to the phantom limb causing continued suffering and distress. It is argued that two independent and potentially dissociable memory components underlie the unified experience of a pain memory. This conceptualization is evaluated in the context of the surgical arena, raising the possibility that under certain conditions post-amputation pain may, in part, reflect the persistent central neural memory trace left by the surgical procedure.

Painful and Non-Painful Phantom Limbs

The Non-Painful Phantom Limb

A distinction is usually made between the painful and non-painful phantom limb (Melzack & Wall 1988). The most salient property of the non-painful phantom is its tingling, "pins and needles" or *paresthetic* quality, but sensations of temperature, posture, length, volume, and movement are also very common (Jensen & Rasmussen 1994).

Table 1 contains excerpts, transcribed verbatim from tape-recorded interviews with amputees describing various phantom sensations and pains they experience. The aim in presenting this material is to convey to the reader the phenomenological experience of a phantom limb as expressed by the subjects in their own words. The approach is purely descriptive and is intended to complement the more quantitative data provided later in the chapter. Excerpts are preceded by the subject's case number, sex, age at the time of interview, side and level of amputation, and time since amputation. These descriptions reveal how dynamic and fluid the phantom limb experience can be, consisting of frequently changing perceptual experiences that depend upon current sensory input, the emotional state and past experience of the individual amputee.

Table 1. *Excerpts from tape-recorded interviews with amputees describing various qualities of phantom sensations and pains. The material is presented according to the type of phantom sensation reported so that excerpts from different subjects appear under separate sub-headings. Excerpts are preceded by the subject's case number, sex, age at time of interview, side and level of amputation, and time since amputation.*

I. Paresthesias /numb sensation

Case E02–Male, aged 62 years; R-above-knee amputation, 3 years prior
"It's getting more. ... Right down to the toes. ... It's just there, that's all. Just seems to have stopped, but I can feel it, you know what I mean? It's not ... paresthesias. It's like kind of a ... let's call it numb. ... Now it's just static. ... It's just like it's numb. ... it's not tingling as much. ... It's just like it was dead ... or numb."

Case E05–Male, aged 61 years; R-above-knee amputation, 2.5 years prior
"I feel right now like there's something. It's not a foot, it's ... it's just the end, you know, before the foot starts, but there's no pain. ... it's a mild, mild, prickly sensation but as a whole ... needles everywhere, you know, not individual, as a whole. It's hard to explain ... you know sometimes you feel pinpricks everywhere ... where what I feel now is the bottom, but not the full foot, like the back ... It feels like the beginning of a numbness or some kind of activity, like pinpricks, but altogether, not separated ... and it's mild. I'm not uncomfortable with it."

Case E08–Male, aged 53 years; L-below-knee amputation, 4 months prior
"It seems to become more frozen or numb again, a little more. Like it's getting ... like if it was there and heavier... If I can compare it, it would be about the same feeling as when ... they freeze your teeth. It doesn't feel cold, but it feels like it's getting thick, clumsy, that's it, thick."
"It's getting more frozen — if I may use this expression. It's not cold, but it's getting like heavier, numb completely. It's going above the ankle a little in the front only. I don't feel anything in the back. The heel and the back of the ankle, I don't feel, but the front there, where the arch of the foot is, I feel it ... on the left side only."

II. Temperature

Case E04–Female, aged 59 years; R-shoulder disarticulation , 8 years prior
"That left hand is getting cool ... I don't think it's *cool*, it's almost as though there were ice in the veins; *cool*, *cool*. Not quite cold enough to get frostbite, but cool."
"I can feel the fingertips sort of pulsing but cool, and then there's the ... the heel of my hand. The elbow's there, but not doing much of anything ... Now it's warm in my upper arm, or just above the elbow. Just warm *there*, not overall warm ... and expanding, pulsing ... my pinky finger is throbbing as though in sympathy to where it's expanding."

Table 1. *Continued*

Case E05
"Now I feel like I could feel my knee. ... Without pain, yah, but it's cold. I never felt that before. I felt my knee because it was cold at the end... not the stump ... it seemed like it was further than my stump and it felt *cold*, but felt like a knee, like I would touch my knee and it would feel cold. Now I start to feel my foot again ... heavy. ... Heavier and uh ... I feel my knee, now. Boy that's a new sensation!"

Case E20–Male, aged 23 years; R-above-knee amputation, 2 months prior
"The pain ... the pain, it's different. It's not *pain*. It's like if you froze your hands outside and then you go in. It's hot, it burns, but it's very, very low. It's hot, I feel my foot like, like it was frozen ... as if you had frozen it outside in the snow and it's coming back, softly. Like it's thawing. It seems a little like that."

III. Pressure/constriction

Case E04
"Um ...... I don't know how to explain that to you: If you have a knot and it loosens, you know, like a muscle spasm type thing, I just felt that in my elbow ... and now my hand is tingling."

Case E07–Female, aged 31 years; R-below-knee amputation, 5.8 years prior
"Um, in the back of my ankle, I feel it. A squeezing ... and also a tingle, like freezing cold."

Case E14–Female, aged 31 years; L-below-knee amputation, 1.5 months prior
"... this is what hurts the most .... the pressure ... on the {phantom} foot, it's tight ... the cramp, it's all tight."

IV. Somatosensory memories

Case E04
"... the hand is tingling now and I'm well aware of the elbow, somewhere between the elbow and the hand. I feel as though it's full of edema, extra fluid where it doesn't belong. ... When I say edema, I remember the feeling I had when I wore the sleeve. That's what it brings to mind. This was long before the amputation when I used to wear a sleeve to keep the swelling in the arm down, you know."
"OK now, my hand seems to be starting to drain. ... It's like draining it from edema. It's as though it were trickling out, and it's a little cooler. I guess I explain it that way because it reminds me of how my hand and arm felt when I was in that machine at the hospital having the edema pumped out. I can't really say... it's as though my arm were up and the fluid was leaving it. Now, it still feels swollen. ... There's the draining feeling, leaving the finger tips, going down the finger into the palm of the hand, through the palm, into this part [the heel of her hand], then it just doesn't happen. I mean there's

Table 1. *Continued*

nothing there: The wrist is there, but it isn't part of the draining ... well, it's not draining anymore, now it's throbbing."
"My thumb feels the way it did when I first was losing the sensation ... the feeling of being asleep, but more ... fat and being asleep. ... That strange tingling feeling."

Case E06–Female, aged 61 years; R-above-knee amputation, 5.5 years prior
"... and that's where I had the pain. I'm just thinking of that now. You know when I had the bypasses? The side of my leg, that's where it was so sore, where I'm getting those [pains] there now. That's how I knew that I had a blockage ... it was sore down the side of my leg."
"It's down the side of the leg again. When I went in there [the hospital], I had the pain on the side of my leg which told me that something was wrong, you know. That's when I had no circulation. And it's the same kind of pain I got, like down the side of my leg on the outside."

Case E14
"... when I had my accident, the bottom of my foot was torn away. I feel that it [the phantom pain] originates there ... I had so much pain under my foot that the phantom pain has stayed ... I had so much pain underneath."

Case E20
"I just had a pain in my leg. Bone pain. When I was a kid, I had a pain like that in my leg. Well, like eight, nine, ten years ago. I had pain in my leg. You know in my bone. Like my bone hurt. You know, some kids get that — when they grow up — It's the same thing I got."

V. Weight

Case E04
"I'd say that there was a heaviness almost as though I had a breast again. Not quite a phantom pain, but ... as though I'm supporting weight."
"A tight feeling in the upper arm, heavy, ... a load .... almost the way it would be if you were lifting weights I imagine, and the muscles are all tense."

Case E05
"I start to feel my foot, but without pain, ... a weight. ... the foot is starting to form completely."

Case E06
"The heaviness ... It isn't *so* heavy, so I can feel the leg from the knee down. [When the leg feels heavy] it just feels heavy and I can't distinguish ... the knee from the foot."

Table 1. *Continued*

VI. Posture/position

Case E04
"It's cool and comfy and quiet at my side. Instead of the hand being out here [arm outstretched] it's sort of against the body like this [hanging by her side]."

Case E12–Female, aged 73 years; L-above-knee amputation, 1.8 years prior
"Now I can't even bend my toes. It's like they're paralyzed. ... usually I *think* I can move them."

VII. Other phantom sensations and pains

Case E04
"There's a feeling in the elbow, as though I've been batting a tennis ball around and it's tired ... and it's cool again. The fingers don't seem to be so spread eagle ... I feel the whole palm like a ... sort of a wave or something going over it, and it comes back and goes over it ... the hand is cool ... the elbow feels just ... full."
"This is really a dichotomy. My normal reaction is to ignore the pain and I have the feeling that you'd like me to concentrate on it ... My arm's just there. It's not cool but it's not hot and invading my mind ...It's not as cool as it was before ... but it's not drawing attention to itself. ... I know that when I start thinking about my arm it feels it has licence to hurt, so I guess one of the things I try to do is *not* think about it. It's sort of like keeping the lid on Pandora's Box."

Case E05
"It's funny, I felt just then, I felt my knee again, but not good ... not a pain, but not cold like a little while ago. Like nerves was working inside, inside the knee. ... I didn't feel the coldness that I did a while ago. That coldness felt good."

Case E11–Female, aged 54 years; R-above-knee amputation, 2 years prior
"The only way I can describe it [the phantom] now, is like looking out the window ... but the window is frosted. You see what is there, but you don't see the sharp edges of everything. Or, if you touch somebody but there's something on the skin so you don't touch the skin, but you feel the skin, you feel ... Oh, I don't know, something like that ... but it can be very intense even if it is like that."
"It's painful because the feeling is excessive, but it's not a pain like if you cut yourself or banged yourself. It's not that kind of pain. I can't call it a pain. It's not a pain. It's not a *physical* pain, I would say, because that [motioning to the space below the stump] is not physical ... and it is. So, how can I describe something that is physical and is not? It's physical in the way that I feel it, but it's not there. So how do you describe something like that? So it's painful but it's not a pain. I don't know what else to say."

Recent studies estimate the incidence of the non-painful phantom at approximately 80% to 100% (Jensen & Rasmussen 1994). In fact, the presence of a non-painful phantom is so common that it is considered a "normal" sequela of amputation. It is standard practice to prepare the patient pre-operatively for its subsequent occurrence (Butler, Turkal, & Seidl 1992; McGrath & Hillier 1992; Sherman 1989). Much of the variability in the prevalence rate of the non-painful phantom can be attributed to between-study differences in the length of time between amputation and interview.

The frequency of occurrence of a painless phantom does not appear to be related to the extremity, side, level of amputation, age, gender, or reason for amputation (Jensen, Krebs, Nielsen, & Rasmussen 1984; Jensen & Rasmussen 1994). There is considerably more variability in the estimates of the duration of the non-painful phantom. In some amputees, the phantom may disappear within days or weeks of the amputation. In others, it remains unchanged for up to 60 years (James, 1887; Jensen & Rasmussen 1994).

Phantom Limb Pain

For many amputees, a distressing problem is phantom limb pain. The distinction between a painful and painless phantom is not a clear cut one, but for purposes of description and classification it useful to separate them (Melzack & Wall 1988; Wall 1981). Painful phantom experiences vary along a number of dimensions which include intensity, quality, location, frequency, and duration. Many patients report a painful intensification of the paresthesias (i.e., dysesthesias) that define the non-painful phantom limb. Some sufferers describe bouts of paroxysmal shooting pain that travel up and down the limb. Others report the phantom to be in a cramped or otherwise unnatural posture that gives rise to excruciating pain. Many amputees describe the pain in the phantom limb as indistinguishable from the pain they experienced in the limb prior to amputation. In still others, the phantom may be immobile or paralyzed so that attempts to move it generate pain. Finally, the phantom is often the seat of an intense burning pain as if the hand or foot were being held too close to an open flame. Frequently amputees suffer from several types of pain (Jensen & Rasmussen 1994). Phantom limb pain appears to be equally prevalent among men and women, and does not appear to be related to side, level, age, or cause of amputation (Jensen, Krebs, Nielsen, & Rasmussen 1985; Jensen & Rasmussen 1994).

Early reports suggested the risk of developing phantom limb pain after amputation to be extremely low. Prevalence estimates ranged between 1% and 10% (Ewalt et al. 1947; Randall et al. 1946). Unfortunately, these studies drastically under-estimated the frequency of phantom limb pain. Recent surveys based on several thousand amputees reveal that between 78% (Sherman, Sherman, & Parker 1984) and 85% of patients (Sherman & Sherman 1983) continue to experience significant amounts of phantom limb pain more than 25 years after amputation. Even the more conservative estimates far exceed the earlier figures. Using a very conservative criterion, Sherman and Sherman (1983) estimated no less than 51% of their sample of 1,200 amputees continued to live in pain more than two and a half decades after losing their limbs. According to recent prospective studies (Jensen et al. 1985; Nikolajsen, Ilkjaer, Krøner, Christensen, & Jensen 1997a), the incidence of phantom limb pain ranges between 50% and 71% over a 2-year period, with a reduction in the frequency and duration of attacks over time (Jensen et al. 1985). Equally striking is the low success rate of treatments for phantom limb pain: in the long term only 7% of patients are helped by the more than 50 types of therapy used to treat phantom limb pain (Sherman 1989).

The different qualities of phantom limb pain, its high prevalence and incidence, and low treatment success rate point to the complexity of the problem and suggest that there is not just one cause of phantom limb pain. The development and severity of this disorder are determined by the interaction of multiple inputs which vary across individuals and include past experience with pain and the immediate physiological, motivational and psychological states of the individual. There is an urgent need for clinical investigations into the physiological mechanisms and psychological processes associated with phantom limb pain as well as for placebo-controlled clinical trials and outcome studies aimed at modifying these mechanisms and processes once they have been isolated.

Fading, Telescoping, and Shrinking of the Phantom Limb

In the majority of cases, the normal phantom undergoes a number of predictable changes within several years of amputation (Jensen et al. 1984; Jensen et al. 1985; Jensen & Rasmussen 1994). These include fading, telescoping, and shrinking. Immediately after amputation the phantom limb usually feels of normal size and length, but with time, the proximal portions begin to fade and soon disappear (Figure 1). After some fading has occurred, the phantom limb usually consists of only the extremity and major joints (Figure 1C). These are felt at a normal distance from the body. The intervening parts have disappeared so that the phantom hand or foot feels as if it were hanging, unattached, in empty space. In the case of an amputation performed at the shoulder, the phantom limb may consist of only the lower arm and hand, with a gap between the shoulder stump and the phantom elbow (Figure 2). In approximately one third of amputees, a process of "telescoping" (Guéniot, 1861) begins. Among upper extremity amputees, the phantom is perceived gradually to approach the stump so that the hand is located in phenomenal space on a level with the elbow of the other arm. As the process continues, the gap between the stump and phantom continues to close; the amputee may find that the hand is protruding from, or attached to, the end of the stump. Later, the phantom hand may retract into the stump so that only the tips of the fingers jut out (Figure 1B). In some cases, eventually even these may disappear completely and permanently into the stump.

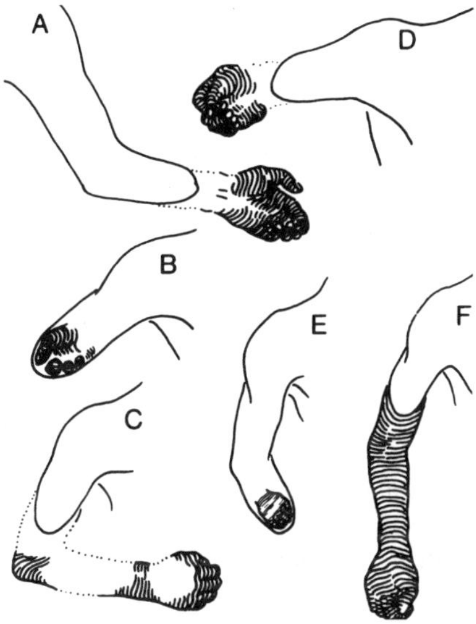

Figure 1. *Illustrations of phantom limbs in various stages of fading, telescoping, and shrinking after amputation of the upper extremity. A: Below-elbow amputation with phantom limb of normal size and length. B: Above-elbow amputation with phantom fingers completely telescoped into the stump. C: Above-elbow amputation with normal length phantom limb. After some fading has occurred the phantom consists of the elbow, wrist and fingers. D: Above-elbow amputation with telescoped phantom hand attached to the stump. E: Below-elbow amputation with telescoped phantom hand. Note also the marked shrinking of the phantom and its position within the stump. F: Above-elbow amputation with phantom of normal size and length before fading has occurred. Adapted from Solonen (1962) with permission.*

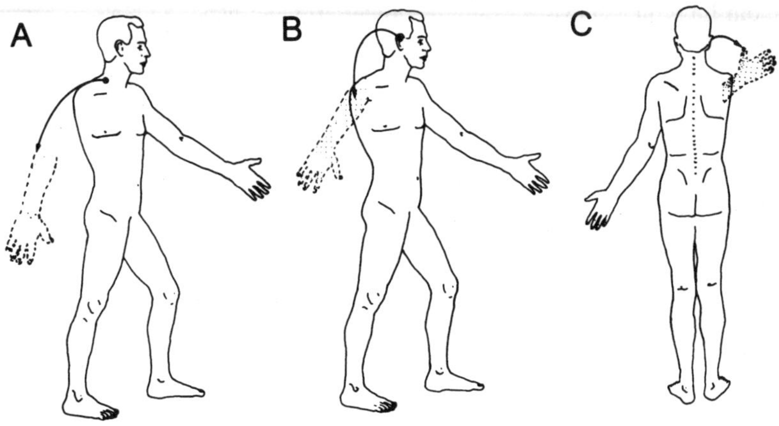

Figure 2. *Illustrations of a patient who sustained a complete fore-quarter amputation of his right shoulder in a work accident and later developed phantom limb pain. The figurines depict the process of telecscoping following a series of treatments with transcutaneous elecrical nerve stimulation. Dots represent points where stimulation was applied. Arrows indicate site of referred phantom limb sensations. A: The patient reported a phantom limb of normal length that consisted of only the lower arm and hand, with a gap between the shoulder stump and phantom elbow. During stimulation applied at a point above the clavicle, the patient reported that his phantom hand began to swell and become warm. B: In response to stimulation applied at a point on his right ear, he remarked that his phantom arm had "telescoped" into the stump so that the elbow protruded from the stump. C: Later, stimulation of the same point resulted in a further retraction of the phantom, leaving only the wrist and hand attached to the stump. Adapted from Katz and Melzack (1987) with permission.*

There are times when a completely telescoped phantom will temporarily lengthen so that the hand or foot is once again felt at a normal distance from the stump (Cronholm 1951; James 1887; Riddoch 1941). More rarely, the converse also occurs; a phantom which is already telescoped may temporarily retract completely into the stump, or one which is of normal, or shortened length, may become even shorter (Haber 1958; Henderson & Smyth 1948). The circumstances and stimuli which bring about these changes are extremely varied and range from peripheral stimulation of the stump and other regions of the body to more central influences.

When Guéniot (1861) first introduced the phenomenon of telescoping, he also remarked that it might be accompanied by a marked shrinking of the phantom to the dimensions of a child's limb (Figure 1E). This gradual diminution in perceived size or volume occurs in both upper and lower limb amputees.

The extent of shrinking that occurs is quite variable. In spite of the uniformity of the process, the conscious experience of the shrinking phantom is a highly individual phenomenon. Adult amputees have reported the phantom to be the size of a doll's hand or a baby's hand (Browder & Gallagher 1948), a silver dollar (Livingston 1943), and even as small as a postage stamp (Morgenstern 1964).

Cortical Maps and Phantom Limbs

Factors governing the fading, telescoping, and shrinking of the phantom are not well understood. The gradual fading of the phantom is thought to represent a perceptual correlate of the re-establishment of control over hyperactive or spontaneously active cells which subserve the phantom (Carlen, Wall, Nadvorna, & Steinbach 1978; Wall 1981). The gradual telescoping and shrinking have been hypothesized to depend upon input from intact peripheral fibers located in the stump. These experiences appear to be perceptual markers of the short- and long-term reorganizational changes that occur after amputation in central nervous system structures including somatosensory cortex (Katz 1992b; Merzenich et al. 1984). The process of cortical reoccupation involves an orderly topographic expansion of adjacent parts of the hand into the deprived region and appears to progress in a proximo-distal direction. This process parallels the perceptual experience of telescoping in which the hand or foot is gradually felt to approach the stump. Thus, the perceived distance between the phantom and the stump may be a function of the distance separating their respective representations in the cortical map (Merzenich et al. 1984).

Evidence of a link between the telescoping process and cortical reorganization is suggested by the differential sensory acuity of stumps of amputees with "telescoped" and "extended" (i.e., normal length) phantom limbs (Haber 1955). Point localization is significantly enhanced in above-elbow amputees whose phantoms are perceived to be inside the stump as compared to those who report phantom limbs of normal length. Light touch and two-point discrimination thresholds also show greater stump sensitivity among amputees with telescoped phantom limbs. These findings suggest that as a result of the central readjustment of cutaneous inputs after amputation, the distal region of the stump takes over the tactile and sensory functions of the amputated hand.

Referred Phantom Limb Sensations

The observation that cells in re-occupied cortex respond to new inputs from skin surfaces on the stump and adjacent digits (Merzenich et al. 1984) raises the questions of where (to which body part) a stimulus would be localized when applied to a novel receptive field and whether the referred location differs as a function of the length of the phantom. Reports of sensations referred to the phantom limb when the stump is stimulated provide further support for the suggestion that a process of central reorganization after amputation involves an expansion of stump inputs into brain regions originally representing the amputated limb. For example, Pitres (1897) notes that when the stump is pricked or scratched lightly, a sensation with the appropriate quality of experience, is felt at precise points of the phantom extremity. One subject reported "droplets of sweat trickle down the absent hand" (p. 183) whenever the stump perspires. James (1887) remarks how a breeze directed at the stump is felt as a breeze on the phantom foot, and Gallinek (1939) reports that placing a pillow at the end of the stump is felt at the sole of the phantom foot. In response to a touch on the stump, one of Haber's (1956) subjects with a telescoped phantom remarked "Gee! It feels just like you are touching my hand" (p. 629). Similarly, Morgenstern (1964) describes a subject with bilateral lower extremity amputations and phantoms of shorter than normal length who reported that stimulation of the stump gave rise to dual percepts that "are very hard to describe, as there are separate sensations in the stump and in the foot which appear to come from the same point" (p. 61).

Cronholm (1951) systematically studied the pattern of referred phantom limb sensations elicited by applying a variety of stimuli to the stump. Light touch produced a distinct sensation that specific points on phantom hand had been touched. Stimulation with objects of different temperatures elicited appropriate sensations of heat or cold in the phantom limb. The data reveal a remarkable isomorphism and consistency between the site and quality of the stimulus applied at the stump and the referred sensations experienced in the phantom limb.

Other, more recent, studies have confirmed and extended these findings. Phantom sensations may be referred to the phantom limb when a variety of body regions, remote from the stump, are stimulated, including the face (Ebert et al. 1994; Halligan, Marshall, & Wade 1994; Halligan, Marshall, Wade, Davey, & Morrison 1993; Ramachandran, Stewart, & Rogers-Ramachandran 1992), chest, and axilla (Ramachandran et al. 1992). In most cases, these results have been interpreted as evidence for the remapping hypothesis. However, when the degree of cortical reorganization was actually measured by magnetic source imaging, it did not correlate with referred phantom sensations induced by stimulation of the face (Ebert et al. 1994).

The process of telescoping may be use-dependent. Kallio (1950b) surgically cleaved below-elbow stumps so that the two branches could function as a "forcepslike gripping organ" without the need of a prosthesis. After an extensive post-operative training program, the branches of the stump were capable of pronation, supination, grasping, and of opening and closing at a rate which approximated that of normal fingers. Two to six years later, 36% of the patients reported a cleft phantom hand in which certain fingers had fused or others had disappeared in accommodating to the shape of the stump (Figure 3). The phantom had shortened so that it coincided with the tips of the branches or was completely within the stump. Opening and closing the branches of the stump were accompanied by corresponding movements in the phantom hand.

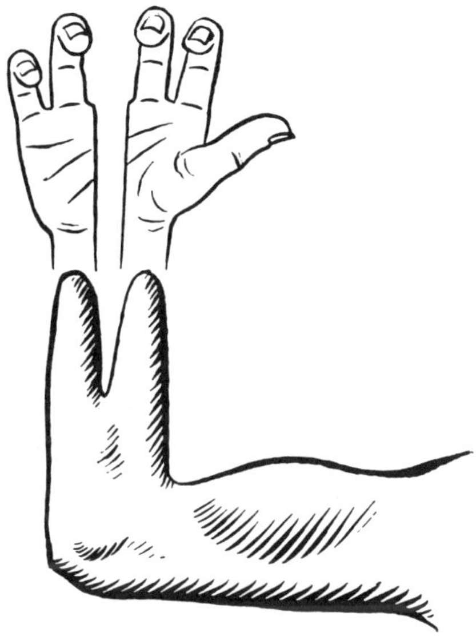

Figure 3. *Illustration of the use-dependent changes in the phantom limb following a post-operative training program. Below-elbow stumps were surgically cleaved so the two branches could function in opposition. After training, the phantom fingers were reported to coincide with the two branches of the stump. Opening and closing the branches of the stump were accompanied by corresponding movements in the phantom hand, Reproduced from Kallio (1950b) with permission.*

Taken together, these observations support the hypothesis that the perception of the size and length of the phantom correspond to a process of central reorganization involving an expansion of stump inputs into cortical areas subserving parts of the lost limb. Moreover, with repetitive use of the stump, there appears to be an adaptive restructuring of the phantom so that it eventually conforms to the combined visual and kinesthetic percept of the stump.

Phantom Limbs and the Sympathetic Nervous System

Recently, Sherman (1994) has argued that phantom limb pain is not a unitary syndrome, but a symptom class, with each class subserved by different etiologic mechanisms. For example, one class of phantom limb pain which is characterized by a cramping quality is associated with electromyographic spike activity in muscles of the stump whereas burning phantom limb pain shows no such association (Sherman & Arena 1992). Katz and Melzack (1990) have identified a class of phantom limb pain which resembles in quality and location a pain experienced in the limb before amputation. Although the precise physiological mechanisms that underlie these somatosensory pain memories are unknown, the presence of pre-amputation pain clearly is a necessary condition for these phantom pains to develop.

Another class of phantom limb pain may come about through involvement of the sympathetic nervous system although its role in triggering or maintaining pathological pain has been a source of considerable confusion and debate (Campbell, Raja, Selig, Belzberg, & Meyer 1994; Jänig 1990; Nathan 1989; Ochoa, Torebjörk, Marchettini, & Sivak 1985; Schott 1993). Sympathetic nervous system involvement in pain has been attributed to a cycle of sympathetic-efferent somatic-afferent activity in which neural and/or vascular mechanisms participate. Pain is hypothesized to arise from sympathetically-triggered ephaptic transmission (Jänig 1985), sympathetic activation of nociceptors (Campbell, Meyer, Davis, & Raja 1992a; Devor 1983), or low threshold mechanoreceptors which terminate on sensitized spinal cord cells (Roberts 1986), and injury-induced alteration in the pattern of postganglionic cutaneous vasoconstrictor neurons which lose their normal thermoregulatory function leading to trophic changes and ischemia (Jänig 1985).

Despite frequent assertions that the sympathetic nervous system is involved in the production and maintenance of phantom limb pain, surprisingly few studies have actually examined peripheral sympathetic nervous system activity at the stump and contralateral limb. Sliosberg (1948) studied 141 amputees and found that the stump was cooler than the intact limb in 94 patients but he did not relate the temperature difference to the presence or absence of phantom limb pain. Kristen et al. (1984) reported that a "patchy asymmetrical temperature" distribution of stump thermograms was significantly more frequent among stump pain sufferers than in patients who were free from stump pain, but thermograms were no different for patients with or without phantom limb pain.

In contrast, Sherman and colleagues (Sherman 1984; Sherman & Bruno 1987) observed a negative correlation between temperature at the stump and the presence of burning, tingling or throbbing phantom limb and stump pain indicating that reduced blood flow to the stump is associated with increased levels of pain. Repeated measurements of the same patients on different occasions revealed that lower temperatures at the stump relative to the contralateral limb were associated with greater intensities of phantom limb and stump pain suggesting that the reduced blood flow was in some way causally tied to the pain. However, in the majority of cases, the relationship between phantom pain and limb temperature was confounded by co-existing stump pain so that it is not possible to unambiguously attribute the presence of phantom limb pain to altered blood flow at the stump.

Katz (1992a) followed up this line of inquiry and compared skin conductance and surface skin temperature of the stump and contralateral limb in amputees reporting phantom limb pain (Group PLP), non-painful phantom limb sensations (Group PLS), or no phantom limb at all (Group No PL). The results showed that although mean skin temperature was lower at the stump than the contralateral limb in all groups, the difference was significant for Groups PLP and PLS, but not Group No PL (Figure 4). Stump-intact limb temperature differences in excess of −1°C were associated with the presence of a phantom limb in the absence of concomitant stump pain (Table 2). Group differences in pressure sensitivity thresholds or skin conductance levels were not significant.

These results suggest that the presence of a phantom limb, whether painful or painless, is related to the sympathetic-efferent outflow of cutaneous vasoconstrictor fibers in the stump and stump neuromas. The related finding that stump skin conductance responses over time correlated significantly with the intensity of phantom limb paresthesias, but not other qualities of sensation, supports the hypothesis (outlined below) of a sympathetic-efferent somatic-afferent mechanism involving both sudomotor and vasoconstrictor fibers. The most parsimonious explanation of these findings is that the paresthetic or dysesthetic component of the phantom limb may be triggered by sympathetic-efferent activity.

Individual Differences in the Psychophysical Correlates of Phantom Limb Sensations

Although a normal phantom occurs whenever nerve impulses from the periphery are blocked or otherwise removed (Wall 1981), it is also true that direct stimulation

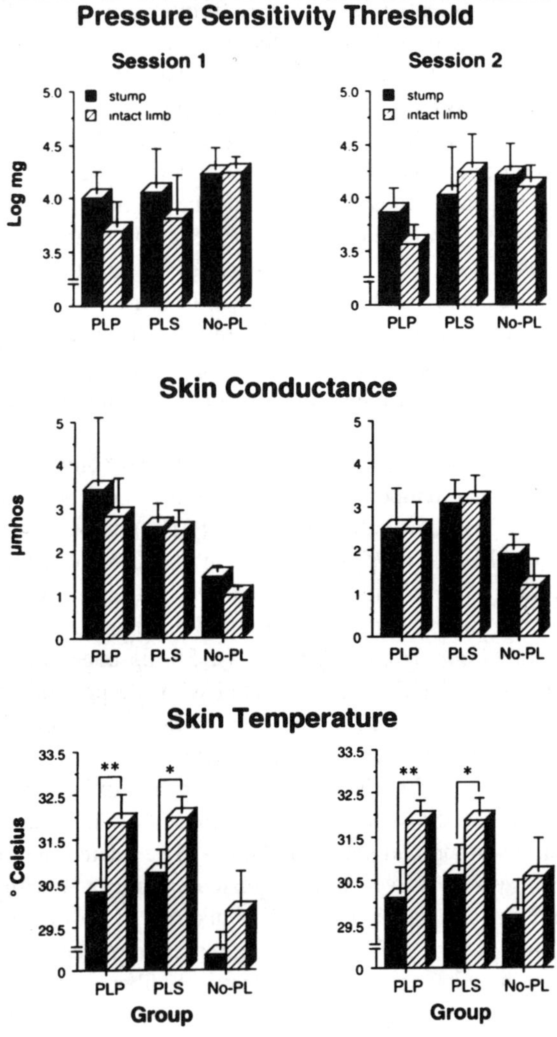

Figure 4. *Mean pressure sensitivity thresholds, skin conductance and skin temperature of the stump and contralateral limb displayed for 3 groups of amputees on 2 sessions separated by at least 24 hours. PLP refers to phantom limb pain; PLS, non-painful phantom limb sensations; No PL, no phantom limb at all. Mean stump skin temperature was significantly lower than the contralateral limb for Groups PLP (** $p < .005$) and PLS (* $p < .05$) but not Group No PL. Reproduced from Katz (1992a) with permission.*

Table 2. *Mean stump-intact limb difference scores for pressure sensitivity thresholds (PST), skin conductance (SC), and skin temperature (ST) presented for 3 groups of amputees on 2 sessions separated by at least 24 hours. Standard deviations are shown in parentheses. Stump-intact limb difference scores were obtained by subtracting measurements taken at the intact limb from those at the stump. Negative difference scores indicate that relative to the intact limb the stump is lower in skin temperature, lower in skin conductance, and more sensitive to applied pressure.*

	Session 1					
	Group PLP (n = 11)		Group PLS (n = 9)		Group No PL (n = 8)	
PST (log mg)	0.31	(1.3)	0.25	(1.2)	-0.004	(0.5)
SC (μmhos)	0.61	(3.0)	0.11	(0.7)	0.43	(0.4)
ST (°Celsius)	−1.59*	(1.8)	-1.26*	(1.3)	-0.88	(1.9)
	Session 2					
	Group PLP (n = 11)		Group PLS (n = 9)		Group No PL (n = 8)	
PST (log mg)	0.30	(0.6)	-0.21	(0.6)	0.11	(0.7)
SC (μmhos)	0.02	(1.7)	-0.06	(1.5)	0.74	(0.9)
ST (°Celsius)	-1.75	(1.8)*	-1.25	(1.5)*	-0.85	(2.0)

* significantly different ($p < 0.05$) from Group No PL.
Reproduced from Katz (1992a) with permission.

of the amputation stump frequently exaggerates the tingling or paresthetic quality of sensation typical of the painless phantom limb (Carlen et al. 1978). Careful questioning of amputees reveals that the non-painful phantom limb is not perceived as a static phenomenon. The paresthetic quality of sensation, which defines the phantom limb percept, is in a constant state of flux, with changes occurring in intensity, body part, or both (Table 1). Katz et al. (1989) reported on a subject with a right above-the-knee amputation whose phantom consisted of a numb sensation that defined a region including the lateral three phantom toes. Within this circumscribed area, he experienced rapid "waves of numbness" that increased and decreased the intensity of the involved phantom parts. As shown in Figure 5, stump skin conductance levels measured at the amputation stump correlated significantly over time with the intensity of paresthesias experienced in his phantom toes. In a subsequent study (Katz 1992a), other individuals also showed striking relationships between phantom limb paresthesias (e.g., numb and tingling sensations) and stump skin conductance responses (Figures 5, 6).

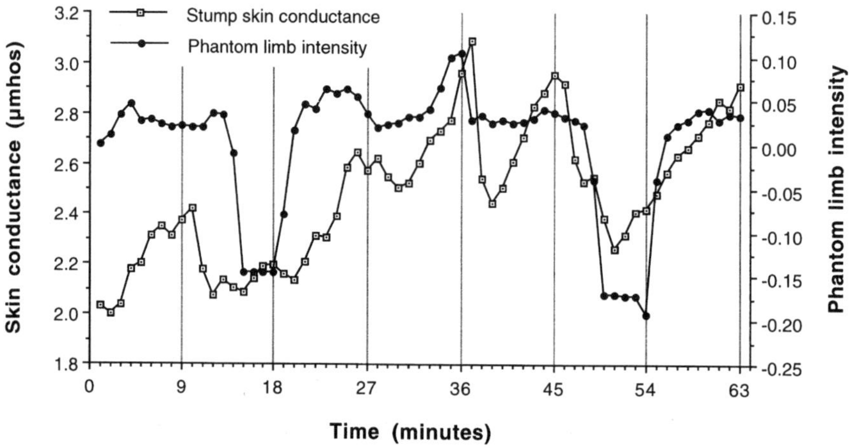

Figure 5. *A minute-by-minute plot of the relationship between stump skin conductance and the intensity of non-painful phantom limb paresthesias for a subject with an amputation above the knee and paresthesias referred to the phantom foot and toes. Skin conductance was continuously measured at the stump over a 63-minute period while the subject monitored the intensity of the phantom limb by turning a dial. Phantom limb intensity ratings have been transformed so that a value of 0.0 represents the intensity at the start of the session and deviations from zero correspond to increases and decreases in phantom limb intensity. Each data point represents a mean of 30 values consecutively sampled at 2 second intervals. Note that changes in the intensity of paresthesias (described by the subject as increases and decreases in "numb" sensations referred to the phantom toes) occur in concert with changes in stump skin conductance. Reproduced from Katz et al. (1989) with permission.*

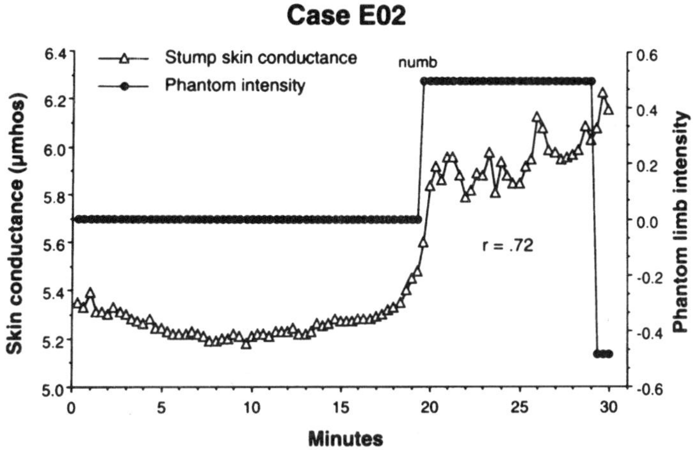

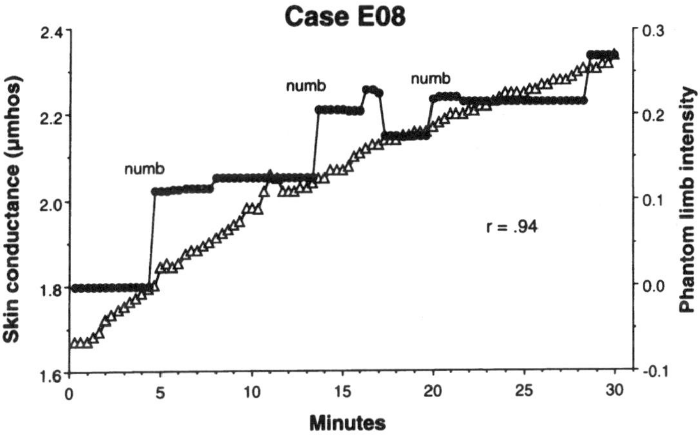

Figure 6. *Plots of the relationship between stump skin conductance and the intensity of phantom limb paresthesias for two subjects with non-painful phantom limb paresthesias. Skin conductance was measured at the stump over a 30 minute period while the subjects monitored the intensity of the phantom limb by turning a dial. Each data point represents a mean of 3 values consecutively sampled at 10 second intervals. Changes in the intensity of paresthesias (described as increases and decreases in "numb" sensations referred to the phantom limb) occur in concert with changes in stump skin conductance. Also shown is the correlation coefficient describing the strength of the relationship between the two variables and the subjects' descriptions of the quality of the phantom sensation. Reproduced from Katz (1992a) with permission.*

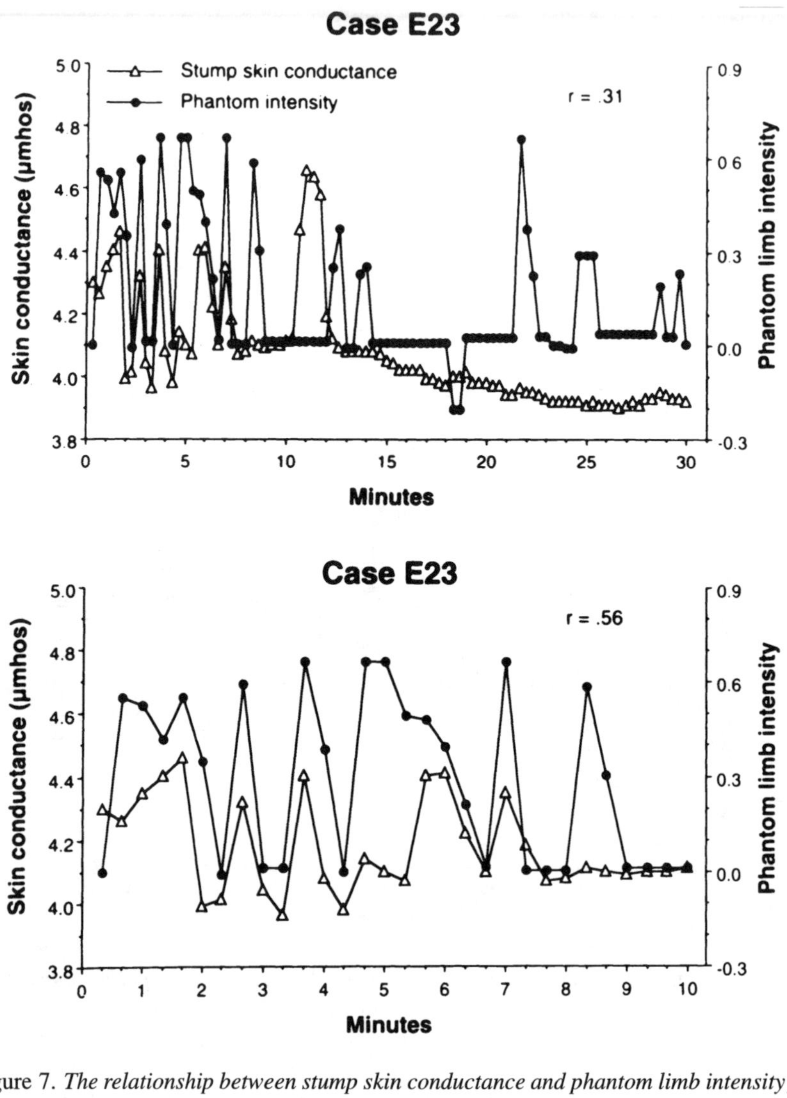

Figure 7. *The relationship between stump skin conductance and phantom limb intensity for another amputee with phantom limb paresthesias shown for a 30 minute session (top panel). For ease of viewing, the bottom panel shows only the first 10 minutes of the same session when the two measures showed a prominent tendency to covary. All changes in phantom limb intensity were described by the subject as increases and decreases in "numbness" experienced in the phantom foot. Reproduced from Katz (1992a) with permission.*

One mechanism that has been proposed to account for the paresthetic component of the phantom limb is a cycle of sympathetic-efferent somatic-afferent activity (Katz 1992a; Katz et al. 1989). It is hypothesized that changes in the intensity of phantom limb paresthesias reflect the joint activity of cholinergic (sudomotor) and noradrenergic (vasomotor) post-ganglionic sympathetic fibers on primary afferents located in the stump and stump neuromas. Release of acetylcholine and norepinephrine from post-ganglionic sympathetic fibers produces transient vasoconstriction and heightened skin conductance responses. As well, neurotransmitter release onto apposing peripheral fibers trapped in stump neuromas increases primary afferent discharge. This information is transmitted rostrally where it gives rise to referred phantom sensations upon reaching central structures subserving the amputated parts of the limb. The moment-to-moment fluctuations in the intensity of phantom limb paresthesias reported by many amputees may, in part, reflect a cycle of sympathetic-efferent somatic-afferent activity. Increases in the intensity of phantom limb paresthesias would follow bursts of sympathetic activity and decreases would correspond to periods of relative sympathetic inactivity (Katz 1992a; Katz et al. 1989). If central sensitization has also developed either through prior injury, trauma during amputation, or peripheral inflammation, or, if the sympathetic-sensory coupling involves nociceptors (Roberts 1986) the sensation may be one of dysesthesia.

The possibility that heightened electrodermal activity at the stump occurs as a *consequence* of the perception of a change in the intensity of paresthesias does not appear to be tenable. As depicted in Figure 8, shooting pains, somatosensory memories, and phantom limb movements do not also correlate with stump skin conductance (Katz 1992a). That is, changes in stump skin conductance are related only to the perception of paresthesias (Figures 4–6) and not to other qualities of sensation (Figure 8).

The precise role of post-ganglionic sudomotor fibers in generating phantom limb paresthesias is not known. The possibility exists that the relationship between stump skin conductance levels and phantom limb paresthesias reflects a direct cholinergic-afferent coupling mechanism (Diamond 1959) but peripheral sudomotor blockade with atropine in patients with sympathetically-maintained pain failed to have an immediate analgesic effect suggesting that the cholinergic limb of the sympathetic nervous system does not contribute to SMP (Glynn, Stannard, Collins, & Casale 1993). Another possibility is that since stump skin conductance provides a more accurate indication of post-ganglionic discharge than surface skin temperature, and sudomotor and vasomotor fibers tend to discharge in tandem (Bini, Hagbarth, Hynninen, & Wallin 1980), skin conductance responses may merely be a marker for an adrenergic-afferent coupling

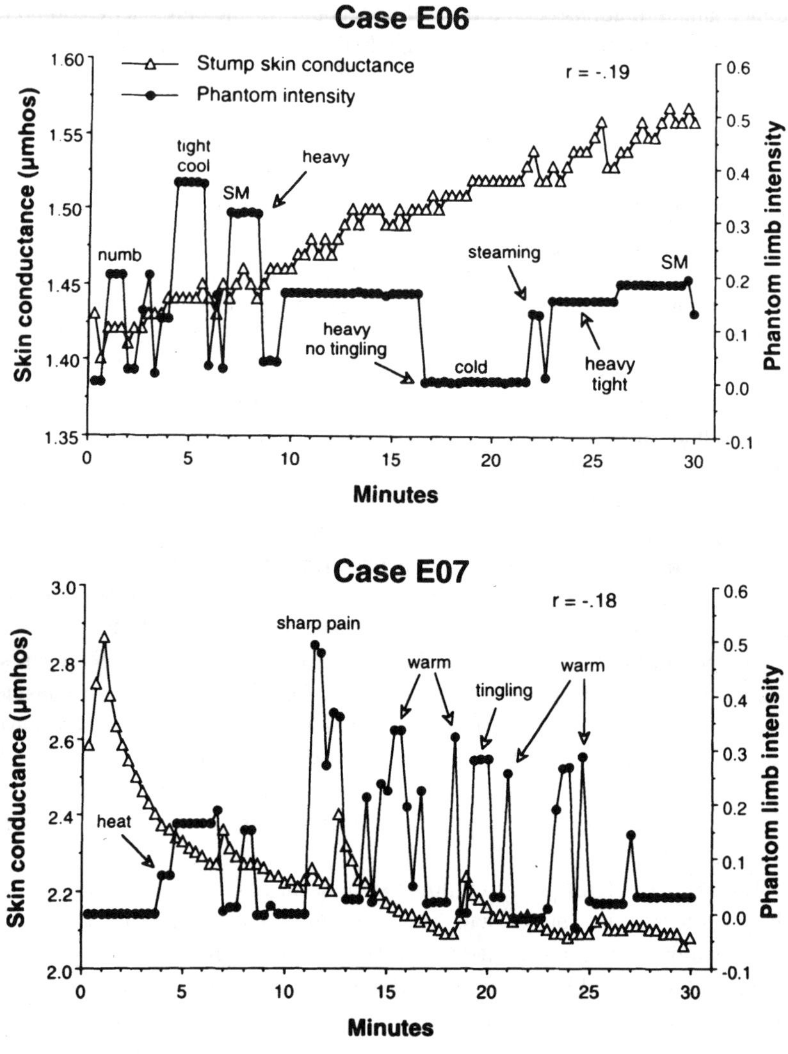

Figure 8. *Plots of the relationship between stump skin conductance and various qualities of phantom limb pain for 2 subjects in Group PLP. Note that unlike the plots in earlier figures there is no relationship between stump skin conductance and the intensity of phantom limb pain. Reproduced from Katz (1992a) with permission.*

mechanism generated by epinephrine release following activity in post-ganglionic vasomotor fibers.

There are several lines of indirect evidence to support the hypothesis that moment-to-moment fluctuations in the intensity of phantom limb paresthesias reflects sympathetic-afferent coupling. First, sympathetic activity in the form of skin conductance responses and changes in skin temperature reflect the activity of post-ganglionic sudomotor and vasomotor fibers, respectively (Bini et al. 1980; Hagbarth, Hallin, Hongell, Torebjörk, & Wallin 1972). Multiunit sympathetic activity recorded from skin nerve fascicles in awake humans shows a strong relationship to effector organ responses including vasoconstriction and sweat gland activity (Bini et al. 1980; Hagbarth et al. 1972). These studies demonstrate that bursts of activity in sudomotor and vasomotor fibers are reliably followed by transient electrodermal responses and plethysmographic signs of vasoconstriction within the region of skin subserved by the sympathetic fibers under study.

Second, intraneural recordings from sensory nerve fascicles in conscious humans reveals a remarkably strong relationship between the perception of non-painful paresthesias and spontaneous bursting activity in afferent fibers (Nordin, Nyström, Wallin, & Hagbarth 1984; Ochoa & Torebjörk 1980). Finally, non-noxious percutaneous electrical stimulation of afferent nerves located in the stump of forearm amputees produces paresthesias referred to a localized region of the phantom hand but not the stump. Subsequent alterations in the amplitude of electrical stimulation are paralleled by corresponding perceptual changes in the intensity of phantom limb paresthesias (Anani & Körner 1979).

Taken together, these studies suggests that the paresthetic component of the phantom limb may in part represent the perceptual correlate of a central autonomic mechanism that operates on peripheral structures. In the following section, this mechanism is elaborated to explain how psychological and emotional processes might alter phantom limb sensations through their actions on the sympathetic nervous system. Direct support for this hypothesis is not available and would require that changes in the intensity of phantom limb paresthesias (or dysesthesias) be correlated with microneurographic recordings from post-ganglionic sympathetic and primary afferent fibers in amputation stump neuromas.

Psychological and Emotional Processes Influence Phantom Limb Experience

The idea that emotional and psychological processes can cause pain traditionally has been tied to the notion of psychopathology. However, it is becoming increasingly clear that under certain circumstances (e.g., after amputation) pain may be triggered by these processes in psychologically healthy individuals as well. It is commonly accepted that anxiety or stress influences pain perception and subsequent behavior (Merskey 1989). The aggravation or alleviation of pain referred to phantom body parts also may be mediated in part by psychological processes that alter anxiety levels (Kolb 1954). Phantom breast pain after mastectomy is provoked by emotional distress in 6% of women 3 weeks after surgery and in 29% one year later (Krøner, Krebs, Skov, & Jørgensen 1989). Fifty percent of lower extremity amputees report that attacks of phantom limb pain are triggered by emotional distress (Jensen et al. 1985) as long as 7 years after amputation (Krebs, Jensen, Krøner, Nielsen, & Jørgensen 1985). A combination of progressive relaxation training and EMG biofeedback of stump and forehead muscles produces significant reductions of phantom limb pain and anxiety (Sherman 1976) that are sustained for up to 3 years (Sherman, Gall, & Gormly 1979). Finally, stress levels and pain intensity ratings sampled over a 180 day observation period correlate significantly for most amputees (Arena, Sherman, & Bruno 1990).

There are also examples of psychological or emotional processes precipitating transient but profound alterations in the quality and intensity of phantom limb sensations. These processes include concentration (Morgenstern 1964) distraction, (Parkes 1973), relaxation (Sherman 1976; Sherman et al. 1979), fright (Henderson & Smyth 1948), forceful reminders of the events that led to amputation (Simmel 1956), and witnessing cruel and violent acts (Pilowsky & Kaufman 1965; Stengel 1965). One amputee, interviewed by the present writer described his reaction to an accident involving his wife by reporting "... goose bumps and cold shivering down the phantom [leg]. It went through me. Everything emotional will get you that". Another amputee stated, "It's like everything I feel goes there — the good and the bad".

A Centrally-Triggered Sympathetic-Efferent Somatic-Afferent Mechanism

The material presented above indicates that cognitive and affective processes reliably trigger transient pains or sensations referred to the phantom limb. The model schematically represented in Figure 9 outlines a mechanism through which cognitive and affective processes associated with higher cortical and limbic centers may alter phantom limb sensations. The reciprocal connections between cortical, limbic and lateral hypothalamic structures are well documented (Brodal 1981; Smith & DeVito 1984). The lateral hypothalamus is involved in the control and integration of neural activity associated with affectively-charged behavior (Brodal 1981; Melzack & Casey 1968; Smith & DeVito 1984) and has direct projections to the lateral horn of the spinal cord. The intensity of phantom limb paresthesias and dysesthesias may thus be modulated by higher brain centers involved in cognitive and affective processes *via* a multi-synaptic network of descending inputs that impinges on pre-ganglionic sympathetic neurons producing diffuse peripheral autonomic discharge and activation of primary afferent fibers located in stump neuromas.

Occasionally, the effects of intense affect (e.g., fright, horror) are experienced diffusely over the entire body as *cutis anserina* associated with pilomotor contraction (i.e., "goose bumps"). Among amputees, however, a more frequent occurrence is that the perception of less salient events and emotions precipitate these sensations throughout only the phantom limb. The tendency for affectively-charged and psychologically-meaningful experiences to be referred to the phantom limb, but not to other parts of the body, is consistent with two lines of evidence suggesting that the threshold for impulse generation is lower both in regenerating primary afferents in the stump and in deafferented central cells subserving the phantom limb than it is in the intact nervous system.

First, regenerating sprouts, which are trapped in a neuroma, are exceedingly sensitive to the post-ganglionic sympathetic neurotransmitters norepinephrine (Wall & Gutnick 1974) and acetylcholine (Diamond 1959), and they discharge rapidly when these substances are present. In contrast, intact peripheral fibers do not show this chemosensitivity, and thus have a higher threshold compared with regenerating sprouts. Second, the loss of afferent nerve impulses (deafferentation) resulting from amputation produces a disinhibition of cells in the dorsal horn and more rostral sensory structures giving rise to the perception of a phantom limb (Melzack & Loeser 1978; Wall 1981). This consequence of deafferentation implies that the threshold for detecting sympathetically-triggered afferent impulses arising from stump neuromas should be lower than at other, intact body sites since stump impulses would be subject to less inhibition upon reaching the spinal cord. This is consistent with the observation that the threshold for detecting sensations in the phantom limb during stimulation of the stump is lower than at the site of stimulation itself (Carlen et al. 1978).

Another possibility (Campbell, Meyer, & Raja 1992b) is that amputation leads to increased expression of alpha adrenergic receptors located on mechanoreceptors or nociceptors in stump neuromas. This hypothesis would explain the perception of phantom limb paresthesias or dysesthesias in the absence of regional sympathetic hyperactivity or trophic changes at the stump. Taken together, these observations may explain the puzzling finding that only after amputation does the (phantom) limb become the site of affectvely- or cognitively-triggered sensations.

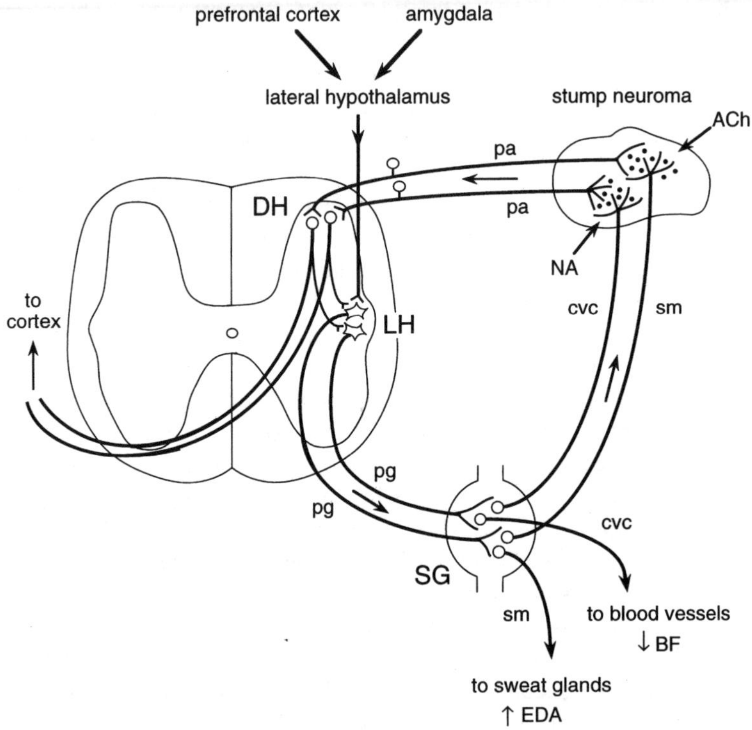

Figure 9. *Schematic diagram illustrating a mechanism of sympathetically-generated phantom limb paresthesias. Spontaneous sympathetic activity or excitatory inputs descending from cortex (e.g., due to the perception of a salient event, loud noise, thought, feeling, etc.) increase the discharge rate of pre-ganglionic (pg) sympathetic neurons with cell bodies in the lateral horn (LH) of the spinal cord and terminals in the sympathetic ganglion (SG). These neurons excite post-ganglionic noradrenergic (NA) cutaneous vasoconstrictor (cvc) and cholinergic (ACh) sudomotor (sm) fibers that impinge on effector organs (vascular smooth muscle and sweat glands) in the stump and on sprouts from large diameter primary afferent (pa) fibers that have been trapped in a neuroma. The release of ACh and NA on effector organs results in increased electrodermal activity (EDA) and decreased blood flow (BF) to the stump. Release of these chemicals in the neuroma activates primary afferents that project to spinal cord dorsal horn (DH) cells subserving the amputated parts of the limb. These neurons, in turn, feed back to the pre-ganglionic sympathetic neurons and project rostrally where the impulses contribute to the perception of phantom limb paresthesias. If DH cells have been sensitized due to injury, or nociceptive primary afferents are activated, then the perception may be one of dysesthesias.*

Treatment and treatment implications

The majority of interventions for phantom limb pain lack the rigorous control conditions and adequate sample sizes to conclude with certainty that specific treatments are more effective than no treatment or placebo treatment. Chabal's (1992) findings provide the strongest evidence in support of an adrenergic sympathetic-sensory coupling mechanism underlying stump pain and possibly phantom limb pain as well. The results of early studies showing that local anesthetic infiltration into the sympathetic chain (Livingston 1938; Livingston 1943) and sympathectomy (Bailey & Moersch 1941; Kallio 1950a) at least temporary relieve phantom limb pain also suggest that sympathetic ganglion blocks or surgical sympathectomies are effective because they block the release of norepinephrine from the peripheral sympathetic terminals.

It should be noted, however, that pain relief in response to a local anesthetic sympathetic block may be due to factors other than sympathetic blockade. Diffusion of the agent to the dorsal roots resulting in small fiber block or a systemic action of the local anesthetic are limitations of diagnostic sympathetic blocks which reduce the specificity of the test (Raja 1993). The lack of permanency of sympathectomy for phantom limb pain (Kallio 1950a) may be due to a variety of factors including inadequacy of diagnosis, extent of sympathectomy, surgical skill and confusion about anatomy (Campbell et al. 1994). The finding that beta-adrenergic receptor blockade does not seem to be effective in relieving phantom limb pain (Scadding, Wall, Wynn Parry, & Brooks 1982) is consistent with the negative results of propranolol for treatment of SMP in non-amputees (Campbell, Raja, & Meyer 1993).

Phantom limb pain and stump pain respond well to epidural or spinal administration of local anesthetics or opioids (Jacobson & Chabal 1989; Jacobson, Chabal, & Brody 1989; Jacobson, Chabal, Brody, Mariano, & Chaney 1990). While the relevant assessments to determine the presence of SMP were not established in these studies, the possibility remains that the continuous sympathetic blockade achieved by epidural infusions of local anesthetic agents may prove effective in the management of patients with SMP (Campbell et al. 1994). To date, neither the phentolamine test (Raja, Treede, Davis, & Campbell 1991), nor regional infusions of guanethidine have been tried for phantom limb pain. Raja (1993) has published guidelines for evaluating patients suspected of having SMP.

Finally, it is noteworthy that mental stress and anxiety not only provoke transient increases in the intensity of phantom limb sensations and pain (Arena et al. 1990; Sherman 1976; Sherman et al. 1979), but they also induce reflex bursting activity in cutaneous sudomotor and vasomotor sympathetic fibers

(Delius, Hagbarth, Hongell, & Wallin 1972; Hagbarth et al. 1972). Moreover, distraction or attention diversion (and intense concentration) which reduces phantom limb pain (Morgenstern 1964; Parkes 1973) also diminishes peripheral sympathetic nervous system activity (Hagbarth et al. 1972). These findings provide indirect support for the model shown in Figure 9 and suggest that relaxation training and other cognitive strategies directed at anxiety reduction and increasing self control may be effective in reducing phantom limb pain in certain amputees.

Pain Memories in Phantom Limbs and Deafferented Structures

A striking property of phantom limb pain is the presence of a pain that existed in a limb prior to its amputation (Melzack 1971). This class of phantom limb pain is characterized by the persistence or recurrence of a previous pain, has the same qualities of sensation, and is experienced in the same region of the limb as the pre-amputation pain (Katz & Melzack 1990). Cases studies of amputees have revealed pain "memories" of painful diabetic foot ulcers, bedsores, ganrene, corns, blisters, ingrown toenails, cuts and deep tissue injuries, and damage to joints and bony structures. As well, the phantom limb may assume the same painful posture as that of the real limb prior to amputation, especially if the arm or leg had been immobilized for a prolonged period.

The proportion of amputees who report similar pain before and after amputation may be as high as 79% (Katz & Melzack 1990), although according to prospective studies, the incidence is 10% or less one year after amputation (Jensen et al. 1985; Nikolajsen et al. 1997a). Pain memories in phantom limbs appear to be less common when there has been a discontinuity, or a pain-free interval, between the experience of pain and amputation. Furthermore, compared with pain that is temporally non-contiguous with amputation, pain experienced at or near the time of amputation has a higher probability of persisting into the phantom limb (Jensen et al. 1985; Katz & Melzack 1990; Nikolajsen et al. 1997a).

Pain also persists in patients with deafferentation that does not involve amputation. In these conditions, the involved body part is still present but it is devoid of sensibility due to an interruption in the supply of sensory (afferent) information (i.e., deafferentation). Brachial plexus avulsions, in which the sensory nerve roots supplying the arm and hand are torn from the spinal cord often produce pain that is felt in the deafferented and anesthetic region (Jensen & Rasmussen 1994; Reisner 1981). Similarly, patients with spinal cord injuries

(Berger & Gerstenbrand 1981; Conomy 1973) may complain of pain referred to body parts below the level of the transection. For example, Nathan (1962) described a patient who continued to feel the pain of an ingrown toenail after a complete spinal cord break. As well, patients undergoing spinal anesthesia (Van Bogaert 1934; Wallgren 1954) and those with injuries of the brachial plexus or spinal cord sometimes report that a limb is in the same uncomfortable, often painful, posture it was in prior to the injury of block. These postural phantom sensations do not usually persist beyond several days and in most cases are at least temporarily reversed by competing visual inputs which reveal a dissociation between the real and felt limb(s).

Painful and non-painful sensations also persist or recur after surgical removal or deafferentation of body structures other than the limbs, such as breasts (Krøner, Knudsen, Lundby, & Hvid 1992; Krøner et al. 1989), teeth (Marbach 1996) and internal and special sense organs. Ulcer pain has been reported to persist after subtotal gastrectomy with removal of the ulcer (Gloyne 1954). Patients have reported labor pain and menstrual cramps after total hysterectomy (Dorpat 1971), rectal pain (Boas 1983) and hemorrhoids (Oveson, Krøner, Ørnsholt, & Bach 1991) after removal of the rectum and anus, the burning pain of cystitis after complete removal of the bladder (Brena & Sammons 1979), and the pain of a severely ulcerated cornea after enucleation of an eye (Minski 1943; Nicolodi, Frezzotti, Diadori, Nuti, & Sicuteri 1997).

As noted above, not all somatosenory memories are of painful experiences. Non-painful pre-amputation sensations do recur but they are not as common and tend to include the sensation of objects that were once worn on the limb. These *superadded* sensations (Haber 1956) vary in complexity from such simple somatosensory qualities as the sensation of bandages that once wrapped a wound (Friedmann 1978; Katz & Melzack 1990), a plaster cast (Danke 1981), finger rings, and wristwatches (Friedmann 1978; Haber 1956) to the multi-modal, perceptually integrated phenomenon of a phantom foot clad in a sock and a shoe of specific type and color (Katz & Melzack 1990).

Taken together, these case reports and studies of amputees reveal that pain memories are not merely images or cognitive recollections; they are direct experiences of pain that resemble an earlier pain in location and quality. They are perceptually complex experiences that may even involve information from multiple sensory modalities including visual, olfactory, tactile, and motor compnents that had accompanied the original experience. The precise details of the experiences of pain involve localization, discrimination, affect, and evaluation — that is, all the dimensions of perceptual experience — and these properties are a function of integrated brain activity. It is likely that the outputs of sensitized spinal cells activate the neural structures in the brain that subserve memories of earlier events.

Separate Somatosensory and Cognitive Memory Components Underlie Pain Memories

A closer examination of the phenomenon suggests that the experience of a pain memory reflects the joint activity of two separate memory subsystems with properties and functions specialized for processing somatosensory and cognitive (declarative) information respectively. The somatosensory memory component consists of the same, or very similar, neural circuitry that was activated by the peripheral input prior to amputation. It is a higher-order functional unit that codes the temporal and spatial patterning of nerve impulses specifying the body part, quality of sensation and intensity of the somatosensory experience.

The cognitive memory component contains declarative information related to when and in what context the pre-amputation pain occurred as well as *meta*-information *about* the body part, quality of sensation, and intensity of the pre-amputation experience. The declarative information contained in the cognitive component provides the unique, personal meaning associated with the somatosensory component and provides a basis for the identifying label and response (e.g. "my pain", a corn, diabetic ulcer, etc.). The determination that a current sensory impression has occurred before involves a process of recognition: one must know, or have access to knowledge about, what one has (and therefore has not) previously experienced in order to state whether two experiences separated in time are the same or different.

To clarify the distinction between the two forms of memory, consider an amputee who occasionally feels the painful "hole" on his phantom shin corresponding to a long-standing pre-amputation ulcer as well as the sensation of the bandages that once wrapped the wound. Stripped of the declarative information contained in the cognitive component, which serves to identify and give meaning to the somatosensory qualities of the phantom pain, the sensation of bandages wrapping the wound would probably be described non-specifically in terms of a band of light pressure or tightness around the leg. That is, the somatosensory descriptions used to convey the sensation are the same regardless of whether or not the cognitive component is present. But when the cognitive component has been activated, the descriptive response includes a unique identifying label (e.g., "bandages"), the phantom limb experience is accompanied by a sense of familiarity, and the patient has access to declarative information that ties the somatosensory qualities of the sensation to the original event.

Evidence of a Double Dissociation between Somatosensory and Cognitive Components

There is evidence that it is possible to demonstrate a double dissociation of these two memory components. Evidence of the cognitive component in the absence of the somatosensory component is common and occurs whenever amputees recall details about a pre-amputation pain (e.g., its duration, quality of sensation, location, intensity) without also re-experiencing the somatosensory qualities of that pain (Katz & Melzack 1990). Dissociation of the opposite kind is not as common and is more difficult to demonstrate since without the knowledge (i.e., contents of the cognitive memory component) of what one has felt in the past, the re-activation of the somatosensory qualities of a past pain would be perceived as novel and therefore would not be recognized as having occurred before. Moreover, it is rare to find a situation in which (1) an amputee demonstrates amnesia or forgetting (of the contents of the cognitive memory component) and (2) an independent source had verified the nature of the pain at the time of injury before amputation.

Nevertheless, there are several lines of evidence supporting dissociation of this kind. The first comes from experiments that model the phantom limb in animals (Katz, Vaccarino, Coderre, & Melzack 1991). Sectioning the sciatic and saphenous nerves in the rat is followed by self-mutilation (autotomy) of the denervated hindpaw. It is well established that autotomy is a response to pain or dysesthesias (painful paresthesias or tingling) referred to the anesthetic limb and represents a model of the phantom limb. A brief thermal injury of a specific region of the hindpaw just prior to nerve sections changes the usual pattern of autotomy over the following days. Animals injured before, but not after, nerve sections direct autotomy to the site of prior injury. Since the nerve sections produce a deafferentation of the entire hindpaw, the central effects of the injury are sustained in the absence of further inputs from the hindpaw, implying that painful or dysesthetic sensations are referred specifically to the region of the denervated limb that had received the injury.

The correspondence between the sites of prior injury and subsequent autotomy parallels descriptions of human amputees who report the persistence of a pre-amputation pain or lesion referred to the same location of the phantom limb. In these experiments (Katz et al. 1991), the injury was always induced while the rats were under a general anesthetic, and they were maintained under the general anesthetic until well after the sciatic and saphenous nerve transections had been performed. Thus, although the rats never experienced the thermal injury in an awake state, their behavior in the days after the nerve sections revealed that the effects of the injury were still capable of influencing perception and behavior (in the absence of further inputs from the injured region). These findings provide empirical support for the hypothesis that the unified experience of a pain memory involves two potentially dissociable forms of memory, one of which (the somatosensory component) is independent of the conscious experience of pain.

Lacroix, Melzack, Smith, and Mitchell (1992) recently provided compelling clinical evidence of a dissociation between the cognitive and somatosensory memory components. They report the case of a 16 year-old girl who was born with a congenital deformity of the right foot which was amputated when she was just 6 years old. At the time of the interview 10 years after amputation, the patient reported a flat phantom foot that was stuck in a forward position. This description corresponded to information subsequently obtained from her medical records verifying a right flatfoot which was locked in an equinovalgus position and incapable of movement. Interestingly, the patient was not aware that her foot had been deformed as a child, for she mistakenly described her foot as she "remembered" it prior to amputation as being normal and freely mobile. This case report demonstrates the remarkable capacity of the central nervous system to retain, for years after amputation, a complete representation of the cut-off part, including its somatosensory qualities, proprioceptive sensibility and associated motor program. Moreover, the case demonstrates that the neural circuitry underlying the somatosensory component is capable of being activated and of influencing conscious awareness independent of the cognitive component.

Although separate representations of the somatosensory and cognitive components are formed during repeated occurrences of the pre-amputation pain, such frequent and temporally contiguous activity would result in a tendency for these representations to occur more often together than alone once the limb has been removed. There is evidence that the two memory systems may be reciprocally connected so that activation of either memory component can lead to activation of the other. The presence of the somatosensory component is sufficient to activate the contents of the cognitive component as implied by the process of recognition involved when a patient identifies the somatosensory qualities of the experience as having occurred before. The possibility also exists that the link is bi-directional. One subject in the study by Katz and Melzack (1990) reported that he could reproduce at will the sensation of the "hole" from a gangrenous ulcer he had on the medial aspect of his foot prior to amputation, but if he did not concentrate on it, the somatosensory component remained out of his awareness. It is important to note, however, that activation of the representation underlying the cognitive component is not to be equated with the conscious awareness of thoughts about the past pain, but when such thoughts occur, excitation of the corresponding neural assemblies must have been involved.

Implications of Separate Memory Components

There are important implications associated with the suggestion that separate somatosensory and cognitive memory systems underlie pain that persists after amputation. For one, conscious awareness of the contents of the cognitive memory component is not necessary for the *re-activation* of the somatosensory component (although it may facilitate the process when present). Second, it is clear that the conscious experience of pain is not a necessary condition for the *formation* of the somatosensory memory component. That is, the formation of the somatosensory component can occur even when there is no conscious awareness of pain at the time of injury or trauma (Katz et al. 1992; Katz et al. 1991) or when the cognitive component is not accessible through introspection (Lacroix et al. 1992).

These findings raise the possibility that just as brief, intense pain experienced in a limb shortly before its amputation persists as phantom limb pain memory (Katz & Melzack 1990), the effects of the primary afferent "injury discharge" on spinal cord dorsal horn neurons produced by surgical incision (and subsequent cutting of muscle, nerve, and bone) may also produce lasting changes that later contribute to post-operative pain. This implies that both somatosensory and cognitive systems must be blocked in order to interfere with the formation of a pain memory arising from the surgical procedure (Figure 10).

Patients who have sustained traumatic amputation either by accident, combat-related injury or emergency surgical procedures carried out without anesthetics or analgesics (e.g., in war-ravaged parts of the world) are at highest risk for developing post-amputation problems (Figure 10a). Traumatic amputation would be expected to result in the formation of both the somatosensory and cognitive memory components. The expected outcome would include heightened stump pain (stump hyperalgesia), heightened phantom limb pain intensity, recognition of the somatosensory qualities of the pain and a post-traumatic stress disorder arising from the traumatic events.

Amputation performed under general anesthesia alone (Figure 10b) would interfere with the formation of the *cogntive* but not the *somatosensory* memory component. However, unlike a pain memory that resembles a long-standing pre-amputation lesion, the somatosensory qualities of post-surgical pain would not be recognized by a patient whose surgery was performed under a general anesthetic, since the patient would not have had any conscious experience of pain at the

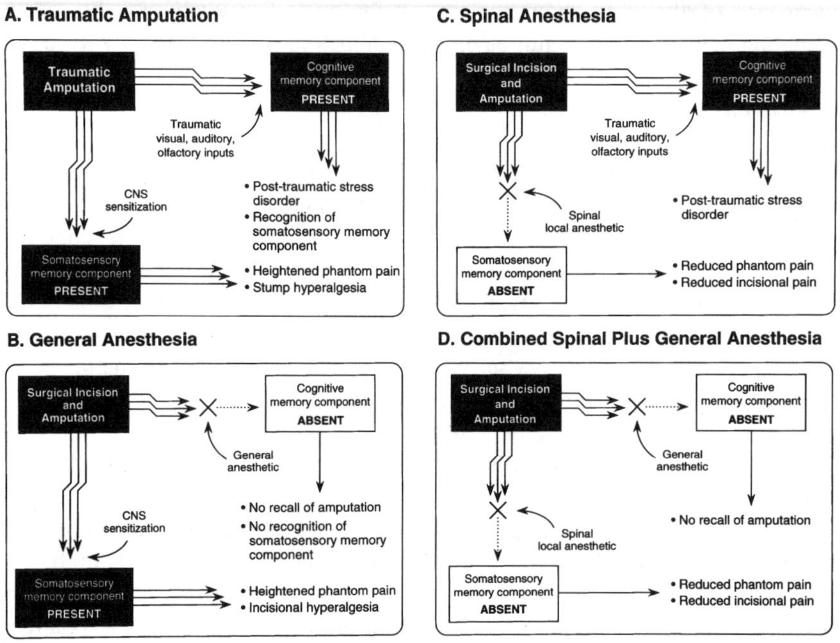

Figure 10. *Predicted post-operative pain status and psychological status following traumatic amputation (A) or surgical amputation performed under general anesthesia (B), spinal local anesthesia (C), or combined spinal local anesthesia plus general anesthesia (D). Reproduced from Katz (1993) with permission.*

time of incision and amputation. Upon awakening from the general anesthetic, the patient's complaints of pain would reflect the persistent central neural memory trace left by the surgical procedure in addition to input from transected fibers in the amputation stump (Wall 1989). This is hypothesized to result in enhanced postoperative phantom limb pain and heightened pain at the site of the incision (incisional hyperalgesia).

Administration of spinal local anesthesia alone (Figure 10c) would block the formation of the *somatosensory* but not the *cognitive* memory component. The pre-incisional spinal blockade would prevent the injury barrage from reaching the CNS resulting in less intense postoperative phantom limb pain and incisional pain. However, in the absence of a general anesthetic, awareness during amputation can produce vivid declarative memories of operating room events that develop into a post-traumatic stress disorder.

Combined use of spinal anesthesia and general anesthesia (Figure 10d) would be expected to interfere with both *somatosensory* and *cognitive* memory systems by blocking the transmission of nociceptive impulses (arising from the cutting of tissue, nerve and bone) at the level of the spinal cord, and by ensuring that the patient is unconscious during the surgical procedure. This validity of this hypothesis has yet to be tested.

Recent studies of patients undergoing thoracic surgery and lower abdominal surgery show that it is possible to *pre-empt* post-operative pain by interrupting the transmission of nerve impulses between the periphery and the spinal cord. Combined use of general anesthesia plus *pre-incisional* epidural administration of an opioid (Katz et al. 1992) or a local anesthetic agent (Katz et al. 1994) is more effective in reducing post-operative pain and analgesic requirements than combined use of general anesthesia plus *post-incisional* (Katz et al. 1994; Katz et al. 1992) administration of the same agent by the same route. These studies support the idea that surgical incision and subsequent noxious intra-operative events sensitize neurons in the dorsal horn of the spinal cord. In the hours and days following surgery, inputs from the wound impinge on a sensitized nervous system which amplifies the peripheral signal and lead to enhanced postoperative pain and a greater need for postoperative analgesia. Blockade of the noxious input associated with surgery prevents the development of the somatosensory memory component and results in less intense pain.

Recent studies of patients undergoing lower limb amputation show that epidural anaesthesia started before and continuing for the duration of surgery (Bach, Noreng, & Tjéllden 1988) or for several days after amptation (Jahangiri, Bradley, Jayatunga, & Dark 1994; Schug, Burrell, Payne, & Tester 1995) appears to confer the most protection from long-term pain (Figure 11). The one exception to this is a recent randomized, controlled trial evaluating the long term effects on phantom limb and stump pain of continuous epidural morphine and bupivacaine administered 18 hours before, during and for about one week after lower limb amputation (Nikolajsen, Ilkjaer, Krøner, Christensen, & Jensen 1997b). By contrast, blockade of late intra-operative and post-operative noxious inputs does not seem alter the developmental course of persistent pain (Elizaga, Smith, Sharar, Edwards, & Hansen 1994; Fisher & Meller 1991; Pinzur, Garla, Pluth, & Vrbos 1996; Schug et al. 1995) probably because the blockade is administered after central sensitization has been established. Uncovering the relative contributions to long-term pain of factors such as preexisting pain, noxious perioperative events, and post-operative pain will enable us to design multi-agent, pre-emptive

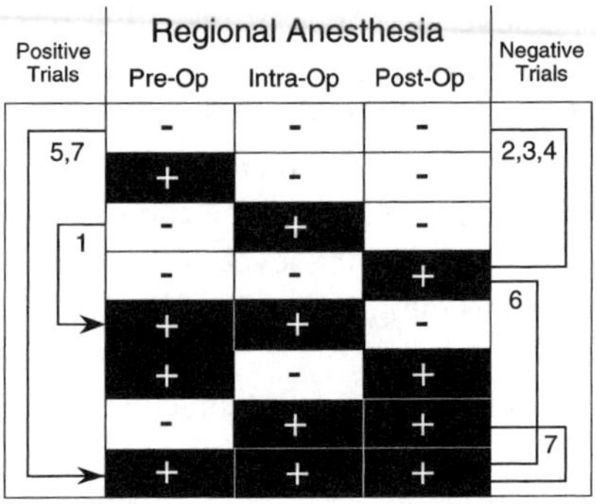

Figure 11. *Administration (+) or non-administration (−) of regional anaesthesia during the pre-operative, intra-operative, and/or post-operative periods shown for clinical trials of patients undergoing limb amputation. Clinical trials with positive (left side of figure) and negative (right side of figure) outcomes are depicted by a line linking treatment conditions. For positive outcomes (# 1,5,7), the arrow points to the treatment condition associated with a significantly reduced incidence of phantom limb pain 6 months or 12 months after amputation Negative outcomes (# 2–4, 6–7) show no difference between treatment conditions in the incidence of long term phantom limb pain. 1 = Bach et al. (1988), 2 = Elizaga et al. (1994), 3 = Fisher and Meller (1991), 4 = Pinzur et al. (1996), 5 = Jahangiri et al. (1994), 6 = Nikolajsen et al. (1997), 7 = Schug et al. (1995). Adapted from Katz (1997) with permission.*

treatments aimed specifically at minimizing the detrimental effects of these factors.

Individual Differences in the Formation and Re-Activation of Pain Memories

Amputation or Deafferentation. When a missing or completely anesthetic limb continues to be the source of pain that resembles an old injury, it is reasonable to assume that the pain is centrally represented. It is unclear, however, whether the interruption of normal sensory nerve impulses (deafferentation) or amputation is necessary for pain memories to develop. The interruption of afferent input associated with amputation or deafferentation may facilitate the central neural changes that contribute to the formation of pain memories by removing normal inhibitory control mechanisms (see Coderre, Katz, Vaccarino & Melzack 1993 for a review).

Alternately, deafferentation may merely provide a condition under which persistent CNS activity becomes obvious to the observer since the peripheral source has been removed or its afferent supply interrupted. This may explain why pain memories are almost exclusively reported to occur in patients with deafferenting lesions and rarely under other circumstances. Examples of recurring pain in the absence of obvious deafferentation include cardiac pain referred to the site of a compression fracture in the upper back sustained 20 years earlier (Henry & Montuschi 1978) and pain, in response to stimulation of the nasal mucosa, referred to teeth that had recently been filled (Hutchins & Reynolds 1947; Reynolds & Hutchins 1948). Noordenbos and Wall (1981) describe seven patients with partial peripheral nerve injury and subsequent pain who underwent nerve resection and graft or ligation. Following a pain-free period all seven re-developed pain of the same quality and in the same location as they had experienced prior to nerve resection, although in some patients the recurrence of pain was restricted to a smaller area within the originally painful region.

If deafferentation or amputation is not a necessary condition for a pain memory to develop, then we must ask why they are reported so infrequently among patients in whom the flow of afferent impulses has not been interrupted. One possibility is that certain peripheral injuries do become represented centrally, but because the peripheral source of pain is so obvious (e.g., a surgical incision), the existence of a central somatosensory component is not even considered. For example, it has been shown that postoperative pain following thoracic surgery is less intense if patients received a general anesthetic plus an epidural opioid or local anesthetic infused *before* incision *versus* a general anesthetic plus an epidural opioid or local anesthetic infused *after* incision (Katz et al. 1994; Katz et al. 1992). Nociceptive impulses during surgery reach the spinal cord and contribute to a state of persistent central sensitization that increases postoperative pain intensity after the patient awakes from the general anesthetic. Blocking nociceptive inputs beforebut not after incision attenuates the development of the central somatosensory component. The obvious source of ongoing pain after surgery (i.e., the incision) may blind the observer to the possibility that the very act of cutting may have set up a permanent representation that amplifies subsequent inputs from the wound.

The possibility that a central somatosensory component may be masked by the more obvious peripheral source of pain is further supported by studies of patients undergoing electrical brain stimulation during neurosurgical procedures. Pain is rarely elicited by test stimuli unless the patient suffers from a long-standing pain problem (Lenz, Kwan, Dostrovsky, & Tasker 1989; Obrador & Dierssen 1966). Electrical stimulation of a variety of subcortical structures in patients with chronic pain frequently evokes pain and in some instances may even reproduces the patient's pain. Although these studies involve patients with central or deafferentation pain, electrical micro-stimulation of the thalamus may even evoke somatosensory pain memories in patients with pain that is not long-standing and that does not involve extensive nerve injury or deafferentation (Davis, Tasker, Kiss, Hutchison, & Dostrovsky 1995; Lenz et al. 1994; Nathan 1985). Nathan (1985) described a patient who underwent thalamic stimulation for a movement disorder. The patient had been suffering from a toothache for 10 days prior to the operation. Electrical stimulation of the thalamus reproduced the toothache. More recently, Lenz et al. (1994) described the case of a woman with unstable angina who, during electrical stimulation of the thalamus, reported "heart pain like what I took nitroglycerin for" except that "it starts and stops suddenly" (p. 121). The possibility that the patient's angina was due to myocardial strain, and not activation of a somatosensory pain memory, was ruled out by demonstrating that EKG, blood pressure, and cardiac enzymes remained unchanged over the course of stimulation. Davis et al. (1995) described a woman who reported pain during thalamic stimulation that resembled the pain she had experienced during labor and delivery. Another patient reported a painful sensation "inside, like my ulcer pain" (p. 373).

Inputs from the periphery. There is evidence that in some cases the reactivation of a pain memory requires a peripheral trigger. Leriche (1947) described a patient who did not experience phantom limb pain until 6 years after amputation, when an injection into the stump instantly and permanently, revived the pain of a former painful ulceration of the Achilles tendon. Nathan (1962, 1985) reported a similar phenomenon after applying noxious stimuli to the stump of an amputee who later re-experienced the pain of an ice-skating injury he had sustained five years earlier when his leg was intact. Katz and Melzack (1990) reported a patient with an amputation below the knee who discovered that when he maximally flexed his knee he could briefly elicit in the phantom limb, the sensation of "the dry, callused, tight skin" he used to feel on the sole of his foot. Another amputee who had suffered from intermittent claudication prior to amputation continued to experience the same pain referred to the phantom calf after walking a short distance. These reports indicate that past pains may be re-experienced months or even years after the original injury, in some cases by a peripheral trigger which provides the input required to activate the central neural structures subserving the memory trace.

Inputs from modalities other than somesthesis. Pain memories sometimes comprise highly complex perceptual phenomena that include components from several modalities which were involved in the original experience. Many pre-amputation pains have corresponding visual elements such as a discolored and festering diabetic ulcer, or a raw, red open surgical wound. Some may even have associated olfactory cues including the foul stench of putrid diabetic ulcers and gangrene. These and other examples (Henderson & Smyth 1948; Jacome 1978; James, 1887; Wallgren 1954) suggest that separate modality-specific sensory memories of the pre-amputation experience may be formed at the time of injury or during episodes of pain. The additional sensory modalities may contribute to the formation of a higher-order functional unit during the contiguous activation of modality-specific representations associated with bouts of pre-amputation pain (Bindra 1978).

The role of vision is especially important since it dominates over other sensory modalities in circumstances involving exteroceptive sensibility. Lower limb amputees frequently report that it was not until they looked under the bed sheets that they realized their limb had been cut off (Gallinek 1939; Simmel 1956). Patients undergoing brachial plexus or spinal blocks, those with complete brachial plexus avulsions, and spinal cored transections all report vivid phantom limbs which are felt to be coincident with the position of the real limb as determined by sight (Bors 1951; Evans 1962; Wynn Parry 1980). This is demonstrated clearly when a patient's deafferented limb is moved from one position to another with his or her eyes closed. Under these circumstances, the felt position of the phantom corresponds to the last seen position of the real limb. However, when the patient's eyes are opened, the phantom is reported to "fuse" with the new position of the real limb as perceived by sight (Bromage & Melzack 1974; Evans 1962; Melzack & Bromage 1973; Wallgren 1954). It is also worth noting that prolonged visual deprivation results in significant increases in cutaneous sensitivity among healthy volunteers who have all their limbs intact (Zubek, Flye, & Aftanas 1964).

These findings demonstrate the powerful influence of vision in determining the phantom limb percept. When there is a discrepancy or contradiction between incoming information from different modalities, or when a state of uncertainty exists based upon somatosensory input alone, additional information is sought *via* the visual sense which usually determines the perceptual experience. Since amputation also results in the loss of visual and tactile information related to the limb, the central influences that normally inhibit established pain traces may be further reduced by the absence of information from these external sources that could otherwise confirm or disconfirm the percept (e.g., of a painful diabetic ulcer) arising from the periphery. Following amputation, the likelihood of re-activation of a pain memory that had a visual component (e.g., a diabetic ulcer) is increased since the potential inhibitory effect of vision has also been removed.

In general, as the number of modalities involved in the pre-amputation pain experience increase (and thus the more sources of potential feedback are removed), the greater is the probability of re-activating a past pain once the limb has been removed since there are fewer senses available to provide a reality-based check (i.e., exert an inhibitory influence) on the perceptual processes generating the phantom.

The use of language. Language may play an important role in the development and re-activation of pain memories since it appears to facilitate integration of information from various sense modalities (Bindra 1978; Marks 1978). In particular, the analogic aspect of the verbal message conveys meaning by likening certain qualities (e.g., sensory) of the pain experience to some other experience — whether fancied or real — and is aided by using such figures of speech as simile, metaphor and hyperbole, or more subtly through allegory. Thus consider one woman's bittersweet description of the "pins and needles" sensation so characteristic of phantoms, as "champagne bubbles and blisters" after a left shoulder amputation simultaneously marked the end of a prolonged period of suffering and the beginning of life without an arm (Janovic & Glass 1985). Or, consider the patient with diabetes mellitus who describes the burning pain of a putrefying and discolored gangrenous ulcer on his toe as "hellfire and brimstone".

The formation of a higher order polymodal representation of the pain is facilitated by the unifying verbal response which captures the entire experience signaled by the contiguous activation of modality-specific representatins arising from separate sensory channels (e.g., visual, olfactory, somatosensory). The foregoing implies that after repeated bouts of pain, information signaling the presence of an injury in one modality would activate corresponding representations in other modalities (e.g., in the absence of input from the painful part after amputation). In this context, language functions to simultaneously access multimodal representations, strengthen their interconnections, and through convergence of input to neo-cortical association areas, facilitate both the formation of a pain memory as well as its re-activation after amputation.

Psychopathology and emotional disturbance. It is not uncommon for proponents of theories of phantom limb pain to discount pain that could not be explained on the basis of current physiological and anatomical knowledge as psychological in origin (Bailey & Moersch 1941; Henderson & Smyth 1948; Lakoff 1990). The practice of relegating certain inexplicable phenomena to the psychological or emotional realm may free the theorist from considering them further, but it changes how the amputee is viewed and treated, and implicitly blames him or her for the pain. It is crucial to differentiate legitimate attempts to explain how psychopathology influences phantom limb experience from attempts to use the label as an explanation.

It has been argued that the similarity of pain before and after amputation represents a psychopathological response to amputation in which the psychological or emotional importance of the pre-amputation pain determines the likelihood of its re-experience in the phantom limb. Henderson and Smyth (1948) describe the case of a soldier who sprained his ankle jumping from a truck and therefore could not keep up with his companions. Shortly after he was wounded in the same leg above the ankle and was taken prisoner. The leg was amputated a few days later but he continued to experience the pain of the ankle sprain. The soldier remarked that had it not been for the sprain, he would not have been captured. Bailey and Moersh (1941) describe a patient whose phantom included the sensation of a wood sliver that had been under the nail of his index finger at the time of amputation. They discuss the importance of "both psychical and physical trauma" at or near the time of amputation and conclude that the persistence of pre-amputation pain represents an "obsession neurosis".

These case reports raise the possibility that emotional and psychological disturbance contribute to pain that persists after amputation but their conclusions should be viewed as hypotheses to be tested in a prospective study of patients scheduled for amputation. In seeking rationale explanations for phantom limb pain, patients, clinicians and researchers may conclude that the significance of the pre-amputation pain was instrumental in its representation in the phantom limb. Furthermore, any psychological theory must take into account the literature documenting the recurrence of corns, ingrown toenails, calluses, etc. which, prior to amputation, are rarely considered psychologically important to the patient.

The only study to compare subjects reporting pain memories with those who did not have phantom limb pain or those who had phantom limb pain that bore no resemblance to their pre-amputation, failed to find any significant inter-group differences in depression, anxiety, or personality (Katz & Melzack 1990). Thus, at the time of interview, approximately 5 years after amputation, there was no evidence to suggest that levels of psychopathology or emotional disturbance were different for subjects who reported phantom limb pain of any type compared to pain-free subjects. However, as noted above, the relationship between emotional disturbance and psychopathology at the time of injury (or the significance of the injury) and the subsequent development of a phantom limb pain memory has yet to be addressed in a prospective study.

Pain memories also occur in certain psychiatric patients in the absence of deafferentation and without positive physical signs of peripheral injury (Bressler, Cohen, & Magnussen 1955; Engel 1959; Szasz 1949). Patents presenting with this clinical picture may obtain a diagnosis of conversion hysteria or embark on a fruitless course of treatment focused at the periphery. In his seminal paper on the "pain-prone patient", Engel (1959) introduced the concept of a pain memory to explain his observation that during emotionally stressful circumstances, certain psychiatric patients reported repeated bouts of pain similar in quality and location to a past pain. The circumstances under which the pains recurred were believed to be symbolic of the traumatic event in which the pain was first experienced. According to Engel (1959):

> "the capacity to experience pain in the first place develops from numerous peripherally induced experiences but thereafter pain experience, like visual or auditory experience, may occur without the corresponding stimulation of the end organ. … The term "pain memories" refers to the ideational complexes, conscious and unconscious, associated with past pain experiences, stimulation of which may later give rise to pain. This pain is not the 'old' pain anymore than the joy evoked by certain memories is the same joy that was felt on the occasion of the original joyous experience" (p. 900–901).

Engel (1959) was careful to leave open the possibility that not all patients suffering from the recurrence of a past pain have pain of psychological origin in the sense that warrants the psychiatric diagnosis of the "pain-prone patient". We do not know the factors responsible for the development and maintenance of pain memories in these patients nor do we know how they differ from the pain memories reported by amputees.

Cognitive and affective processes. A separate but related issue concerns the role played by non-pathological cognitive and affective processes in the development or subsequent expression of pain memories after amputation. Recent work in the field of mood and memory has demonstrated that material with high affective loading is learned best and that memory is enhanced when mood state during recall matches that during acquisition (see Singer & Salovey 1988 for a review). These findings suggest that the role of affect in pain memories might be twofold: (1) to facilitate the formation of the somatosensory and cognitive memory components, perhaps through the peripheral and central release of neuroendocrine products into the general circulation and, (2) to facilitate the re-activation of both memory components by creating a central emotional state similar in affective tone to that experienced prior to amputation, biasing attention, information processing, and memory functioning in favor pain-related material.

For example, traumatic injuries incurred as a result of an accident or an emergency surgical procedure performed without anesthetic form the basis of highly specific and vivid declarative memories (Katz & Melzack 1990) much like "flashbulb memories" that occur after extremely stressful events (Squire 1987). A striking example of a flashbulb memory was reported by a patient with a left, above-the-knee amputation. Prior to amputation, he had undergone an emergency surgical procedure without an anesthetic when a wound on the antero-lateral surface of his left leg rapidly had become infected. "When he [the physician] opened it up, it burned so much, like taking a match and letting it burn ... and I fainted away." Although his left leg was later amputated, he continues to have a persisting awareness of the wound on his phantom leg. He is frequently awakened at night feeling weak, covered in sweat, and in a state of panic. At these moments, he feels the same excruciating pain he experienced during the emergency surgical procedure and feels "[i]t's just like the doctors and nurses are there working on it".

As illustrated, the events surrounding traumatic pre-amputation injuries may be re-experienced accompanied by high levels of anxiety. The nature and severity of the initial traumatic injury, the similarity of pain before and after amputation, and the subsequent disability and suffering suggest a stress-related, post-traumaic chronic pain syndrome precipitated by the initial trauma (Engel 1959; Muse 1985; Muse 1986). In these cases, the stress response associated with the initial trauma may be instrumental in the formation of a pain memory. In addition, specific cognitive or affective domains related to the traumatic event may become sensitized so that they develop the capacity to serve as central triggers for the re-activation of the pain after amputation.

Finally, the nature and origin of the emotional response that accompanies a pain memory requires comment. We have proposed that the unified experience of a pain memory involves information from separate somatosensory and cognitive memory components. However, it is clear that in many cases, pain memories, like most painful experiences, are also accompanied by an aversive emotional state and a desire to be free of the pain (Melzack & Casey 1968; Melzack & Wall 1988). The affective or emotional tone, unlike the somatosensory and cognitive components, does not appear to be a re-activation of a previously stored representation. It is generated on a moment-by-moment basis and is determined by the combined information present in the two memory components. Thus patients modulate their affective response as a joint function of (1) the intensity, quality and location of the sensory-discriminative aspects of the experience and (2) a cognitive appraisal of the somatosensory component including its meaning, expectations about its duration, their ability to cope, and other declarative information.

Summary and Conclusions

The material presented in this chapter reveals that the phantom limb is not perceived as a static entity but as a frequently changing perceptual experience dependent upon the current sensory input, emotional state and past experience of the individual amputee. Phantom limb phenomena range from simple, diffuse sensations of tingling to perceptually complex experiences of pains and lesions that originally were felt in the limb prior to amputation. While phantom pains and other sensations frequently are triggered by the perception of salient events, thoughts, and feelings, there is no evidence that the painful or painless phantom limb is a symptom of a psychological disorder. For many amputees, there appear to be common physiological mechanisms responsible for certain phantom limb pains and phantom sensations. Sub-types of phantom limb pain may be generated by sympathetic-efferent activity (burning, tingling, dysesthesias), cramping in muscles of the stump (cramping phantom limb pain) and re-activation of central neural stuctures involved in somatosensory experience (pain memories). The sympathetic nervous system may provide an important link between higher brain centers involved in cognitive and affective processes and phantom limb sensations through its peripheral actions on primary afferents located in stump neuromas. However, the manner in which this mechanism becomes expressed phenomenologically and perceptually is unique to each individual. The role of individual differences in the conscious experience of phantom limbs is paramount given that amputation not only has removed the limb, but all haptic, tactile and visual information pertaining to the limb as well. Because there are fewer sensory modalities to provide a reality-based check on perceptual activity and conscious experience (as they relate to the phantom limb), these processes are influenced to a greater degree by cognitive and emotional factors than they were prior to amputation when the limb was intact.

References

Anani, A. and Körner, L. 1979. Discrimination of phantom hand sensations elicited by afferent electrical nerve stimulation in below-elbow amputees. *Medical Progress through Technology* 6: 131–135.

Arena, J. G., Sherman, R. A. and Bruno, G. M. 1990. The relationship between situational stress and phantom limb pain: cross-lagged correlational data from six month pain logs. *Journal of Psychosomatic Research* 34: 71–77.

Bach, S., Noreng, M. F. and Tjéllden, N. U. 1988. Phantom limb pain in amputees during the first 12 months following limb amputation, after preoperative lumbar epidural blockade. *Pain* 33: 297–301.

Bailey, A. A. and Moersch, F. P. 1941. Phantom limb. *Canadian Medical Association Journal* 45: 37–42.

Berger, M. and Gerstenbrand, F. 1981. Phantom illusions in spinal cord lesions. In J. Siegfried and M. Zimmermann (eds), *Phantom and stump pain*, 66–73. New York: Springer-Verlag.

Bindra, D. 1978. *A theory of intelligent behavior*. New York: Wiley.

Bini, G., Hagbarth, K. E., Hynninen, P. and Wallin, G. 1980. Thermoregulatory and rhythm-generating mechanisms governing the sudomotor and vasoconstrictor outflow in human cutaneous nerves. *Journal of Physiology (London)* 306: 537–552.

Boas, R. A. 1983. Phantom anus pain syndrome. In J. J. Bonica, U. Lindblom, and A. Iggo (eds), *Advances in pain research and therapy*, Vol. 5: 947–951. New York: Raven Press.

Bors, E. 1951. Phantom limbs of patients with spinal cord injury. *Archives of Neurology and Psychiatry* 66: 610–631.

Brena, S. F. and Sammons, E. E. 1979. Phantom urinary bladder pain - Case report. *Pain* 7: 197–201.

Bressler, B., Cohen, S. I. and Magnussen, F. 1955. Bilateral breast phantom and breast phantom pain. *Journal of Nervous and Mental Disease* 122: 315–320.

Brodal, A. 1981. *Neurological anatomy in relation to clinical medicine (third edition)*. New York: Oxford University Press.

Bromage, P. R. and Melzack, R. 1974. Phantom limbs and the body schema. *Canadian Anaesthetists' Society Journal* 21: 267–274.

Browder, J. G. and Gallagher, J. P. 1948. Dorsal cordotomy for painful phantom limbs. *Annals of Surgery* 128: 456–459.

Butler, D. J., Turkal, N. W. and Seidl, J. J. 1992. Amputation: Preoperative psychological preparation. *Journal of the American Board of Family Practice* 5: 69–73.

Campbell, J. N., Meyer, R. A., Davis, K. D. and Raja, S. N. 1992a. Sympathetically maintained pain: A unifying hypothesis. In W. D. Willis (ed.), *Hyperalgesia and allodynia*. New York, NY: Raven Press.

Campbell, J. N., Meyer, R. A. and Raja, S. N. 1992b). Is nociceptor activation by alpha-1 adrenergic receptors the culprit in sympathetically maintained pain (SMP)? *APS Journal* 1: 3–11.

Campbell, J. N., Raja, S. N. and Meyer, R. A. 1993. Pain and the sympathetic nervous system: connecting the loop. In L. Vecchiet, D. Albe-Fessard, U. Lindblom, and M. A. Giamberadino (eds), *New trends in referred pain and hyperalgesia*, 99–107. Amsterdam: Elsevier.

Campbell, J. N., Raja, S. N., Selig, D. K., Belzberg, A. J. and Meyer, R. A. 1994. Diagnosis and management of sympathetically maintained pain. In H. L. Fields and J. C.

Liebeskind (eds), *Pharmacological approaches to the tratment of chronic pain: New concepts and critical issues*, 85–97. Seattle: IASP Press.

Carlen, P. L., Wall, P. D., Nadvorna, H. and Steinbach, T. 1978. Phantom limbs and related phenomena in recent traumatic amputations. *Neurology, 28*: 211–217.

Chabal, C., Jacobson, L., Russell, L. C. and Burchiel, K. J. 1992. Pain response to perineuromal injection of normal saline, epinephrine, and lidocaine in humans. *Pain* 49: 9–12.

Coderre, T. J., Katz, J., Vaccarino, A. L. and Melzack, R. 1993. Contribution of central neuroplasticity to pathological pain: Review of clinical and experimental evidence. *Pain* 52: 259–285.

Conomy, J. P. 1973. Disorders of body image after spinal cord injury. *Neurology* 23: 842–850.

Cronholm, B. 1951. Phantom limbs in amputees. *Acta Psychiatrica et Neurologica Scandinavica, 72 (Suppl)* 1–310.

Danke, F. 1981. Phantom sensations after amputation: The importance of localization and prognosis. In J. Siegfried and M. Zimmermann (eds), *Phantom and stump pain*, 56–61. New York: Springer-Verlag.

Davis, K. D., Tasker, R. R., Kiss, T. H. T., Hutchison, W. D. and Dostrovsky, J. O. 1995. Visceral pain evoked by thalamic microstimulation in humans. *NeuroReport* 6: 369–374.

Delius, W., Hagbarth, K. E., Hongell, A. and Wallin, B. G. 1972. Manoeuvres affecting sympathetic outflow in human skin nerves. *Acta Physiologica Scandinavica* 84: 177–186.

Devor, M. 1983. Nerve pathophysiology and mechanisms of pain in causalgia. *Journal of the Autonomic Nervous System* 7: 371–384.

Diamond, J. 1959. The effect of injecting acetylcholine into normal and regenerating nerves. *Journal of Physiology (London)* 145: 611–629.

Dorpat, T. L. 1971. Phantom sensations of internal organs. *Comprehensive Psychiatry* 12: 27–35.

Ebert, T., Flor, H., Birbaumer, N., Knecht, S., Hampson, S., Larbig, W. and Taub, E. 1994. Extensive reorganization of the somatosensory cortex in adult humans after nervous system injury. *NeuroReport* 5: 2593–2597.

Elizaga, A. M., Smith, D. G., Sharar, S. R., Edwards, T. and Hansen, S. T. 1994. Continuous regional analgesia by intraneural block: Effect on postoperative opioid requirements and phantom limb pain following amputation. *Journal of Rehabilitation Research and Development* 31: 179–187.

Engel, G. L. 1959. 'Psychogenic' pain and the pain-prone patient. *American Journal of Medicine* 26: 899–918.

Evans, J. H. 1962. On disturbance of the body image in paraplegia. *Brain* 85: 687–700.

Ewalt, J. R., Randall, G. C. and Morris, H. 1947. The phantom limb. *Psychosomatic Medicine* 9: 118–123.

Fisher, A. and Meller, Y. 1991. Continuous postoperative regional analgesia by nerve sheath block for amputation surgery - A pilot study. *Anesthesia and Analgesia* 72: 300–303.

Friedmann, L. W. 1978. *The psychological rehabilitation of the amputee*. Springfield: C. C. Thomas.

Gallinek, A. 1939. The phantom limb. Its origin and its relationship to the hallucinations of psychotic states. *American Journal of Psychiatry* 96: 413–422.

Gloyne, H. F. 1954. Psychosomatic aspects of pain. *Psychoanalytic Review* 41: 135–139.

Glynn, C. J., Stannard, C., Collins, P. A. and Casale, R. 1993. The role of peripheral sudomotor blockade in the treatment of patients with sympathetically-maintained pain. *Pain* 53: 39–42.

Guéniot, M. 1861. D'une hallucination du toucher (ou hétérotopie subjective des extrémités) particulière a certains amputés. *Journal de la Physiologie de l'Homme et des Animaux* 4: 416–430.

Haber, W. B. 1955. Effects of loss of limb on sensory functions. *Journal of Psychology* 40: 115–123.

Haber, W. B. 1956. Observations on phantom-limb phenomena. *Archives of Neurology and Psychiatry* 75: 624–636.

Haber, W. B. 1958. Reactions to loss of limb: Physiological and psychological aspects. *Annals of the New York Academy of Science* 74(14–24): 624–636.

Hagbarth, K. E., Hallin, R. G., Hongell, A., Torebjörk, H. E. and Wallin, B. G. 1972. General characteristics of sympathetic activity in human skin nerves. *Acta Physiologica Scandinavica* 84: 164–176.

Halligan, P. W., Marshall, J. C. and Wade, D. T. 1994. Sensory disorganization and perceptual plasticity after limb amputation: a follow-up study. *NeuroReport* 5: 1341–1345.

Halligan, P. W., Marshall, J. C., Wade, D. T., Davey, J. and Morrison, D. 1993. Thumb in cheek? Sensory reorganization and perceptual plasticity after limb amputation. *NeuroReport* 4: 233–236.

Henderson, W. R. and Smyth, G. E. 1948. Phantom limbs. *Journal of Neurology, Neurosurgery and Psychiatry* 2: 88–112.

Henry, J. A. and Montuschi, E. 1978. Cardiac pain referred to site of previously experienced somatic pain. *British Medical Journal* 2: 1605–1606.

Hutchins, H. C. and Reynolds, O. E. 1947. Experimental investigation of the referred pain of aerodontalgia. *Journal of Dental Research* 26: 3–8.

Jacobson, L. and Chabal, C. 1989. Prolonged relief of acute postamputation phantom limb pain with intrathecal fentanyl and epidural morphine. *Anesthesiology* 71: 984–985.

Jacobson, L., Chabal, C. and Brody, M. C. 1989. Relief of persistent postamputation stump and phantom limb pain with intrathecal fentanyl. *Pain* 37: 317–322.

Jacobson, L., Chabal, C., Brody, M. C., Mariano, A. J. and Chaney, E. F. 1990. A comparison of the effects of intrathecal fentanyl and lidocaine on established postamputation stump pain. *Pain* 40: 137–141.

Jacome, D. 1978. Phantom itching relieved by scratching phantom feet [Letter]. *Journal of the American Medical Association* 240: 2432.

Jahangiri, M., Bradley, J. W. P., Jayatunga, A. P. and Dark, C. H. 1994. Prevention of phantom limb pain after major lower limb amputation by epidural infusion of diamorphine, clonidine and bupivacaine. *Annals of the Royal College of Surgeons of England* 76: 324–326.

James, W. 1887. The consciousness of lost limbs. *Proceedings of the American Society for Psychical Research* 1: 249–258.

Jänig, W. 1985. Causalgia and reflex sympathetic dystrophy: In which way is the sympathetic nervous system involved? *Trends in Neuroscience* 8: 471–477.

Jänig, W. 1990. The sympathetic nervous system in pain: Physiology and pathophysiology. In M. Stanton-Hicks (ed.), *Pain and the sympathetic nervous system*, 17–89. Boston: Kluwer Academic Publishers.

Janovic, J. and Glass, J. P. 1985. Metoclopramine-induced phantom dyskinesia. *Neurology* 35: 432–435.

Jensen, T. S., Krebs, B., Nielsen, J. and Rasmussen, P. 1984. Non-painful phantom limb phenomena in amputees: incidence, clinical characteristics and temporal course. *Acta Neurologica Scandinavica* 70: 407–414.

Jensen, T. S., Krebs, B., Nielsen, J. and Rasmussen, P. 1985. Immediate and long-term phantom pain in amputees: incidence, clinical characteristics and relationship to pre-amputation pain. *Pain* 21: 268–278.

Jensen, T. S. and Rasmussen, P. 1994. Phantom pain and other phenomena after amputation. In P. D. Wall and R. Melzack (eds), *Textbook of Pain* 3: 651–665. Edinburgh: Churchill Livingstone.

Kallio, K. E. 1950a. Permanency of results obtained by sympathetic surgery in the treatment of phantom pain. *Acta Orthopaedica Scandinavica* 19: 391–397.

Kallio, K. E. 1950b. Phantom limb of forearm stump cleft by kineplastic surgery. *Acta Chirurgica Scandinavica* 99: 121–132.

Katz, J. 1992a. Psychophysical correlates of phantom limb experience. *Journal of Neurology, Neurosurgery and Psychiatry* 55: 811–821.

Katz, J. 1992b. Psychophysiological contributions to phantom limbs. *Canadian Journal of Psychiatry* 37: 282–298.

Katz, J. 1993. The reality of phantom limbs. *Motivation and Emotion* 17: 147–179.

Katz, J. 1997. Phantom limb pain. *The Lancet* 350: 1338–1339.

Katz, J., Clairoux, M., Kavanagh, B. P., Roger, S., Nierenberg, H., Redahan, C. and Sandler, A. N. 1994. Pre-emptive lumbar epidural anaesthesia reduces postoperative pain and patient-controlled morphine consumption after lower abdominal surgery. *Pain* 59: 395–403.

Katz, J., France, C. and Melzack, R. 1989. An association between phantom limb sensations and stump skin conductance during transcutaneous electrical nerve stimulation (TENS) applied to the contralateral leg: A case study. *Pain* 36: 367–377.

Katz, J., Kavanagh, B. P., Sandler, A. N., Nierenberg, H., Boylan, J. F., Friedlander, M. and Shaw, B. F. 1992. Preemptive analgesia: Clinical evidence of neuroplasticity contributing to post-operative pain. *Anesthesiology* 77: 439–446.

Katz, J. and Melzack, R. 1987. Referred sensations in chronic pain patients. *Pain* 28: 51–59.

Katz, J. and Melzack, R. 1990. Pain "memories" in phantom limbs: Review and clinical observations. *Pain* 43: 319–336.

Katz, J., Vaccarino, A. L., Coderre, T. J. and Melzack, R. 1991. Injury prior to neurectomy alters the pattern of autotomy in rats. *Anesthesiology* 75: 876–883.

Keynes, G. 1952. *The apologie and treatise of Ambroise Paré containing the voyages made into divers places with many of his writings upon surgery.* Chicago: University of Chicago Press.

Kolb, L. C. 1954. *The painful phantom: psychology, physiology and treatment.* Springfield: C. C. Thomas.

Krebs, B., Jensen, T. S., Krøner, K., Nielsen, J. and Jørgensen, H. S. 1985. Phantom limb phenomena in amputees 7 years after limb amputation. In H. L. Fields, R. Dubner, and F. Cervero (eds), *Advances in pain research and therapy* 9: 425–429. New York: Raven Press.

Kristen, H., Lukeschitsch, G., Plattner, F., Sigmund, R. and Resch, P. 1984. Thermography as a means for quantitative assessment of stump and phantom pains. *Prosthetics and Orthotics International* 8: 76–81.

Krøner, K., Knudsen, U. B., Lundby, L. and Hvid, H. 1992. Long-term phantom bresat syndrome. *Clinical Journal of Pain* 8: 346–350.

Krøner, K., Krebs, B., Skov, J. and Jørgensen, H. S. 1989. Immediate and long-term phantom breast syndrome after mastectomy: incidence, clinical characteristics and relationship to pre-mastectomy breast pain. *Pain* 36: 327–334.

Lacroix, R., Melzack, R., Smith, D. and Mitchell, N. 1992. Multiple phantom limbs in a child. *Cortex* 28: 503–507.

Lakoff, R. 1990. The psychology and psychotherapy of the chronic pain patient. In T. W. Miller (ed.), *Chronic Pain* 2: 499–524. Madison, CT: International Universities Press, Inc.

Lenz, F. A., Gracely, R. H., Hope, E. J., Baker, F. H., Rowland, L. H., Dougherty, P. M. and Richardson, R. T. 1994. The sensation of angina can be evoked by stimulation of the human thalamus. *Pain* 59: 119–125.

Lenz, F. A., Kwan, H. C., Dostrovsky, J. O. and Tasker, R. R. 1989. Characteristics of the bursting pattern of action potential that occurs in the thalamus of patients with central pain. *Brain Research* 496: 357–360.

Leriche, R. 1947. De la douleur comme objet de connaissance. *Le Progrès Médical* 5: 115–129.

Livingston, W. K. 1938. Fantom limb pain. A report of ten cases in which it was treated by injections of procaine hydrochloride near the thoracic sympathetic ganglions. *Archives of Surgery* 37: 353–370.

Livingston, W. K. 1943. *Pain mechanisms*. New York: Macmillan.

Lott, T. L. 1986. Descartes on phantom limbs. *Mind & Language* 1: 242–271.

Marbach, J. J. 1996. Orofacial phantom pain: theory and phenomenology. *Journal of the American Dental Association* 127: 221–229.

Marks, L. E. 1978. *The unity of the senses: Interrelations among the modalities*. New York: Academic Books.

McGrath, P. A. and Hillier, L. M. 1992. Phantom limb sensations in adolescents: A case study to illustrate the utility of sensation and pain logs in pediatric clinical practice. *Journal of Pain and Symptom Management* 7: 46–53.

Melzack, R. 1971. Phantom limb pain: Implications for treatment of pathologic pain. *Anesthesiology* 35: 409–419.

Melzack, R. and Bromage, P. R. 1973. Experimental phantom limbs. *Experimental Neurology* 39: 261–269.

Melzack, R. and Casey, K. L. 1968. Sensory, motivational, and central control determinants of pain. In D. Kenshalo (ed.), *The skin senses* 423–439. Springfield, IL: CC Thomas.

Melzack, R. and Loeser, J. D. 1978. Phantom body pain in paraplegics: Evidence for a central 'pattern generating mechanism' for pain. *Pain* 4: 195–210.

Melzack, R. and Wall, P. D. 1988. *The challenge of pain*. (2nd ed.). New York: Basic Books.

Merskey, H. 1989. Psychiatry and chronic pain. *Canadian Journal of Psychiatry* 34: 329–336.

Merzenich, M. M., Nelson, R. J., Stryker, M. P., Cynader, M. S., Schoppmann, A. and Zook, J. M. 1984. Somatosensory cortical map changes following digit amputation in adult monkeys. *Journal of Comparative Neurology* 224: 591–605.

Minski, L. 1943. Psychological reactions to injury. In W. B. Doherty and D. D. Runes (eds), *Rehabilitation of the war injured*, 115–122. New York: Philosophical Library.

Mitchell, S. W. 1871. Phantom limbs. *Lippincott's Magazine of Popular Literature and Science* 8: 563–569.

Mitchell, S. W. 1872. *Injuries of nerves and their consequences*. Philadelphia: J. B. Lippincott.

Morgenstern, F. S. 1964. The effects of sensory input and concentration on post-amputation phantom limb pain. *Journal of Neurology, Neurosurgery and Psychiatry* 27: 58–65.

Muse, M. 1985. Stress-related, posttraumatic chronic pain syndrome: Criteria for diagnosis, preliminary report on prevalence. *Pain* 23: 295–300.

Muse, M. 1986. Stress-related posttraumatic chronic pain syndrome: Behavioral treatment approach. *Pain* 25: 389–394.

Nathan, P. W. 1962. Pain traces left in the central nervous system. In C. A. Keele and R. Smith (eds), *The assessment of pain in man and animals* 129–134. Edinburgh: Livingstone.

Nathan, P. W. 1985. Pain and nociception in the clinical context. *Philosophical Transactions of the Royal Society of London* 308: 219–226.

Nathan, P. W. 1989. The sympathetic nervous system and pain. *Functional Neurology* 4: 11–15.

Nicolodi, M., Frezzotti, R., Diadori, A., Nuti, A. and Sicuteri, F. 1997. Phantom eye: features and prevalence. The predisposing role of headache. *Cephalalgia* 17: 501–504.

Nikolajsen, L., Ilkjaer, S., Krøner, K., Christensen, J. H. and Jensen, T. S. 1997a. The influence of preamputation pain on postamputation stump and phantom pain. *Pain* 72: 393–405.

Nikolajsen, L., Ilkjaer, S., Krøner, K., Christensen, J. H. and Jensen, T. S. 1997b. Randomised trial of epidural bupivacaine and morphine in prevention of stump and phantom pain in lower-limb amputation. *Lancet* 350: 1353–1357.

Noordenbos, W. and Wall, P. D. 1981. Implications of the failure of nerve resection and graft to cure chronic pain produced by nerve lesions. *Journal of Neurology, Neurosurgery and Psychiatry* 44: 1068–1073.

Nordin, M., Nyström, B., Wallin, U. and Hagbarth, K. E. 1984. Ectopic sensory discharges and paresthesiae in patients with disorders of peripheral nerves, dorsal roots and dorsal columns. *Pain* 20: 231–245.

Obrador, S. and Dierssen, G. 1966. Sensory responses to subcortical stimulation and management of pain disorders by stereotaxic methods. *Confinia Neurologica* 27: 45–51.

Ochoa, J. L., Torebjörk, E., Marchettini, P. and Sivak, M. 1985. Mechanisms of neuropathic pain: Cumulative observations, new experiments, and further speculation. In H. L. Fields, R. Dubner, and F. Cervero (eds), *Advances in pain research and therapy* 9: 431–450. New York: Raven Press.

Ochoa, J. L. and Torebjörk, H. E. 1980. Paresthesia from ectopic impulse generation in human sensory nerves. *Brain* 103: 835–853.

Oveson, P., Krøner, K., Ørnsholt, J. and Bach, K. 1991. Phantom-related phenomena after rectal amputation: prevalence and clinical characteristics. *Pain* 44: 289–291.

Parkes, C. M. 1973. Factors determining the persistence of phantom pain in the amputee. *Journal of Psychosomatic Research* 17: 97–108.

Pilowsky, I. and Kaufman, A. 1965. An experimental study of atypical phantom pain. *British Journal of Psychiatry* 111: 1185–1187.

Pinzur, M. S., Garla, P. G. N., Pluth, T. and Vrbos, L. 1996. Continuous postoperative infusion of a regional anesthetic after an amputation of the lower extremity. A randomized clinical trial. *The Journal of Bone and Joint Surgery* 78(A): 1501–1505.

Pitres, A. 1897. Étude sur les sensations illusoires des amputés. *Annales Médico Psychologiques (Paris)* 55: 5–19: 177–192.

Raja, S. N. 1993. Diagnosis of sympathetically maintained pain: The past, present, and future. *European Journal of Pain* 14: 45–48.

Raja, S. N., Treede, R. D., Davis, K. D. and Campbell, J. N. 1991. Systemic alpha-adrenergic blockade with phentolamine: A diagnostic test for sympathetically maintained pain. *Anesthesiology* 74: 691–698.

Ramachandran, V. S., Stewart, M. and Rogers-Ramachandran, D. C. 1992. Perceptual correlates of massive cortical reorganization. *NeuroReport* 3: 583–586.

Randall, G. C., Ewalt, J. R. and Blair, H. 1946. Psychiatric reaction to amputation. *Research Publications of the Association for Research in Nervous and Mental Disease* 25: 94–115.

Reisner, H. 1981. Phantom sensations (phantom arm) in plexus paralysis. In J. Siegfried and M. Zimmermann (eds), *Phantom and stump pain* 62–65. New York: Springer-Verlag.

Reynolds, O. E. and Hutchins, H. C. 1948. Reduction of central hyper-irritability following block anesthesia of peripheral nerve. *American Journal of Physiology* 152: 658–662.

Riddoch, G. 1941. Phantom limbs and body shape. *Brain* 64: 197–222.

Roberts, W. J. 1986. A hypothesis on the physiological basis for causalgia and related pains. *Pain* 24: 297–311.

Scadding, J. W., Wall, P. D., Wynn Parry, C. B. and Brooks, D. M. 1982. Clinical trial of propranolol in post-traumatic neuralgia. *Pain* 14: 283–292.

Schott, G. D. 1993. Pain and the sympathetic nervous system. In R. Bannister and C. J. Mathias (eds), *Autonomic failure. A textbook of clinical disorders of the autonomic nervous system*, 904–917. Oxford: Oxford University Press.

Schug, S. A., Burrell, R., Payne, J. and Tester, P. 1995. Pre-emptive epidural analgesia may prevent phantom limb pain. *Regional Anesthesia* 20: 256.

Sherman, R. A. 1976. Case reports of treatment of phantom limb pain with a combination of electromyographic biofeedback and verbal relaxation techniques. *Biofeedback and Self Regulation* 1: 353.

Sherman, R. A. 1984. Direct evidence of a link between burning phantom pain and stump blood circulation: a case report. *Orthopedics* 7: 1319–1320.

Sherman, R. A. 1989. Stump and phantom limb pain. *Neurologic Clinics* 7: 249–264.

Sherman, R. A. 1994. What do we really know about phantom limb pain? *Pain Reviews* 1: 261–274.

Sherman, R. A. and Arena, J. G. 1992. Phantom limb pain: Mechanisms, incidence, and treatment. *Critical Reviews in Physical and Rehabilitation Medicine* 4: 1–26.

Sherman, R. A. and Bruno, G. M. 1987. Concurrent variation of burning phantom limb and stump pain with near surface blood flow in the stump. *Orthopedics* 10: 1395–1402.

Sherman, R. A., Gall, N. and Gormly, J. 1979. Teatment of phantom limb pain with muscular relaxation training to disrupt the pain-anxiety-tension cycle. *Pain* 6: 47–55.

Sherman, R. A. and Sherman, C. J. 1983. Prevalence and characteristics of chronic phantom limb pain among American veterans: results of a survey. *American Journal of Physical Medicine* 62: 227–238.

Sherman, R. A., Sherman, C. J. and Parker, L. 1984. Chronic phantom and stump pain among American veterans: results of a study. *Pain* 18: 83–95.

Simmel, M. L. 1956. On phantom limbs. *Archives of Neurology and Psychiatry* 75: 637–647.

Singer, J. A. and Salovey, P. 1988. Mood and memory: Evaluating the network theory of affect. *Clinical Psychology Review* 8: 211–251.

Sliosberg, A. 1948. *Les algies des amputés*. Paris: Masson.

Smith, O. A. and DeVito, J. L. 1984. Central neural integration for the control of autonomic responses associated with emotion. *Annual Review of Neuroscience* 7: 43–65.

Solonen, K. A. 1962. The phantom phenomenon in amputated Finnish war veterans. *Acta Orthopaedica Scandinavica, 54 (Suppl. 3)*: 1–119.

Squire, L. R. 1987. *Memory and brain*. New York: Oxford University Press.

Stengel, E. 1965. Pain and the psychiatrist. *British Journal of Psychiatry* 111: 795–802.

Szasz, T. S. 1949. Psychiatric aspects of vagotomy: IV. Phantom ulcer pain. *Archives of Neurology and Psychiatry* 62: 728–733.

Van Bogaert, L. 1934. Sur la pathologie de l'image de soi (Études anatomo-cliniques). *Annales Médico Psychologiques (Paris)* 14: 519–555: 714–759.

Wall, P. D. 1981. On the origin of pain associated with amputation. In J. Siegfried and M. Zimmermann (eds), *Phantom and stump pain*, 2–14. New York: Springer-Verlag.

Wall, P. D. 1989. To what would Gaston Labat be attending today? *Regional Anesthesia* 14: 261–264.

Wall, P. D. and Gutnick, M. 1974. Ongoing activity in peripheral nerves: The physiology and pharmacology of impulses originating from a neuroma. *Experimental Neurology* 43: 580–593.

Wallgren, G. R. 1954. Phantom experience at spinal anaesthesia. *Annales Chirurgicae et Gynaecologicae Fenniae* 43(Suppl.): 486–500.

Wynn Parry, C. B. 1980. Pain in avulsion lesions of the brachial plexus. *Pain* 9: 40–53.

Zubek, J. P., Flye, J. and Aftanas, M. 1964. Cutaneous sensitivity after prolonged visual deprivation. *Science* 144: 1591–1593.

Individual Differences in Bitter Taste

Dietary Implications

Richard D. Mattes
Purdue University

Gary K. Beauchamp
Monell Chemical Senses Center

Introduction

Taste sensitivity to bitterness has been ascribed a central role in human evolution. It has been argued that most toxic compounds are bitter (Glendinning 1994) and that faced with an ongoing need to select between unfamiliar edible or noxious substances, bitter sensitivity guarded against ingestion of a lethal dose of the latter. It did so by eliciting reactions to purge bitter substances from the oral cavity prior to internalization. Consistent with this view, a rejection response to some bitter solutions is present at birth (Steiner 1979; Bergamasco & Beraldo 1990). So widespread and profound is the dislike for the sensation that the term is reserved to describe the most unpleasant of human experiences — e.g., a bitter divorce, having to swallow bitter medicine or being required to remain until the bitter end of an objectionable event. At the same time, a case may be made that an absolute, widespread rejection of items with any bitterness would be maladaptive. Many wholesome foods have bitter notes and a failure to find them acceptable would limit diet diversity and quality. Thus, an attenuated response could, under conditions of a widely tested, safe and reliable food supply, confer some benefit. Selected items with prominent bitter characteristics (e.g., coffee, alcohol, certain fruits and vegetables) have become highly preferred dietary components by certain individuals. This text will consider factors that may account for individual differences in sensitivity and hedonic responses to bitter taste compounds and the nutritional implications of bitter rejection and acceptance.

Bitter Taste Reception

Fundamental to a consideration of the determinants of individual variability in hedonic responses to bitter food constituents is an understanding of bitter taste reception mechanisms. Due to the broad range of both hydrophobic and hydrophilic compounds that taste bitter, it is commonly assumed that there is more than one mechanism involved in bitter taste transduction. This is supported by recent biophysical studies that identify mechanisms whereby bitter taste compounds interact with membrane receptors and/or channels or intracellular G proteins, phospholipases, or phosphodiesterases resulting in blockage of K^+ channels, opening of Ca^+ channels, activation of phospholipase C or enhanced cAMP degradation (Lindemann 1996). For example, studies in animal models demonstrate that sucrose octaacetate and denatonium chloride (both intensely bitter to humans) probably interact with membrane receptors and stimulate IP_3 levels, which, in turn, free calcium from internal stores and enhance neurotransmitter release. The bitterness of quinine is likely due, in part, to its ability to block K^+ channels resulting in taste receptor cell depolarization. Urea appears to enhance cAMP breakdown via phosphodiesterase and the decreased concentration permits nucleotide-suppressed channels to open leading to cell depolarization. Amphiphilic peptides such as bradykinin may taste bitter due to their direct interaction with G proteins and resultant activation of the IP_3 cascade. There are marked species and even strain differences in the activity of these mechanisms (Whitney & Harder 1994). Whether all apply to humans and are equally expressed in each individual has not been established.

Human psychophysical studies are also consistent with, but do not provide definitive evidence for multiple receptor systems. One line of evidence is based on findings of a lack of association between sensitivity to the bitterness of compounds with varying structures, i.e., phenylthiocarbamide (PTC), propylthiouracil (PROP), quinine sulfate, quinine hydrochloride, urea, caffeine, potassium chloride, picric acid, iso-alpha-acids, L-tryptophan and L-phenylalanine (Blakeslee 1932; Fisher & Griffin 1963; Hall et al. 1975; Bartoshuk et al. 1988; Mela 1989; Schifferstein & Frijters 1991; Tanimura & Mattes 1993). The reasoning derives from the presumption that compounds using a common mechanism will be comparably effective at activating the reception sequence. However, such a view may not be justified since physicochemical factors modifying access of taste molecules to receptors or channels can also influence perception.

A second line of evidence involves cross-adaptation studies, where an individual is adapted to one bitter compound and then exposed to another. These studies indicate that the degree of bitter taste suppression to dissimilar compounds is not as great as that noted when the identical compound is re-sampled (McBurney et al. 1972). This is interpreted as reflecting different transduction mechanisms since perception of compounds sharing a mechanism should be equally affected by modulation of the reception sequence (e.g., by adaptation). Third, suprathreshold taste responsiveness to different bitter compounds also varies. For example, different patterns of responsiveness to caffeine, sucrose octaacetate and magnesium sulfate are observed in individuals more or less sensitive to the bitterness of urea or quinine (Yokomukai, Cowart & Beauchamp 1993). Finally, age-related declines in taste sensitivity may be compound-specific. Whereas children and adults have comparable sensitivity for urea, they differ for quinine (Cowart et al. 1994). Thus, on the basis of the psychophysical evidence, at least three transduction mechanisms have been proposed — one serving thionamide-containing compounds, one for quinine, caffeine and sucrose octaacetate and one for urea and magnesium sulfate (Cowart et al. 1994).

The existence of multiple receptive mechanisms complicates an understanding of individual differences in bitter sensitivity since the factors that influence this trait may exert different influences on each mechanism at different times. At the very least, the apparent inconsistency of findings from various studies may reflect the use of different compounds that are perceived by distinct mechanisms.

Genetics

The most extensive study of a genetic contribution to taste sensitivity has focused on the thionamide-containing compounds, PTC and PROP. A bimodal distribution for sensitivity to PTC was first reported by Fox in 1931 (Fox 1931). Since that time, numerous studies have documented different population-specific prevalence rates for sensitivity to such compounds. Table 1 lists selected studies exemplifying the range of sensitive tasters. Well over 400 populations have been evaluated (Mourant et al. 1976).

Early evidence suggested this could be explained by a single locus model of inheritance (Whissell-Buechy 1990) whereby individuals homozygous recessive for the gene coding sensitivity to such compounds are insensitive and are termed, "non-tasters." Those who are heterozygous or homozygous dominant are "tasters." However, additional studies support a more complex pattern. Bartoshuk et al., (1994) have argued that tasters may be subdivided into "tasters" who are heterozygous for the gene controlling the trait and a group classified as "super-

Table 1. *Reported proportion of PTC/PROP tasters in selected populations*

Population (ref)	% Tasters
Brazilian Indian (Hundley 1960)	99
Peruvian (Paolucci et al. 1971)	98
Egyptian, Sudanese (Lee 1934)	96
Pure American Indians (Levine & Anderson 1932)	94
Ecuadorian Andean (Greene 1974)	93–95
Japanese (Saldanha 1958; Sato & Sata 1989)	93–95
Kenya Africans (Lee 1934)	92
Mixed American Indian X Caucasian (Levine & Anderson 1932)	90
African Americans (Lee 1934)	88–91
Chinese (Barnicot 1951)	89
Ashkenazic Jews (Saldanha 1960)	72
North American Caucasian (Snyder 1931; Allison & Blumberg 1959)	70
Mennonites (Koertvelyessy et al. 1982)	68–80
Greek (salamis Island) (Panyotou et al. 1983)	68
Hindu (Hundley 1960)	66
Aborigines (Northern Territory) (Simmons et al. 1954)	51
Indian (Southern India, Koraput District) (Das & Mukherjee 1964)	48

tasters" who are homozygous dominant and are especially sensitive to the compounds. Further, it has been proposed that there may be sub-groups of non-tasters (Olsen et al. 1989) where some are specifically insensitive to PTC and related compounds and others are more generally insensitive to the bitter taste. As noted above, associations between sensitivity to PTC and other bitter compounds are often weak.

The need to expand the taster status classification scheme may reflect the failings of the simple single locus model of inheritance. Olsen et al. (1989) used pedigree segregation analysis with 1,152 individuals and noted a significantly higher proportion of taster offspring than predicted by the one locus model. Indeed, 18 of the 44 offspring of two non-taster parents were tasters when none were predicted. In addition, significantly greater than expected numbers of tasters were identified from heterozygous matings. Discrepancies in expected and observed distributions were also noted by Whissell-Buechy (1990). Olsen et al. (1989) propose a two-locus or one-locus, three-allel model for PTC taste sensitivity. Their analysis suggests non-tasters may be recessive at one of two loci — one loci with an allel affecting PTC specifically and one controlling more general taste sensitivity. To support their view, they note that other work fails to fit the single locus model (Harris & Kalmus 1951; Das 1956, 1958;

Merton 1958; Reddy & Rao 1989). Further, Kalmus (1958) reported that individuals who were extremely insensitive to PTC were also less sensitive to other bitter compounds (i.e., quinine and brucine) and Frank & Korchmar (1985) noted discrepancies in some non-tasters in reaction time to a wide range of compounds. They estimated in their population that 8.2% were extreme non-tasters and 18.5% were non-tasters.

An additional explanation for the observed inconsistencies with the single locus model may stem from a failure to account for environmental influences on PTC sensitivity. This was acknowledged by Blakeslee (1932), but quantitative support was not available for another 50 years when Morton et al. (1981) conducted a genetic analysis of 393 offspring of 85 monozygotic twin pairs. They reported that 7.9% of the variance in PTC thresholds was attributable to additive genetic effects, 16.6% to dominance effects, 14.2% to maternal effects, 13.7% to common sibship environment and 17.6% to random environmental effects. The overall heritability was only 55%. It was concluded that while PTC taste may be controlled by a major dominant gene, PTC threshold is more influenced by environmental factors. Whether this is due to the susceptibility of a second loci to environmental influences, as suggested by Olsen et al., (1989), has not been tested. Some of the potential environmental influences are discussed below.

Bitter Taste and Health

Based on the view that there is a heritable component for taste sensitivity to selected bitter compounds (i.e., PTC, PROP, quinine) and established genetic influences on various health disorders and personal attributes, associations have been explored between bitter taste and these characteristics. Table 2 is a compilation of reports on such associations. In some instances, a causal relationship was hypothesized. For example, it has been proposed that insensitivity to the bitterness of compounds that inhibit iodine uptake would predispose individuals to goiter (Greene 1974). In other cases associations were explored to determine whether taste responses could provide a rapid, non-invasive index for a mechanism potentially contributing to various health disorders. For instance, the association between bitter taste sensitivity and diabetes may reflect progressing peripheral neuropathy (Terry & Segall 1947). Another motivation was to explore the use of bitter taste responsiveness as a marker for health risk. Assessment of associations between taster status and schizophrenia (Schlosberg & Baruch 1992),

Table 2. *Reported associations between Quinine/PTC/PROP taster status and personal characteristics*

Taste	Index	Relationship
Quinine	Wechsler Adult Intelligence Scale (Fischer et al. 1966)	Digit Symbol Performance (R=0.4) Extreme insensitive tasters — compensated Extreme sensitive tasters — internalized
	Systemic reactivity (Fischer et al. 1966)	More sensitive tasters react to lower doses of certain pharmacologic agents (e.g., stelazine) Shorter reaction time in more sensitive tasters (serial seven test)
	Paroxysmal vascular headache (Fischer & Griffin 1961)	Higher incidence in non-tasters
	Down's syndrome (Fischer et al. 1962)	No sensitive tasters among parents of affected children
	Cigarette Smoking (Fischer et al. 1966)	Fewer heavy smokers among sensitive tasters
	Body habitus (Fischer et al. 1966)	Higher prevalence of ectomorphs among sensitive tasters and endomorphs among less sensitive tasters
PROP/PTC	Wechsler Adult Intelligence Scale (Mascie-Taylor et al. 1983)	Non-tasters more placid, relaxed, practical, and scored higher on visual-spatial component of IQ test (AH5) internalized
	Beck Depression Inventory (Whittemore 1986)	Higher level of depression among tasters (r=0.2394)
	Schizophrenia (Schlosberg & Baruch 1992)	Higher incidence of non-tasters among non-paranoid schizophrenics
	Taste reactivity (Frank & Korchmar 1985)	Non-tasters are slower
	Visual Motor perception (Greene 1974)	Non-tasters more deficits with low iodine intake (Kendall=0.25)

Taste	Index	Relationship
	Body habitus (Fischer et al. 1966)	Higher prevalence of ectomorphs among sensitive tasters and endomorphs among less sensitive tasters
	Paroxysmal vascular headache (Fischer & Griffin 1961)	Higher incidence in non-tasters
	Congenital athyrotic cretins (Fraser 1961; Shepard 1961)	Higher incidence in non-tasters
	Toxic goiter (Kitchin et al. 1959)	Higher incidence among tasters
	Nodular goiter (Harris et al. 1949; Kalmus 1971)	Higher incidence among non-tasters
	Duodenal ulcer (Kaplan et al. 1965; Kaplan et al. 1964b)	Higher incidence in more sensitive tasters
	Glaucoma (Becker et al. 1966)	Higher incidence of open angle glaucoma among non-tasters, lower incidence of non-tasters among closed angle glaucoma patients
	Diabetes (Terry & Segall 1947)	Higher incidence of non-tasters
	Cancer (breast, cervix, ovaries) (Milunicova et al. 1969)	Lower incidence among non-tasters
	Tuberculosis (Beiguelman 1964a; Saldanha 1956)	Lower incidence among non-tasters
	Leprosy (Beiguelman 1964a; Beiguelman 1964b)	Lower incidence in non-tasters
	Down's syndrome (Fischer et al. 1962)	Higher incidence of non-tasters in parents, especially fathers of affected children

depression (Whittemore 1986), psychometric variables (Mascie-Taylor et al. 1983) and tuberculosis and leprosy (Beiguelman 1964a) were prompted by an hypothesized pleotrophic effect. Although numerous associations have been identified, their veracity has not been established. In many cases, no attempts to replicate the findings have been undertaken. Where this has occurred, conflicting observations are often reported. In contrast to the work cited in Table 2, other studies have failed to note differences between tasters and non-tasters of PTC and mental illness (Shepard 1961), intelligence quotient (Shepard 1961) and toxic goiter (Harris et al. 1949). Additional work will be required to reconcile these apparently conflicting findings. Clinically, there has been little interest in the use of a taste test for risk assessment, diagnostic or prognostic purposes, or assessment of pathologic mechanisms. This is likely due to questions about the strength of association between taste responses and the various clinical dependent variables and concern about the reliability and sensitivity of taste testing.

Age

Complaints of diminished taste sensitivity are common among the elderly. Psychophysical studies using bitter stimuli have not verified substantive changes. Some note no significant changes with age (Byrd & Gertman 1959). Weiffenbach et al., (1982) observed only a non-significant trend for rising thresholds (i.e., sensitivity decreased) to quinine sulfate in a sample of 23–88 year olds. Comparable shifts were observed for males and females. The regression coefficient was 0.008. Glanville et al. (1964) estimated that thresholds for quinine increased from age 16 to 55 by 0.066 thresholds for males and 0.043 thresholds for females using serial half dilutions of quinine sulfate starting with a $1.20X10^{-2}$M solution. This translates to a shift of one threshold unit in 15 years for males and 23 years for females. An incremental sex difference is not consistently observed, but where it is noted, males have a sharper decline than females (Glanville et al. 1964; Fikentscher et al. 1977). Bartoshuk et al. (1986) observed a significantly lower sensitivity for quinine among a smaller and older sample of elderly relative to a sample of young adults, but no difference in PROP thresholds. In a larger sample (n=137) comprised of healthy young and elderly individuals, Cowart (1989) observed only a non-significant trend for decreased sensitivity to quinine with age. Further, the group data may not faithfully represent changes at the individual level. Weiffenbach et al., (1982) noted that there was increasing variance in threshold values with age indicating that while some individuals exhibit no shift in sensitivity, a sub-set of individuals experience a marked shift. It is not known whether the changes seen in the latter subgroup are attributable to aging *per se* or influences of other biological processes such as effects of emerging health disorders. Sampling biases resulting in differential test performance may also accentuate apparent age discrepancies (Cowart 1989) (e.g., a more highly educated young population may perform better on tests).

An explanation for some of the variation in study findings may relate to the taste stimuli used for testing. Aging appears to differentially affect the various bitter transduction mechanisms. As noted above, the young and elderly have similar thresholds for the bitterness of urea while, there is a decline in sensitivity to quinine sulfate with age (Cowart et al. 1994). An interaction with smoking has also been reported. Larger age-related declines in threshold sensitivity have been reported among smokers (Krut et al. 1961; Kaplan et al. 1965) that improve with smoking cessation (Peterson et al. 1968).

The literature related to aging effects on PTC taste status is inconclusive. Early evidence suggests there is a higher proportion of super-tasters among children than adults (Blakeslee 1932) and there are small declines in sensitivity to PTC with age (Lee 1934; Harris & Kalmus 1949). Kalmus and Trotter (1962) reported a 3% mean annual increase in thresholds. A small (slope of the regression line = 0.031), but significant decline was also reported by Olsen et al., (1989) using the Fels Longitudinal Growth Study data. They noted that a small number of adults appeared to lose their ability to sense PTC. One recently identified factor that may account for the age effect on PROP sensitivity may be the number of taste receptors on the anterior tongue. There is a correlation between PROP sensitivity and fungiform papillae and taste bud density. The number of these structures may decline with age, but generally, the association between taste sensitivity and taste bud numbers is weak (Mistretta 1984; Miller & Reedy 1990; Catalanotto et al. 1993; Lehman et al. 1995). In contrast, Morton et al. (1981) observed no age effect on PTC threshold, and Whissell-Buechy (1990) found the antimodes of the PTC taste distributions of children were higher than those of adults (i.e., the children were less sensitive), although by only one dilution step. Thus, whether age affects PTC taster status is not clear, but should an effect be identified, it will likely be subtle.

Studies of suprathreshold scaling ability indicate there is little or no decrement of intensity ratings among the aged. In one study, individuals over the age of 40 had shallower slopes of psychophysical intensity functions than those 20–39 years of age (Weiffenbach et al. 1986). No further declines were noted in individuals ranging from 40–56, 57–70 and 70+ years of age. Using magnitude matching, Bartoshuk et al., (1986) observed no substantive diminution of intensity ratings for strong quinine solutions in the elderly. A statistically significant decrement in intensity ratings for quinine was observed by Cowart (1989) when responses were obtained with category scales, but the effect was marginal when data collected with a magnitude matching procedure were assessed.

Assuming some true decline in bitter taste sensitivity or intensity does occur with aging, the practical significance remains an open question. The quality is generally viewed as unpleasant so the loss of sensitivity to an unpleasant sensation may not be undesirable from a sensory perspective (such a loss would be more problematic if it were relied upon to make safe food choices). However, the overall flavor of food reflects the main and interactive effects of all sensory input and to this end, differential declines can lead to altered overall flavor perception. The elderly reportedly experience larger masking effects of taste interactions (i.e., they experience sharper reductions of sensitivity to the component parts of mixtures than the young) (Stevens 1996). Thus, their perception of complex flavors may be more severely affected by a change in sensitivity to bitterness. The implications of subtle shifts in flavor perception, where a low level of bitterness may contribute to a pleasant sensation (e.g., in wines), are difficult to predict.

Sex

Studies of chemosensory function generally reveal no sex effects or a slightly greater sensitivity for females. With respect specifically to bitter taste, Cowart did not observe a significant sex effect for quinine thresholds in a large sample of healthy adults representing a wide segment of the lifecycle (Cowart 1989). Sex effects were noted for salt (NaCl) and sour (citric acid) thresholds. No effects of sex on analyses of suprathreshold ratings were reported. There is some evidence that females are better able to correctly identify the quality of a bitter taste stimulus (Meiselman & Dzendolet 1967; Cowart 1989). The effect of sex on PTC sensitivity was recently reviewed (Bartoshuk et al., (1994). A reanalysis of several older studies demonstrates females are able to detect the bitterness of PTC at lower concentrations than males. Females also have lower thresholds for PROP, rate the intensity of suprathreshold concentrations as more intense and are disproportionately represented in the super-taster sub-group (Bartoshuk et al.,1994). Findings that females have a higher density of fungiform papillae and larger number of taste buds on the anterior tongue supports a hypothesis that this accounts for the sensory testing findings. However, other studies have not observed sex differences in PTC taste acuity (Parr 1934; Morton et al. 1981) or proportions of female supertasters (Whissell-Buechy & Wills 1989). Further, one group reported a one dilution-step higher antimode for taster-status in females compared to males (Whissell-Buechy 1990). Because the most recent data indicate the presence of a sex difference and plausible physiological basis, acceptance of a sex effect is growing, but additional study is required to verify the effect and establish its magnitude.

Tobacco Use

It is widely believed that cigarette smoking adversely influences taste sensitivity. In controlled studies, bitter taste thresholds (e.g., quinine, caffeine) are comparable before and after smoking a cigarette (Krut et al. 1961; Pangborn et al. 1967). Further, no significant difference in sensitivity has been noted following two week periods of smoking and abstinence (Pangborn & Trabue 1973). The literature is inconsistent on the effects of chronic smoking (Pangborn & Trabue 1973; McBurney & Moskat 1975). Smoking has not been found to exert a marked effect on PTC/PROP sensitivity (Kalmus 1971), although, again, there are conflicting data on this point (Kaplan et al. 1964a). Although smoking and age have been shown to exert only limited independent effects on bitter taste sensitivity, combined, a more substantive effect is reported (Fischer et al. 1966) such that quinine sensitivity declines more markedly in aging smokers.

Dietary Implications

While taste clearly plays an important role in food selection, not all facets of the sense hold reliable predictive power for ingestion. Indeed, attempts to document associations between measures of taste sensitivity (i.e., thresholds) or intensity judgements of suprathreshold stimulus concentrations and estimates of dietary intake have generally failed (Mattes 1985; Mattes & Mela 1986). This may be due to the fact that some taste attributes are not intrinsically motivating with respect to feeding behavior. Instead, such measures are only the substrate upon which hedonic impressions are formed and safety information is conveyed. The perceived pleasantness and wholesomeness of oral stimuli are more tightly coupled with ingestive behavior, but are also influenced by numerous additional factors (e.g., cost, convenience, cultural and religious beliefs) which attenuate the effects of such input.

Nevertheless, interest in a regulatory role for bitter taste sensitivity in human feeding has remained strong. This has been bolstered by several points. First, the association between an unpleasant sensation and food rejection is stronger than that between an appealing taste and acceptance (Randall & Sanjur 1981). Unpalatable foods are easily and reliably rejected where the food supply is ample, nutritious and readily accessible. When there is a belief that rejection of a set of foods holds little or no adverse consequence, a decision based on sensory property is straightforward. Thus, because bitterness is generally regarded as an unpleasant sensation, foods with this characteristic are typically avoided. In contrast, decisions about ingesting a given item are highly complex. In western nations, there is a wide array of highly palatable foods competing for selection. The desirability of sensory variety, health concerns about excessive consumption of specific items (e.g., high fat foods and weight gain), cost, convenience, cultural norms and a host of other issues contribute to ingestive decisions. Thus, a prominent appealing sensory note in a food does not ensure its ingestion on a regular basis. Second, the role of bitter taste sensitivity in food selection has been ascribed particular importance because of the hypothesized causal relationship between the ability to taste bitter compounds and risk of toxin exposure. It is purported that individuals insensitive to bitterness would be less likely to reject foods containing toxic bitter compounds. Most heavily studied is goitrogen exposure because of evidence that PTC/PROP non-tasters have a higher incidence of nodular and toxic goiter (Harris et al. 1949; Kitchin et al. 1959; Kalmus 1971), but exposure to other pharmacologically active compounds such as caffeine and ethanol have also been considered (Mattes 1994). Third, there has been a more recent realization that avoidance of foods with bitter notes may reduce diet diversity and pose a risk to nutritional status. Bitter notes are prevalent in many nutrient dense foods such as cruciferous vegetables, red meat, certain citrus fruits and selected dairy products.

Three approaches have been taken in studies of bitter taste and food intake. One explores the associations between sensitivity to a specific compound and ingestion of foods with dissimilar compounds, but possessing some key functional chemical group (e.g., PROP taste status and foods with thionamide-containing moieties). Second, an association between bitter taste sensitivity and either general food dislikes or avoidances of items with bitter taste notes has been sought (e.g., PROP sensitivity and ingestion of dairy products). Third, studies have sought a relationship between sensitivity to and ingestion of the same specific bitter compound (e.g., caffeine).

With respect to the first approach, Mattes & Labov (1989) had a sample of 282 individuals rate their hedonic impression and frequency of consumption of

31 foods containing compounds demonstrated to inhibit iodine uptake by the thyroid. No association between PTC taster status and either liking or frequency of consumption of the foods was observed. Similarly, another study observed no evidence of an association between PTC taster status and reported consumption of cruciferous vegetables, which contain bitter compounds with thionamide moieties (Jerza-Latta et al. 1990). The lack of association between PTC taster status and goitrogen exposure is not surprising because the hypothetical arguments made regarding insensitivity to the bitter taste and acceptance of goitrogen-containing bitter foods have not been clearly supported by published research. Assessment of a population with a high prevalence of goiter revealed no association between PTC taste sensitivity and thyroid size, although a weak correlation with visual-motor perception (an index of thyroid status) was noted= 0.25 (Greene 1974). No attempt was made to assess goitrogen intake. Further, there is a similar (Harris et al. 1949) or lower (Kitchin et al. 1959) prevalence of insensitive bitter tasters among patients with toxic diffuse goiter, a disorder potentially responsive to goitrogen intake. While there is presently little support for the hypothesized causal relationship between bitter taste sensitivity, dietary goitrogen intake and thyroid disorders, it should be noted that in no study was actual intake of purported problematic foods quantitated. Further, the procedures for assessing taster status may not have been optimal.

Several, studies have explored a more general association between bitter taste and dietary choice. Fischer et al., (1961) had 48 individuals complete a questionnaire eliciting information about the incidence of dislikes and aversions for a list of 118 foods. An association between sensitivity to both PROP and quinine and food dislikes was reported whereas no significant relationship was noted with other taste qualities. However, the correlation was of a low order (r=0.272) which accounted for a small percentage of the variance (7.5%) in food likes. A follow-up study involving a larger (n=187) and older (mean=38 y/o) population responding to questionnaires about the acceptability of a smaller number of common foods yielded comparable results (Glanville & Kaplan 1965). Correlations between quinine and PROP thresholds and food dislikes were r=0.319 and r=0.480, respectively. Korslund & Eppright (1967) reported a non-significant inverse trend between thresholds for quinine and number of food dislikes among children. Similar, non-significant, results were obtain with 13 and 14 year olds (Jefferson & Erdman 1970). Krondl et al. (1983) assessed genetic influences on food preferences and intake with 13 monozygotic and 10 dizygotic twin pairs and observed an association between PTC sensitivity and preference for only 2 of 24 foods (unsweetened grapefruit juice, green beans). Another study with children found PROP sensitivity inversely related to liking of cheese and directly related to liking of milk (Anliker et al. 1991). However, these were only 2 of 11 foods tested and the associations were in different directions and only apparent on one of three assessment measures. Thus, there is, at best, weak support for an association between sensitivity to one bitter compound and general food dislikes. This may be because sensitivity to one bitter compound is not necessarily related to sensitivity for another (Mela 1989; Schifferstein & Frijters 1991; Tanimura & Mattes 1993; Yokomukai et al. 1993) and the bitterness of foods stems from a wide range of compounds. Secondly, the lists of foods used in most studies have been heavily weighted with bitter items and this could result in a floor effect. If only a weak bitter note is sufficient to render most foods unpalatable, then they will be rejected by tasters and non-tasters leaving little room for discrimination. Indeed, based on their energy contribution, bitter foods contribute little to total intake (Mattes 1985). Third, there are numerous factors in addition to sensory properties that influence food preferences.

Several additional studies have explored PROP-taster responses to non-bitter dietary components. The most recent work has focused on dietary fat. Tepper and Nurse (1997) reported that PROP tasters were better able to discriminate between salad dressings containing 10% or 40% fat compared to non-tasters. The performance of medium tasters and supertasters was comparable. Three additional reports are available in abstract form only. One noted that PROP super-tasters assigned higher creaminess ratings to a high fat dairy product than medium or non-tasters (Duffy et al. 1996). No differences were observed at medium or low fat concentrations. Another observed a significant negative association between PROP sensitivity and fat intake (r=0.29), but no significant association with fat hedonics (Dabrila et al. 1995). In contrast, a third report noted that "high tasters" assigned higher hedonic ratings to high fat cream cheese samples and non-tasters rated the low fat samples as least pleasant (Tuorila et al. 1996). The association between PROP sensitivity and fat perception is hypothesized to derive from the observation that more sensitive PROP tasters have higher numbers of fungiform taste buds and these are innervated by trigeminal fibers that presumably mediate the perception of fat. This view warrants further exploration, but the lack of association between taste bud number and taste sensitivity (Mistretta 1984; Miller & Reedy 1990; Catalanotto et al. 1993; Lehman et al. 1995) raises questions about its veracity. The dietary implications of these bitter taste-fat intake relationships are not known.

One group has reported that PROP tasters exhibit a reduced liking for high concentrations of sucrose due to an altered ability to perceive the nonsweet components of the sugar (Looy & Weingarten 1992). However, psychophysical studies have indicated that the qualitative aspects of sucrose and saccharin are rated comparably by PROP tasters and non-tasters (Rankin & Marks 1992) and another study failed to observe differences in hedonic responses to either sweetener (Drewnowski et al. 1997).

Hypothesizing that the bitterness of ethanol would discourage consumption by sensitive tasters, an association between PTC/PROP taste status and alcoholism has been examined. An inverse relationship has been reported (Peeples 1962), but not supported by other work (Reid et al. 1968; Smith 1972; Swinson 1973; Pelchat & Danowski 1992; Kranzler et al. 1996). Additional studies show no relationship between PROP taster status and perceived bitterness of wine (Noble 1994) or beer (Mela 1990) and that alcohol ingestion does not alter sensitivity to the bitterness of the principle bittering agent in beer (Guinard et al. 1996).

The third line of research has explored associations between taste sensitivity for a specific bitter food component and ingestion of that component. Taste thresholds for isohumalones are significantly higher in beer consumers (Tanimura & Mattes 1993). Assuming a functional association exists, the question of causality arises. Consumption may be facilitated by lower bitter sensitivity or use may decrease sensitivity. One attempt to experimentally evaluate the latter possibility failed to reveal an effect of intake on taste (Mela et al. 1992). It has also been reported that coffee drinkers/caffeine consumers have higher thresholds for the bitterness of caffeine (Mela et al. 1992; Tanimura & Mattes 1993; Tanimura 1994). The significance of this observation is unclear since caffeine is not the predominant source of bitterness in the primary dietary sources of the compound (i.e., coffee, tea).

While the evidence summarized above has focused on the permissive role of low bitter taste sensitivity on intake, potential nutritional concerns also arise for those with acute senses. Because omnivores may not possess the ability to distinguish between toxic and non-toxic foods on the basis of bitterness (Glendinning 1994), a general rejection response to all bitter foods may constrain diet diversity and, as a consequence, quality (Jacobs et al. 1978). Adults view bitter vegetables as less palatable (Drewnowski 1996) and an association between taste acceptability and perceived tolerance to vegetables has been noted in the elderly (Zimmerman & Krondl 1986). No large-scale dietary study in free-living individuals has been undertaken to explore this issue. In contrast to this concern, the bitter notes of foods have also prompted populations to modify their food preparation practices with a resulting increase in diet quality. For example, the Aymara prepare unripened potatoes with clay to reduce their bitterness, but in so doing, potentially toxic compounds are rendered inactive (Johns & Duquette 1991).

Motivation to Consume Bitter Foods

Reflecting the state of the literature, this discussion has focused on evidence pertaining to an inhibitory effect of bitterness on food intake. However, there are a number of distinctly bitter foods and beverages that are widely enjoyed and consumed. Against a backdrop depicting bitter taste as a mechanism to avoid toxin ingestion, such behavior poses interesting questions about the factors that guide human feeding. What innate or acquired attributes motivate an individual to override such a fundemental characteristic? Limited evidence pertaining to bitterness is available on this issue.

Personality traits constitute one set of factors that may influence decisions about ingestion of bitter items. Theories regarding optimal level of arousal hold that organisms seek to achieve a given state of arousal, in part, by selective exposure to stimuli with varying sensory and physiological properties as well as culturally defined valence. To the degree that bitterness elicits a sense of danger and intrigue, ingestion of items with this attribute could enhance the level of arousal. Individuals scoring high on the Sensation Seeking Scale (Zuckerman 1979) and Varseek scale (Van Trijp et al. 1992) have higher intakes of the bitter compound, caffeine (Mattes 1994). Caffeine intake was also negatively correlated with scores on the General Neophobia Scale (Pliner & Hobden 1992). However, no associations were observed with another bitter food constituent, alcohol. Whether this indicates the purported arousing property of bitterness was not influential on intake or was overridden by other factors such as the differing pharmacologic effects of the compounds is not known.

Early experiences may impact on the acceptability of bitter compounds. The best example of this may be found in the responses of infants to protein hydrolysate formulas which have been described as bitter as well as having a very unpleasant flavor, probably due to volatile compounds produced during hydrolyses. Infants less than four months of age will readily accept such formulas with no sign of displeasure. In contrast, infants first given these formulas at seven or more months of age strongly reject them, exhibiting facial expressions of extreme displeasure (Mennella & Beauchamp 1996). If, however, infants are fed these diets from an early age, they will readily accept them at seven months and older (Mennella & Beauchamp, unpublished observations; see also Beauchamp & Mennella 1996). Much remains to be understood about the long term effects of early exposure to later acceptability, including even what sensory characteristics underlie the rejection, but if bitterness is one of them, the data are consistent with the hypothesis that early exposure to bitterness may render it less unpleasant.

Dietary experience could also account for increased intake. For a variety of reasons, including cultural norms, individuals may obtain considerable exposure to bitter items. Increased exposure reduces neophobia and increases acceptance of foods (Pliner 1982; Pliner et al. 1993). However, there is evidence for an inverse association between palatability and exposure effects. Pleasant novel items show more rapid and marked increases in acceptance than unpleasant, including bitter, novel items (Pliner 1982; Mattes 1994). In fact, in one study specifically exploring exposure effects on bitter acceptance, 10 days of exposure led to no measureable shift in hedonic responses to novel bitter foods whereas consistent shifts were noted with the same level of exposure to sweet and salty foods (Mattes 1994). The test foods were not associated with expected or experienced pharmacologic effects, as would be the case for items containing caffeine or ethanol. Study participants were required to ingest the test foods in the forms provided which accentuated their bitterness.

However, under normal conditions, consumers are free to modify the sensory properties of foods to enhance their appeal. Commonly consumed bitter items are frequently modified. For example, the bitterness of caffeinated beverages is often blunted by the addition of cream and/or sweetener, the bitterness of salad greens is typically reduced by the addition of various salad dressings and the bitterness of ethanol in spirits is reduced through addition of different flavored mixers, chilling and dilution. Thus, perhaps the rewarding properties of bitter food constituents can exert their influence only if the sensory note is muted. Studies of acquired bitter acceptance involving longer exposure times and allowing participants the freedom to self-modify the sensory properties of bitter foods are needed to better understand the importance of dietary experience on ingestion of foods with bitter taste components.

The level of ingestion of bitter items may also be related to the susceptibility of individuals to the pharmacologic effects many of them exert. In some instances, bitter items are stimulatory and the sensations produced are viewed as desirable. Alcohol is an example where self-reported ingestion is related to the degree of alteration of bodily sensations and the enjoyment it produces (Mattes 1994). Alternatively, lack of sensitivity to undesirable physiological and behavioral effects may play a permissive role in consumption where there are other incentives (e.g., cultural) to ingest bitter foods. Alcoholics (Mello, & Mendelson 1970; Nagoshi & Wilson 1987; Vogel-Sprott & Chipperfield 1987; deWit & McCracken 1990) are less sensitive to the pharmacologic properties of ethanol and regular users can develop a tolerance (Zuckerman 1979; Mitchell & Herlong 1986). Avoidance of malaise can also prompt use of bitter foods. Many consume caffeinated beverages to prevent the onset of symptoms of caffeinism rather than to produce a rewarding sensation (Silverman et al. 1992).

Summary

There are wide individual differences in sensitivity to the taste of bitterness. There is strong evidence for a genetic component to this variation for selected compounds, with lesser contributions by age, sex or smoking habit. Bitter taste may hold some predictive power for susceptibility to various health conditions, but the associations between measures of threshold sensitivity or scaling ability and food preferences and intake are weak. Hedonic responsiveness is more closely related to food selection. Generally, items with pronounced bitter notes are not highly preferred or consumed. The tendency to reject bitter foods may have been, and continue to be, beneficial since many such items contain toxins. However, avoidance of bitter foods may also limit diet diversity and access to needed nutrients. In western nations where food safety is nearly assured and nutrient density is high, these competing consequences of bitter rejection are not readily apparent. Predictions may be made regarding their relative value under other conditions, but currently there is scarce evidence for a substantive association. The motivation to consume bitter items among populations with access to convenient, inexpensive wholesome food has not been well defined. Individual differences in personality traits, responsiveness to cultural practices and pharmacologic reactivity may be involved. A better understanding of the factors influencing ingestion of bitter foods, should provide important insights on the more general controls of human feeding.

References

Allison, A. C. and Blumber B. S. 1959. "Ability to taste phenylthiocarbamide among Alaskan Eskimos and other populations". *Human Biology* 31: 352–359.

Anliker, J. A., Bartoshuk, L., Ferris, A. M. and Hooks, L. D. 1991. "Children's food preferences and genetic sensitivity to the bitter taste of 6-*n*-propylthiouracil (PROP)". *American Journal of Clinical Nutrition* 54: 316–20.

Barnicot, N. A. 1950–1951. "Taste deficiency for phenylthiourea in African Negroes and Chinese." *Annnals of Eugenics* 15: 248–254.

Bartoshuk, L. M., Duffy, V. B. and Miller, I. J. 1994. "PTC/PROP Tasting: Anatomy, Psychophysics, and Sex Effects". *Physiology & Behavior* 56: 1165–1171.

Bartoshuk, L. M., Rifkin, B., Marks, L. E. and Bars, P. 1986. "Taste and Aging". *J Gerontology* 41: 51–57.

Bartoshuk. L. M., Rifkin, B., Marks, L. E. and Hooper, J. E. 1988. "Bitterness of KCl and benzoate: related to genetic status for sensitivity to PTC/PROP". *Chemical Senses* 13: 517–528.

Beauchamp, G. K. and Mennella, J. A. 1996. "Early feeding and the acquisition of flavor preferences". In Boulton, J., Laron, Z. and Rey, J. (eds.) Long-term consequences of early feeding. *Nestle series workshop book 36*, 163–177. Philadelphia: Lippincott-Raven Publishers.

Becker, B., Kolker, A. E. and Ballin, N. 1966. "Thyroid Function and Glaucoma". *American Journal of Ophthalmology* 61: 997–999.

Beiguelman, B. 1964a. "Taste Sensitivity to Phenylthiourea among Patients affected with both Tuberculosis and Leprosy". *Acta Geneticae Medicae et Gemellologiae* 13: 190–192.

Beiguelman, B. 1964b. "Taste Sensitivity to Phenylthiourea and Leprosy". *Acta Geneticae Medicae et Gemellologiae* 13: 193–196.

Bergamasco, N. H. P. and Beraldo, K. E. A. 1990. "Facial Expressions of Neonate Infants in Response to Gustatory Stimuli". *Brazilian Journal of Medical and Biological Research* 23: 245–249.

Blakeslee, A. F. 1932. "Genetics of sensory thresholds: Taste for phenyl thio carbamide". *Proceedings National Academy of Science* 18: 120–130.

Byrd, E. and Gertman, S. 1959. "Taste sensitivity in aging persons". *Geriatrics* 14: 381.

Catalanotto, F. A., Bartoshuk, L. M., Ostrom, K. M., Gent, J. F. and Fast, K. 1993. "Effects of anesthesia of the facial nerve on taste". *Chemical Senses* 18: 461–470.

Cowart, B. J. 1989. "Relationships between Taste and Smell across the Adult Life Span". *Annals of the New York Academy of Sciences* 561: 39–55.

Cowart, B. J., Yokomukai, Y. and Beauchamp, G. K. 1994. "Bitter Taste in Aging: Compound-Specific Decline in Sensitivity". *Physiology & Behavior* 56: 1237–1241.

Dabrila, G. M., Bartoshuk, L. M. and Duffy, V. B. 1995. "Preliminary Findings of Genetic Taste Status Association with Fat Intake and Body Mass Index in Adult Females". *Journal of The American Dietetic Association* A-41.

Das, S. R. 1956. "A contribution to the heredity of the PTC taste character based on a study of 845 sib-pairs". *Annals of Human Genetics* 20: 334–343.

Das, S. R. 1958. "Inheritance of the PTC taste character in man: An analysis of 126 Rarhi Brahmin families of West Bengal". *Annals of Human Genetics* 22: 200–212.

Das, S. R. and Mukherjee, D. P. 1964. "Phenylthiocarbamide taste sensitivity survey among the Pareng Gadaba, the Ollaro, Gadaba and the Konda Paroja of Koraput District, Orissa". *Acta Geneticae et Statisticae Medicae* 14: 168: 76.

deWit, H. and McCracken, S. G. 1990. "Ethanol self-administration in males with and without an alcoholic first-degree relative". *Alcoholism: Clinical and Experimental Research* 14: 63–70.

Drewnowski, A. 1996. "From Asparagus to Zucchini: Mapping Cognitive Space for Vegetable Names". *American College of Nutrition.* 15: 147–153.

Drewnowski, A. 1990. "Genetics of Taste and Smell". *World Review of Nutrition and Dietetics* 63: 194–208.

Drewnowski, A., Henderson, S. A. and Shore, A. B. 1997. "Genetic Sensitivity to 6-n-Propylthiouracil (PROP) and Hedonic Responses to Bitter and Sweet Tastes". *Chemical Senses* 22: 27–37.

Duffy, V. B., Tym, A., Bartoshuk, L. M., Lucchina, L. A. and Snyder, D. J. 1996. "Perceived Creaminess of High-Fat Milk Products Varies with Genetic Taste Status". *Chemical Senses* 74: 19.

Fikentscher, R., Roseburg, B., Spinar, H. and Bruchmuller, W. 1977. "Loss of taste in the elderly: sex differences". *Clinical Otolaryngology* 2: 183–189.

Fischer, R. and Griffin, F. 1961. ""Taste-Blindness" and Variations in Taste-Threshold in Relation to Thyroid Metabolism". *Journal of Neuropsychiatry* 3: 98–104.

Fischer, R. and Griffin, F. 1963. "Quinine dimorphism: a cardinal determinant of taste sensitivity". *Nature* 200: 343–347.

Fischer, R., Griffin, F., England, S. and Garn, S. M. 1961. "Taste Thresholds and Food Dislikes". *Nature* 191: 1328.

Fischer, R., Griffin, F. and Rockey, M. A. 1966. "Gustatory Chemoreception in Man: Multi-Disciplinary Aspects and Perspectives". *Perspectives in Biology and Medicine* 9: 549–577.

Fischer, R., Kaplan, A. R., Griffin, F. and Sting, D. G. 1962. "Abnormal Congregation of Insensitive ("Non"-) Tasters Among Parents of Children with Down's Syndrome". *American Journal of Mental Deficiency* 67: 849–855.

Fox, A. L. 1931. Six in Ten "Tasteblind". *Science News Letter*. 19: 249.

Frank, R. A. and Korchmar, D. L. 1985. "Gustatory Processing Differences in PTC Tasters and Non-Tasters: A Reaction Time Analysis". *Physiology & Behavior* 35: 239–242.

Fraser, G. R. 1961. "Cretinism and Taste Sensitivity to Phenylthiocarbamide". *The Lancet* 280: 964–965.

Glanville, E. V. and Kaplan, A. R. 1965. "Food Preference and Sensitivity of Taste for Bitter Compounds". *Nature* 205: 851–843.

Glanville, E. V., Kaplan, A. R. and Fischer, R. 1964. "Age, Sex, and Taste Sensitivity". *Journal of Gerontology* 19: 474–478.

Glendinning, J. I. 1994. "Is the bitter rejection response always adaptive?". *Physiology & Behavior* 56: 1217–1227.

Greene, L. S. 1974. "Physical Growth and Development, Neurological Maturation, and Behavioral Functioning in Two Ecuadorian Andean Communities in Which Goiter Is Endemic". *American Journal of Physical Anthropology* 41: 139–152.

Guinard, J. X., Zoumas-Morse, C., Dietz, J., Goldberg, S., Holz, M., Heck, E. and Amoros, A. 1996. "Does Consumption of Beer, Alcohol, and Bitter Substances Affect Bitterness Perception?". *Physiology & Behavior* 59: 625–631.

Hall, M. J., Bartoshuk, L. M., Cain, W. S. and Stevens, J. C. 1975. "PTC taste blindness and the taste of caffeine". *Nature* 253: 442–443.

Harris, H., Kalmus, H. 1951. "The distribution of taste thresholds for phenylthiourea of 384 sib pairs". *Annals of Eugenics* 16: 226–230.

Harris, H., Kalmus, H. and Trotter, W. R. 1949. "Taste Sensitivity to Phenylthiourea in Goitre and Diabetes". *The Lancet* 257: 1038–1039.

Hundley, L. R. 1960. "Taste Test Papers". *Carolina Tips.*

Jacobs, W. W., Beauchamp, G. K. and Kare, M. R. 1978. "Progress in animal flavor research". In: R. W. Bullard, (ed.) *Flavor chemistry of animal foods*, 1–20. Washington, DC: American Chemical Society.

Jefferson, S. C. and Erdman, A. M. 1970. "Taste Sensitivity and Food Aversions of Teenagers". *Journal of Home Economics* 62: 605–608.

Jerzsa-Latta, M. J., Krondl, M. and Coleman, P. 1990. "Use and Perceived Attributes of Cruciferous Vegetables in Terms of Genetically-mediated Taste Sensitivity". *Appetite* 15: 127–134.

Johns, T. and Duquette, M. 1991. "Detoxification and mineral supplementation as functions of geophagy". *American Journal of Clinical Nutrition* 53: 448–56.

Kalmus, H. 1958. "Improvements in the classification of the taster genotype." *Annals of Human Genetics* 22: 222–230.

Kalmus, H. 1971. "Genetics of Taste". *Handbook of Sensory Physiology, Chemical Senses & Taste*, 165–179.

Kalmus, H. and Trotter, W. R. 1962. "Direct assessment of the effect of age on P. T. C. sensitivity". *Annals of Human. Genetics* 26: 145–149.

Kaplan, A. R., Fischer, R., Glanville, E., Powell, W., Kamionkowski, M., Fleshler, B. 1964b. "Differential taste sensitivities in duodenal and gastric ulcer patients". *Gastroenterology* 47: 604–609.

Kaplan, A. R., Glanville, E. and Fischer, R. 1965. "Cumulative effect of age and smoking on taste sensitivity in males and females". *Journal of Gerontology* 20: 335–337.

Kaplan, A. R., Glanville, E. V. and Fischer, R. 1964a. "Taste Thresholds for Bitterness and Cigarette Smoking". *Nature* 202: 1366.

Kitchin, F. D., Howel-Evens, W., Clarke, C. A., McConnell, R. B. and Sheppard, P. M. 1959. "PTC taste response and thyroid disease". *British Medical Journal* 1: 1069–1074.

Koertvelyessy, T. A., Crawford, M. H. and Hutchinson, J. 1982. "PTC Taste Threshold Distributions and Age in Mennonite Populations". *Human Biology* 54: 635–646.

Korslund, M. K. and Eppright, E. S. 1967. "Taste Sensitivity and Eating Behavior of Preschool Children". *Journal of Home Economics* 59: 168–170.

Kranzler, H. R., Moore, P. J. and Hesselbrock, V. M. 1996. "No Association of PROP Taster Status and Paternal History of Alcohol Dependence". *Alcoholism: Clinical and Experimental Research* 20: 1496–1500.

Krondl, M., Coleman, P., Wade, J. and Milner, J. 1983. "A Twin Study Examining the Genetic Influence on Food Selection". *Human Nutrition: Applied Nutrition* 37A: 189–198.

Krut, L. H., Perrin, M. J. and Bronte-Stewart, B. 1961. "Taste Perception in Smokers and Non-Smokers". *British Medical Journal* 1: 384–388.

Lee, B. F. 1934. "A Genetic Analysis of Taste Deficiency in the American Negro". *Ohio Journal of Science* 34: 337–42.

Lehman, C. D., Bartoshuk, L. M., Catalanotto, F. C., Kveton, J. F. and Lowlicht, R. A. 1995. "Effect of Anesthesia of the Chorda Tympani Nerve on Taste Perception in Humans". *Physiology & Behavior* 57: 943–951.

Levine, P. and Anderson, A. S. 1932. "Observations on taste blindness". *Science* 75: 497–498.

Lindemann, B. 1996. "Taste Reception". *Physiological Reviews* 76: 719–766.

Looy, H. and Weingarten, H. P. 1992. "Facial Expressions and Genetic Sensitivity to 6-*n*-propylthiouracil Predict Hedonic Response to Sweet". *Physiology & Behavior* 52: 75–82.

Mascie-Taylor, C. G. N., McManus, I. C., MacLarnon, A. M. and Lanigan, P. M. 1983. "The Association Between Phenylthiocarbamide (PTC) Tasting Ability and Psychometric Variables". *Behavior Genetics* 13: 191–196.

Mattes, R. 1985. "Gustation as a determinant of ingestion: methodological issues". *American Journal of Clinical Nutrition* 41: 672–683.

Mattes, R. D. 1994. "Influences on Acceptance of Bitter Foods and Beverages". *Physiology & Behavior* 56: 1229–1236.

Mattes, R. and Labov, J. 1989. "Bitter taste responses to phenylthiocarbamide are not related to dietary goitrogen intake in human beings". *Journal of The American Dietetics Association* 89: 692–694.

Mattes, R. and Mela, D. J. 1986. "Relationships between and among selected measures of sweet-taste preference and dietary intake". *Chemical Senses* 11: 523–539.

McBurney, D. H. and Moskat, L. J. 1975. "Taste thresholds in college-age smokers and nonsmokers". *Perception & Psychophysics* 18: 71–73.

McBurney, D. H., Smith, D. V. and Shick, T. R. 1972. "Gustatory cross-adaptation: sourness and bitterness". *Perception & Psychophysics* 11: 228–232.

Meiselman, H. L. and Dzendolet, E. 1967. Variability in gustatory quality identification. *Perception & Psychophysics* 2: 496.

Mela, D. J. 1989. "Bitter taste intensity: the effect of tastant and thiourea taster status". *Chemical Senses* 14: 31–135.

Mela, D. J. 1990. "Gustatory perception of isohumulones:influence of sex and thiourea taster status". *Chemical Senses* 15: 485–490.

Mela, D. J., Mattes, R. D., Tanimura, S. and Garcia-Medina, M. R. 1992. "Relationships Between Ingestion and Gustatory Perception of Caffeine". *Pharmacology Biochemistry and Behavior* 43: 513–521.

Mello, N. K. and Mendelson, J. G. 1970. "Experimentally induced intoxication in alcoholics". *Pharmacology and Experimental Therapeutics* 173: 101–116.

Mennella, J. A. and Beauchamp, G. K. 1996. "Developmental changes in the acceptance of protein hydrolysate formula. *Journal of Developmental Behavior and Pediatrics* 19: 13–19.

Merton, B. B. 1958. "Taste senstivity to PTC in 50 Norwegian families with 176 children. Confirmation of the hypothesis of single gene inheritance. *Acta Genetica* 8: 114–128.

Miller, I. J. and Reedy, F. E. 1990. "Variations in human taste bud density and taste intensity perception". *Physiology and Behavior* 47: 1213–1219.

Milunicova, A., Jandova, A. and Skoda, V. 1969. "Phenylthiocarbamide tasting ability and malignant tumors". *Human Heredity* 19: 398–401.

Mistretta, C. M. 1984. "Aging effects on anatomy and neurophysiology of taste and smell". *Gerontology* 3: 131–136.

Mitchell, M. C. and Herlong, H. F. 1986. "Alcohol and nutrition: Caloric value, bioenergetics, and relationship to liver damage". *Annual Review of Nutrition* 6: 457–474.

Morton, C. C., Cantor, R. M., Corey, L. A. and Nance, W. E. 1981. "A Genetic Analysis of Taste Threshold for Phenylthiocarbamide". *Acta Geneticae Medicae et Gemellologiae* 30: 51–57.

Mourant, A. E., Kopec, A. C. and Domaniewska-Sobczak, K. 1976. "The distribution of the human blood groups". *Oxford Monographs on Medical Genetics*, 2nd ed. London: Oxford Univ. Press.

Nagoshi, C. T. and Wilson, J. R. 1987. "Influence of family alcoholism history on alcohol metabolism, sensitivity and tolerance". *Alcoholism: Clinical and Experimental Research* 11: 392–398.

Noble, A. C. 1994. "Bitterness in Wine". *Physiology & Behavior* 56: 1251–1255.

Olsen, J., Boehnke, M., Neiswanger, K., Roche, A. F. and Siervogel, R. M. 1989. "Alternative Genetic Models for the Inheritance of the Phenylthiocarbamide Taste Deficiency". *Genetic Epidemiology* 6: 423–434.

Panayotou, T., Kritsikis, S. and Bartsocas, C. S. 1983. "Taste Sensitivity to Phenylthiocarbamide in the Salamis Island Population (Greece)". *Human Heredity* 33: 179–180.

Pangborn, R. M. and Trabue, I. M. 1973. "Gustatory responses during periods of controlled and ad lib cigarette smoking". *Perception & Psychophysics* 1: 139–144.

Pangborn, R. M., Trabue, I. M. and Barylko-Pikielna, N. 1967. "Taste, odor, and tactile discrimination before and after smoking". *Perception & Psychophysics* 2: 529–532.

Paolucci, A. M., Ferro-Luzzi, A., Modiano, G., Morpurgo, G., Kanashiro, V. H. 1971. "Taste sensitivity to phenylthiocarbamide (PTC) and endemic goiter in the India natives of Peruvian Highlands". *American Journal of Physical Anthropology* 34: 427–430.

Parr, L. W. 1934. "Taste blindness and race." *Journal of Heredity* 25: 187–190.

Peeples, E. E. 1962. Taste sensitivity to phenylthiocarbamide in alcoholics. Unpublished Master's thesis, Stetson Univeristy, Deland, FL.

Pelchat, M. L. and Danowski, S. 1992. "A Possible Genetic Association Between PROP-Tasting and Alcoholism". *Physiology & Behavior* 51: 1261–1266.

Peterson, D. I., Lonergan, L. H. and Hardinge, M. G. 1968. "Smoking and taste perception". *Archives of Environmental Health* 16: 219–222.

Pliner, P. 1982. "The effects of mere exposure on linking for edible substances". *Appetite* 3: 283–290.

Pliner, P. and Hobden, K. 1992. "Development of a scale to measure the trait of food neophobia in humans". *Appetite* 19: 105–120.

Pliner, P., Pelchat, M. and Grabski, M. 1993. "Reduction of neophobia in humans by exposure to novel foods". *Appetite* 20: 111–123.

Randall, E. and Sanjur, D. 1981. "Food Preferences-Their Conceptualization and Relationship to Consumption". *Ecology of Food and Nutrition* 11: 151–161.

Rankin, K. M. and Marks, L. E. 1992. "Effects of context on sweet and bitter tastes: Unrelated to sensitivity to PROP (6-*n*-propylthiouracil)". *Perception & Psychophysics* 52: 479–486.

Reddy, B. M. and Rao, D. C. 1989. "PTC taste sensitivity revisited: Complete sorting test supports residual family resemblance". *Genetics and Epidemiology.* 6: 413–421.

Reid, N. C. R. W., Brunt, P. W., Bias, W. B. 1968. Genetic characteristics and cirrhosis: A controlled study of 200 patients. *British Medical Journal* 2: 463–465.

Saldanha, P. H. 1956. "Apparent pleiotropic effect of genes determining taste thresholds for phenylthiourea". *Lancet* 11: 74.

Saldanha, P. H. 1958. "Taste thresholds for phenylthiourea among Japanese". *Annals of Human Genetics* 22: 380–384.

Saldanha, P. H. 1960. "Taste thresholds for phenylthiourea among Ashkenazic Jews. *Science* 129: 150–151.

Sato, T. and Sata, O. 1989. "Taste thresholds of Japanese dental students to phenylthiocarbamide". *Chemical Senses* 14: 847–852.

Schifferstein, H. N.J and Frijters, J. E. R. 1991. "The perception of the taste of KCl, NaCl and quinineHCl is not related to PROP-sensitivity". *Chemical Senses* 16: 303–317.

Schlosberg, A. and Baruch, I. 1992. "Phenylthiocarbamide (PTC) Testing in Paranoid and Nonparanoid Schizophrenic Patients". *XI Itl. Congress of Dietetics, Jerusalem Israel* 3/22–27/92 Prog. Abst. 66.

Shepard, T. H. 1961. "Phenylthiocarbamide Non-Tasting Among Congenital Athyrotic Cretins: Further Studies in an Attempt to Explain the Increased Incidence". *Journal of Clinical Investigation* 40: 1751–1757.

Silverman, K., Evans, S. M., Strain, E. C. and Griffiths, R. R. 1992. "Withdrawal syndrome after the double-blind cessation of caffeine consumption". *New England Journal of Medicine* 327: 1109–1114.

Simmons, R. T., Graydon, J. J. and Semple, N. M. 1954. "A blood group genetical survey in Australian aborigines". *American Journal of Physical Anthropology* 12: 599–606.

Smith, S. E. 1972. Taste thresholds in drug addicts and alcoholics. *British Journal of Addiction* 67: 317–321.

Snyder, L. H. 1931. "Inherited taste deficiency". *Science* 74: 151.

Steiner, J. E. 1979. "Human facial expressions in response to taste and smell stimulation". *Advances in Child Development and Behavior.* 13: 257.

Stevens, J. C. 1996. "Detection of Tastes in Mixture with Other Tastes: Issues of Masking and Aging". *Chemical Senses* 21: 211–221.

Swinson, R. P. 1973. Phenylthiocarbamide taste sensitivity in alcoholism. *British Journal of Addiction.* 68: 33–36.

Tanimura, S. 1994. "A Research Note: Comparison of Time-Intensity and Threshold Measures for Determining Bitter Taste Sensitivity of Caffeine User and Nonuser". *Journal of Sensory Studies* 9: 217–222.

Tanimura, S. and Mattes, R. 1993. "Relationships Between Bitter Taste Sensitivity and Consumption of Bitter Substances". *Journal of Sensory Studies* 8: 31–41.

Tepper, Beverly J. and Nurse, Ricky J. 1997. "Fat Perception is Related to PROP Taster Status". *Physiology & Behavior* 61: 949–954.

Terry, M. C. and Segall, G. 1947. "The Association of Diabetes and Taste-Blindness". *Journal of Heredity* 38: 135–137.

Tuorila, H., Urala, N., Lähteenmäki, L. and Rita, H. 1996. "The effect of KCL and fat content on perceived characteristics of cream cheese in PROP tasters and non-tasters". ECRO XII abstr. p. 213.

Van Trijp. H. C. M., Lähteenmäki, L. and Tuorila, H. 1992. "Variety seeking in the consumption of spread and cheese". *Appetite* 18: 155–164.

Vogel-Sprott, M. and Chipperfield, B. 1987. "Family history of problem drinking among young male social drinkers: Behavioral effects of alcohol". *Journal of Studies on Alcohol* 48: 430–436.

Weiffenbach, J. M., Baum, B. J. and Burghauser, R. 1982. "Taste Thresholds: Quality Specific Variation with Human Aging". *Journal of Gerontology* 37: 372–377.

Weiffenbach, J. M., Cowart, B. J. and Baum, B. J. 1986. "Taste Intensity Perception in Aging". *Journal of Gerontology* 41: 460–468.

Whissell-Buechy, D. 1990. "Genetic basis of the phenylthiocarbamide polymorphism". *Chemical Senses* 15: 27–37.

Whissell-Buechy, D. and Wills, C. 1989. "Male and female correlations for taster (P. T. C.) phenotypes and rate of adolescent development". *Annals of Human Biology* 16: 131–146.

Whitney, G. and Harder, D. B. 1994. "Genetics of bitter perception in mice. *Physiology and Behavior* 56: 1141–1147.

Whittemore, P. B. 1986. "Phenylthiocarbamide (PTC) Tasting and Reported Depression". *Journal of Clinical Psychology* 42: 260–263.

Yokomukai, Y., Cowart, B. J. and Beauchamp, G. K. 1993. "Individual differences in sensitivity to bitter-tasting substances". *Chemical Senses* 18: 669–681.

Zimmerman, S. A. and Krondl, M. M. 1986. "Perceived intolerance of vegetables among the elderly". *Journal of The American Dietetic Association* 86: 1047–1051.

Zuckerman, M. 1979. "Sensation seeking: Beyond the optimal level of arousal". *New York: Lawrence Erlbaum.*

Individual Differences in Visual Imagination Imagery

Alan Richardson
University of Western Australia

All the situations in which visual imagination imagery has been reported share a common characteristic; varied sensory information, especially from the external world, has been reduced in quality and/or quantity so that it is rendered psychologically irrelevant. Under these circumstances the end state is usually one of sleep. It is in this twilight state, between a waking orientation of readiness to react to any external demands or internal needs, and a total disappearance of this orientation in sleep and dreaming, that a residual level of cognitive alertness enables the observer to become aware of internally generated sensory percept like phenomena, i.e. imagination images.

Though the best known situation, under which these events occur is the period that precedes sleep at the end of each day, other naturally occurring situations, produced by monotonous sleep inducing activities (e.g. long spells of lorry-driving, Moseley 1953) have been found to produce similar imaginal consequences. Situations that have been deliberately contrived for the experimental investigation of visual imagination imagery or for related purposes include: *hallucinogenic drug intoxicants* (e.g. Klüver 1928; Ardis and McKellar 1956) which, according to West (1962) are "both sensory poisons and diencephalic stimulants" (p. 288); *hypnosis* (e.g. Kubie and Margolin 1944; Sheehan 1979) which induces an alert trance like state; *meditation* (e.g. Carrington 1968; Mavromatis 1987, Chapter Five and Appendix III); *perceptual isolation* (e.g. Bexton, Heron and Scott 1954; Zuckerman and Cohen 1964); *photic* and *pulse current* stimulation (e.g. Smythies 1960; Knoll and Kugler 1959) especially with frequencies in the alpha and theta range (e.g. Glicksohn 1986; Richardson and McAndrew 1990); *relaxed wakefulness* (e.g. Foulkes and Fleisher 1975) *sleep deprivation* (e.g. West, Morris and Lubin 1962; Brauchi and West 1959) and the period of *sleep onset* known as the hypnagogic state (e.g. Foulkes, Spear and Symonds 1966; Vogel 1991).

What, then, is imagination imagery and how can it be distinguished from other types of imaginal experience? When this question has been answered a description of the main phenomenological attributes of visual imagination imagery will be given prior to a discussion of what is known concerning the personal characteristics of those who are most and least likely to notice and report on one or more of these attributes. The chapter will conclude with a discussion of how these individual differences might help to explain the experiences reported and finally, of what future directions research and theory might take.

Four Types of Spontaneous Visual Imagery

All types of mental imagery can be found in modalities other than the visual (Richardson 1969, 1983, 1994) but it is with the visual mode that this chapter is concerned.

After Imagery

Sometimes, and perhaps more accurately, this type of imagery has been referred to as involving an after-sensation i.e. a persistence of the original stimulus in the sensory apparatus. Details of the conditions that affect the experience of peripherally stimulated visual after-images are provided by Brown (1965). It is sufficient to note here that the necessary stimulus conditions require a stable (unmoving) retinal registration which may be achieved either by prolonged staring at the contrasting stimulus object (e.g. a black cross on a white ground) or by its brief but intense illumination. Not everyone has the experience of a visual after-image under these conditions and as Woodworth (1938) observed, "Many students require some practice before seeing the after-image, because it is one of those subjective phenomena which our whole practical life leads us to disregard." (p. 557). Reinhold (1957) showed, experimentally, that with practice the mean number of seconds necessary to become aware of a visual after-image declined over a series of 16 trials. As will be shown in relation to visual imagination imagery, knowing what to look for and learning how to attend to its various manifestations are among the necessary personal characteristics of those who most readily have this experience.

Eidetic Imagery

Since the work of Ahsen (1977) it has become necessary to distinguish between *structural eidetic images*, which have a special meaning within the context of his diagnostic and therapeutic system and *typographic eidetic images* which have been studied experimentally, by Haber (1979) and others. These latter images are experienced by about five percent of primary school age children (Richardson and Harris 1986) but are almost unknown amongst adolescents and adults. The experimental situation requires the subject to scan a high contrast picture stimulus for a period of approximately 30 seconds. When the picture is removed the eidetic child continues to see features of the original stimulus on any plain white surface that has been substituted. Like the after-image the content of a typographic eidetic image can be literally *seen* on an external surface. Unlike the after-image the content of an eidetic image does not shift with movements of the eyes but can be scanned like any physically present picture. Those most likely to experience this type of imagery appear to be at the developmental stage described by Werner (1948) where the 'inner world' of imaginal events has not yet become clearly differentiated from the 'outer world' of perceived events. Some support for this interpretation was obtained by Richardson (1986) who found that eidetikers (i.e. Those who show the most consistent (reliable) eidetic responses to a set of four stimulus pictures) are also more likely, than comparable non-eidetikers, to admit being confused about the source of different remembered events.

Thought Imagery

Once called *memory imagery* (Richardson 1969) it was renamed *thought imagery* (Richardson 1983) because the same percept-like experiences may occur when anticipating future events as well as when recalling past events. The conditions for its spontaneous arousal usually involve the blocking (frustration) of some goal directed but, typically, non-conscious thought process. As a result of the confusion and uncertainty thus engendered, visual and other (e.g. auditory) thought images are likely to surface into conscious awareness. Originally reported by Fox (1914) this process was experimentally confirmed by Sheehan and Lewis (1974). Spontaneous thought imagery is, clearly, different from both after-imagery and typographic eidetic imagery in that it does not result from the retinal *fixation* of a stimulus or from the *scanning* of a stimulus. In addition, the image obtained is not literally *seen* but is, typically, unlocalized and somewhat hazy and incomplete. However, it is the only type of imagery that can be voluntarily produced and controlled (Richardson 1994).

Imagination Imagery

Like after-imagery and typographic eidetic imagery this type possesses the characteristic of being literally *seen*–so much so that its content has often been described as "realer than real." Though eidetic imagery sometimes includes a visual element that was not present in the original stimulus, this is rare. However, the opposite is true of visual imagination imagery; its most marked characteristic being the *novelty* of its content. It is never merely reproductive and only rarely incorporates some recognisable feature from some remembered event. Its difference from thought imagery (memory imagery) was early mentioned by Ogden (1913) and by Perky (1910), who wrote of her own study,

> "There were, on the one hand, images of recognised and particular things, figuring in a particular spatial context, on a particular occasion and with definite personal reference; and there were, on the other hand, images with no determination of context, occasion or personal reference." (p. 436)

The first of these imagery types she called "images of memory" — (thought images), and the second she called "images of imagination".

Imagination images may exhibit a variety of colours, forms, locations, and movements but each one in a series most often appears more like a set of snapshots than a continuous film strip; this may, in part, be associated with the fact that they are usually of short duration, often no more than two or three seconds. As noted earlier they are most likely to occur when attention has been withdrawn from the external world and while the observer is still relatively alert and self consciously aware. In summary it may be said that visual imagination images are typically *autonomous*, (spontaneous), *novel, super distinct in detail, vividly coloured*, often succeeding each other in *fairly rapid succession* and capable of *changing size and shape* (i.e. Showing some form of movement).

Phenomenological Attributes Of Visual Imagination Imagery

These will be described under the headings of colour, form, location and movement.

Colour

Visual imagination imagery is often coloured and not merely in the non-colours of black or white. When colours appear, as they usually do, they are sometimes reported as, initially, no more than swirling masses which, later, form themselves into faces or other objects. The seeing of faces, often grotesque or humorous is extremely common, especially under condition of sleep onset.

In a study of sleep onset experiences by Richardson (1982), 39% of the females (n=26) and 32% of the males (n=12), who had imagination images, also reported seeing moving masses of bright colour. The presence of colour has also been studied under conditions of hallucinogenic drug intoxication (Siegel and Jarvik 1975) and photic stimulation (Richardson and McAndrew 1990). The same set of nine colour categories was employed in both theses studies. The order from most to least frequently reported, in this latter study was: white, black (grey), yellow, red (maroon, pink), green, blue, orange, violet (purple) and brown (tan).

Form

These vary in complexity from mere *flashes of light*, through a great variety of simple *geometric patterns* (Klüver's 1928, 'form constants') to *faces and objects* and eventually, *integrated scenes* containing people, often in landscape settings. Thirty different geometrical patterns were printed in a booklet and presented to the forty females who had taken part in a photic stimulation experiment conducted by Richardson and McAndrew (1990). The frequency with which each pattern was recognised as having been seen during photic stimulation was relatively the same for the twenty females who had been selected because they had a disposition to notice inner states (high scorers on a six item Private Self-consciousness Scale) and for the twenty who lacked this disposition (low scorers on this Scale). The patterns and their order from most to least frequent were as follows: large circles (19 high and 20 low PSC scores), arcs, straight parallel lines, tunnels, cones and cylinders, small circles, waves, spirals, triangles, radiations, parallel figures, ripples, quadrangles, amorphous specks, horizontal ovals, masses, small line designs, 'V' radiations, multiple figures, gratings, lattices, poles, crosses, radials, odd figures, diamond constructions, combined figures, kaleidoscopes, bilateral duplications, fingers, snakes and cobwebs (one high and zero low PSC scores). Two patterns — honeycomb and cherries — were reported by no one from either PSC group.

That a consistent hierarchy of form complexity may exist was first reported by Hebb (1954) as a result of the early studies on perceptual isolation effects that he and his colleagues conducted at McGill University. He wrote,

> "It appears that the activity has a rather regular course of development from simple to complex. The first symptom is that the visual field, when the eyes are closed, changes from a dark to a light colour; next there are reports of dots of light, lines or simple geometrical patterns. All 14 subjects reported such imagery which was a new experience for them. The next step, reported by 11 subjects, is seeing something like wallpaper patterns. Then come isolated objects, without background, reported by 7 out of 14, and finally integrated scenes usually containing dreamlike distortions, reported by 3 of the 14." (p. 416)

A similar hierarchy was noted by Leuner (1963) for subjects who had received hallucinogenic drugs. Only in an eight hour perceptual isolation study reported by Freedman, Grunebaum, Stare and Greenblatt (1962) was there a specific contrary finding reported. Two studies have found that this complexity hierarchy forms a highly reliable four item cumulative (Guttman) scale. The first, by Myers and Murphy (1962) obtained these results from data provided under perceptual isolation conditions while, the second, by Richardson and McAndrew (1990) employed photic stimulation. Thus, those who experience a higher form of complexity will be more likely to experience all lower forms of complexity to produce a reliable scale, scored: (4) for integrated scenes; (3) for objects and faces; (2) for geometric patterns; and, (1) for flashes of light.

Location

The visual content of an imagination image may appear as if *behind the eyeballs* or *in the head* or, it may be projected as if seen *in the external world* or *outside beyond one's body*. In the Richardson (1982) study a large pool of first year psychology students from the University of Western Australia had been given a questionnaire concerned with a wide range of subjective experiences that might or might not have been familiar to them. The data from all those aged between 17 and 20, who had also claimed that their responses were trustworthly (86 females, 52 males) were analysed and of those claiming to have experienced imagination imagery at sleep onset (66 females, 37 males) 63% of the females and 62% of the males answered 'Yes' to the question, "Do any of the visual experiences appear to be located 'out there' in the external world?" Thus an apparent external location is, perhaps, the most common position for the content of a visual imagination imagery to appear. This observation has been noted by most other workers in this field (see Mavromatis 1987).

Because an external location is where we see visually perceived objects in the real world it would not be surprising to find that some people, however briefly, mistake their externally located visual imagination images for actual percepts. Indeed, this is so. For example, Freedman et al. (1962) in their perceptual isolation study report that one of their subjects tried to eat an imaged salad. The question now arises as to whether any reliable person variables have been found that differentiate those who are most likely to give reality status to what they see 'out there' from those who accept these same events as subjective phenomena generated from within themselves. There is one, and it has been found to operate in a number of different experimental situations as well as among hallucinating alcoholics. By definition a visual hallucination is a projected visual imagination image which the imager believes to be something actually existing in the external world. The concept that begins to make sense of this misattribution is that of *boundary confusion*; "an inability to discriminate whether experiences represent inside of the body or outside of the body events." (Fisher 1962 p. 249) but which, because the experience is so real, is often assumed to be a genuine external event. It is this inability to maintain clear perceptual boundaries that has been called *field dependence* (in contrast to field independence) by Witkin, Lewis, Hertzman, Machover, Meissner and Wapner (1954). It is measured by the Rod and Frame Test (RFT) and the Embedded Figures Test (EFT). In the former the field dependent person finds it more difficult to make accurate judgments of the gravitational uprightness of a moveable rod when the sides of the frame within which it is placed deviate from the vertical. In the latter the field dependent person has more difficulty in identifying a known geometric figure when it is embedded in a larger pattern of distracting lines. Holt and Goldberger (1959), in a perceptual isolation study, found no difference in the frequency with which imagination images were reported by field dependent and field independent subjects but noted that field dependent subjects were more likely to attribute their imagery to an external source. Again, in another perceptual isolation study by Silverman, Cohen, Shmavonian and Greenberg (1961) four out of 11 field dependent observers reported 'meaningful' visual imagination images which they believed, at the time, to have an external source, compared with none of the nine field independent observers. In research on the Perky effect (Segal and Nathan 1964) Segal (1964) reported that boundary confusion was more likely among those who were field dependent. These subjects tended to misidentify the stimulus as part of their own imagery, they were also less familiar with their inner world of subjective experiences as measured by some of the subscales of the As (1962) questionnaire. This misidentification finding was replicated by David and Glicksman (1976).

Hallucinating psychotic patients without delusions were found, by Taylor (1956) to be more field dependent than a comparable sample of delusions-only patients. Finally in a study by Bergman and Agren (1974) employing both the RFT and the EFT it was found that recovering alcoholics with a history of hallucinatory experiences were significantly more field dependent than a comparison group of non-hallucinatory alcoholics.

Movement

In the Siegel and Jarvik (1975) study on the effects of hallucinogenic intoxication eight movement patterns were identified in the imagination images reported by their subjects. These were: aimless ('things floating around'), concentric ('motion toward the centre'), explosive, horizontal (right or left), oblique (any linear motion at an angle other than 90 or 180 degrees to the observer's mid-line axis), pulsating (twinkling, flickering, throbbing), rotational (circular motion, clockwise or anti clockwise) and vertical (up and down).

When these movement patterns were analysed in the photic stimulation study undertaken by Richardson and McAndrew (1990) the order from most to least frequent was found to be: pulsating, reported by 25 out of the 40 young women involved, followed by, explosive rotational, vertical, aimless, concentric, horizontal and oblique, reported by seven of them. Pulsating movements had been reported as the most frequent pattern of movement in the Siegel and Jarvik (1975) investigation and, as one of their subjects had said, "No matter what else the imagery is doing, no matter how it's moving, it's always flickering and this is the *basso continue* of it's motion." (p. 127)

Personal Characteristics Of Those Most And Least Likely To Experience Visual Imagination Images

Surveys and experimental investigations have both shown that most people have experienced visual imagination images of some kind under the conditions described and discussed above. Why do not all people have these experiences?

Surveys

In the most comprehensive survey to be described, Richardson, Mavromatis, Mindel and Owens (1981) gave the following question to a representative sample of 600 individuals (300 females and 300 males) aged between 20 and 80 and living in the Merseyside district of Northern England: "Do you experience, or have you experienced imagery when you are just falling asleep?". As has been found in other modern surveys approximately one quarter answered 'No' or reported that they had never experienced sleep onset imagery of this kind. In this study a five point frequency scale was employed with the following results: 24% of the females and 26% of the males answered 'Never' followed by 14% of the females and 21% of the males who answered 'Seldom', 31% of the females and 32% of the males who answered 'Occasionally', 18% of the females and 13% of the males who answered 'Fairly often' and, 12% of the females and 7% of the males who answered 'Frequently'. It was found that sleep onset (hypnagogic) imagery was less common among the men than among the women and in those of higher occupational status than in those of lower occupational status. Men and women in their sixties and seventies reported the lowest incidence. No association was found between the frequency with which images were reported and scores obtained on a verbal intelligence scale (Mill Hill Vocabulary) and on a non-verbal intelligence scale (Raven's Progressive Matrices).

In the Richardson (1982) survey mentioned earlier the basic question had asked, "Do you ever find that when you become drowsy but have not yet fallen asleep you lose your train of thought and experience different types of suddenly appearing images thoughts or sensations?" A total of 23% of the females and 29% of the males answered 'No'. When those answering 'No' were compared with those answering 'Yes' on a five-item Dissociation Scale (Richardson 1984, p. 204) it was found, for both females and males, when separately analysed, that significantly more dissociation experiences had been reported by those who had reported themselves as having experienced some kind of imagination image at sleep onset. Perhaps, this is not surprising as some of the experiences described by items on the Dissociation Scale are not unlike some of the non-visual experiences commonly reported at sleep onset. For example, "...the feeling that part of your body (such as a limb) was really not part of you" or having "... the impression that the walls or ceiling were moving or changing size even though you were wide awake and knew that this was impossible".

Finally, Glicksohn (1989) administered a questionnaire to 140 first year students of psychology at Tel Aviv University in Israel (102 females and 38 males). The critical question asked, "When you are on the verge of sleep do you experience imagery?" The same response categories were employed as those adopted by Richardson et al. (1981). Overall, 27% answered 'Never'. No significant association was found between answers to this question and another that asked, "Do you usually pay attention to your subjective experiences." However, another question which asked, "Do you experience imagery when you're just beginning to awake?" was significantly associated with answers to the "subjective experiences" question. It has often been assumed that this hypnopompic imagery, occurring at the onset of waking, is essentially the same as hypnagogic (sleep onset) imagery; both occur when in a drowsy but relatively alert state. Richardson et al. (1981) had also noted some differences between the two states (e.g. hypnopompic imagery is less frequently reported) and concluded."... hypnagogic and hypnopompic imagery should be distinguished in future research, despite the phenomenological and physiological similarities between the two states." (p. 96)

It will have been noticed that in none of these surveys has any specific reference been made to visual imagery in the critical question asked. However, evidence available in reviews of the literature (e.g. Mavromatis and Richardson 1984; Mavromatis 1987) suggests that visual phenomena predominate during the sleep onset period.

In a smaller investigation, not worthy of being called a survey, Richardson (1980) administered a questionnaire, based on one constructed by Schachter and Crovitz (1977), to 36 female and 14 male third year psychology students at the University of Western Australia (mean age 24). The critical question was, "How frequently do you experience suddenly appearing images, thoughts or sensations when you become drowsy but before falling asleep?" Seven response categories were employed ranging from 'Never' (Scored zero) to 'Everyday' (Scored 6). Those who reported experiencing imagination imagery frequently (categories 3–6) when compared with those who experienced imagination imagery infrequently (categories 0–2) were found to score significantly higher on both an eight item Imagination Imagery scale (Barber and Wilson 1979) and on a 28-item version of Tellegen and Atkinson's (1974) Absorption Scale. Voluntary visual imaging ability as measured by the five relevant items from Sheehan's (1967) modification of Betts' QMI did not discriminate between these two groups. Three unexpected but statistically significant results were obtained from this study; all require replication and interpretation before they can be treated as anything more than chance happenings. Those who most frequently experienced imagination imagery at sleep onset reported themselves as less likely to be confused by road signs or 'turned round' (i.e. not easily confused as to direction); were better able to recognise emotional expressions in the facial test developed by Ekman and Friesen (1975) and, were more likely to remember their dreams, as measured by the Hiscock and Cohen (1973) Dream Recall Frequency (DRF) questionnaire. Some further details of this small study were reported in Richardson (1983).

Experiments

Turning now to some of the experimental investigations in which the occurrence or non-occurrence of imagination images has been related to individual differences on measures of personality, the following results have been obtained.

Meditation

Maupin (1969) defined meditation as a state of "deep passivity combined with awareness." (p. 180). In an earlier paper (Maupin 1965) he reported the results of a study in which 28 male students had volunteered to take a small battery of tests prior to completing a series of 10 meditation sessions, each of 45 minutes duration. The principal tests were designed to measure *tolerance for unrealistic experiences* (the most successful of which was based on a Rorschach measure devised by Klein, Gardner and Schlesinger 1962) and, *capacity for adaptive regression*. This latter concept was measured by the verbal free associations produced to the words DRY and HOUSE. Independent raters scored these associations in terms of the appearance of spontaneous imagery in none, one or both sets (Score range: 0–2).

Depth of meditation was judged from interview data obtained after each of the 10 sessions. Five depth levels (A, B, C, D and E) were identified ranging from light (A. dizzyness and foggyness) to profound (E. concentration and detachment) in which visual imagery may come into prominence. Two independent judges agreed on the placement of 25 out of the 28 subjects into one or other of three groups: A profound, or 'high' group consisting of six subjects who had obtained at least one E level response pattern; a 'moderate' group of 10 subjects who had obtained at least one C (pleasant body sensations) or D (vivid breathing sensations) level response pattern; and a light or low' group of 12 subjects who had obtained only A or B (relaxation and calmness) response patterns. It was concluded that, "Capacity for regression and tolerance for unrealistic experience significantly predicted response to meditation…" (p.197). If meditation can result in a sequence of deepening states in which increasingly bizarre and possibly threatening experiences may occur then, it makes theoretical sense that the capacity to regress (i.e. go 'deeper') and to tolerate what emerges, will be relevant personality characteristics.

Perceptual Isolation

In two studies (Holt and Goldberger 1959; Goldberger and Holt 1961) subjects reclined on a comfortable bed for an eight hour isolation period while wearing halved table tennis balls over their eyes and listening, to the constant masking sound of 'white noise' through padded earphones. Prior to each of these experiments all those taking part had been given a large battery of tests. When frequency of visual imagery reports were correlated with test scores only two replicated findings were obtained; one was with Paul's test of memory style and the other with Block's MMPI scale of neurotic under-control. These tests were interpreted, respectively, as measuring *intellectual flexibility* and *emotional freedom* both of which were thought to facilitate the acceptance of imaginal experiences as part of an adaptive reaction to perceptual isolation. That individual difference variables are critical to an understanding of the occurrence of visual imagination imagery is nowhere clearer than in the research conducted under conditions of perceptual isolation. Variations in the frequency of imaginal reports is unrelated to: the amount and type of visual restriction (e.g. total darkness, diffuse or patterned light, or homogeneous white light); the amount and type of movement restriction (e.g. sitting upright, reclining at an angle or prone or supine *or* suspended in a tank of water or placement in an 'iron lung'); or the duration of confinement. In regard to this latter it has been found that some subjects reported images after only 10 minutes of confinement (Ziskind and Augsburg 1962) while others failed to report any after two weeks. (Zubek, Welch and Saunders 1963).

Photic Stimulation

In an investigation by Freedman and Marks (1965) subjects reclined on a bed in a darkened room. With eyes closed a stroboscope emitted its flashes from a position approximately one inch in front of the subject's nose. Flash frequency and other conditions were varied. Any visual experiences were to be reported and were later coded for colour and form. When frequency of reports of visual imagination imagery was correlated with scores on a variety of tests the following results were obtained. Those who experienced most images showed more emotional responsiveness to external stimuli, as measured by the Rorschach colour sum ratio; higher self ratings on imaginative ability, though not higher scores on the Barron-Welsh art scale, and, a history of experiencing naturally occurring imagination imagery at sleep onset.

Richardson and McAndrew (1990) employed three levels of photic stimulation (6, 10 and 18Hz) aimed at driving the corresponding theta, alpha and beta EEG patterns. No EEG data were obtained but it was found that high scores on the four step cumulative scale of visual imagination imagery complexity (described earlier) occurred significantly more often at the 6 and 10Hz frequencies than at the 18Hz (waking) frequency and, significantly more often at the 6 than at the 10Hz frequency. The 40 female undergraduates who took part had been selected on the basis of high (n=20) and low (n=20) scores on a modified (six item) scale of Private Self-consciousness (PSC) designed to emphasise differences in *internal state awareness* (i.e. the disposition to pay attention to inner states) rather than *self-reflectiveness* (i.e. the disposition to think about oneself). Overall, those who were disposed to pay attention to their inner states experienced significantly more complex visual imagination imagery than those who were not so disposed. This difference was maintained when separate analyses were undertaken under the 6 and 10Hz conditions but not under the 18Hz condition. It is of interest that the high PSC group obtained significantly higher scores than the low PSC group on the Richardson (1984) scales for the measurement of Dissociation and Peak experiences.

Sleep Onset

In a study by Foulkes, Spear, and Symonds (1966), subjects were awakened during the descending Stage 1 EEG period that precedes sleep. They were then asked what had been passing through their minds just beforehand. Their tape recorded answers were rated on an eight point (0–7) scale of dreamlike fantasy. Personality measures were also obtained from the California Personality Inventory and from the TAT. When scores on these personality measures were correlated with ratings on the dreamlike fantasy scale (visual imagination imagery?) it was found that the more dreamlike the experiences the more self-accepting, socially poised and non-rigid was the experiencer. The authors' interpretation of their results was that:

> "...the hypnagogic dream might profitably be viewed as an ego-controlled excursion into inner thoughts and feelings following the ego's voluntary decathexis of sensory input from the external world. Subjects with rigid defenses against impulse-life tend to resist any encroachment of such regressive mental content upon wakeful levels of ego-functioning, and thus experience little dreamlike content at sleep onset." (p. 286)

Explanations

What has been said so far has been aimed at making clear the phenomena to be explained and the special role of some individual differences in personality that might contribute to an explanation. It is no more than a crude beginning to a set of complex problems. We possess a range of stimulus conditions, some relatively imprecise, like the administration of an hallucinogenic drug, others relatively more precise, like the presentation of a specific frequency of photic stimulation, but all capable of producing one or more phenomena from the large repertoire of what we have chosen to call visual imagination imagery. That these stimulus conditions may not produce *any* of these phenomena in approximately 25% of large unselected samples is more readily explained when the data on individual differences have been taken into account. However, other factors must also be considered. For example, some people who report never having had a sleep onset image may drop off to sleep as soon as their heads hit the pillow. Others may never have paid attention to such phenomena because, as Woodworth (1938) observed, in relation to the after-image experience, they are subjective events "which our whole practical life leads us to disregard" (p.557). If, in addition, the intensity of visual (or other) imagination imagery experiences is weak (due perhaps to genetic or related biological causes) it is hardly surprising that nothing is 'seen'. Again, McKellar (1979), among others, has noted that when some people are alerted to the potential phenomena associated with sleep onset they begin to experience them. This latter observation is consistent with the finding (Richardson and McAndrew 1990) that more complex visual imagination imagery is experienced by those who have an habitual disposition to pay attention to inner states. Where the vividness and complexity of their imagery is likely to be intense and, even threatening in it content, some individuals, who also lack tolerance for unrealistic experiences and are rigid and defensive in their adaptive strategies, may be expected to deny such experiences both to themselves and to others.

From all that has been said it would seem that explanations in this, as in many other areas of psychology, will require an interaction approach in which variations in the *stimulus situation* (as indexed by EEG, EOG, regional blood flow and, perhaps, other physiological measures) variations in the *sensory apparatus*, mentioned by Horowitz (1964) (e.g. the retinal ganglionic network and anatomic bodies within the eyeball itself), variations in *present motivation* (e.g. expectancies) as well as differences in more enduring *personality dispositions*, may all play a part.

Future Directions

The recommendations that follow have been classified under four headings: conceptual, methodological, theoretical and functional.

Conceptual

It would be advantageous to future research and theory if an agreed upon terminology could be achieved. In the past a variety of terms have been used to describe what has, here, been called, visual imagination imagery. For example, Myers and Murphy (1962) used the term *reported visual sensations;* Scheibel and Scheibel (1962) favoured *non-object-bound sensations* and Sedman, (1966), called them *pseudo-hallucinations.* In most of the sleep onset literature (e.g. McKellar and Simpson 1954) the term *hypnagogic* imagery has been employed for the obvious reason that it occurs during the hypnagogic state (Schacher 1976). But a single name, like the one suggested, would avoid unnecessary confusion.

Methodological

Some methods of inducing different levels of drowsiness are easier for the experimenter to arrange and, make fewer demands on the subjects. For this reason meditation and photic stimulation may be preferred to hallucinogenic drug intoxication procedures, perceptual isolation or even laboratory investigations of sleep onset. Apart from the process of selecting subjects on various person variables and inducing various expectations prior to an experiment, attempts need to be made to train those who claim never to have had a naturally occurring visual imagination image or who fail to experience one during an experiment. Such training procedures would need to describe the kind of visual phenomena that might be encountered and encourage the state of passive awareness that facilitates the observation of these phenomena when they occur. A related requirement is the development of a set of descriptors and associated illustrations to aid in the communication of all the major phenomena of imagination imagery that may be experienced. Method of reporting has shown no consistent differences in the number or complexity of images reported during perceptual isolation (Zuckerman and Cohen 1964) though duration of confinement sets an obvious limit when events must be recalled over long periods. In a one-hour isolation period Morgan and Bakan (1965) found no difference in the number or vividness of images reported under conditions of *delay* (reporting afterwards), *voluntary* (reporting from time to time throughout the hour) or *continuous* (reporting when ever an event occurred). However, this last method of reporting was the only one during which no subject fell asleep. In studies of sleep onset where 'awakening' procedures are employed there is always the possibility that this disruption will distort the experience that is to be reported. Nevertheless, the experiences are usually so 'real' and percept-like that an observer is able to describe them as if describing an actual physical event without any observable influence on what is happening.

Theoretical

In the present context the major theoretical problem concerns the relationship of visual imagination imagery to the spontaneous visual imagery of the dream on one side and the spontaneous visual imagery of waking life, on the other side. The evidence, such as it is, suggests that the phenomenological differences of each imagery type can be placed on a rough continuum. In waking life the visual thought imagery that may come into awareness when attention is shifted from the demands of action in relation to the external world, is typically sketchy and lacking in detail, often incomplete and unlocalised, as was noted in an earlier section. The content will, usually, involve familiar people, places and objects based on remembered or, at least, known events. However, as attention is withdrawn from the external world a state of relaxed wakefulness will deepen into the drowsy state preceding sleep and, the observer may become absorbed in the more novel and increasingly detailed and colourful imagery of this hypnagogic state. Finally when the I-Me distinction associated with conscious awareness has been completely obliterated in sleep the more bizarre imagery of dreams may begin to manifest itself. What is needed is objective indexing of these changes in state so that they can be correlated, as far as this is possible, with changes in the phenomenological experiences reported. Many attempts, of this kind have been made (e.g. Foulkes et al. 1966; Vogel, Foulkes and Trosman 1966) and it is to be hoped that they will be continued using better EEG and other physiological monitoring techniques than were available in the past. (e.g. Rowley, Stickgold and Hobson 1998)

Functional

One critical question remains. Of what use is visual imagination imagery? What function(s) does it serve? Apart from its entertainment value and possible aesthetic interest what, if anything, does it contribute to our more general adaptive endeavours? Perhaps, its chief contribution is made by its central defining characteristic. The content of visual imagination imagery, in its more complex forms, provides us with *novelty*. Like the images of sleep the images of drowsiness may provide the solution to a problem or present a new way of understanding something. (e.g. Montangero 1993)However, unlike dreams which may be difficult to interpret, the briefer duration of the visual imagination image is invariably transparent in its meaning. For it to have the kind of creative potential suggested there must be some prior concern that is sufficiently powerful to have provoked prior thought. When incubation has done its work the *illumination phase* of problem solving often emerges in the form of a visual imagination image. Silberer (1909) was among the first to discuss this functional property of visual imagination imagery and he named it, the *autosymbolic* phenomenon. An example from my own experience occurred before sleep in the form of a vividly coloured rocket, of the large firework kind. It was angled ready for take-off but, almost immediately, I noticed that it was made of solid wood and was incapable of going anywhere. Its meaning was instantly obvious and related to an idea that I had been working on. In that moment I knew, with complete certainty, that this idea was not going to work — it was not going to get off the ground. Anecdotal evidence of how more productive novel ideas and solutions to problems have appeared to many individuals in their visual imagination imagery has been widely reported (e.g. Ghiselin 1952; Mavromatis 1987, Chapter 8) but experimental evidence is sparse indeed (e.g. Harman, McKim, Mogar, Fadiman and Stolaroff 1966).

Concluding Comment

In the distant past (and perhaps, in the present) the phenomena of visual imagination imagery has contributed to a belief in ghosts (apparitions) and other supernatural visitations. In the 1950's and 1960's, as a result of so-called 'brainwashing' and the 'prisoners' cinema' reported by POW's during the Korean war, funds were made available for research into these phenomena. More recently, reports of visitations and abductions by aliens seem to have become more common. Perhaps the time is right for research funds to become available, once again. The results of a new round of sustained research would, undoubtedly, increase our scientific understanding of these fascinating and potentially valuable subjective experiences. They might, also, help to reduce some of the personal and social anxieties associated with the misinterpretation of these experiences.

References

Ahsen, A. 1977. Eidetics: An overview. *Journal of Mental Imagery* 1: 5–38.

Ardis, J. A. and McKellar, P. 1956. Hypnagogic imagery and mescaline. *Journal of Mental Science* 102: 22–29.

As, A 1962. Non-hypnotic experiences related to hypnotisibility in male and female college students. *Scandinavian Journal of Psychology* 3: 112–121.

Barber, T. X. and Wilson, S. C. 1979. Guided imagining and hypnosis: Theoretical and empirical overlap and convergence in a new Creative Imagination Scale. In A. A. Sheikh and J. T. Shaffer (eds), *The potential of fantasy and imagination*, 67–88. New York: Brandon House.

Bergman, H. and Agren, G. 1974. Cognitive style and intellectual performance in relation to the progress of alcoholism. *Quarterly Journal of Studies in Alcoholism* 35: 1242–1255.

Bexton, W. H., Heron, W. and Scott, T. H. 1954. Effects of decreased variation in the sensory environment. *Canadian Journal of Psychology* 8: 70–76.

Brauchi, J. T. and West, L. J. 1959. Sleep deprivation. *Journal of the American Medical Association* 171: 11–14.

Brown, L. J. 1965. Afterimages. In C. H. Graham (ed.) *Vision and visual perception*, 479–503. New York: Wiley.

Carrington, P. 1986. Meditation as an access to altered states of consciousness. In B. B. Wolman and M. Ullman (eds) *Handbook of states of consciousness*, 487–523. New York: Van Nostrand Reinhold.

David, O. and Glicksman, M. 1976. Cognitive style and the Perky effect. *Perceptual and Motor Skills* 42: 432–434.

Ekman, P. and Friesen, W. V. 1975. *Unmasking the face.* Englewood Cliffs, New Jersey: Prentice-Hall.

Fisher, S. 1962. Body image boundaries and hallucinations. In L. J. West (ed.) *Hallucinations*, 249–260. New York: Grune & Stratton.

Foulkes, D. and Fleisher, S. 1975. Mental activity in relaxed wakefulness. *Journal of Abnormal Psychology* 84: 66–75.

Foulkes, D., Spear, P. S. and Symonds, J. D. 1966. Individual differences in mental activity at sleep onset. *Journal of Abnormal Psychology* 71: 280–286.

Fox, C. 1914. The conditions which arouse mental images in thought. *British Journal of Psychology* 6: 420–431.

Freedman, S. J., Grunebaum, H. U., Stare, F. A. and Greenblatt, M. 1962. Imagery in sensory deprivation. In L. J. West (ed.) *Hallucinations*, 108–117. New York: Grune and Stratton.

Freedman, S. J. and Marks, P. A. 1965. Visual imagery produced by rhythmic photic stimulation: Personality correlates and phenomenology. *British Journal of Psychology* 56: 95–112.

Ghiselin, B. 1952. (ed.) *The creative process.* New York: Mentor

Glicksohn, J. 1986. Photic driving and altered states of consciousness: An exploratory study. *Imagination, Cognition and Personality* 6: 167–182.

Glicksohn, J. 1989. The structure of subjective experience: Interdependencies along the sleep — wakefulness continuum. *Journal of Mental Imagery* 13: 99–106.

Goldberger, L. and Holt, R.R 1961. *A comparison of isolation effects and their personality correlates in two divergent samples.* A. S. D. Tech. Rep. 61–417. Wright-Patterson A. F. B., Ohio.

Haber, R. N. 1979. Twenty years of haunting eidetic imagery: Where's the ghost? *Behavioral and Brain Sciences* 2: 583–629.

Harman, W. W., McKim, R. H., Mogar, R. E., Fadiman, J. and Stolaroff, M. J. 1966. Psychodelic agents in creative problem solving: A pilot study. *Psychological Reports* 19: 211–227.

Hebb, D. O. 1954. The problem of consciousness and introspection. In J. F. Delafresnaye (ed.). *Brain mechanisms and consciousness*, 402–421. Oxford: Blackwell.

Hiscock, M. and Cohen, D. B. 1973. Visual imagery and dream recall. *Journal of Research in Personality* 7: 179–188.

Holt, R. R. and Goldberger, L. 1959. *Personological correlates of reactions to perceptual isolation.* WADC Tech. Rep. 59–753. Wright-Patterson A. F. B., Ohio.

Horowitz, M. J. 1964. The imagery of visual hallucinations. *Journal of Nervous and Mental Disease* 138: 513–523.

Klein G., Gardner, R. and Schlesinger, H. 1962. Tolerance for unrealistic experience: A study of generality of a cognitive control. *British Journal of Psychology* 53: 41–55.

Klüver, H. 1928. *Mescal: The divine plant and its psychological effects.* London: Kegan, Paul, Trench, Trubner.

Knoll, M. and Kugler, J. 1959. Subjective light pattern spectroscopy in the electroencephalographic range. *Nature* 184: 1823.

Kubie, L. and Margolin, S. 1944. The process of hypnotism and the nature of the hypnotic state. *American Journal of Psychiatry* 100: 611–622.

Leuner, H. 1963. The interpretation of visual hallucinations. Series 3 of *Psychopathology and pictorial expression: An international iconographical collection.* Sandoz.

McKellar, P. 1979. Between wakefulness and sleep: Hypnagogic fantasy. In A. A. Sheikh and J. T. Shaffer (eds), *The potential of fantasy and imagination*, 189–197. New York: Brandon House.

McKellar, P. and Simpson, L. 1954. Between wakefulness and sleep: Hypnagogic imagery *British Journal of Psychology* 45: 266–276.

Maupin, E. W. 1965. Individual differences in response to a Zen meditation exercise. *Journal of Consulting Psychology* 29: 139–145.

Maupin, E. W. 1969. On meditation. In C. T. Tart (ed.) *Altered states of consciousness: A book of readings*, 177–189. New York: Wiley.

Mavromatis, A. 1987. *Hypnagogia: The unique state of consciousness between wakefulness and sleep.* London: Routledge and Kegan Paul.

Mavromatis, A. and Richardson, J. T. E. 1984. Hypnagogic imagery. In A. A. Sheikh (ed.). *International review of mental imagery* 1: 159–189.

Montangero, J. 1993. Dream problem-solving, and creativity. In C. Cavaller and D. Foulkes (eds). *Dreaming and cognition*, 93–113. New York: Harvester Wheatsheaf.

Morgan, R. F. and Bakan, P. 1965. Sensory deprivation, hallucinations and other sleep behavior as a function of position, method of report, and anxiety. *Perceptual and Motor Skills* 20: 19–25.

Moseley, A. L. 1953. Hynagogic hallucinations in relation to accidents. *American Psychologist* 8: 407.

Myers, T. I. and Murphy, D. B. 1962. Reported visual sensation during brief exposure to reduced sensory input. In L. J. West (ed.), *Hallucinations*, 118–134. New York: Grune & Stratton.

Ogden, R. M. 1913. Experimental criteria for differentiating memory and imagination in projected visual images. *Psychological Review* 30: 378–410.

Perky, C. W. 1910. An experimental study of imagination. *American Journal of Psychology* 21: 422–452.

Reinhold, D. B. 1957. Effect of training on perception of after-images. *Perception and Motor Skills* 7: 198.

Richardson, A. 1969. *Mental imagery.* London: Routledge & Kegan Paul.

Richardson, A. 1980. Unpublished data.

Richardson, A. 1982. Unpublished data.

Richardson, A. 1983. Imagery: Definition and types. In A. A. Sheikh (ed.), *Imagery: Current theory research, and application*, 3–42. New York: Wiley.

Richardson, A. 1984. *The experiential dimension of psychology.* St Lucia, Qld.: Queensland University Press.

Richardson, A. 1986. A follow-up study of nine typographic eidetikers. *Psychologia: An international Journal of Psychology in the Orient* 29: 165–175.

Richardson, A. 1994. *Individual differences in imaging: Their measurement, origins, and consequences.* New York: Baywood.

Richardson, A. and Harris, L. J. 1986. Age trends in eidetikers. *Journal of Genetic Psychology* 147: 303–308.

Richardson, A. and McAndrew, F. 1990. The effects of photic stimulation and Private self-consciousness on the complexity of visual imagination imagery. *British Journal of Psychology* 81: 381–394.

Richardson, J. T. E., Mavromatis, A., Mindel, T. and Owens, A. C. 1981. Individual differences in hypnagogic and hypnopompic imagery. *Journal of Mental Imagery* 5: 91–96.

Rowley, J. T., Stickgold, R. and Hobson, J. A. 1998. Eyelid movements and mental activity at sleep onset. *Consciousness and Cognition* 7: 67–84.

Schachter, D. L. 1976. The hypnagogic state: A critical review of the literature. *Psychological Bulletin* 83: 452–481.

Schachter, D. L. and Crovitz, H. F. 1977. 'Falling' while falling asleep: Sex differences. *Perceptual and Motor Skills* 44: 656.

Scheibel, M. E. and Scheibel, A. B. 1962. Hallucinations and the brain stem reticular core. In L. J. West (ed.), *Hallucinations*, 15–35. New York: Grune & Stratton.

Sedman, G. 1966. A comparative study of pseudo-hallucinations, imagery and true hallucinations. *British Journal of Psychiatry* 112: 9–17.

Segal, S. J. 1964. Personal communication.

Segal, S. J. and Nathan, S. 1964. The Perky effect: Incorporation of an external stimulus into an imagery experience under placebo and control conditions. *Perceptual and Motor Skills* 18: 385–395.

Sheehan, P.W 1967. A shortened form of Betts' Questionnaire upon Mental Imagery. *Journal of Clinical Psychology* 23: 386–389.

Sheehan, P. W. 1979. Imagery processes and hypnosis: An experiential analysis of phenomena. In A. A. Sheikh and J. T. Shaffer (eds), *The potential of fantasy and imagination*, 89–103. New York: Brandon House.

Sheehan, P. W. and Lewis, S. E. 1974. Subjects' reports of confusion in consciousness and the arousal of imagery. *Perceptual and Motor Skills* 38: 731–734.

Siegel, R. K. and Jarvik, M. E. 1975. Drug-induced hallucinations in animals and man. In R. K. Siegel and L. J. West (eds), *Hallucinations: Behavior, experience and theory*, 81–161. New York: Wiley.

Silberer, J. R. 1909. Report on a method of eliciting and observing certain symbolic hallucination-phenomena (Chapter 8) and, On symbol formation (Chapter 3. In D. Rapaport (ed.)), *Organization and pathology of thought: Selected sources*, 195–233. New York: Columbia University Press.

Silverman, A. J., Cohen, S. I., Shmavonian, B. M. and Greenberg, G. 1961. Psychophysiological investigations in sensory deprivation. *Psychosomatic Medicine* 23: 48–61.

Smythies, J. R. 1960. The stroboscopic patterns III: Further experiments and discussion. *British Journal of Psychology* 51: 247–255.

Taylor, J. M. 1956. A comparison of delusional and hallucinatory individuals using field dependency as a measure. Unpublished doctoral dissertation, Purdue University. Cited by Witkin, H. A., Dyk, R. B., Faterson, H. F., Goodenough, D. R. and Karp, S. A. *Psychological differentiation: Studies of development*. New York: Wiley, 1962.

Tellegen, A. and Atkinson, G. 1974. Openness to absorbing and self-altering experiences ('absorption'). A trait related to hypnotic susceptibility. *Journal of Abnormal Psychology* 83: 268–277.

Vogel, G. W. 1991. Sleep onset mentation. In S. J. Ellman and J. S. Antrobus (eds) *The mind in sleep: Psychology and psychophysiology*, 125–142. New York: Wiley.

Vogel, G., Foulkes, D. and Trosman, H. 1966. Ego functions and dreaming during sleep onset. *Archives of General Psychiatry* 14: 238–248.

Werner, H. 1948. *Comparative psychology of mental development* (Rev. Edn). New York: Follett.

West, L. J. 1962. A general theory of hallucinations and dreams. In L. J. West (ed.), *Hallucinations*, 275–291. New York: Grune and Stratton.

West, L. J., Morris, G. O. and Lubin, A. 1962. Illusions, hallucinations and sleep loss. In L. J.West (ed.) *Hallucinations*. New York: Grune & Stratton.

Witkin, H. A., Lewis, H. B., Hertzman, M., Machover, K., Meissner, P. B. and Wapner, S. 1954. *Personality through perception.* New York: Harper.

Woodworth, R. S. 1938. *Experimental psychology.* New York: MacMillan.

Ziskind, E. and Augsburg, T. 1962. Hallucinations in sensory deprivation — method or madness. *Science* 137: 992–993.

Zubek, J. P., Welch, G. and Saunders, M. G. 1963. Electroencephalographic changes during and after 14 days of perceptual deprivation. *Science* 139: 490–492.

Zuckerman, M. and Cohen, N. 1964. Sources of reports of visual and auditory sensations in perceptual isolation experiments. *Psychological Bulletin* 62: 1–20.

Daydreaming Characteristics Across the Life-Span

Age Differences and Seven To Twenty Year Longitudinal Changes

Leonard M. Giambra
National Institute on Aging

It has happened to each of us, a spontaneous shift of attention from external stimuli to the contents of consciousness, i.e., we have daydreamed. Did you daydream as much 6, 13 or 20 years ago as you do now? As a college senior do you daydream as much as when a freshman? As a thiry-something do you daydream as much as when a twenty-something? As a middle-aged business or professional person do you daydream as much, as intensely, about the future or about success or sex as when you were thirty-something or a college senior. As a newly-retired senior citizen do you daydream in the same manner as when you were a middle-aged citizen? After 20 years of retirement do you daydream in the same manner as when you first retired? These questions will be addressed by this paper.

Data based — as contrasted with psychoanalytic or psychodynamic based — studies of daydreaming have taken two forms, psychometric and experimental. In this paper we will report on data collected by psychometric techniques which rely upon retrospective memory — for a complete review of experimental work see Giambra (1995), Singer (1978), Klinger (1990).

The definition of daydreaming and a daydream is tied to its long usage in the English language. In psychology there is no universally accepted definition. For a psychometric perspective this has the potential to muddle outcomes; individuals might use different definitions even when provided with a definition and different instruments may define daydreaming differently. This situation has hampered our understanding of daydreaming and has confused its study. In this paper, we will define a daydream as a thought or image which occurs spontaneously — not deliberately recalled from memory or directly elicited by a perceptual stimulus — and is unrelated to the task at hand. That is, a daydream is an internally initiated and generated spontaneous switch in the contents of consciousness unrelated to the task at hand. The contents of daydreams may be fantastic in nature but are more likely to be mundane. Thus, a daydream may be a fantasy, but need not be, and is not taken as interchangeable term for the same phenonomena — however it is acknowledged that both psychologists and nonpsychologists often use the terms interchangeably.

What initiates daydreaming? Is it determined by a biological rhythm? Kripke and Sonnenschein (1978) have provided evidence of a greatly increased likelihood of daydreaming approximately every 90 minutes. Giambra et al. (1988–1989) have provided evidence of circadian waxing and waning of daydreaming. Thus, daydreaming seems to have a biologically-based cyclicality. Age changes in circadian and ultradian rhythms may modify the occurrence of daydreams (see Woodruff 1985; Schroots and Birren 1990; Prinz, Dustman, & Emmerson 1990 for reviews of the influence of age on biological rhythms). Overlaying cyclical necessity seems to be situational opportunity. When the external world does not demand one's full attentional resources one seems to daydream more. Antrobus (1968) and Giambra (1995) have shown quite clearly that an inverse relationship exits between time spent in daydreaming and the information processing demands of the external world. Older adults process information more slowly (Salthouse 1985) and older adults often do more poorly in divided attention and attention-switching tasks (McDowd & Birren 1990) than younger adults. Given equivalent information processing demands and attention-switching tasks older adults would be expected to do less daydreaming than younger adults. Finally, Klinger (1971, 1990) has proposed and shown convincing evidence that the "current concerns" and "unfinished business" of a individual have a strong influence on the likelihood of daydreams. Parks, Klinger, & Perlmutter (1988–89) have shown fewer current concerns in the elderly which may be responsible for the reduced number of daydreams reported.

What determines the content of a daydream? Content may also be biologically determined. As the time since last eating or drinking increases, our daydreams may be of food or water. As conditions change which challenge our biological equilibrium do our daydreams turn to actions which can restore that equilibrium? Clearly, we have daydreams which go beyond biological utility or necessity. Klinger (1996) has provided evidence that people are especially and subliminally sensitive to external information related to their current concerns and that this may initiate — especially when the concern has an emotional overlay or influence — or determine the content of, daydreams. Further evidence comes from data showing congruence of the current concern hierarchy with specific daydream content likelihoods (Klinger 1978). Thus, to the extent that aging affects biological cycles and affects the current concerns of individuals, we should expect that age will affect the frequency and content of daydreams.

These potential explanations of daydreaming frequency and content are not tested in this paper. We seek to provide basic descriptive data on daydreaming likelihood and characteristics across the adult lifespan. These basic data form a database which constains both present and future potential explanations. We know from earlier studies by Giambra (1974, 1977a, 1997b, 1977–1978, 1979–1980, 1980, 1993; Giambra & Grodsky 1991–1992) and McCraven & Singer (1961) that adult age differences and seven year age changes do occur. This paper expands on these earlier works by increasing the size and diversity of the age group samples and by increasing the size and diversity of the seven year longitudinal sample and adding 13 year and 20 year longitudinal samples.

Following the Method description this paper is divided into seven additional parts and a General Discussion. In the first part, response honesty is examined by looking at scales concerned with willingness to reveal oneself and with acceptance of daydreaming. In the second part, scales measuring the frequency and intensity of daydreaming are examined. Scales measuring the extent that daydreams are oriented to the present, past or future comprise the third part. Emotional reactions in and to daydreams are examined in the fourth part. Imagery in daydreams is examined in the fifth part. The sixth part examines actual content of daydreams; specifically, scales which measure the likelihood of having daydreams which are concerned with problem solving, bizarre-improbable things and actions, sexual activity, heroic actions, achievement, fear of failure, hostile actions and wishes, and feeling of guilt. In all parts, we look at age differences across adulthood and age changes that occur in approximately 7, 13, and 20 years across adulthood. We examine women and men separately and look for similarities and differences. Finally, we make comparisons across scales to determine relative importance and strength.

Method

Participants

Overview. The recruitment of participants began in 1971 and continued through 1996. This included individuals who were tested only once and individuals who were tested as many as six times over a 24 year period. Most longitudinal participants were men and women who were volunteers in the Baltimore

Longitudinal Study on Aging (BLSA; Shock et al. 1984); the remainder were their relatives and friends. BLSA participants were from all over the United States with about 80% living within 150 miles of Baltimore. Cross-sectional participants who were college students were recruited from Miami University (Ohio) and schools in Maryland. Older non-BLSA participants were recruited through senior citizen organizations in the Baltimore Metropolitan area and from civic and service organizations in the Baltimore and St. Louis Metropolitan areas and Southwestern Pennsylvania. All participants were told when they were recruited that they would be completing a questionnaire on imaginal processes.

Cross-Sectional Sample. The sample consisted of 1782 women and 1545 men from 17 to 95 years of age. Of these, 597 women and 1009 men were BLSA participants. The distribution by age was: (a) 17–24 yrs, 677 W, 478 M; (b) 25–34 yrs, 278 W, 182 M; (c) 35–44 yrs, 216 W, 143 M; (d) 45–54 yrs, 187 W, 160 M; (e) 55–64 yrs, 186 W, 222 M; (f) 65–74 yrs, 142 W, 174 M; (g) 75–84 yrs, 82 W, 165 M; (h) 85–95 yrs, 14 W, 21 M. BLSA participants made of from 37% to 79% of the age groups for women and 84% to 100% of the age groups for men, except for the 17–24 year age interval which contained less than 5%. Table 1 provides a description of the sample. In general, the sample was made up of individuals from urban or suburban areas, of a Protestant religion, of the middle or upper-middle class, White, and married.

Longitudinal samples. Three two-point longitudinal periods were used: 5.45 to 9.54 years ($M = 6.9$ yrs, $SD = 0.9$ yrs; 367 W, 519 M), 11.45 to 16.67 years ($M = 13.6$ yrs, $SD = 1.1$ yrs; 230 W, 398 M), and 17.40 to 23.44 years ($M = 20.0$ yrs, $SD = 1.4$ yrs; 72 W, 218 M). These represent the maximum sample sizes since not all participants responded to all items of the IPI; for example, see Table 2 for the age distribution of these three longitudinal samples for participants who responded to all items of Scale 1 of the IPI. The Age-at-First-Testing(by decades) X Sex analyses of longitudinal change variances, for each longitudinal interval, reported in the results were restricted to those decades where at least 10 men and 10 women provided data — hence the decades tested were different for each longitudinal interval. For men, all longitudinal participants were members of the BLSA. For women, in the 5.45 to 9.54 year period, 80% were from the BLSA; in the 11.45 to 16.67 year period, 77% were from the BLSA; in the 17.40 to 23.44 year period, 52% were from the BLSA; the remainder were wives, women friends, and relatives of the male BLSA participants. After the first testing, 18 men and 9 women from the BLSA refused to participate in a longitudinal repeat. Table 3 provides a description of the longitudinal samples by residency, religion, self-rated socio-economic class, educational attainment, and marital status.

Table 1. *A Demographic Description of Cross-Sectional Sample*

Age Group (Yrs)	17–24		25–34		35–44		45–54		55–64		65–74		75–95	
Gender	F[a]	M	F	M	F	M	F	M	F	M	F	M	F	M
Residency														
Farm or Rural	6[b]	7	10	15	13	15	16	13	13	13	18	16	7	8
Fewer than 20,000	33	25	24	29	20	19	19	23	23	19	25	23	32	30
20,000 to 250,000	26	24	28	25	24	20	28	22	32	25	25	24	26	26
More than 250,000	35	44	38	31	43	46	37	42	32	44	32	36	36	36
Religion														
Protestant	41	33	46	50	51	57	67	61	71	68	80	71	73	78
Jewish	7	7	4	7	4	3	6	9	7	10	2	7	2	7
Catholic	33	42	28	25	34	31	17	24	13	15	10	12	13	6
Other	19	16	20	16	12	7	10	6	8	6	5	9	8	8
Atheist	1	2	2	1	0	2	1	0	2	2	3	2	4	1
Self-Rated Socio-Economic Class														
Lower/Lower-Middle	15	13	22	16	10	4	8	3	4	5	7	5	4	7
Middle-Middle	49	45	50	48	39	41	37	38	39	27	42	40	49	42
Upper-Middle	34	37	26	34	45	48	48	48	49	56	45	43	41	41
Upper	2	5	2	3	5	7	8	11	9	12	7	12	5	10
Race, Self-Described														
Caucasian/White	76	83	87	90	93	90	91	94	93	94	95	97	97	100
Negroid/Black	21	14	10	8	6	9	9	5	7	6	3	4	3	0
Mixed/Other	3	3	3	2	1	1	1	1	1	0	2	0	0	0
Education														
12 Yrs or Less	7	9	11	6	12	8	16	10	18	10	22	9	14	12
College 1–3 Yrs	78	74	28	26	22	15	23	13	17	10	20	14	20	10
College 4–5 Yrs	12	15	32	40	29	34	27	22	30	28	23	23	34	24
Post-Graduate 1–5 Yrs	1	1	23	26	33	43	29	53	26	50	29	53	28	51
Technical/Other	1	1	6	3	4	1	5	2	9	2	7	1	3	3
Marital Status (Current)														
Married	3	3	58	56	81	86	74	91	80	89	63	84	40	83
Divorced/Separated	0	0	10	8	13	3	13	4	8	9	7	10	9	1
Widowed	0	0	1	0	1	1	3	0	9	0	19	3	43	15
Never Married	97	97	31	36	5	10	11	5	4	2	12	3	8	2

Table 1 *(Continued)*

a. F = Female, M = Male.
b. The entries are the percentage of the total sample of each gender in each age group who fall into a category of each demographic descriptor — may not add up to 100% due to rounding.
Note. Within each gender, a Chi Square Test indicated a significant age effect, $p <$ .05, for each demographic descriptor whether or not the 17–24 year old age group was excluded. A Chi Square Test indicated a significant gender effect, $p < .05$, for the (a) 17–24 year old group for residency and race, (b) 25–34 year old group for no demographic descriptor, (c) 35–44 year old group for education, (d) 45–54 year old group for education and marital status, (e) 55–64 year old group for education and marital status, (f) 65–74 year old group for education and marital status, and (g) 75–95 year old group race, education and marital status.

Procedure. Aspects of daydreaming were determined from participant responses to the items of selected scales of the 344 item *Imaginal Processes Inventory* (IPI; Giambra 1980; Singer & Antrobus 1970). The IPI was usually taken alone or in small groups. For those 17–24 years old the IPI was usually completed in larger groups during a single session with a proctor present or nearby. Non-BLSA women 24 years and older usually completed the IPI at home after receiving it in the mail. BLSA participants usually completed the IPI while on a regularly scheduled visit to the Gerontology Research Center, Baltimore, Maryland. Instructions and approximately 50 items were completed in small groups; the IPI was finished when participants were alone and in the privacy of their rooms. Some inactive BLSA participants received the IPI by postal service and completed it at home.

Each participant was given a brief explanation of daydreaming and the purposes of the study. Each participant was provided with examples of daydreaming behavior and urged to "Make a distinction between thinking about an immediate task you're performing, e.g., working, doing school work, thinking directly about it while doing it and daydreaming which involves thought unrelated to a task you are doing or else thoughts that go on while you are getting ready for sleep or during a long bus, plane, or train ride." Relevant demographic information was also obtained from each participant prior to attempting the IPI.

Scoring the Imaginal Processes Inventory. Each item has five options on a continuum implying frequency or quantity. The options were assigned values of 0, 1, 2, 3 or 4 according to their ordinal position on the implied continuum — negatively phrased items were appropriately transposed. The five options of the

Table 2. *Daydreaming Frequency Scale, Age-at-First-Testings, Group Sizes for the Longitudinal Intervals*

	Age-at-1st-Testing Age Group (Yrs)	Longitudinal Interval (Yrs) 5.5 to 9.5	11.5 to 16.7	17.4 to 23.4
Women	17–24	6	6	3
	25–34	56	40	12
	35–44	51	34	16
	45–54	61	40	14
	55–64	61	46	12
	65–74	42	22	1
	75–84	27	4	0
Men	17–24	5	4	2
	25–34	84	67	34
	35–44	71	65	33
	45–54	95	90	43
	55–64	105	95	41
	65–74	61	31	11
	75–84	35	2	0

items of Scale 1 (Daydreaming Frequency) changed with each item. The items of the remaining daydream characteristic scales had the following five options: (a) "definitely not true for me or strongly uncharacteristic of me," (b) "usually not true for me," (c) "usually true for me," (d) "true for me," (e) "very true for me or strongly characteristic of me." The minimum score for all scales was zero. The maximum score for all scales was 4 times the number of items assigned the scale. All scales, except Scale 3, were based upon responses to 12 different items resulting in a maximum score of 48; Scale 3 (Absorption in Daydreaming) had 20 items and a maximum score of 80. The scales reported in this study along with their internal consistency and test-retest reliability are presented in Table 4. Prior to the presentation of the results of analyses performed on each scale, a more complete description of each scale is given.

Response Honesty

Results

Self-Revelation. This scale indicated the extent to which each participant was

Table 3. *A Demographic Description of the Longitudinal Samples*

Longitudinal Interval (Yrs)	5.5–9.5		11.5–16.7		17.4–23.4	
Gender	F[a]	M	F	M	F	M
Residency						
Farm or Rural	18[b]	15[c]	20	17[c]	22	11[c]
Fewer than 20,000	25	22	22	19	30	17
20,000 to 250,000	31	22	33	22	28	26
More than 250,000	27	40	26	42	20	46
Religion						
Protestant	69	68	70	68	60	70
Jewish	6	7	4	7	6	7
Catholic	14	18	17	20	23	15
Other	9	6	7	5	8	6
Atheist	2	1	2	1	4	1
Self-Rated Socio-Economic Class						
Lower/Lower-Middle	6	5	6	5	10	5
Middle-Middle	42	38	39	34	37	31
Upper-Middle	47	47	49	51	49	56
Upper	5	11	5	9	4	8
Race, Self-Described						
Caucasian/White	96	95	97	95	100	94
Negroid/Black	3	5	3	5	0	6
Mixed/Other	1	0	1	0	0	0
Education						
12 Yrs or Less	14	7[c]	9	8[c]	11	7[c]
College 1–3 Yrs	17	12	17	10	22	7
College 4–5 Yrs	29	29	33	31	32	34
Post-Graduate 1–5 Yrs	35	51	34	51	30	51
Technical/Other	5	1	7	1	6	1
Marital Status (Current)						
Married	73	84[c]	83	87	85	86
Divorced/Separated	10	4	5	6	6	10
Widowed	7	1	3	0	6	2
Never Married	10	11	9	4	4	2

Table 3. *Continued*

a. F = Female, M = Male.
b. The entries are the percentage of the longitudinal sample of each gender who fall into a category of each demographic descriptor — may not add up to 100% due to rounding errors.
c. A significant gender effect, $p < .05$.

Note. Chi Square Tests indicated some significant age effects, $p < .05$. The 25–34 year olds tended to have a smaller proportion of Protestants and the 75–84 year olds tended to have a larger proportion of Protestants than the 35–74 year olds [ages are at first testing]. The 25–34 year olds tended to have a larger proportion of individuals whose self-rated socio-economic class was lower-middle and lower class. For men, with increased age there occurred an increasing proportion of postgraduate education, from 28% in 25–34 year olds to 69% in 75–84 year olds. For women, the 35–44 year olds had clearly the highest level of education. Never marrieds occurred in a much higher proportion for 25–34 year olds and for 75–84 year old women. Widowhood also occurred in a much higher porportion of 75–84 year old women.

willing to reveal himself or herself honestly while completing the IPI. Examples of items are: "I like to talk about my problems." "I don't like being a subject in an experiment and answering a personality test." "I like to observe my reactions to things and to other people." "I feel uncomfortable when someone asks me a personal question."

Age differences. An Age Group X Sex ANOVA showed a significant effect of sex and age, but not their interaction, see Table 5. Women had somewhat greater mean scale values, i.e., greater self-revelation, than men and older participants had lesser values than younger participants, see Table 5. A scale value of 12 may be interpreted as "usually not true" and a scale value of 24 may be interpreted as "usually true." Thus, even the least willing age groups had mean values closer to "usually true" than "usually not true" in their tendency toward self-revelation.

Age changes. Analyses of variance of the changes for the longitudinal intervals indicated that the interval resulted in a significant decrease in self-revelation scores for the 5.5–9.5 year interval ($M = -0.6$, $F(1,593) = 8.41$, $p < .01$, partial eta squared = .014), the 11.5–16.7 year interval ($M = -1.2$, $F(1,415) = 18.44$, $p < .001$, partial eta squared = .043), and 17.4–23.4 year interval ($M = -1.9$, $F(1,118) = 11.78$, $p < .01$, partial eta squared = .091). The effect of the longitudinal interval was not significantly, $p < .05$, affected by sex, age-at-first-testing, or their interaction for all three periods.

Table 4. *Daydreaming Characteristic Scales: Internal Consistency and Test-Retest Reliability*

Scale	Internal Consistency	Test-Retest Correlation Interval (Yrs)			
		< 2.01	5.5–9.5	11.5–16.7	17.4–23.4
Frequency and intensity					
Daydreaming Frequency (#1)	.91	.72	.64	.58	.55
Absorption in Daydreaming (#3)	.90	.69	.71	.67	.51
Hallucinatory-Vividness of Daydreaming (#16)	.88	.62	.61	.60	.50
Temporal setting					
Present-Oriented Daydreams (#10)	.65	.41	.46	.42	.38
Future in Daydreams (#11)	.80	.63	.59	.54	.57
Past in Daydreams (#12)	.84	.72	.66	.61	.53
Emotional reactions					
Positive Reactions in Daydreaming (#5)	.83	.68	.61	.51	.40
Frightened Reactions to Daydreams (#6)	.84	.40	.58	.55	.47
Imagery					
Visual Imagery in Daydreaming (#7)	.84	.58	.61	.54	.45
Auditory Imagery in Daydreaming (#8)	.89	.67	.61	.50	.48
Content					
Problem Solving Daydreams (#9)	.84	.62	.58	.53	.56
Bizarre-Improbable Daydreams (#13)	.82	.69	.63	.57	.47
Sexual Daydreams (#19)	.93	.70	.75	.70	.52
Heroic Daydreams (#20)	.90	.48	.68	.62	.59
Achievement-Oriented Daydreams (#15)	.90	.81	.71	.62	.59
Fear of Failure Daydreams (#17)	.86	.42	.64	.54	.50
Hostile Daydreams (#18)	.90	.61	.64	.61	.65
Guilt Daydreams (#21)	.88	.41	.62	.55	.48
Other					
Acceptance of Daydreaming (#4)	.76	.51	.58	.57	.53
Self-Revelation (#28)	.73	.67	.69	.63	.60

Note. Cronbach's alpha was used to determine internal consistency; it is the mean of the value calculated for men and women separately, based upon the first testing sample. The test-retest interval was as indicated, the correlation is for men and women combined; all correlations, $p < .001$.

Table 5. *Daydreaming Characteristic Scales: ANOVA Results and Means by Age Group for All Participants Tested for the First Time*

Scale	Sex[a]	Age Groups							Standard Deviations	ANOVA Effects[b]		
		17–24	25–34	35–44	45–54	55–64	65–74	75–84		Age	Sex	A X S
Response honesty												
Self-Revelation (#28)	F	27.2	25.1	22.9	23.7	21.8	20.2	19.9	5.3–7.2	***[c]	***	ns
	M	25.5	22.3	21.4	21.5	20.3	19.8	20.1	5.0–6.7	13[d]	< 1	
Acceptance of Daydreaming (#4)	F	33.5	34.6	35.5	35.5	34.0	33.2	32.1	5.0–6.1	***	***	ns
	M	32.7	34.4	34.1	32.5	32.2	32.2	30.9	4.9–6.6	2	< 1	
Frequency and intensity												
Daydreaming Frequency (#1)	F	28.9	26.2	23.1	23.1	19.0	18.2	16.6	7.6–9.4	***	**	ns
	M	27.6	24.3	22.3	20.4	19.5	18.2	15.6	8.0–9.0	19	< 1	
Absorption in Daydreaming (#3)	F	39.2	35.7	31.5	31.7	28.3	26.7	26.8	9.2–12.8	***	***	
	M	36.4	30.3	29.5	27.3	25.9	24.6	22.7	8.3–12.0	15	2	ns
Hallucinatory-Vividness of Daydreaming (#16)	F	11.5	8.9	6.8	7.8	6.4	6.6	7.4	5.7–7.5	***	ns	*
	M	11.3	7.1	8.2	7.4	6.8	6.7	6.3	5.4–7.0	9	< 1	
Temporal setting												
Present-Oriented Daydreams (#10)	F	24.8	25.4	25.9	26.4	25.6	25.9	25.2	4.9–6.0	***	***	ns
	M	23.3	23.7	24.4	24.8	24.4	23.1	23.3	4.1–5.4	1	2	
Future in Daydreams (#11)	F	29.8	27.4	26.5	26.2	26.0	24.2	23.9	6.0–6.9	***	**	ns
	M	28.4	27.7	25.5	25.4	24.1	23.8	22.7	6.0–6.7	8	< 1	
Past in Daydreams (#12)	F	24.6	24.0	22.6	24.1	23.8	24.9	26.4	6.4–8.1	***	***	ns
	M	24.4	22.6	22.6	21.3	22.4	24.3	24.6	6.2–7.4	2	< 1	
Emotional reactions												
Positive Reactions in Daydreaming (#5)	F	26.5	25.9	23.9	23.9	21.9	20.7	20.4	6.2–7.2	***	***	ns
	M	25.7	24.3	24.0	21.9	20.2	20.4	18.3	6.0–6.8	10	< 1	
Frightened Reactions to Daydreams (#6)	F	17.4	15.0	12.8	13.3	12.9	12.2	13.1	5.1–7.1	***	***	ns
	M	16.1	12.3	11.8	11.6	10.5	11.4	10.9	5.5–7.3	10	1	

Table 5. *Continued*

Scale	Sex[a]	Age Groups							Standard Deviations	ANOVA Effects[b]		
		17–24	25–34	35–44	45–54	55–64	65–74	75–84		Age	Sex	A X S
Imagery												
Visual Imagery in Daydreaming (#7)	F	24.3	23.4	21.1	20.7	18.9	18.6	19.2	6.1–7.7	***	ns	ns
	M	24.0	22.0	21.8	20.4	19.3	20.0	17.7	5.8–7.4	8		
Auditory Imagery in Daydreaming (#8)	F	20.8	18.6	15.7	16.4	14.7	14.0	15.3	6.8–9.2	***	ns	ns
	M	21.3	17.4	16.7	14.7	13.8	14.3	12.8	6.3–8.1	11		
Content												
Problem Solving Daydreams (#9)	F	23.4	24.0	24.4	24.6	22.6	21.7	20.9	6.9–7.8	***	***	ns
	M	22.8	22.9	22.7	21.3	20.1	20.3	18.6	6.8–7.6	2	1	
Bizarre-Improbable Daydreams (#13)	F	17.4	16.0	13.9	13.8	13.5	13.8	15.6	4.9–7.3	***	***	ns
	M	19.5	17.3	15.8	15.7	15.5	16.7	16.1	5.6–7.7	6	1	< 1
Sexual Daydreams (#19)	F	23.0	19.0	16.1	13.4	9.5	7.8	8.1	6.3–9.3	***	***	***
	M	25.9	21.9	20.6	17.8	15.8	14.6	11.7	7.0–9.0	29	5	
Heroic Daydreams (#20)	F	11.3	8.7	6.5	6.0	5.3	4.3	4.8	4.8–7.8	***	***	ns
	M	15.0	11.2	9.9	9.1	7.5	6.7	6.1	5.8–8.3	15	3	< 1
Achievement-Oriented Daydreams (#15)	F	17.4	15.9	14.0	13.9	10.3	8.6	9.6	6.0–9.2	***	***	ns
	M	19.2	17.5	15.8	14.0	13.0	10.9	10.5	7.0–8.5	12	< 1	
Fear of Failure Daydreams (#17)	F	10.6	8.7	7.9	7.6	7.2	6.5	7.9	4.6–6.3	***	*	ns
	M	12.2	9.4	8.3	8.7	7.5	7.3	6.8	5.2–6.3	8	< 1	
Hostile Daydreams (#18)	F	12.6	10.2	9.1	8.3	6.8	6.5	5.9	4.8–7.8	***	***	ns
	M	15.7	12.1	11.0	9.6	8.3	8.1	6.1	5.3–8.3	13	< 1	
Guilt Daydreams (#21)	F	9.0	6.5	5.0	4.8	4.5	4.5	5.3	4.4–6.2	***	***	ns
	M	10.7	7.4	6.0	6.1	5.4	5.6	5.0	5.0–6.8	12	< 1	

a. F = Female, M = Male

b. The 85–95 year old age group was omitted since sample sizes were less than 20. The Age X Sex ANOVA included the age groups indicated. The degrees of freedom were Age (6), Sex (1), Age X Sex (6), Error (2707 to 3077).

c. Indicates significance level, ns $p > .05$, * $p < .05$, ** $p < .01$, *** $p < .001$.

d. Indicates effect size, partial eta squared converted to a percentage for all significant effects.

Acceptance of Daydreaming

Another indicator of the willingness of participants to honestly answer questions about their daydreaming was Scale 4, Acceptance of Daydreaming. This scale indicated the extent to which an individual considered daydreaming as common, natural, and not revealing psychological maladjustment. Participants with low acceptance might cloak their true daydreaming characteristics by under reporting negative components and over reporting positive components.

Age differences. An Age Group X Sex ANOVA showed a significant effect of sex and age, but not their interaction, see Table 5. Women had somewhat greater mean scale values, i.e., greater acceptance than men, see Table 5. A scale value of 24 may be interpreted as "usually true" and a value of 36 as "true"; Table 5 shows all age group means closer to 36 than 24. Thus, every age group of both sexes accepted daydreaming as normal and desirable. We could reasonably expect high acceptance to lead to response honesty.

Age changes. Analyses of variance of changes for the longitudinal intervals indicated that the interval resulted in a significant decrease in acceptance of daydreaming scores only for the 5.5–9.5 year interval ($M = -0.8$, $F(1,581) = 10.10$, $p < .01$, partial eta squared = .017). Age-at-first-testing significantly affected the amount of change for the 5.5–9.5 year interval ($F(5,581) = 3.65$, $p < .01$, partial eta squared = .030), the 11.5–16.7 year interval ($F(4,412) = 2.36$, $p < .054$, partial eta squared = .022), and the 17.4–23.4 year interval ($F(3,149) = 7.09$, $p < .001$, partial eta squared = .125) — age in combination with sex also significantly affected the amount of change for the 17.4–23.4 year interval ($F(3,149) = 2.93$, $p < .05$, partial eta squared = .056). The changes were consistent with the increase in mean values followed by the decrease in mean values indicated in the age differences displayed in Table 5. For the 17.4–23.4 year interval, the age by sex interaction resulted from the positive changes being greater for men than for women.

Summary and Discussion

It is very clear that reduced self-revelation with increased age was not simply the result of birth cohort differences. Changes within individuals were in the same direction as cohort differences and longer longitudinal intervals yielded larger decreases in willingness to reveal oneself. However, absolute levels of self-revelation willingness were high and intraindividual decreases were small even over 17.4–23.4 years. Acceptance of daydreaming was extremely high for all age groups and age changes were consistent with 35–54 year old women and 25–44 year old men having the highest acceptance — again suggesting that differences were not substantially due to birth cohort differences.

High levels of willingness to self-revelation, very high levels of acceptance of daydreaming, and small decreases in willingness to self-revelation, even for the 17.4–23.4 year longitudinal period, all suggest that there was little support for attributing any age differences and age changes on the scales reported hereafter to age differences or changes in self-revelation and acceptance of daydreaming.

Frequency and Intensity of Daydreaming

Results

Daydreaming Frequency. The items of the Daydreaming Frequency Scale have options which indicate different quantitative estimates of daydreaming frequency. The scale, by rescaling each item on a 0 to 4 basis and summing across the 12 items, gives a relative value to daydreaming frequency. Hence a scale value of zero indicates absolutely no daydreaming while a scale value of 48 indicates the maximum level of daydreaming frequency — but not 48 daydreams. Gold, Teague, and Jarvinen (1981) obtained correlations between this scale's values and frequency of daydreaming obtained from a diary kept for a one week period and obtained values from .36 to .87 for four small samples of college students.

Age differences. The Age X Sex ANOVA yielded a significant age effect, 19% variance accounted for, and a significant sex effect, but not a significant age by sex interaction, see Table 5. Daydreaming likelihood decreased with age and women reported somewhat higher levels than men. The scale correlation with age was −.44 for women and −.45 for men.

To make less abstract the meaning of this age shift in daydreaming likelihood the distribution of responses to two items of the Daydream Frequency Scale are examined. Table 6 shows the percentage of each age group who endorsed each optional choice for these two items. The percentage of participants who said they daydream "infrequently" showed large and consistent increases from the 17–24 year old group (W = 3.4%, M = 5.2%) to the 75 years and older group (W = 39.5%, M = 61.9%) while those who said they daydream "many times daily" show a less dramatic but reverse trend (from 35.4% to 14.8% or 9.5%). As the age groups become older the distribution shifted from unimodal at "a few times daily" to bimodal at "infrequently". For "When not paying close attention to some job, book or TV, I tend to be daydreaming __ of the time" the modal response was "10%" for all age groups except the 17–24 year olds whose mode was "50%" for women and "25%" for men. The modal percentage increased with increased age. The percentage endorsing the 0% daydreaming time increased with increased age while the percentage endorsing 75% daydreaming time decreased with increased age.

Age changes. Analyses of variance of changes for the longitudinal intervals indicated that the interval resulted in a significant decrease in daydreaming frequency scores for the 5.5–9.5 year interval ($M = -1.4$, $F(1,737) = 23.64$, $p < .001$, partial eta squared = .031), the 11.5–16.7 year interval ($M = -2.3$, $F(1,520) = 35.68$, $p < .001$, partial eta squared = .064), and 17.4–23.4 year interval ($M = -2.4$, $F(1,197) = 13.13$, $p < .001$, partial eta squared = .063). The effect of the longitudinal interval was not significantly, $p > .05$, affected by sex, age-at-first-testing, or both in combination for all three intervals.

Using a procedure described in Giambra et al. (1995), see also Appendix A, to maximize sample sizes the longitudinal samples were reconstituted into six-year-interval, age-at-later-testing, male-female combined groups — sex did not affect age changes as tested for each age-at-later-testing group. The daydreaming frequency score changes for each of the maximized age-at-later-testing longitudinal groups is presented in Table 7. The use of maximized sample age-at-later-testing groups allowed for two additional analyses and for comparisons of changes for a specific age from three earlier ages. The first analysis was a determination, for each age-at-later-testing group at each longitudinal interval, of the significance of the daydreaming frequency score change. The second analysis was a determination of the significance of the difference among the daydreaming frequency score changes for the three longitudinal intervals. Table 7 summarizes these analyses for the Daydreaming Frequency Scale. When comparisons of daydreaming frequency scale changes were made between longitudinal intervals only two age-at-later-testing groups had significant differences between the changes, the 76–81 years and 82–87 years. Of the 28 longitudinal changes obtained in the three longitudinal intervals, 12 were significantly different from zero.

Statistically, these procedures were very conservative. Thus, significant changes for any age group and between longitudinal periods suggest true changes and true differences. In general, longer longitudinal intervals producted greater decreases in daydreaming frequency and for the 76–81 and 82–87 year olds these differences were significant

Table 6. *Daydreaming Frequency Scale: Percentage of Each Age Interval Endorsing Each Item-Alternative for Two Items, First Testing*

"I daydream	Years	Infrequently	Once Weekly	Once Daily	A Few Times Daily	Many Times Daily"
Females	17–24	3.4	2.2	8.6	50.4	35.4
	25–34	7.2	4.0	10.1	48.7	30.0
	35–44	12.0	4.6	12.0	41.7	29.6
	45–54	12.8	3.7	10.7	45.5	27.3
	55–64	27.0	5.4	9.7	37.3	20.5
	65–74	27.3	1.4	7.2	43.9	20.1
	75–84	39.5	6.2	3.7	35.8	14.8
Males	17–24	5.2	2.3	10.5	46.5	35.4
	25–34	8.8	3.8	11.5	48.9	26.9
	35–44	9.1	4.2	11.9	58.7	16.1
	45–54	22.0	5.0	9.4	45.3	18.2
	55–64	22.1	8.6	13.1	41.9	14.4
	65–74	25.3	6.9	14.4	44.8	8.6
	75–84	44.8	6.7	15.3	27.6	5.5
	85–95	61.9	4.8	4.8	19.0	9.5

"When I an not paying close attention to some job, book or TV, I tend to be daydreaming	Years	0%	10%	25%	50%	75% of the time"
Females	17–24	1.8	24.4	24.1	31.1	18.6
	25–34	3.6	41.2	22.4	19.1	13.7
	35–44	6.6	52.6	16.9	12.7	11.3
	45–54	9.2	47.3	19.6	15.8	8.2
	55–64	17.3	57.3	15.1	7.6	2.7
	65–74	18.1	56.5	13.8	10.1	1.4
	75–84	15.6	68.8	10.4	5.2	---
Males	17–24	2.7	25.8	30.0	24.7	16.8
	25–34	3.3	42.9	24.7	18.1	11.0
	35–44	7.7	49.0	21.0	16.1	6.3
	45–54	10.1	57.9	20.1	7.5	4.4
	55–64	9.2	65.1	15.6	7.3	2.8
	65–74	14.0	64.3	16.4	3.5	1.8
	75–84	24.2	58.6	12.7	3.2	1.3
	85–95	42.9	42.9	14.3	---	---

Table 7. *Daydream Frequency Scale, Maximum Age-at-Later-Testings Samples: Mean Change Scores (Later — Earlier) and Results of Analysis of Variance between Longitudinal Intervals for Change Scores within Each Age-at-Later-Testing*

Age-at-Later-Testing	Change in Score From When ___ Years Younger			Between Longitudinal Interval ANOVA Results				Significant $p < .05$ Contrasts
					Partial	– Error –		
Group (Yrs)[a]	6.8[b]	13.3[c]	19.4	*F*	Eta**2	*df*	*MS*	
28–33	+2.4	----	----	----	-----	---	----	
34–39	–1.6[d]	–0.1	----	< 1	-----	108	49.0	
40–45	–1.2[d]	–1.4	----	< 1	-----	204	51.8	
46–51	–0.7	–2.1[d]	–1.1	< 1	-----	281	59.1	
52–57	–0.6	–1.1	–1.2	< 1	-----	267	72.5	
58–63	–1.6[d]	–0.7	–2.9[d]	1.00	-----	310	58.8	
64–69	–2.1[d]	–2.5[d]	–2.6	< 1	-----	315	60.1	
70–75	–1.0	–2.7[d]	–2.4	1.53	-----	288	59.1	
76–81	–1.1	–1.2	–4.1[d]	2.20	-----	249	53.9	(6.8, 19.4)
82–87	–1.7[d]	–4.6[d]	–6.1[d]	4.34*	.0685	118	39.9	(6.8, 13.3)(6.8, 19.4)
88–95	+3.1	–1.6	----	2.75	-----	34	68.0	

* $p < .05$, ** $p < .01$, *** $p < .001$

a, b, c. These are means, the Longitudinal Intervals were, respectively, 5.5 to 9.5 yrs, 11.5 to 16.7 years, and 17.4 to 23.4 years.

d. Indicates change score within an age group-longitudinal interval combination was significantly, $p < .05$, different from zero.

Note. Analysis of variance was one-way repeated measures between Longitudinal Intervals on Change Scores. *df* = degrees of freedom, *MS* = Mean Square. The sample sizes for the 6.8, 13.3, and 19.4 year Longitudinal Intervals, respectively, for each age-at-later-testing group were: 28–33 (25, 1, 0), 34–39 (95, 15, 0), 40–45 (144, 62, 4), 46–51 (152, 105, 57), 52–57 (154, 84, 32), 58–63 (194, 90, 29), 64–69 (186, 103, 29), 70–75 (170, 93, 28), 76–81 (137, 84, 31), 82–87 (73, 33, 15), 88–95 (23, 13, 4). Includes age groups with an *N* of 10 or more. Similar sample sizes were obtained for other scales presented in subsequent tables.

Absorption in Daydreaming

This scale indicated the extent to which an individual is self-absorbed in daydreaming. It represents the degree of influence that an individual's daydreaming has on his or her life. For example, items deal with repetitiveness of daydreams, influence on mood, desire to maintain particular daydreams, attentional pull or attraction of some daydreams, etc. There are 20 items, minimum score of 0 and maximum score of 80. A score of 20 indicates "usually not true" while a score of 40 indicates "usually true for me".

Age differences. The Age X Sex ANOVA yielded significant age (15% of variance accounted for) and sex effect effects, but not their interaction, see Table 5. Decreased means occurred with increased age — means decreased from levels at "usually true for me" to levels at "usually not true for me" — and women reported greater levels of absorption than men. The scale correlation with age was −.36 for women and −.41 for men. To summarize, absorption in daydreaming clearly declined with cohort to levels suggesting that there is little absorption in daydreaming in old age.

Age changes. Analyses of variance of changes for the longitudinal intervals indicated that the interval resulted in a significant decrease in absorption in daydreaming scores for the 5.5–9.5 year interval ($M = -1.3$, $F(1, 652) = 12.74$, $p < .001$, partial eta squared = .019) and the 11.5–16.7 year interval ($M = -1.8$, $F(1, 436) = 15.78$, $p < .001$, partial eta squared = .035), but not the 17.4–23.4 year interval ($M = -1.5$, $F(1, 128) = 2.24$, $p > .05$). The effect of the 5.5–9.5 year longitudinal interval interacted with sex ($F(1, 652) = 4.17$, $p < .05$, partial eta squared = .006) but not age-at-first-testing or both together ($F < 1$). Women showed a greater decrease ($M = -2.0$) than men ($M = -0.5$). The magnitude of the effect of the 11.5–16.7 year longitudinal interval was affected by sex ($F(1,436) = 6.14$, $p < .05$, partial eta squared = .014) but not age-at-first-testing or both together ($F(4,463) < 1.86$). Women showed a greater decrease ($M = -2.9$) than men ($M = -0.7$). The effect of the 17.4–23.4 year longitudinal interval interval did not interact with sex ($F(1,128) = 1.27$, $p > .05$) nor with age-at-first-testing nor both together ($F(2,128) < 1.81$).

Using a procedure, described in Giambra et al. (1995) and Appendix A, to maximize sample sizes the longitudinal samples were reconstituted into six-year-interval, age-at-later-testing groups. An ANOVA determined that sex significantly affected longitudinal change in the 34–39 year and 58–63 year groups within the 5.5–9.5 year longitudinal interval; women showed a large decrease while men showed a small increase, see Table 8. When comparisons of absorption in daydreaming scale changes were made between longitudinal intervals only two age-at-later-testing groups had significant differences among the changes, 76–81 years and 82–87 years. Of the 33 longitudinal changes reported in Table 8, 9 were significantly different from zero.

Summary. Longitudinal change in absorption in daydreaming was age dependent, strongly for women and less so for men. Furthermore, larger decreases with longer longitudinal intervals did not take place until individuals reached age 64–69 years. These decreases were generally significantly different from zero and from each other.

Table 8. *Absorption in Daydreaming Scale, Maximum Age-at-Later-Testings Samples: Mean Change Scores (Later — Earlier) and Results of Analysis of Variance between Longitudinal Intervals for Change Scores within Each Age-at-Later-Testing*

Age-at-Later-Testing	Change in Score From When ___ Years Younger			Between Longitudinal Interval ANOVA Results				Significant $p < .05$ Contrasts
					Partial	– Error –		
Group (Yrs)	6.8[a]	13.3[b]	19.4[c]	*F*	Eta**2	*df*	*MS*	
28–33	+0.1	----	----	--------	-----	---	----	
34–39	−1.3	+3.3	----	2.57	-----	89	73.6	
40–45	−1.1	+1.0	----	2.57	-----	174	65.6	
46–51	−0.2	−1.9	+2.1	2.28	-----	223	64.5	(13.3, 19.4)
52–57	−0.8	−1.1	+0.4	< 1	-----	234	81.8	
58–63 [Women]	−3.9	−2.3	+1.9	1.21	-----	90	94.3	
58–63 [Men]	+0.5	−0.9	−1.6	< 1	-----	191	62.9	
64–69	−2.1[d]	−2.5[d]	−4.6[d]	< 1	-----	306	77.3	
70–75	−1.3[d]	−2.4[d]	−4.4	1.61	-----	256	71.2	
76–81	−0.1	−0.7	−5.6[d]	4.24*	.0367	223	72.0	(6.8, 19.4) (13.3, 19.4)
82–87	0.0	−2.5	−6.0[d]	3.34*	.067	93	60.4	(13.3, 19.4)
88–95	−0.8	−0.9	----	< 1	-----	26		

* $p < .05$, ** $p < .01$, *** $p < .001$

a, b, c. These are means, the Longitudinal Intervals were, respectively, 5.5 to 9.5 years, 11.5 to 16.7 years, and 17.4 to 23.4 years.

d. Indicates change score within an age group-longitudinal interval combination was significantly, $p < .05$, different from zero.

Note. See "Note" of Table 7.

Hallucinatory-Vividness of Daydreaming

This scale indicated how much the daydreams of the individual seem life-like and real. Items of this scale ask for judgments regarding how hard it is to distinguish daydreams from real life, how real the images and voice seem, and the extent to which they are tempted to interact with the people who appear in their daydreams.

Age differences. Sex X Age ANOVA found a significant age effect (9% of variance accounted for) and a signifiant interaction, see Table 5. All age groups had means which were less than 11.4, interpretable as "usually not true;" 17–24 year olds had the greatest mean. For 25–34 years and older groups the means were substantially smaller than the 17–24 year olds, but not much different from each other. For women, increasing age showed no consistently decreasing means.

For men, there was a consistent decrease from 35 years old and older. The correlation with age was −.25 for both men and women.

Age changes. Analyses of variance of changes for the longitudinal intervals indicated only two significant effects, both in the 5.5–9.5 year interval, the effect of age on the longitudinal change ($F(5,738) = 7.46$, $p < .001$, partial eta squared = .048) and the effect of sex on the longitudinal change ($F(1,738) = 5.67$, $p < .05$, partial eta squared = .008). The age effect on change was the result of younger age groups showing decreases in hallucinatory-vividness while the older age groups reported mean increases. The sex effect occured because women showed a small decrease while men showed a small increase. The longitudinal change in hallucinatory-vividness of daydreaming was not significant, $p > .05$, for all three intervals (all $F(1,184–738) < 2.44$); likewise, for the age x sex interaction (all $F < 1.54$).

The longitudinal samples were reconstituted into six-year interval, age-at-later-testing groups, to maximize sample size. Sex significantly affected longitudinal change in the 34–39 year group within the 5.5–9.5 year longitudinal interval; women showed a very small decrease while men showed a small increase, see Table 9. When comparisons of hallucinatory-vividness in daydreaming scale changes were made between longitudinal intervals only the 46–52 year old age-at-later-testing group showed a significant difference between changes. Of the 30 longitudinal changes in Table 9, only two were significantly different from zero.

Summary. Both the longitudinal and cross sectional outcomes suggest that there was little in the way of hallucinatory-vivid daydreaming at any age and little change with age, even over 17.4–24.4 year intervals.

Summary and Discussion

The pattern suggested by these outcomes is that daydreaming, in terms of both frequency and absorption or dominance of attention show a gradual reduction with increased age. Young adults were likely to daydream frequently and to have their attention captured by daydreams; old adults were likely not to daydream and when they are having a daydream to be easily distracted from it; in between the young and the elderly we saw a gradual movement from one condition to the other. The pattern occurred both between individuals of different ages and with individuals as they aged. The intraindividual change in daydreaming frequency was clear and occurred at all ages; however, there was good evidence that these changes accelerated with age. The intraindividual change in absorption in daydreaming was less clear for younger adults but much stronger for older adults

Table 9. *Hallucinatory-Vividness of Daydreaming Scale, Maximum Age-at-Later-Testings Samples: Mean Change Scores (Later — Earlier) and Results of Analysis of Variance between Longitudinal Intervals for Change Scores within Each Age-at-Later-Testing*

Age-at-Later-Testing	Change in Score From When ___ Years Younger			Between Longitudinal Interval ANOVA Results				Significant $p < .05$ Contrasts
					Partial	– Error –		
Group (Yrs)	6.8[a]	13.3[b]	19.4[c]	*F*	Eta**2	*df*	*MS*	
28–33	−1.1	----	----	-----	-----	---	----	
34–39	−0.8	−0.6	----	< 1	-----	106	21.8	
40–45	−0.2	+1.0	----	< 1	-----	201	21.0	
46–51	−0.5	−0.4	+1.3	2.05	-----	266	20.8	(6.8, 19.4)
52–57	−0.7	+0.1	+0.3	< 1	-----	251	30.9	
58–63	+0.1	−0.6	−0.3	< 1	-----	311	27.0	
64–69	−0.7	−0.7	−0.9	< 1	-----	328	26.1	
70–75	0.0	−0.7	−0.7	< 1	-----	295	26.1	
76–81	+1.0[d]	+1.0	−0.2	< 1	-----	261	26.3	
82–87	+1.8[d]	−0.1	+0.8	1.79	-----	110	23.7	
88–95	+1.9	+2.9	----	< 1	-----	33	52.1	

* $p < .05$, ** $p < .01$, *** $p < .001$

a, b, c. These are means, the Longitudinal Intervals were, respectively, 5.5 to 9.5 years, 11.5 to 16.7 years, and 17.4 to 23.4 years.

d. Indicates change score within an age group-longitudinal interval combination was significant, $p < .05$, from zero.

Note. See "Note" of Table 7.

or, more precisely, as individuals became old from middle-age. The occurrence of daydreams of an hallucinatory or vivid nature were uncommon at all ages, becoming more uncommon after age 24 years with some further reduction thereafter. Because of the uncommonness of hallucinatory-vivid daydreams there was little room for intraindividual change and few age groups showed much change.

Temporal Setting

The temporal setting of thoughts — the relative number concerned with the past, the present, or the future — in general and daydreams in particular would seem to be a function of the age of the adult individual (Kastenbaum 1982; Thomae 1991, 1992; Wigdor 1980) — a young adult has a long future and a short past and an old-old adult has a short future and a long past. Cameron (1972,

1977–1978) using a consciousness sampling technique on large community-based, adult lifespan samples found no evidence that the young adults thought less about the past than the older adults. Thoughts about the present and the past were, respectively, the most and second most likely at any age. There was evidence of a moderate decrease in thoughts about the future and a moderate increase in thoughts about the present from age 20 to age 65+ years. Surprisingly, teenagers showed the greatest proportion of thoughts of the past and the smallest proportion of thoughts about the present. There was evidence presented that these results may be confined to Americans. Ghanians and Iranians found future-oriented thoughts most likely and presented-oriented thoughts as least likely; past-oriented thoughts increased while future-oriented and present-oriented thoughts decreased with age. The shortening of one's future perspective in the elderly has, in general, been found (Thomae 1992; Wigdor 1980). However, that shortening is not overwhelming in terms of the proportion of individuals who evidence shortening nor in terms of the years that they look ahead if they have foreshortened their future perspective. Further, Cameron et al. (1977–78) has found a greater percentage (27%) of older adults thoughts extend more than five years into the future than any younger age group. As might be expected, Cameron found that older adults had a greater percentage (20%) of thoughts that extended more than five years into the past. However, other variables such as health, age of death of parents, desire for change, positive or negative view of the future, and control of one's activities play important moderating roles. "A dominant past orientation may be representative for isolated, lonely elderly. For the majority of active community aged, futurity is still an important aspect of their lives (Thomae 1992, p. 115)." Because current concerns and unfinished business are an important source of daydream content then it would be reasonable that the temporal orientation, most likely the present, of those concerns would be expressed in daydreams. Other evidence points to a modest reduction in future orientation and a modest increase in past orientation in the elderly.

Results

Present-Oriented Daydreams. This scale measured the extent to which the daydreams of the individual were set in the present. For example, items ask how much daydream events relate to their current life, relate to their current problems, and show a preference for the presence over the past or future.

Age differences. The Sex X Age ANOVA found a significant age effect (1% of variance accounted for) and a signifiant sex effect (2% of variance accounted for), see Table 5. The middle-aged groups showed somewhat greater means than young and elderly groups. Women had greater mean values than men in all age groups. Clearly, age differences account for little variance in the likelihood of daydreaming about the present — all means were at "usually true for me" values.

Age changes. Analyses of variance of changes for the longitudinal intervals indicated that the interval resulted in a significant decrease in present-oriented daydreams scores for the 5.5–9.5 year interval ($M = -0.4$, $F(1,637) = 4.47$, $p < .05$, partial eta squared = .007), but not the 11.5–16.7 year interval ($F < 1$) and the 17.4–23.4 year interval $F(1,129) = 3.83$, $p < .06$). Magnitude of longitudinal changes was determined by age-at-1st-testing only for the 11.5–16.7 year interval ($F(4,442) = 2.71$, $p < .05$, partial eta squared = .024; the 25–34 and 65–74 year old groups showed increases and the in-between age groups showed decreases in present-oriented daydreams).

The longitudinal samples were reconstituted into six-year-interval, maximize sample size, age-at-later-testing groups. When comparisons of present-oriented daydreaming scale changes were made among longitudinal intervals, see Table 10, only the 34–39 year age-at-later-testing group showed a significant difference among the changes. Of the 29 longitudinal changes reported in Table 10, only seven were significantly different from zero. In general, the pattern of longitudinal changes was consistent with the age differences in that movement to middle-age from the 20's and 30's increased the present temporal setting in daydreams and movement from middle-age to old age decreased the present temporal setting in daydreams.

Future in Daydreams

This scale measured the extent to which the daydreams of the individual were set in the future. For example, items ask how much daydream events involve thinking ahead, about what might happen in the future, and their lives in the future.

Age differences. The Sex X Age ANOVA found a significant age effect (8% of variance accounted for) and a signifiant sex effect, see Table 5. Group means decreased with increased age for both men and women. Women had greater mean values than men in all age groups. The correlation with age was −.27 for women and −.31 for men. Age differences showed a decrease in futuristic daydreaming with increased age.

Age changes. Analyses of variance of changes for the longitudinal intervals indicated that the interval resulted in a significant decrease in future in daydreams scores for the 5.5–9.5 year interval ($M = -0.7$, $F(1,669) = 8.33$, $p < .01$,

Table 10. *Present-Oriented Daydreaming Scale, Maximum Age-at-Later-Testings Samples: Mean Change Scores (Later — Earlier) and Results of Analysis of Variance between Longitudinal Intervals for Change Scores within Each Age-at-Later-Testing*

Age-at-Later-Testing	Change in Score From When ___ Years Younger			Between Longitudinal Interval ANOVA Results				Significant $p <$ .05 Contrasts
					Partial	– Error –		
Group (Yrs)	6.8[a]	13.3[b]	19.4[c]	*F*	Eta**2	*df*	*MS*	
28–33	+1.9[d]	--	--	----	---	--	--	
34–39	0.0	+4.5[d]	--	8.32**	.0855	89	22.9	
40–45	−0.1	+0.4	--	< 1	---	186	25.4	
46–51	−0.5	−0.2	+0.7	< 1	---	230	21.2	
52–57	−0.6	−1.1	−0.6	< 1	---	218	18.7	
58–63	−0.1	−1.3[d]	+0.3	2.40	---	278	21.4	(6.8, 13.3)
64–69	−0.5	−0.8	−2.0[d]	1.22	---	304	22.5	
70–75	−0.8[d]	−0.9	−2.1	< 1	---	264	22.8	
76–81 [Women]	+1.0	+1.5	--	< 1	---	63	20.4	
76–81 [Men]	−1.0	−1.5[d]	−1.7	< 1	---	171	32.0	
82–87	0.0	−0.2	−0.1	< 1	---	90	18.6	
88–95	−1.9[d]	--	--	----	---	--	--	

* $p < .05$, ** $p < .01$, *** $p < .001$

a, b, c. These are means, the longitudinal interval were, respectively, 5.5 to 9.5 years, 11.5 to 16.7 years, and 17.4 to 23.4 years.

d. Indicates change score within an age group-longitudinal interval combination was significantly, $p < .05$, different from zero.

Note. See "Note" of Table 7.

partial eta squared = .012), the 11.5–16.7 year interval ($M = -1.0$, F(1,467 = 11.78, $p < .01$, partial eta squared = .025) but not the 17.4–23.4 year interval (F < 1). However, age-at-first-testing did determine the level of decrease for the 17.4–23.4 year longitudinal interval ($F(2,139) = 4.83$, p < .01, partial eta squared = .065); the 25–34 year old group showed an increase ($M = 2.2$) while the 35–44 and 45–54 year old groups showed a decrease ($M = -1.8$ and -1.0, respectively).

The longitudinal samples were reconstituted into six-year-interval, maximum sample size, age-at-later-testing groups. When comparisons of future in daydreams scale changes were made among longitudinal intervals, see Table 11, the 64–69 and 70–75 year age-at-later-testing group showed a significant difference among the changes. Of the 30 longitudinal changes reported in Table 11, only six were significantly different from zero. Both age differences and age changes point to less daydreaming about the future with increased age, and the greatest decreases occurred for individuals as they became 64 or 65 years and older.

Table 11. *Future in Daydreams Scale, Maximum Age-at-Later-Testings Samples: Mean Change Scores (Later — Earlier) and Results of Analysis of Variance between Longitudinal Intervals for Change Scores within Each Age-at-Later-Testing*

Age-at-Later-Testing	Change in Score From When ___ Years Younger			Between Longitudinal Interval ANOVA Results				Significant $p < .05$ Contrasts
Group (Yrs)	6.8[a]	13.3[b]	19.4[c]	*F*	Partial Eta**2	-Error- *df*	*MS*	
28–33	−1.4	----	----	-------	-----	---	----	
34–39	+0.2	−1.4	----	1.00	-----	100	29.1	
40–45 [Women]	−0.4	+2.1	----	2.95	-----	84	39.2	
40–45 [Men]	−1.2	−1.6	----	< 1	-----	110	33.8	
46–51	−0.6	−0.2	+0.8	< 1	-----	238	26.9	
52–57	−0.6	−0.5	−0.8	< 1	-----	238	33.2	
58–63	−0.8	−0.1	+0.7	< 1	-----	295	35.2	
64–69	−0.6	−2.4[d]	+0.4	3.86*	.0248	304	34.8	(6.8, 13.3)(13.3, 19.4)
70–75	+0.1	−1.4[d]	−2.7[d]	3.83*	.0268	278	33.4	(6.8, 19.4)
76–81	−1.4[d]	−0.9	−1.5	< 1	-----	243	31.1	
82–87	−1.7[d]	−4.0[d]	−2.5	1.82	-----	97	29.5	
88–95	+1.7	−1.7	----	2.43	-----	28	21.5	

* $p < .05$, ** $p < .01$, *** $p < .001$

a, b, c. These are means, the longitudinal interval were, respectively, 5.5 to 9.5 years, 11.5 to 16.7 years, and 17.4 to 23.4 years.

d. Indicates change score within an age group-longitudinal interval combination was significantly, $p < .05$, different from zero.

Note. See "Note" of Table 7.

Past in Daydreams

This scale measured the extent to which the daydreams of the individual were set in the past. For example, items querried how often daydream events relate to their immediate and distant past, relate to their past experiences, relate to their youth, and show a preference for the past over the present or future.

Age differences. The Sex X Age ANOVA found a significant age effect (2% of variance accounted for) and a signifiant sex effect, see Table 5. The middle-aged groups showed somewhat smaller means than young and elderly groups. Women had somewhat greater mean values than men in all but one age group.

Age changes. Analyses of variance on changes for the longitudinal intervals resulted in only one significant and two near-significant effects. Magnitude of longitudinal changes was determined by age-at-1st-testing for the 5.5–9.5 year interval ($F(5,686) = 2.71$, $p < .05$, partial eta squared = .016). The changes were as expected from the cross-sectional means, younger groups decreased while middle-aged and young-old groups increased in daydreaming about the past.

The longitudinal samples were reconstituted into six-year interval, maximize sample size, age-at-later-testing groups. When comparisons of past in daydreaming scale changes were made among longitudinal intervals, the 70–75 and 76–81 year age-at-later-testing groups showed a significant difference among the changes, see Table 12. Of the 30 longitudinal changes reported in Table 12, only six were significantly different from zero. While age differences and age changes were consistent in the sense that young and old daydreamed more about the past that middle-aged adults the change from middle-age to old age was particularly salient. Table 12 shows significant increases and generally larger increases in likelihood of daydreaming about the past for longer longitudinal intervals.

Comparisons Among Temporal Setting Scales

Cross-sectional sample. A measure of the relative tendency to daydream about the past, present, and future was obtained by observing the relative magnitudes of the means of the scales measuring past, present, and future settings in daydreams. To determine if the differences in the means, see Table 5, were statistically different an Age Group by Sex by Temporal Scales (repeated) ANOVA was carried out. A significant effect occurred for the difference between temporal scales ($F(2,5346) = 48.71$, $p < .001$, partial eta squared = .018), for the effect of sex on this difference ($F(2,5346) = 3.02$, $p < .05$, partial eta squared = .001), and the effect of age on this difference ($F(12,5346) = 21.51$, $p < .001$, partial eta squared = .046). The order was future ($M = 25.9$), present ($M = 24.8$), and past ($M = 23.8$). Both men and women showed this order. However, women showed a greater difference (1.3) than men (0.7) between the future and present, but women showed a smaller difference (0.7) than men (1.5) between the present and the past. When the differences among the temporal setting scales was examined at each age group that differences were significant for all age groups except the 65–74 year olds. The future was more prominent than the past until age 65–74 years where it became equally prominent; at 75–84 years the past became more prominent than the future. The future was more prominent than the present until age 45–54 where it became equally prominent until age 75–84 where it became less prominent. The present was more prominent than the past from 25 to 64 years old and was less prominent in the 75–84 year olds.

Table 12. *Past in Daydreams Scale, Maximum Age-at-Later-Testings Samples: Mean Change Scores (Later — Earlier) and Results of Analysis of Variance between Longitudinal Intervals for Change Scores within Each Age-at-Later-Testing*

Age-at-Later-Testing	Change in Score From When ___ Years Younger			Between Longitudinal Interval ANOVA Results				Significant $p<.05$ Contrasts
					Partial	– Error –		
Group (Yrs)	6.8[a]	13.3[b]	19.4[c]	*F*	Eta**2	*df*	*MS*	
28–33	–0.8	----	----	-------	-----	---	----	
34–39	–1.0	–0.7	----	< 1	-----	97	23.8	
40–45	0.0	0.0	----	< 1	-----	197	32.6	
46–51	+0.1	–0.7	–0.4	< 1	-----	242	31.3	
52–57 [Women]	–1.3	–2.2[d]	–4.2	1.29	-----	91	30.2	
52–57 [Men]	+0.6	+0.7	+1.0	< 1	-----	143	31.8	
58–63	+0.3	+0.7	+0.3	< 1	-----	296	29.8	
64–69	+0.9[d]	+0.9	+1.5	< 1	-----	319	32.3	
70–75	+1.0[d]	+2.8[d]	+1.3	3.08*	.0209	289	32.4	(6.8, 13.3)
76–81	+0.2	+1.8[d]	+3.6[d]	5.28**	.0412	246	32.2	(6.8, 13.3)(6.8, 19.4)
82–87	+0.9	+1.9	–0.4	< 1	-----	101	36.1	
88–95	+1.4	+3.4	----	< 1	-----	33	37.0	

* $p<.05$, ** $p<.01$, *** $p<.001$

a, b, c. These are means, the longitudinal interval were, respectively, 5.5 to 9.5 years, 11.5 to 16.7 years, and 17.4 to 23.4 years.

d. Indicates change score within an age group-longitudinal interval combination was significantly, $p<.05$, different from zero.

Note. See "Note" of Table 7.

Longitudinal sample. A measure of the relative change over time in the tendency to daydream about the past, present, and future was obtained by comparing the magnitude of the mean changes for the scales measuring past, present, and future settings in daydreams. To determine if the mean changes were statistically different an Age-at-1st-testing by Sex by Temporal scales (repeated) ANOVA was carried out for each longitudinal period. Significant effects occurred in the 11.5–16.7 year interval for the difference among the temporal scales ($F(2,796)=5.27$, $p<.01$, partial eta squared = .013) and in the 17.4–23.4 year interval for the interaction of age on that difference ($F(6,290)=2.86$, $p<.05$, partial eta squared = .056). For the 11.5–16.7 year interval the present and future daydream setting showed negative mean changes (*M*'s = –0.7 and –0.8, respectively) and past daydream settings showed a positive mean change ($M=+0.7$). In the 17.4–23.4 year interval the age interaction resulted from the previously described tendency of the past setting to increase in the oldest individuals while the future setting tended to decrease.

Summary and Discussion

The pattern for both cohort differences and age changes was, as follows: the likelihood of daydreams with a future temporal setting decreased with increased age in adulthood; the likelihood of a past temporal setting decreased then increased with age; the likelihood of a present temporal setting increased then decreased with age; the differences in magnitude among the scales were small at all ages except for the 17–24 year olds where the future was clearly greatest. Thus, one's age does influence the time setting of one's daydreams and changes in age result in changes in the likelihood of a time setting. As an expression of the individual's current concerns the future setting appears to be the most strongly influenced by age; sometimes because of an increased orientation to present — brought about by increased unfinished business or mounting daily concerns — and sometimes because of an increased orientation to the past. Changes in the temporal orientation of a person's daydreams may thus provide cues to the changes in the degree to which they must deal with unfinished business and the press and immediacy of their current concerns.

Emotional Reactions

Three important components of emotion are expression, experience, and control (Gross, Carstensen, Pasupathi et al. 1997; Schulz 1985). Emotional responses to, and in, daydreams are an expression of emotion in terms of physiological response or arousal and an experience of emotion, i.e., an affective or feeling state associated with or brought about by daydream. Control of emotions associated with daydreams is minimal, in the sense that daydreams and the emotions associated with them occur spontaneously. Control could be instituted by cutting off the daydream through shifting attention to something in the environment or by deliberately thinking of something else. These control actions could reduce, but not eliminate, the emotions engendered by and in the daydreams. Emotions may be further classified as positive (desireable or pleasant) and negative (undesireable or unpleasant) (Filip 1996). Theories of emotion and speculations regarding life experiences in general, and emotional experiences in particular, as well as putative changes associated with physiological responses associated with aging lead to conflicting expectations regarding emotional experiences and the relative likelihood of positive and negative emotional experiences (Filip 1996; Magai & McFadden 1996; Schultz 1985). Experimental studies have been somewhat clearer.

Gross et al. (1997) studied that relationship of emotional experience, emotional expression and emotional control in divergent adult lifespan samples. They found increases in positive emotional experience and selective decreases in negative emotional experience. Also, found was evidence of greater emotional control, especially with regard to effective regulation of the inner experience of emotion — as opposed to external expression — with greater regulation resulting in decreasing the experience of negative emotions. Because daydreams have an essentially uncontrolled or spontaneous nature this position could lead to the expectation of a greater level of negative emotional experience in daydreams than in consciously controlled aspects of mental life. Other studies, see Filip, (1996) and Gross et al. (1997) for a review, found decreases with increased age in both positive and negative emotion experience and intensity of those experienced emotions. Costa and McCrae (1988) report facets of personality measuring "positive emotions," "hostility," and "depression" which were negatively correlated with age in a cross-sectional sample — six year longitudinal and cross-sequential samples failed to show any decrease on these facets. In studies where individuals were asked to recall and re-experience intense emotional life episodes no age differences were observed in rated intensity of the experienced emotion and in the ability to re-experience the episode.

Results

Positive Reactions in Daydreaming. This scale indicated positive emotional and affective responses to, and tone of, the daydreams recalled. Items were concerned with daydreams which aroused and excited, which brought a smile to their face, which had pleasant emotions, and which thrilled the daydreamer.

Age differences. The Age X Sex ANOVA yielded significant age (10% of variance accounted for) and sex effects, but not their interaction, see Table 5. Decreased means occurred with increased age — means decrease from levels somewhat above, to levels somewhat below, "usually true for me" and women reported about 5% higher levels than men. The scale correlation with age was −.27 for women and −.38 for men.

Age changes. Analyses of variance of changes for the longitudinal intervals showed a significant, $p < .001$, decrease for the 5.5–9.5 ($M = -1.2$, $F(1{,}664) = 23.06$, partial eta squared = .034), the 11.5–16.7 ($M = -1.8$, $F(1{,}456) = 34.57$, partial eta squared = .070), and for the 17.4–23.4 ($M = -2.6$, $F(1, 189) = 19.70$, partial eta squared = .094) year intervals. The only other significant effect was sex for the 5.5–9.5 year interval ($F(1,664) = 5.87$, $p < .05$, partial eta squared = .009); women showed a greater mean decrease (-1.7) than men (-0.6) — the magnitude of the sex difference remained for both longer intervals

The longitudinal samples were reconstituted into six-year interval, age-at-later-testing groups to maximized sample sizes. Sex significantly affected longitudinal change in the 34–39 year old group within the 5.5–9.5 year longitudinal interval and the 58–63 year groups within the 5.5–9.5 and 11.5–16.7 year longitudinal intervals; women showed a large decrease while men showed a small increase or decrease, see Table 13. When comparisons of positive reactions in daydreaming scale changes were made between longitudinal intervals only two age-at-later-testing groups had significant contrasts between the changes, 58–63 years [men] and 64–69 years. Of the 33 longitudinal changes reported in Table 13, 16 were significantly different from zero. Clearly, age changes followed age differences and as groups, men especially, got older the magnitude of the decrease in positive reactions in daydreaming tended to become greater.

Frightened Reactions in Daydreaming

This scale indicated negative emotional and affective responses to, and tone of, daydreams. Items were concerned with daydreams which depressed or frightened, which upset, which terrified, which were unpleasant, and which resulted in muscular tension.

Age differences. The Age X Sex ANOVA yielded significant age (10% of variance accounted for) and sex effects, but not their interaction, see Table 5. Means decreased rapidly from 17–24 to 35–44 years and remained stable thereafter. Fightened reactions were at the "usually not true for me" level, except for the 17–24 year olds and 25–34 year old women which were closer to the "usually true" level. Women showed greater means than men. The scale correlation with age was −.26 for women and −.28 for men.

Age changes. Analyses of variance of changes for the longitudinal intervals produced the following significant effects, $p < .05$, on changes; all others were not significant: (a) age-at-first-testing for the 5.5–9.5 year interval ($F(5,697) = 2.26$, partial eta squared = .016), (b) sex for the 11.5–16.7 year interval ($F(1,474) = 5.16$, partial eta squared = .011), and (c) Age X Sex interaction for the 17.4–23.4 year interval ($F(3,179) = 2.77$, partial eta squared = .044). The differential effect of age for the 5.5–9.5 year interval was the most likely the result of a decease for the 25–34 year olds ($M = -0.8$) and an increase for the 75–84 year olds ($M = 2.1$); from 35 to 74 years little change occurred. For the 11.5–16.7 year

Table 13. *Positive Reactions in Daydreaming Scale, Maximum Age-at-Later-Testings Samples: Mean Change Scores (Later — Earlier) and Results of Analysis of Variance between Longitudinal Intervals for Change Scores within Each Age-at-Later-Testing*

Age-at-Later-Testing	Change in Score From When ___ Years Younger			Between Longitudinal Interval ANOVA Results				Significant $p < .05$ Contrasts
					Partial	– Error –		
Group (Yrs)	6.8[a]	13.3[b]	19.4[c]	*F*	Eta**2	*df*	*MS*	
28–33	+0.8	----	----	-----	-----	---	----	
34–39	–0.5	+1.4	----	1.29	-----	101	31.3	
40–45	–1.3[d]	–1.5[d]	----	< 1	-----	184	24.5	
46–51	–0.9[d]	–2.1[d]	+0.1	2.34	-----	235	26.1	
52–57	–0.7	–1.1	–2.6[d]	1.52	-----	246	29.6	
58–63 [Women]	–2.7[d]	–3.7[d]	–0.8[e]	< 1	-----	92	50.3	
58–63 [Men]	–0.4	–0.5	–3.8[d]	3.02	-----	207	36.3	(6.8, 19.4)(13.3, 19.4)
64–69	–0.8	–2.1[d]	–3.3[d]	3.62*	.0233	303	30.3	(6.8, 19.4)
70–75	–0.8	–1.0	–3.0[d]	1.46	-----	257	37.5	
76–81	–1.2[d]	–1.5[d]	–3.6[d]	1.64	-----	232	37.6	
82–87	–1.1	–3.5[d]	–2.8	1.48	-----	116	47.9	
88–95	–1.3	–2.2	----	< 1	-----	30	33.1	

* $p < .05$, ** $p < .01$, *** $p < .001$

a, b, c. These are means, the Longitudinal Intervals were, respectively, 5.5 to 9.5 years. 11.5 to 16.7 years, and 17.4 to 23.4 years.

d. Indicates change score within an age group-longitudinal interval combination was significantly, p < .05, different from zero.

e. $N < 10$.

Note. See "Note" of Table 7.

interval women showed a decrease ($M = –0.9$) and men showed a small increase ($M = 0.4$). The Age X Sex interaction for the 17.4–23.4 year interval was difficult to interpret. Women showed greater *absolute* mean changes than men, respectively, 2.2 and 0.7 — the sum of the mean changes was essentially zero — with the greatest difference between men and women in the 25–34 year old (–4.9) and 55–64 year old (2.3) groups.

The longitudinal samples were reconstituted into six-year interval, age-at-later-testing groups to maximized sample sizes. Sex significantly affected longitudinal change in the 34–39 year, 58–63 year, and 64–69 year old groups within the 5.5–9.5 interval; women showed a large absolute change while men showed a small absolute change, see Table 14. When comparisons of frightened reactions to daydreams scale changes were made between longitudinal intervals no significant differences between longitudinal periods were found. Of the 35 longitudinal changes reported in Table 14, only two were significantly different from zero. There was little evidence for age differences and age changes in frightened reactions in and to daydreams except for the younger ages. There was some suggestion that reaching old age may somewhat increase frightened reactions intraindividually. However, levels tended to be low at all ages and indicated little in the way of frightening daydreams.

Comparisons Between Emotional Reaction Scales

Cross-sectional sample. A measure of the relative tendency of daydreams to have positive and negative emotional responses was obtained by observing the magnitude of the means of the positive and negative reaction scales. To determine if the differences in the means, see Table 5, were statistically different an Age Group by Sex by Emotional Reaction Scales (repeated) ANOVA was carried out. A significant effect occurred for the difference between emotional reaction scales ($F(1,2750) = 2774.02$, $p < .001$, partial eta squared = .502) and the effect of age on this difference ($F(6,2750) = 8.58$, $p < .001$, partial eta squared = .018). Positive reactions ($M = 22.7$) were much more likely than negative reactions ($M = 13.0$); both men and women responded this way. The difference between emotional reaction scales was significant for all age groups.

Positive reactions exceeded negative reactions in decreasing amounts as the age groups increased from 25–44 years ($M_{\text{Difference}} = 11.5$) to 75–84 years ($M_{\text{Difference}} = 7.4$); the 17–24 year old group's mean difference was 9.3.

Longitudinal sample. A measure of the relative change, over time, in the tendency to have daydreams with positive or negative emotional responses was obtained by comparing the magnitude of the mean changes for these two scales. To determine if the mean changes were statistically different an Age-at-1st-testing by Sex by Emotional Reaction Scales (repeated) ANOVA was carried out for each longitudinal period. A significant repeated measures factor effect occurred for all longitudinal intervals: 5.5–9.5 years ($F(1,601) = 18.11$, $p < .001$, partial eta squared = .029); 11.5–16.7 years ($F(1,407) = 6.90$, $p < .01$, partial eta squared = .017); and 17.4–23.4 years ($F(1,158) = 4.26$, $p < .05$, partial eta squared = .026). For the 5.5–9.5 year interval, age-at-1st-testing determined the difference between the mean changes of the two emotional reaction scales ($F(5,601) = 2.87$, $p < .05$, partial eta squared = .023). For the three intervals there was a decrease (-1.2, −1.2, and −1.5, respectively) for the positive reactions and little change for the negative reactions (0.2, –0.1, and –0.1, respectively). For the 5.5–9.5 year interval, age group influenced the difference (positive minus negative reactions)

Table 14. *Frightened Reactions to Daydreaming Scale, Maximum Age-at-Later-Testings Samples: Mean Change Scores (Later — Earlier) and Results of Analysis of Variance between Longitudinal Intervals for Change Scores within Each Age-at-Later-Testing*

Age-at-Later-Testing	Change in Score From When ___ Years Younger			Between Longitudinal Interval ANOVA Results				Significant $p<.05$ Contrasts
Group (Yrs)	6.8[a]	13.3[b]	19.4[c]	*F*	Partial Eta**2	– Error – *df*	*MS*	
28–33	−1.3	----	----	-----	-----	---	----	[None]
34–39	−0.7	+0.2	----	< 1	-----	102	32.3	
40–45	−0.3	−0.4	----	< 1	-----	200	35.9	
46–51	−0.4	−0.8	+0.3	< 1	-----	248	29.2	
52–57	−0.8	−0.8	+0.3	< 1	-----	240	36.0	
58–63 [Women]	−1.4[d]	−0.5	−0.9[e]	< 1	-----	108	24.2	
58–63 [Men]	+0.4	−0.2	−1.8	1.42	-----	190	27.0	
64–69 [Women]	+1.4	+0.1	+0.3[e]	< 1	-----	104	32.1	
64–69 [Men]	−0.4	−0.3	−0.2	< 1	-----	209	23.3	
70–75	+0.2	+0.1	−1.1	< 1	-----	287	26.1	
76–81	+0.6	+1.2[d]	+1.2	< 1	-----	237	28.3	
82–87	+0.6	−0.7	+1.2	< 1	-----	105	37.3	
88–95	+1.0	----	----	-----	-----	---	----	

* p <.05, ** p <.01, *** p <.001

a, b, c. These are means, the Longitudinal Intervals were, respectively, was 5.5 to 9.5 years, 11.5 to 16.7 years, and 17.4 to 23.4 years.

d. Indicates change score within an age group-longitudinal interval combination was significantly, *p* <.05, different from zero.

e. *N* <10.

Note. See "Note" of Table 7.

between the two emotional reaction scale mean changes; with similar values for the 25–34, 45–54, and 55–64 year old groups (0.5, −0.8, −0.5, respectively) and disparate values for the 35–44, 65–74, and 75–84 year groups (−1.6, −2.4, −3.6, respectively).

Summary and Discussion

It is clear, both cross-sectionally and longitudinally, that age influences emotions in, and to, daydreams. Positive reactions dominate at all ages with less dominance with increased age. Relative to 17–24 year olds, both positive and negative emotional reactions decrease. For negative reactions, age has little effect once early middle-age has arrived. For positive reactions, age acts to reduce such reactions until old age. In the oldest individuals, change in positive reactions were markedly greater than change in negative reactions. Increased age seems to result in less emotional experience associated with daydreams which are spontaneous and less subject to control. Furthermore, these results seem to be at odds with emotional experience in situations where control can be exercised. In those studies positive emotions seem to remain high and relatively unchanged with increased age while negative emotions were reduced (Gross et al. 1997).

Imagery

Visual mental imagery may be partitioned into four aspects: image generation, image maintenance, image inspection, and image transformation (Dror & Kosslyn 1994). Auditory mental imagery can easily be conceived as having generation, maintenance, and transformation; inspection may be possible but seems less likely, more difficult, and more problematical. Images must be generated and maintained during a daydream. Image transformation may occur while image inspection is rationally possible but seems unlikely. Dror and Kosslyn (1994) show clearly that the older adult has impairment of image generation and transformation and weak impairment of image maintenance — impairment was defined as disproportionate slowing and error-making with increased difficulty. Johnson and Rybash (1993) in their review found considerable evidence for age effects on image transformation — usually the mental rotation task — but suggest that the outcomes were the result of an "attention shift" artifact in the image transformation tasks because of the lack of an age effect in a mental rotation experiment where no attention shift was required. Johnson and Rybash report additional studies by Johnson where image generation was not particularly age sensitive but image maintenance was strongly age sensitive. Finally, in a survey study, Giray, Roodin, Altkin et al. (1985) found that 60–94 year olds reported more frequent eidetic imagery than 20–59 year olds. This was a clearly anomalous in terms of its outcome and, because eidetic images represent the most vivid and "true" of generated visual images, it is in need of replication and may be the result of sampling bias. Despite Giray et al. (1985), the age effects reported in the literature on image generation, maintenance and transformation in the elderly would predict reduced imagery in the daydreams of the aged.

Results

Visual Imagery In Daydreams. This scale reported the extent and clarity of visual imagery in daydreams. Items were concerned with daydreams which were like "pictures in my mind," which incuded seeing things and people moving around, were in color, and which contained "scenes."

Age differences. The Age X Sex ANOVA yielded only a significant age effect (8% of variance accounted for), see Table 5. Decreased means occurred with increased age — means decreased from levels somewhat above, to levels somewhat below, "usually true for me." The correlation with age was −.28 for women and −.30 for men.

Age changes. Analyses of variance of changes for the longitudinal intervals showed a significant, $p < .05$, decrease for the 5.5–9.5 year interval ($M = -0.6$, $F(1{,}615) = 5.85$, partial eta squared = .009) and the 17.4–23.4 year interval ($M = -1.1$, $F(1{,}175) = 4.22$, partial eta squared = .024. The effects of age, sex, and their interaction on longitudinal changes were not significant, $p > .05$.

The longitudinal samples were reconstituted into six-year-interval, age-at-later-testing groups to maximized sample sizes. Sex significantly affected longitudinal change in the the 46–51 year group within the 11.5–16.7 year longitudinal interval; women showed a large decrease while men showed a small decrease, see Table 15. When comparisons of visual imagery in daydreams scale changes were made between longitudinal intervals no significant effects were obtained. Of the 30 longitudinal changes reported in Table 15, five were significantly different from zero.

Summary. Although the 11.5–16.7 year longitudinal interval failed to show a significant decrease in visual imagery in daydreams the longer and shorter intervals did show significant, but small decreases. When individual age groups were examined positive changes indicated in the cohort differences were evident and in one case significant. Thus, age effects on visual imagery seem to be real, but small.

Auditory Imagery in Daydreams

This scale reported the extent and apparent clarity of auditory imagery in daydreams. Items were concerned with daydreams which included music, which were like listening to the radio, which included voices, and which included conversations between the individual and others.

Age differences. The Age X Sex ANOVA yielded only a significant age effect (11% of variance accounted for), see Table 5. Decreased means occurred with increased age — means decreased from levels somewhat below "usually true for me" to levels somewhat above "usually not true for me." The correlation with age was −.27 for women and −.38 for men.

Table 15. *Visual Imagery in Daydreams Scale, Maximum Age-at-Later-Testings Samples: Mean Change Scores (Later — Earlier) and Results of Analysis of Variance between Longitudinal Intervals for Change Scores within Each Age-at-Later-Testing*

Age-at-Later-Testing	Change in Score From When ___ Years Younger			Between Longitudinal Interval ANOVA Results				Significant $p<.05$ Contrasts
					Partial	– Error –		
Group (Yrs)	6.8[a]	13.3[b]	19.4[c]	*F*	Eta**2	*df*	*MS*	
28–33	+0.5	----	----	-----	-----	---	----	[None]
34–39	−1.8[d]	−0.5	----	< 1	-----	94	40.0	
40–45	−1.0	−1.1	----	< 1	-----	175	48.9	
46–51 [Women]	−1.3	−3.2[d]	−1.4	< 1	-----	85	34.4	
46–51 [Men]	+0.4	+0.5	+1.7	< 1	-----	143	27.6	
52–57	−0.4	−0.7	−0.3	< 1	-----	228	35.6	
58–63	−0.7[d]	−0.5	−2.6[d]	1.43	-----	282	33.4	
64–69	0.0	0.0	−1.4	< 1	-----	287	31.8	
70–75	−0.1	+0.1	−0.6	< 1	-----	238	31.1	
76–81	−0.1	+0.3	−0.9	< 1	-----	223	33.9	
82–87	+1.5[d]	+0.2	----	< 1	-----	84	32.0	
88–95	+0.9	+0.7	----	< 1	-----	25	28.0	

* $p<.05$, ** $p<.01$, *** $p<.001$

a, b, c. These are means, the Longitudinal Intervals were, respectively, 5.5 to 9.5 years, 11.5 to 16.7 years, and 17.4 to 23.4 years.

d. Indicates change score within an age group-longitudinal interval combination was significantly, $p<.05$, different from zero.

Note. See "Note" of Table 7.

Age changes. Analyses of variance of changes for the longitudinal intervals showed a significant: (a) age-at-1st-testing effect ($F(5,598)= 4.99$, $p < .001$, partial eta squared = .040; the means for the 25–34 through 75–84 year old were, respectively, −1.4, −2.1, −0.8, 0.1, 0.2, 3.2) and Age X Sex interaction ($F(5,598) = 4.07$, $p<.01$, partial eta squared = .033; due primarily to 75–84 year old women having an increase of 6.5 and 75–84 year old men having a decrease of −0.1) for the 5.5–9.5 year interval and (b) effect of the longitudinal period ($M = -0.8$, $F(1,417) = 5.67$, $p<.05$, partial eta squared = .013) for the 11.5–16.7 year interval. No effects were significant for the 17.4–23.4 year interval, $p>.05$.

The longitudinal samples were reconstituted into six-year intervals age-at-later-testing groups to maximized sample sizes. Sex significantly affected longitudinal change in the the 82–87 year group within the 5.5–9.5 year longitudinal interval; women showed a large increase while men showed essentially no change, see Table 16. When comparisons of auditory imagery in daydreams scale changes were made between longitudinal intervals one significant effect — for the 58–63 year olds — was obtained, see Table 16. Of the 29 longitudinal changes reported in Table 16, 5 were significantly different from zero.

Table 16. *Auditory Imagery in Daydreams Scale, Maximum Age-at-Later-Testings Samples: Mean Change Scores (Later — Earlier) and Results of Analysis of Variance between Longitudinal Intervals for Change Scores within Each Age-at-Later-Testing*

Age-at-Later-Testing	Change in Score From When ___ Years Younger			Between Longitudinal Interval ANOVA Results				Significant $p<.05$ Contrasts
					Partial	– Error –		
Group (Yrs)	6.8[a]	13.3[b]	19.4[c]	*F*	Eta**2	*df*	*MS*	
28–33	–2.9	----	----	-----	-----	---	----	
34–39	–1.2	0.0	----	< 1	-----	89	40.0	
40–45	–1.8[d]	–2.0	----	< 1	-----	177	45.8	
46–51	–0.5	–1.9[d]	+0.1	1.59	-----	223	39.8	
52–57	–0.1	–0.7	–2.4	1.40	-----	208	42.1	
58–63	–0.6	–1.2	–4.7[d]	4.33*	.0338	248	40.6	(6.8, 19.4) (13.3, 19.4)
64–69	–0.5	–0.9	–1.0	< 1	-----	263	37.6	
70–75	+0.3	+0.5	–1.0	< 1	-----	232	39.3	
76–81	+0.5	+0.4	–0.7	< 1	-----	209	41.7	
82–87[e]	+1.8	+2.2	0.0	< 1	-----	90	51.9	
88–95	+3.8[d]	----	----	-----	-----	---	----	

* $p<.05$, ** $p<.01$, *** $p<.001$

a, b, c. These are means, the Longitudinal Intervals were, respectively, 5.5 to 9.5 years, 11.5 to 16.7 years, and 17.4 to 23.4 years.

d. Indicates change score within an age group–longitudinal interval combination was significantly, $p<.05$, different from zero.

e. Significant sex effect on longitudinal change for the 6.3 year interval; women's mean of 6.1 ($t(15)=3.07$, $p<.01$) and men's mean of –0.1 ($t(35)=-0.09$, $p>.05$). However, for the 13.3 year interval $N<10$ for both men and women so separate ANOVAs for men and women were not run.

Note. See "Note" for Table 7.

There was much discordance between the age changes observed here and the age differences displayed in Table 5. This was especially true because the change for the 17.4–23.4 year interval was not significant and because all the older age groups showed increases in auditory imagery for 5.5–9.5 year and 11.5–16.7 year longitudinal intervals. Hence the effect of age on auditory imagery remains less clear.

Comparisons Between Imagery Scales

Cross-sectional sample. A measure of the relative tendency of daydreams to have visual and auditory imagery in daydreams was obtained by comparing the magnitude of the means of the visual and auditory imagery scales. To determine if the differences in the means, see Table 5, were statistically different an Age Group by Sex by Imagery Scales (repeated) ANOVA was carried out. A significant effect occurred for the difference between imagery scales ($F(1,2571) = 1247.95$, $p < .001$, partial eta squared = .327), for the effect of sex on the difference ($F(1,2571) = 4.62$, $p < .05$, partial eta squared = .002), the effect of age on the difference ($F(6,2571) = 11.32$, $p < .001$, partial eta squared = .026), and the combined effect of the age and sex ($F(6,2571) = 2.47$, $p < .05$, partial eta squared = .006). Overall, visual imagery ($M = 20.8$) was greater than audiory imagery ($M = 16.2$); furthermore, this difference was significant for all age groups. Women had a smaller mean difference (4.4) between the scales than men (5.1); the sex difference was significant in the 45–54, 55–64, and 65–74 year old groups. The mean difference was smallest in the 17–24 year olds (3.1) and 75–84 year olds (4.4) and greatest in the 35–44 year olds (5.3). Women showed this pattern while men diverged from it — the 25–34 year olds had the second smallest mean difference between the scales.

Longitudinal sample. A measure of the relative change over time in the tendency to have daydreams with visual or auditory imagery was obtained by comparing the magnitude of the mean changes for these two scales. To determine if the mean changes were statistically different an Age-at-1st-testing by Sex by Daydream Imagery Scales (repeated) ANOVA was carried out for each longitudinal period. A single significant effect occurred, the interaction of imagery type, sex, and age in the 5.5–9.5 year interval ($F(5,538) = 2.94$, $p < .05$, partial eta squared = .027). The difference between the changes for the two imagery scales was less than one for both men and women between 25 and 54 years old at age-at-1st-testing and for men in the 55–64 year old group and for women in the 65–74 year old group. The greatest differences between the two scales occurred in the 55–64 year old women (−1.7), 65–74 year old men (−1.7), and the 75–84 year old women (−5.0) and men (+1.1). Note also that 75–84 year old women showed large longitudinal increases in visual imagery (2.6) and auditory imagery (7.6) while all other age group-sex combinations showed longitudinal decreases or essential no changes in either visual or auditory imagery.

Summary and Discussion

Both age differences and age changes were clear and mutually confirmatory for visual imagery in daydreams but not for auditory imagery in daydreams. Image generation, maintenance and transformation in daydreams was reduced with increased age for visual imagery. Auditory imagery seemed to be relatively low at all age groups and thus left little room for further age-related decreases. Longitudinally, there appeared to be in the oldest age groups a tendency to have a large increase in auditory imagery accompanied by some increase in visual imagery, especially in women. These disparate results need replication — if replicated then these increases in daydream imagery may be the result increased opportunity or occurrence of psychiatric disorders (auditory imagery often accompanies psychiatric disorders of a schizoid nature).

Daydream Content

Results

Problem Solving Daydreams. This scale indicated the occurrence of daydreams whose content provide, or are about, solutions to personal, practical, and intellectual problems of concern to the individual daydreamer. The items of the scale were about solving problems of family and friends, resolving "tricky situations," practical significance of their daydreams, surprise solutions and fresh approaches to problems, and alternate solutions to life's unfinished "things."

Age differences. The Age X Sex ANOVA yielded a significant age (2% of variance accounted for) and sex effect but not their interaction, see Table 5. Decreased means do not begin until age 55–64 years for women and age 45–54 years for men; for 75–84 year olds the means represent a decrease of 15% and 19%, respectively, for the women and men from their maximum values. The scale correlation with age was –.07 for women and –.20 for men. Women show greater means than men at all age groups; all means were at or somewhat below an "usually true for me" interpretation

Age changes. Analyses of variance of changes for the longitudinal intervals showed a significant change in the 5.5–9.5 year interval ($M = -1.1$, $F(1,707) = 17.92$, $p < .001$, partial eta squared = .025) and the 11.5–16.7 year interval ($M = -1.1$, $F(1,489) = 10.04$, $p < .01$, partial eta squared = .020), but not the 17.4–23.4 year interval ($M = -0.8$, $F(1,190) = 2.24$, $p > .05$). Age-at-1st-testing significantly influenced the level of change in the 11.5–16.7 year ($F(4,489) = 3.85$, $p < .01$, partial eta squared = .031) and 17.4–23.4 year intervals ($F(3,190) = 4.30$, $p < .01$, partial eta squared = .064. For the 11.5–16.7 year interval the changes went from positive to increasing negative — for the 25–34, 35–44, 45–54, 55–64, and 65–74 year old age groups the changes were, respectively, 0.9, –0.1, –1.4, –2.6, and –2.2. For the 17.4–23.4 year interval the changes went from decreasing positive to increasing negative — for the 25–34, 35–44, 45–54, and 55–64 year old age groups the changes were, respectively, 1.3, 0.8, –2.1, and –3.3. Sex and the Age X Sex interaction did not significantly affect change, $p > .05$.

Summary. Longitudinal changes appeared to track age differences suggesting little change until middle and old age. Longitudinal change for the longest interval seemed to be smaller than that of the two shorter intervals. Significant longitudinal changes found within age-at-later-testing groups suggests that intraindividual change may be larger than group differences.

Bizarre-Improbable Daydreams

This scale indicated the occurrence of daydreams whose content was of an unusual and unrealistic nature. The items of the scale were about "utter impossible situations," weird science fiction, "...things I know will never be possible for me," being a different person, not being realistic, and daydreams containing unusual people and events.

Age differences. The Age X Sex ANOVA yielded a significant age (6% of variance accounted for) and sex effect but not their interaction, see Table 5. Means decreased until a minimum in the 55–64 year old group then increased thereafter. The scale correlation with age was –.20 for both men and women. Women had lesser means than men; means were interpretable as intermediary between "usually true for me" and "usually not true for me" to "usually not true for me" at the minimum.

Age changes. Analyses of variance of changes for the longitudinal intervals showed a significant change for the 5.5–9.5 year interval ($M = +0.6$, $F(1,719) = 7.74$, $p < .01$, partial eta squared = .011) only. Age-at-1st-testing significantly affected change levels only in the 5.5–9.5 year interval ($F(5,719) = 3.09$, $p < .01$, partial eta squared = .021); the changes went from negative to increasing positive — for the 25–34, 35–44, 45–54, 55–64, 65–74, and 75–84 year old age groups the changes were, respectively, –0.7, 0.7, –0.2, 0.5, 0.8, and 2.3. Sex significantly affected change levels, ($M_{Women} = -0.7$, $M_{Men} = +0.5$), only in the 11.5–16.7 year interval ($F(1,486) = 4.87$, $p < .05$, partial eta squared = .010. The Age X Sex interaction did not significantly affect change levels, all $F\text{s} < 1.20$, $p > .05$.

Summary. The cross-sectional differences indicated a U-shaped age function. The longitudinal changes appear to be consistent with this function only for the older individuals, generally showing an increase. Except for young and old subjects the level of bizarre-improbable contents seems to be low.

Sexual Daydreams

This scale indicated the occurrence of daydreams whose content was of an erotic or sexually arousing nature. According to Leitenberg and Henning (1995) the items of this scale are more likely to be endorsed by men than women — women are more likely to fantasize about romantic and interpersonal love while men are more likely to fantasize about erotic or arousing relationships. The items of the scale were about physical attractiveness to the opposite sex, having sex, having intense sex, making love, "having sexual relations with someone I am fond of," arousing great desire in someone, and having daydreams sexually arouse you.

Age differences. The Age X Sex ANOVA yielded a significant age effect (29% of variance accounted for — by far the largest of all the content scales), sex effect (5% of variance accounted for — the largest of all the content scales), and their interaction (< 1% of variance accounted for), see Table 5. Decreased means occurred for both men and women at each succeeding decade, a decrease, from youngest group to oldest group, of 65% for women and 55% for men. Means went from an interpretation of "usually true for me" to somewhat less likely than "usually not true for me." Women had smaller means than men at each decade with increasing differences from 35 to 74 years of age. All items of this scale showed men having greater means than women in all age groups except Item 199 "I imagine myself to be physically attractive to people of the opposite sex;" Item 187 "My daydreams about love are so vivid, I actually feel they are occurring;" and Item 254 "While traveling on the train or bus my idle thoughts turn to love." For item 199 neither the sex effect nor the sex by age interaction was significant. For items 187 and 254, women had greater means than men in the 17–24 and 25–34 year old age groups. The scale correlation with age was −.56 for women and −.53 for men.

Age changes. Analyses of variance of changes for the longitudinal intervals showed a significant interval effect for 5.5–9.5 years ($M = -0.7$, $F(1,656) = 7.03$, $p < .01$, partial eta squared = .011), for 11.5–16.7 years ($M = -2.3$, $F(1,455) = 45.57$, $p < .001$, partial eta squared = .091), and for 17.4–23.4 years ($M = -4.0$, $F(1,185) = 34.11$, $p < .001$, partial eta squared = .156). Age-at-1st-testing significantly affected the level of change only for the 5.5–9.5 year longitudinal period

($F(5,656) = 3.04$, $p < .05$, partial eta squared = .023); the changes became less negative then positive with increasing age until they became positive — for the 25–34, 35–44, 45–54, 55–64, 65–74, and 75–84 year old groups, the changes were, respectively, −2.0. −1.4, −1.5, +0.1, −0.7, and +1.3.

Summary. Age had a very strong effect on the tendency to sexual daydreams of an erotic or arousing nature. Intraindividual change mirrored age differences and longer longitudinal intervals yield larger decreases than shorter intervals for virtually all ages.

Heroic Daydreams

This scale indicated the occurrence of daydreams whose content was of a heroic or self-sacrificing nature. The items of the scale were about preventing a political killing, volunteering for an important scientific experiment, saving someone from a fire or drowning or drug addiction or an highjacking, and saving the family from danger or financial ruin.

Age differences. The Age X Sex ANOVA yielded a significant age (15% of variance accounted for — the second strongest effect of age) and sex effect (3% of variance accounted for — the second strongest effect of sex) but not their interaction, see Table 5. Decreased means occurred with increased age, a drop of 58%. Heroic daydreams were not common going from "usually not true for me" in 17–24 year olds to somewhat above "definitely not true for me" in 75–84 year olds. Women had much lower means than men. The scale correlation with age was −.40 for women and −.32 for men.

Age changes. Analyses of variance of changes showed a significant decrease for 11.5–16.7 year ($M = -0.8$, $F(1,472) = 7.39$, $p < .01$, partial eta squared = .015) and 17.4–23.4 year ($M = -2.0$, $F(1,174) = 15.31$, $p < .001$, partial eta squared = .081) intervals. Neither age-at-1st-testing nor sex nor their interaction significantly affected the levels of change for any longitudinal interval.

Summary. Age differences were strong with greater differences occurring in the younger part of the age span. Intraindividual change was strong especially in women and in the longer longitudinal intervals. We saw heroic daydreams as relatively unlikely even in the youngest age group and become much less likely with the older and oldest age groups.

Achievement-Oriented Daydreams

This scale indicated the occurrence of daydreams whose content was about life achievement, social recognition, business achievement, and development of things vital to society. The items of the scale were about accomplishing a difficult task, being respected by colleagues, exceeding parents' expectations, "receiving the highest honor in my field of work," being "promoted to a better position," being regarded as an expert, and belonging to "an organization for successful individuals."

Age differences. The Age X Sex ANOVA yielded a significant age (12% of variance accounted for) and sex effect but not their interaction, see Table 5. Decreased means occurred with increased age, a decrease of 45% from youngest to oldest; from an interpretation somewhat below "usually true" to somewhat below "usually not true." Women had smaller means than men except for the 45–54 year olds where they were essentially the same. The scale correlation with age was −.32 for women and −.37 for men.

Age changes. Analyses of variance of changes for the longitudinal intervals showed a significant effect (decrease) only for 11.5–16.7 years ($M = -1.3$, $F(1,420) = 13.87$, $p < .001$, partial eta squared = .032). Age-at-1st-testing significantly affected the level of change only for the 5.5–9.5 year interval ($F(5,590) = 3.58$, $p < .01$, partial eta squared = .029) — the 25–34 year old group showed a positive change while the older groups showed a negative change; for the 25–34, 35–44, 45–54, 55–64, 65–74, and 75–84 year old groups, the changes were, respectively, +0.8, −1.8, −0.4, −1.0, −1.1, and −1.6. Neither sex nor the Age X Sex interaction significantly affected the level of change for any interval. In general, for participants with the same initial level of achievement-oriented daydreaming, the older you were the greater the decrease in achievement-oriented daydreaming.

Summary. Large age group differences were obtained with the greatest means occurring in the younger age groups. However, achievement-oriented daydreams were not well-represented in daydreams at any age, but especially among the oldest participants. Virtually all ages showed a decrease for all longitudinal intervals with selection factors reducing the change for the longest interval. When initial level was controlled older adults tended to show greater decreases in achievement-oriented content than younger adults.

Fear of Failure Daydreams

This scale indicated the occurrence of daydreams whose content was about failure in life and profession and failing loved ones. The items of the scale were about fearing "meeting new responsibilities in my life," not being promoted, giving a bad impression, fearing failure in loved ones, fearing failure to complete an important job or task, financial loss, not living up to parents' expectation, and lossing or failing at one's job.

Age differences. The Age X Sex ANOVA yielded a significant age (8% of variance accounted for) and sex effect but not their interaction, see Table 5. Decreased means occurred with increased age; however, there was some indication of an increase fear of failure in the oldest old. Fear of failure content was uncommon; "usually not true" in 17–24 year old and approaching "definitely not true" thereafter. Women had somewhat smaller means than men except in the 75–84 year olds. The scale correlation with age was −.21 women and −.29 for men.

Age changes. Analyses of variance of changes for the longitudinal intervals showed a significant effect (decrease) only for 11.5–16.7 years ($M = -0.7$, $F(1,431) = 5.56$, $p < .05$, partial eta squared = .013). Neither age nor sex nor their interaction significantly affected the level of change for all intervals.

Summary. Fear of failure does not appear as a strong component of daydreaming content for any age group. Furthermore, the likelihood of fear of failure content shows a tendency to decrease within the individual with increased age; although there was some evidence that the oldest old show an increase.

Hostile Daydreams

This scale indicated the occurrence of daydreams whose content was of a hostile and hurtful nature. The items of the scale were about "physically hurting someone I hate," seeking revenge, "telling off my parents," deliberately annoying people, "getting even," hatred of "those whose morals and values are not in accord with my own, "clashing with my parents over trivial matters," and becoming angry and antagonistic toward others.

Age differences. The Age X Sex ANOVA yielded a significant age (13% of variance accounted for) and sex effect but not their interaction, see Table 5. Decreased means occurred with increased age, a decrease of 53% for women and 61% for men; from an interpretation at "usually not true" in the 17–24 year olds to one approaching "definitely not true" in 75–84 year olds. The scale correlation with age was −.30 for women and −.41 for men.

Age changes. Analyses of variance of changes for the longitudinal intervals showed a significant or near significant decrease for 5.5–9.5 years ($M = -0.5$, $F(1,645) = 3.34$, $p < .07$, partial eta squared = .005), for 11.5–16.7 years ($M = -1.7$, $F(1,437) = 31.32$, $p < .001$, partial eta squared = .067), and for 17.4–23.4 years ($M = -2.5$, $F(1,166) = 25.14$, $p < .001$, partial eta squared = .132). Sex significantly affected the level of change for the 17.4–23.4 year interval ($M_{\text{Women}} = -3.8$, $M_{\text{Men}} = -1.3$), $F(1,166) = 6.58$, $p < .05$, partial eta squared = .038). Age-at-1st-testing and the interaction of age and sex did not significantly affect levels of change.

Summary. Hostile daydream content was uncommon at all ages, with older individuals showing considerably less hostile daydream content than their younger cohorts. Intraindividual decreases were pervasive at all ages except the very oldest; longer longitudinal intervals resulted in greater decreases.

Guilt Daydreams

This scale indicated the occurrence of daydreams whose content was about feelings of guilt or engaging in guilt-inducing actions. The scale items were about being caught stealing or at other crimes, being caught a telling a lie, feeling "tortured by the images of the sins I have committed," feeling guilty about taking advantage of some less fortunate or escaping punishment or cheating in a game or going against one's religious beliefs, and damaging something borrowed from a friend.

Age differences. The Age X Sex ANOVA yielded a significant age (12% of variance accounted for) and sex effect but not their interaction, see Table 5. Decreased means occurred with increased age, a decrease of 47%; from an interpretation somewhat below "usually not true" in 17–24 year olds to one approaching "definitely not true" in 75–84 year olds. The scale correlation with age was −.28 for women and −.32 for men.

Age changes. Analyses of variance of changes for the longitudinal intervals showed a significant or near significant decrease for 11.5–16.7 years ($M = -0.5$, $F(1,464) = 3.81$, $p < .052$, partial eta squared = .008) and 17.4–23.4 years ($M = -0.8$, $F(1,171) = 4.02$, $p < .05$, partial eta squared = .023). Age, sex, and their interaction did not significantly affect the change magnitudes.

Summary. Guilty daydreams were not very likely at any age. Despite initial low levels, there was clear evidence of intraindividual decreases in guilty daydreams in all longitudinal intervals, especially the longer intervals.

Comparisons Among Daydream Content Scales

Cross-sectional sample. A measure of the relative strength of different daydream contents was obtained by comparing the magnitudes of the daydream content scales. To determine if the differences in the means, see Table 5, were statistically different an Age Group by Sex by Daydream Content Scales (repeated) ANOVA was carried out separately for the positive (problem solving, bizarre-improbable, sexual, heroic, and achievement-oriented) and negative (fear of failure, hostile, and guilt) daydream content. A significant effect occurred for the differences among positive content scales ($F(4,9604) = 1068.10$, $p < .001$, partial eta squared = .308) and among negative content scales ($F(2,5228) = 296.48$, $p < .001$, partial eta squared = .102) scales, for the effect of sex on the difference among positive content scales ($F(4,9604) = 56.75$, $p < .001$, partial eta squared = .023) and negative content scales ($F(2,5228) = 10.80$, $p < .001$, partial eta squared = .004), the effect of age on the differences among positive content scales ($F(24,9604) = 33.78$, $p < .001$, partial eta squared = .078) and negative content scales ($F(12,5228) = 12.78$, $p < .001$, partial eta squared = .029), and the combined effect of the age and sex only for positive content scales ($F(24,9604) = 1.98$, $p < .01$, partial eta squared = .005).

Based upon the means across all seven age groups, the order of the scales was Problem Solving (22.2), Achievement-Oriented (16.6), Sexual (16.1), Bizarre-Improbable (15.8), Hostile (9.3), Fear of Failure (8.4), Heroic (8.1) and Guilt (6.2) Daydreams. For men this order was maintained, the means were, respectively, 21.2, 18.3, 16.7, 14.4, 10.1, 9.4, 8.6, and 6.6. For women, the order was reversed between second and third and between sixth and seventh; the means were, respectively, 23.1, 13.8, 14.9, 12.8, 8.5, 6.7, 8.1, and 5.7. Based upon the means across both sexes, the order of the age groups was 17–24 (16.6), 25–34 (14.3), 35–44 (13.0), 45–54 (12.2), 55–64 (10.8), 65–74 (10.3), and 75–84 (10.0) years old. Table 17 shows the eight content scales ranked by magnitude of means within an age group for women and men separately. In no case did a content scale maintain a constant rank across all age groups and both sexes. The Problem Solving Daydream Scale was ranked first for women for all age groups and for men for all age groups except 17–24 year olds where it was ranked second — the Sexual Daydreams Scale was ranked first. The Hostile Daydream Scale was ranked fifth for men for all age groups and for women for all age groups except 55–64 and 75–84 year olds. The Guilt Daydream Scale was ranked eighth for men for all age groups and for women for all groups except the 65–74 and 75–84 year olds where the Heroic Daydreams Scale ranked eighth. Most notable shifts in rank occurred for the Bizarre-Improbable Scale which moved from third or fourth in the younger groups to second in the older groups and for the Sexual Daydreaming Scale which moved from first or second in the younger groups to third in the older groups. Most notable disparity between men and women in the rank change which occurred with increased age was for the Heroic Daydream Scale and the Fear of Failure Scale — heroic daydreams became more important and fear of failure daydreams became less important for men, the opposite was true for women.

Table 17 also shows the eight content scales converted to a percentage of the eight scale total within an age group. This procedure mantains the ranks and also assigns a relative weighting. Most notable was the increase in percentage with increased age for problem solving and bizarre-improbable daydreams and a decrease in percentage with increased age for sexual and heroic daydreams.

Table 17. *Daydream Content Scales: Relative Strength within an Age Group, Cross-Sectional Data, Men and Women Separate*

Rank of Scale Means (Within an Age Group)	Age Groups													
	17–24		25–34		35–44		45–54		55–64		65–74		75–84	
	F	M	F	M	F	M	F	M	F	M	F	M	F	M
Problem Solving Daydreams (#9)	1	2	1	1	1	1	1	1	1	1	1	1	1	1
Sexual Daydreams (#19)	2	1	2	2	2	2	4	2	4	2	4	3	4	3
Bizarre-Improbable Daydreams (#13)	3	3	3	4	4	3	3	3	2	3	2	2	2	2
Achievement-Oriented Daydreams (#15)	3	4	4	3	3	3	2	4	3	4	3	4	3	4
Hostile Daydreams (#18)	5	5	5	5	5	5	5	5	6	5	5	5	6	5
Heroic Daydreams (#20)	6	6	6	6	7	6	7	6	7	6	8	7	8	5
Fear of Failure Daydreams (#17)	7	7	6	7	6	7	6	7	5	6	5	6	5	7
Guilt Daydreams (#21)	8	8	8	8	8	8	8	8	8	8	7	8	7	8

Percentage of total of content scales (Within an age group)	Age groups													
	17–24		25–34		35–44		45–54		55–64		65–74		75–84	
	F	M	F	M	F	M	F	M	F	M	F	M	F	M
Problem Solving Daydreams (#9)	19	16	22	19	25	21	27	21	28	22	29	22	27	23
Sexual Daydreams (#19)	18	18	17	18	17	19	14	17	12	17	11	16	10	14
Bizarre-Improbable Daydreams (#13)	14	14	15	14	14	14	15	15	17	17	19	18	20	20
Achievement-Oriented Daydreams (#15)	14	14	15	15	14	14	15	14	13	14	12	12	12	13
Hostile Daydreams (#18)	10	11	9	10	10	10	9	9	9	9	9	9	8	8
Heroic Daydreams (#20)	9	11	8	9	7	9	6	9	7	8	6	7	6	8
Fear of Failure Daydreams (#17)	8	9	8	8	8	8	8	8	9	8	9	8	10	8
Guilt Daydreams (#21)	7	8	6	6	5	5	5	6	6	6	6	6	7	6

Note. F = Females, M = Males

Longitudinal sample. A measure of the relative change over time in the tendency to have daydreams of various contents was obtained by comparing the magnitude of the changes for the five positive content scales and for the three negative content scales. To determine if the mean changes were statistically different an Age-at-1st-Testing by Sex by Content Scales (repeated) ANOVA was carried out for each longitudinal period and for positive and negative content scales. Different content scales showed significantly different mean changes for positive content for all longitudinal periods and for negative content for the two longer periods: (a) 5.5–9.5 years (positive content, $F(4,1916) = 4.08$, $p < .01$, partial eta squared = .009), (b) 11.5–16.7 years (positive content, $F(4,1316) = 7.02$, $p < .001$, partial eta squared = .021; negative content, $F(2,782) = 10.12$, $p < .001$, partial eta squared = .025), and (c) 17.4–23.4 years (positive content, $F(4,448) = 6.39$, $p < .001$, partial eta squared = .054; negative content, $F(2,280) = 8.17$, $p < .001$, partial eta squared = .055). For the positive content scales, these effects appear to be primarily due to the Bizarre-Improbable Scale showing an increase while the other scales usually showing a decrease during a longitudinal period. For the negative content scales, these effects appear to be primarily the result of a large decrease for the Hostile Daydream Scale and small mean changes for the Fear of Failure and Guilt Scales. Age-at-1st-testing significantly affected the differences among the content scales for the: (a) 5.5–9.5 year interval (positive content, $F(20,1916) = 2.36$, $p < .01$, partial eta squared = .024), (b) 11.5–16.7 year interval (negative content, $F(8,782) = 2.80$, $p < .01$, partial eta squared = .028), and (c) 17.4–23.4 year interval (positive content, $F(12,448) = 2.58$, $p < .01$, partial eta squared = .065). For positive content scales, the effect of age on longitudinal changes appeared to be: (a) for the 5.5–9.5 year interval, due to relatively large increases for the 75–84 year old age-at-1st-testing group for sexual, heroic, and achievement-oriented daydream content while most of the younger age groups showed little change or a decrease; in addition, the 25–34 year old group showed a relatively large increase in achievement-oriented content; (b) for the 17.4–23.4 year interval, due to the 25–34 year old age-at-1st-testing group showing a relatively large increase in problem solving and achievement-oriented content and to the 55–64 year old group showing the largest decreases in problem solving, sexual, and achievement-oriented content and largest increase in bizarre-improbable content. For negative content, for the 11.5–16.7 year interval, the effect of age on longitudinal changes was the result of hostile content showing relatively large decreases in the 25–34 and 65–74 year old groups and moderate decreases in fear of failure and hostile daydream content in the 35–44, 45–54, and 55–64 year old groups. Sex significantly affected the difference among negative content scales for the 11.5–16.7 year interval ($F(2,782) = 3.26$, $p < .05$, partial eta squared = .008) and the 17.4–23.4 year interval ($F(2,280) = 3.39$, $p < .05$, partial eta squared = .024). For negative content, the effect of gender on longitudinal change appeared to be due to small gender differences in change in hostile and guilt content and a large gender difference in fear of failure content — women showed a greater decrease than men, approximately a 2:1 ratio — for the 11.5–16.7 year and 17.4–23.4 year longitudinal intervals.

Relationships Among All Scales, Age, and Sex

For the cross-sectional sample, a principle components analysis using maximum likelihood estimators was carried out on the intercorrelations of age, sex, and the scales measuring response honesty, frequency-intensity, temporal setting, emotional reactions, imagery, and content of daydreams. Table 18 presents the outcome of the analysis after a Varimax othogonal rotation. Only Factor 6 showed a substantial loading on age (−.83). Other substantial loadings were on sexual daydream content (.47), daydream frequency (.44), and self-revelation (.35). Only Factor 4 (Content Practicality) showed a substantial loading on Sex (.34).

For each of the longitudinal samples, a principle components analysis using maximum likelihood estimators was carried out on the intercorrelations of age-at-1st-testing, sex, and longitudinal changes on the scales measuring response honesty, frequency-intensity, temporal setting, emotional reactions, imagery, and content of daydreams. Table 18 presents the outcome of the analyses after each had a Varimax rotation. It is noteworthy that Factors 1 (Negative Aspects of Daydreaming), 2 (Positive Aspects of Daydreaming), 3 (Imagery/Clarity of Daydreams) and 4 (Content Practicality) appeared for all three longitudinal intervals and for the cross-sectional sample. This supports the notion that these aspects of daydreaming move together with regard to level (absolute value) both for different age groups and for individuals as they age. Furthermore, Positive Aspects of Daydreaming has age-at-1st-testing account for 2.3%, 4.0%, and 5.3% of the variance of the factor for the 5.5–9.5 year, 11.5–16.7 year, and 17.4–23.4 year intervals, respectively. Also, age-at-1st-testing accounted for 4.4% of the variance of Imagery/Clarity of Daydreams factor for the 5.5–9.5 year interval and 9.6% of the variance of Factor 6 for the 17.4–23.4 year interval — Factor 6 also had Past in Daydreams (.54) and Achievement-Oriented Daydreams (-.33) and Sex (.29) load on it. Thus, age differentially affected the longitudinal changes for Positive Aspects of Daydreaming for all three longitudinal periods, for Imagery/Clarity of Daydreams for the 5.5–9.5 year longitudinal period, and for the Past in Daydreams and Achievement-Oriented Daydreams for the 17.4–23.4 year longitudinal period.

General Discussion

These results are consistent with Giambra's earlier findings, daydream frequency and intensity decrease with age in adulthood. We have seen that this occurred both within individuals over periods as long as 24 years and between different age groups. Using methods which do not depend upon retrospective recall but do depend upon self-report Giambra (1989) has corroborative evidence, during very easy vigilance tasks and during reading (Grodsky & Giambra 1990–1991; Giambra & Godsky 1991–1992), that reduced daydreaming occurs with increased age. Using an indirect measure which did not depend upon self-report, Einstein and McDaniel (1997) also reported less daydreaming with older than with younger age groups.

What might account for reduced daydreaming with increased age? The studies of Giambra using contemporaneous reporting of daydreaming and the Einstein and McDaniel study using indirect and non-self-report provide counter-evidence to the hypothesis that this study's results were an artifact of poorer memory in older adults. These studies, as well as high levels of a willingness to self-revelation and positive views of daydreaming at all ages provide counter-evidence to deliberate or unconscious self-censorship in reporting of daydreaming at any age. Other potential explanations of the age decline in daydreaming frequency are age differences in attention, opportunity, use of alternatives to daydreaming, a less productive central nervous system, and less need to day-dream. Clear evidence has been provided by Giambra (1995) and Antrobus (1968) that as the demands of the outside world increase, daydreaming decreases. Older adults process outside information at a slower rate tha younger adults (Cerella 1985; Myerson, Hale, Wagstaff, Poon, & Smith 1990; Salthouse,1985). With more of their attentional resources devoted to processing external information there would be less for processing internally generated information and thus daydreaming. Giambra's vigilance task studies with very little in the way of information processing demands provide counterevidence to the attentional resource hypothesis. If older adults had more daily situations in which they were actively processing external information then we would expect that situation to result in less daydreaming. We have no evidence to support this conjecture.

Table 18. *Factor Analysis of Daydreaming Characteristic Scales, Sex, and Age Intercorrelations for the Cross-sectional Sample and Changes in Daydreaming Characteristic Scales, Sex, and Age-at-1st-Testing Intercorrelations for the Three Longitudinal Samples*

	Sample			
	Longitudinal (Yrs)			Cross-Sectional
	5.5–9.5	11.5–16.7	17.4–23.4	
Factor 1: Negative Aspects of Daydreaming				
Variance Accounted for:	21.4%	22.0%	26.5%	31.1%
Guilt Daydreams (#21)	.77	.80	.75	.87
Fear of Failure Daydreams (#17)	.76	.75	.89	.82
Heroic Daydreams (#20)	.64	.59	.68	.66
Hostile Daydreams (#18)	.65	.61	.61	.65
Frightened Reactions to Daydreams (#6)	.55	.47	.52	.56
Achievement-Oriented Daydreams (#15)	.48	.36	.49	.45
Hallucinatory-Vividness of Daydreaming (#16)	.39	.35	.43	.45
Absorption in Daydreaming (#3)	.36	.32	.39	.32
Sexual Daydreams (#19)	.34	.23&[a]	.54	.32
Factor 2: Positive Aspects of Daydreaming				
Variance Accounted for:	7.7%	4.7%	9.2%	8.8%
Problem Solving Daydreams (#9)	.56	.50	.55	.73
Acceptance of Daydreaming (#4)	.47	.43	.46	.59
Future in Daydreams (#11)	.38	.49	.37	.58
Positive Reactions in Daydreaming (#5)	.62	.50	.88	.56
Achievement-Oriented Daydreams (#15)	.53	.55	.37	.52
Absorption in Daydreaming (#3)	.48	.27&	.68	.37
Daydreaming Frequency (#1)	.46	.30&	.61	.34
Heroic Daydreams (#20)	.24&	.33	.16&	.27&
Age (Yrs)	−.15&	−.20$[b]	−.23&	−.11&
Sexual Daydreams (#19)	.26&	.19&	.37	.30&
Factor 3: Imagery/Clarity of Daydreams				
Variance Accounted for:	4.5%	8.6%	5.0%	4.1%
Auditory Imagery in Daydreaming (#8)	.78	.79	.74	.81
Visual Imagery in Daydreaming (#7)	.65	.69	.68	.73
Hallucinatory-Vividness of Daydreaming (#16)	.37	.42	.49	.49
Sexual Daydreams (#19)	.34	.34	.30&	.25&
Heroic Daydreams (#20)	.13&	.20&	.38	.15&
Achievement-Oriented Daydreams (#15)	.08&	.16&	.37	.08&
Age (Yrs)	.21$	.11&	.08&	−.11&
Self-Revelation (#28)	.20$	.01&	.04&	.12&

	Sample			
	Longitudinal (Yrs)			Cross-Sectional
	5.5–9.5	11.5–16.7	17.4–23.4	
Factor 4: Content Practicality				
Variance Accounted for:	4.0%	2.7%	4.1%	3.8%
Bizarre-Improbable Daydreams (#13)	.57	.55	.76	.57
Present-Oriented Daydreams (#10)	–.55	–.37	–.49	–.55
Problem Solving Daydreams (#9)	–.36	–.55	–.18&	–.28&
Acceptance of Daydreaming (#4)	–.25&	–.39	–.30&	–.16&
Heroic Daydreams (#20)	.28&	.32	.02&	.35
Sex (F = 0, M = 1)	.03&	.06&	.01&	.34
Achievement-Oriented Daydreams (#15)	.23&	.13&	.08&	.33
Factor 5: [No consistent name]				
Variance Accounted for:	2.4%	3.1%	2.9%	4.3%
Absorption in Daydreaming (#3)	.61	.69	.16&	.74
Daydreaming Frequency (#1)	.19&	.44	–.09&	.42
Frightened Reactions to Daydreams (#6)	.23&	.29&	.45	.43
Past in Daydreams (#12)	.19&	.27&	.02&	.32
Hallucinatory-Vividness of Daydreaming (#16)	.40	.44	.10&	.28&
Self-Revelation (#28)	–.03&	.11&	.49	.10&
Sex (F = 0, M = 1)	.17$	.19$	.04&	–.19&
Positive Reactions in Daydreaming (#5)	.28&	.44	.09&	.27&
Factor 6: Name variable				
Variance Accounted for:	1.9%	1.9%	4.1%	4.6%
Age (Yrs)	–.08&	.05&	.31$	–.83
Sexual Daydreams (#19)	.06&	.33	.11&	.47
Daydreaming Frequencey (#1)	.05&	.07&	–.04&	.44
Self-Revelation (#28)	.13&	.27$	.04&	.35
Past in Daydreams (#12)	.43	.28$	.54	–.06&
Acceptance of Daydreaming (#4)	.45	.21&	–.26&	.05&
Achievement-Oriented Daydreams (#15)	–.14&	–.09&	–.33	.20&
Sex (F = 0, M = 1)	.03&	.06&	.29$	–.16&

a. & indicates that this loading was included for this factor on a different sample, but less than .316 — less than 10% of variance accounted for.

b. $ indicates highest loading for that variable, but less than .316.

Note. All entries are loadings (factor-item correlations) which account for 10% or more of variance, unless otherwise indicated. Loadings were estimated using the maximum likelihood procedure. The number of factors was determined by eigenvalue magnitude, i.e., until less than 1.0. Factors underwent a Varimax rotation. The communalities for Age, Sex, Scales # 1, 3, 4, 5, 6, 7, 8, 9, 10, 11, 12, 13, 15, 16, 17, 18, 19, 20, 21, and 28 were, respectively: .76, .19, .52, .95, .47, .54, .62, .71, .80, .70, .31, .42, .21, .49, .63, .56, .71, .54, .60, .70, .81, and .23 for the cross-sectional sample; .10, .04, .27, .78, .51, .49, .43, .51, .68, .48, .33, .17, .30, .39, .50, .51, .61, .47, .33, .62, .61, and .09 for the 5.5–9.5 year longitudinal sample; .08, .05, .33, .69, .47, .51, .37, .58, .70, .62, .14, .26, .29, .41, .53, .56, .59, .43, .41, .64, .67, and .13 for the 11.5–16.7 year longitudinal sample; .21, .09, .42, .66, .55, .85, .63, .61, .63, .46, .29, .31, .35, .67, .65, .53, .82, .47, .54, .74, .61, and .28 for the 17.4–23.4 year longitudinal sample.

Indeed, folk wisdom would have the elderly engaging in fewer situations where they are in a demanding information processing environment and thus more daydreaming would be expected, as might be the situation for individuals confined to their homes or in an assisted-care facility due to limiting physical difficulties. The BLSA participants were not in this situation since they were overwhelmingly active community dwelling individuals.

When the situation allows for more daydreaming older adults might be "choosing" alternative behaviors. Two kinds of alternative behaviors are falling asleep or napping and deliberately directing attention to external events. In high likelihood daydreaming situations like lectures, vigilance tasks, and many daily tasks falling asleep instead of daydreaming is a viable option. Since older adults are more likely than younger adults to have sleep disturbance (Morgan 1992; Woodruff 1985) and reduced sleep-onset latency during the daytime it would appear that less daydreaming may results because the older individual is more likely to be sleeping. Laboratory studies (Giambra 1989, 1995) using vigilance tasks found less daydreaming in older adults even after individuals who fell asleep, even for only a minute or two, were omitted from the analyses. However, for this study's IPI data those individuals who fall asleep as an alternative cannot be determined and thus the actions may have acted to increase the young-old disparity. Some individuals when in a high daydream likelihood situation may deliberately focus on something in the environment or direct their attention to deliberate planning and other directed thinking to reduce or eliminate daydreaming. There is, however, no evidence that this behavior is more likely among older than younger adults.

Because all daydreams are thoughts and all thoughts must result from activity in the brain or central nervous system any biological changes which degrade its functioning may reduce its daydream production. There have been many studies, based upon post-mortem analyses (see Coleman & Flood 1987; Johnson & Rybash 1993, and Scheibel 1996 for a review), which indicate neuronal loss (but see Rapp & Gallagher 1996 and Wickelgren 1996 for counter-evidence), reduction in the size of many neurons, and the increased presence of plaques and tangles in older adults. Changes in neurotransmitter production also has been documented (Rossor 1992). These changes probably degrade the functioning of the CNS and hence probably impact negatively on thought frequency or thought length. Another possibility is that these changes interfer with the movement of thoughts into consciousness and thus cannot be experienced as daydreams. Perhaps, daydream reduction might be taken as an early sign of a deteriorating CNS.

Klinger (1971, 1977, 1978, 1987, 1996) has presented much evidence that daydreams and their contents are initiated or controlled by the unfinished business and interupted tasks (goal-oriented) of the individual which he labels their "current concerns." He and his colleagues (Parks et al. 1988–1989) have provided evidence of fewer current concerns in older adults. Evidence has also been provided that the attention of individuals is sensitively tuned to information in their environment that is related to their current concerns and that these environment cues result in current concern related thoughts and daydreams (Klinger 1993, 1994, 1996; Klinger, Barta, & Maxeiner 1987; Nikula, Klinger, & Larson-Gutman 1993). Poor sight and hearing in the elderly may reduce the apprehension of these cues or current concern related information and thus reduce the frequency of daydreams initiated by them. Fewer current concerns and reduced awareness of current concern related information may combine to reduce daydreaming frequency in the elderly. On the other hand, reduced sensory input in the elderly does make more likely an environment conducive to more daydreaming, by reducing the compelling attentional quality of external stimuli (Giambra, Grodsky, Swartz, & Bernard 1997–1998).

We have seen that the content of daydreams as well as the relative likelihood of the different contents does change with age. Evidence for ethnic (Giambra 1981, 1982) and cultural (Giambra & Stone 1982–1983) influences on daydream content is consistent with age-related differences. Cultures, ethnic groups, and age/cohort groups all are likely to have different current concerns or different priorities or salience to their varied concerns and unfinished business. For example, sexual activity, achievement goals, and temporal perspective and horizons all can be heavily influenced by the age and past experiences of the individuals and thus influence or determine the likelihood of daydreams about sexuality, achievement, and the future or past, as evidenced in this study. These outcomes suggest we can use a person's daydreams to help us determine their current concerns and unfinished business, not as wishfulfillment or as an expression of suppressed desires, but as the problem solving activity of an efficient biological system operating in an essentially uncontrollable environment.

Appendix A

Maximizing Age Group Representation. Some longitudinal participants were tested as many as four times, not including short-term test-retest repeats. Table A1 shows three hypothetical longitudinal participants who were last tested at age 56. Participant 1 (P1) was tested twice; Participant 2 (P2) was tested three times; and Participant 3 (P3) was tested four times. Each of these participants had 6 years

Table A1. *An Illustration of How to Maximize Sample Size for a Longitudinal Period for a Particular Age-at-Later-Testing: Age at Testing of Three Hypothetical Longitudinal Participants*

Participant	Longitudinal period (years)		Age at later testing	. . . . Testing			
	Maximum	Used		Last-3	Last-2	Last-1	Last
P1	6	6	56			50	56
P2	12	6	56		44	50	56
P3	18	6	56	38	44	50	56
P2	12	6	50		44	50	56
P3	18	6	50	38	44	50	56
P3	18	6	44	38	44	50	56
P2	12	12	56		44	. . . .	56
P3	18	12	56	38	44	. . . .	56
P3	18	12	50	38	. . . .	50	56

between testings and a different initial testing age. P1 had one 6-year longitudinal period (50–56 years), P2 had two 6-year longitudinal periods (44–50 and 50–56 years), and P3 had three 6-year longitudinal periods (38–44, 44–50, 50–56 years). Therefore, P1 contributed information on longitudinal change for one 6-year interval, P2 contributed information on two 6-year intervals, and P3 contributed information on three 6-year intervals. Thus, if the maximum information on 6-year longitudinal change between 50 and 56 years of age were to be obtained, all three participants would contribute; for 44–50 years, two participants (P2, P3) would contribute; and for 38–44 years, one participant (P3) would contribute. The cost of this gain in information at specific ages is that longitudinal change estimates for different ages come from interdependent samples instead of independent samples, as was the case in the earlier ANOVA analyses. A similar maximization of sample size at a particular age interval can occur for the 12 year longitudinal periods depicted in Table A1. With the 12 year longitudinal period, for example, P2 and P3, could contribute to the 44–56 year interval; and P3 could contribute to the 38–50 year interval.

This method of aggregating longitudinal participants permits a longitudinal period one-way ANOVA for each age-at-later-testing. An ANOVA was carried out for each age-at-later-testing interval with two or more longitudinal periods consisting of samples of at least 10 men or women.

Acknowledgments

The data for this study was collected while the author was a Research Psychologist with the Intramural Research Program, National Institute on Aging. This article is a summary of several papers currently in press or under review.

I would like to acknowledge the invaluable help of Cathy Dent of the BLSA, Tom Traynor, Renee Baldi, and Alicia Grodsky in the data collection.

Correspondence with the author should be sent to 204 Saint Dunstan's Rd., Baltimore, MD 21212.

References

Antrobus, J. S. 1968. "Information theory and stimulus independent thought." *British Journal of Psychology* 59: 423–430.

Cameron, P. 1972. "The generation gap: Time orientation." *Gerontologist* 12, Part I, 117–119.

Cameron, P., Desai, K. G., Bahador, D. and Dremel, G. 1977–1978. "Temporality across the life-span." *International Journal of Aging and Human Development* 8: 229–259.

Cerella, J. 1985. "Information processing rates in the elderly." *Psychological Bulletin* 98: 67–83.

Coleman, P. D. and Flood, D. G. 1987. "Neuron numbers and dendritic extent in normal aging and Alzheimer's Disease." *Neurobiology of Aging* 8: 521–545.

Costa, P. T. Jr. and McCrae, R. R. 1988. "Personality in adulthood: A six year longitudinal study of self-reports and spouse ratings on the *NEO Personality Inventory*." *Journal of Personality and Social Psychology* 54: 853–863.

Dror, I. E. and Kosslyn, S. M. 1994. "Mental imagery and aging." *Psychology and Aging* 9: 90–102.

Einstein, G. O. and McDaniel, M. A. 1997. "Aging and mind wandering: Reduced inhibition in older adults?" *Experimental Aging Research* 23: 343–354.

Filip, S. 1996. "Motivation and emotion." In J. E. Birren and K. W. Schaie (eds) *Handbook of the psychology of aging* 4: 218–235. San Diego: Academic Press.

Giambra, L. M. 1973. "Daydreaming in males from seventeen to seventy-seven; a preliminary report." *Proceedings of the 81st Convention of the American Psychological Association* 8: 769–770.

Giambra, L. M. 1974. "Daydreaming across the the life span: Late adolescent to senior citizen." *International Journal of Aging and Human Development* 5: 115–140.

Giambra, L. M. 1977a. "Daydreaming about the past: The time setting of spontaneous thought intrusions." *The Gerontologist* 17: 35–38.

Giambra, L. M. 1977b. "A factor analytic study of daydreaming, imaginal process, and temperament: A replication on an adult male life-span sample." *Journal of Gerontology* 12: 675–680.

Giambra, L. M. 1977–1978. "Adult male daydreaming across the life span: a replication and further analyses." *International Journal of Aging and Human Development* 8: 197–228.

Giambra, L. M. 1979–1980. "Sex differences in daydreaming and related mental activity from the late teens to the early nineties." *International Journal of Aging and Human Development* 10: 1–34.

Giambra, L. M. 1980. "A factor analysis of the items of the *Imaginal Processes Inventory.*" *Journal of Clinical Psychology* 36: 383–409.

Giambra, L. M. 1981. "Daydreaming, attention processes, and curiosity in White Americans: Religious, educational, economic, and residency influences for a life span sample." *Journal of Clinical Psychology* 37: 262–275.

Giambra, L. M. 1982. "Daydreaming: A black-white comparison for 17–34 year olds." *Journal of Personality and Social Psychology* 42: 1146–1156.

Giambra, L. M. 1983. "Sexual daydreams in 40 to 60 year old women: The influence of menopause, sexual activity, and health." In J. Shorr, G. Sobel-Whittington, P. Robin, and J. Connella (eds) *Imagery: Theoretical and clinical applications* 3: 297–303. New York: Plenum.

Giambra, L. M. 1988–1989. "The influence of subject-experimenter sexual congruence on the frequency of task-unrelated imagery and thought: Further evidence." *Imagination, Cognition and Personality* 8: 247–258.

Giambra, L. M. 1989. "Task-unrelated thought frequency as a function of age: A laboratory study." *Psychology and Aging* 4: 136–143.

Giambra, L. M. 1993. "The influence of aging on spontaneous shifts of attention from external stimuli to the contents of consciousness." *Experimental Gerontology* 28: 485–492.

Giambra, L. M. 1995. "A laboratory method for investigating influences on switching attention to task-unrelated imagery and thought." *Consciousness and Cognition* 4: 1–21.

Giambra, L. M., Arenberg, D., Zonderman, A. B., Kawas, K. and Costa, P. T. Jr. 1995. "Adult life span changes in immediate visual memory and verbal intelligence." *Psychology and Aging* 10: 123–139.

Giambra, L. M. and Grodsky, A. 1989. "Task-unrelated images and thoughts while reading." In J. E. Shorr, P. Robin, J. A. Connella, and M. Wolpin (eds) *Imagery: Current perspectives*, 27–31. New York: Plenum.

Giambra, L. M. and Grodsky, A. 1991. "Aging, imagery, and imagery vividness in daydreams: Cross-Sectional and longitudinal perspectives." In R. Kunzendorf (ed.) *Mental imagery*, 23–34. New York: Plenum.

Giambra, L. M. and Grodsky, A. 1991–1992. "The influence of age on the frequency of spontaneous task-unrelated thought intrusions during reading." *Imagination, Cognition and Personality* 11: 367–379.

Giambra, L. M., Grodsky, A., Swartz, D. B. and Bernard, M. E. 1997–1998. "Task-unrelated image and thought frequency during chronic auditory sensory deprivation:

A laboratory study with the severely hearing-impaired." *Imagination, Cognition, and Personality* 17: 179–189.

Giambra, L. M., Rosenberg, E. H., Kasper, S., Yee, W. and Sack, D. A. 1988–1989. "A circadian rhythm in the frequency of spontaneous task-unrelated images and thoughts." *Imagination, Cognition and Personality* 8: 307–312.

Giambra, L. M. and Stone, B. 1982–1983. "Australian-American differences in daydreaming, attentional processes, and curiosity: First findings based on retrospective reports." *Imagination, Cognition, and Personality* 2: 23–35.

Giambra, L. M. and Traynor, T. D. 1978. "Depression and daydreaming: An analysis based on self-ratings." *Journal of Clinical Psychology* 34: 14–25.

Giray, E. F., Roodin, P. A., Altkin, W. A., Flagg, P. and Yoon, G. 1985. "A life span approach to the study of eidetic imagery." *Journal of Mental Imagery* 9: 21–32.

Gold, S. R., Teague, R. C. and Jarvinen, P. 1981. "Counting daydreams." *Journal of Mental Imagery* 5: 129–132.

Grodsky, A. and Giambra, L. M. 1990–1991. "The consistency across vigilance and reading tasks of individual differences in the occurrence of task-unrelated and task-related images and thoughts." *Imagination Cognition, and Personality* 10: 39–52.

Gross, J. J., Carstensen, L. L., Pasupathi, M., Tsai, J., Skorpen, C. G. and Hsu, A. Y. C. 1997. "Emotion and aging: Experience, expression, and control." *Psychology and Aging* 12: 590–599.

Johnson, S. H. and Rybash, J. M. 1993. "A cognitive neuroscience perspective on age-related slowing: Developmental changes in the functional architecture." In Cerella, J., Rybash, J., Hoyer, W., Commons, M. L. (eds) *Adult information processing: Limits on loss* 143–173. San Diego: Academic Press.

Kastenbaum, R. 1982. "Time course and time perspective in later life." In C. Eisdorfer (ed.) *Annual review of gerontology and geriatrics* 3: 80–101. New York: Springer.

Klinger, E. 1971. *Structure and functions of fantasy*. New York: Wiley.

Klinger, E. 1977. *Meaning and void: Inner experience and the incentives in peoples lives*. Minneapolis: University of Minnesota Press.

Klinger, E. 1978. "Modes of normal conscious flow." In K. S. Pope and J. L. Singer (eds) *The stream of consciousness: Scientific investigations in the flow of human experience*, 225–258. New York: Plenum.

Klinger, E. 1990. *Daydreaming: Using waking fantasy and imagery for self-knowledge and creativity*. Los Angeles: Tarcher.

Klinger, E. 1992. "Motivation and imagination." *Psychologische Beitrage* 34: 127–142. Reprinted in T. Gjesme and R. Nygard (eds, 1996), *Advances in motivation*, 269–284. Oslo: Scandinavian University Press.

Klinger, E. 1993. "What will they think of next? Understanding daydreaming." In G. G. Brannigan and M. R. Merrens (eds), *The undaunted psychologist*, 143–154. New York: McGraw-Hill.

Klinger, E. 1994. "On living tomorrow today: The quality of inner life as a function of goal expectations." In Z. Zaleski (ed.), *Psychology of future orientation*, 97–106. Lublin: Towarzystwo Naukowe KUL.

Klinger, E. 1995. "Effects of motivation and emotion on thought flow and cognition: Assessment and findings." In P.E. Shrout and S.T. Fiske (eds), *Personality research, methods, and theory: A Festschrift honoring Donald W. Fiske*, 257–270. Hillsdale, NJ: Erlbaum.

Klinger, E. 1996. "The contents of thoughts: Interference as the downside of adaptive normal mechanisms in thought flow." In I.G. Sarason, B.R. Sarason, and G.R. Pierce (eds), *Cognitive interference: Theories, methods, and findings*, 3–23. Hillsdale, NJ: Lawrence Erlbaum Associates.

Klinger, E., Barta, S.G. and Maxeiner, M.E. 1980. "Motivational correlates of thought content frequency and commitment." *Journal of Personality and Social Psychology* 39: 1222–1237.

Kripke, D.F. and Sonnenschein, D. 1978. "A biologic rhythm in waking fantasy." In K.S. Pope and J.L. Singer (eds), *The stream of consciousness*, 321–334. New York: Plenum.

Leitenberg, H. and Henning, K. 1995. "Sexual fantasy." *Psychological Bulletin* 117: 469–496.

Magai, C. and McFadden, S.H. (Eds). 1996. *Handbook of emotion, adult development, and aging*. San Diego: Academic Press.

McCraven, V. and Singer, J.L. 1961. "Some characteristics of adult daydreaming." *Journal of Consulting Psychology* 51: 151–164.

McDowd, J.M. and Birren, J.E. 1990. "Aging and attentional processes." In J.E. Birren and K.W. Schaie (Eds,) *Handbook of the psychology of aging*, 3rd edition 222–233. San Diego: Academic Press.

Morgan, K. 1992. "Sleep in normal and pathological aging." In J.C. Brocklehurst, R.C. Tallis, and H, M. Fillit (eds) *Textbook of Geriatric Medicine and Gerontology* 4: 122–128. Edinburgh: Churchill Livingstone.

Myerson, J., Hale, S., Wagstaff, D., Poon, L.W. and Smith, G.A. 1990. "The information loss model: A mathematical theory of age-related cognitive slowing." *Psychological Review* 97: 475–487.

Nikula, R., Klinger, E. and Larson-Gutman, M.K. 1993. "Current concerns and electrodermal reactivity: Responses to words and thoughts." *Journal of Personality* 61: 63–84.

Parks, C.W., Jr., Klinger, E. and Perlmutter, M. 1988–1989. "Dimensions of thought as a function of age, gender, and task difficulty." *Imagination, Cognition, and Personality* 8: 49–62.

Prinz, P.N., Dustman, R.E. and Emmerson, R. 1990. "Electrophysiology and aging." In J.E. Birren and K.W. Schaie (Eds,) *Handbook of the psychology of aging* 3: 135–149. San Diego: Academic Press.

Rapp, P.R. and Gallagher, M. 1996. "Preserved neuron number in the hippocampus of aged rats with spatial learning deficits." *Proceedings of the National Academy of Science* 93: 9926–9930.

Rossor, M.N. 1992. "Neurochemistry of the aging brain and dementia." In J.C. Brocklehurst, R.C. Tallis, and H, M. Fillit (eds) *Textbook of Geriatric Medicine and Gerontology* 4: 290–301. Edinburgh: Churchill Livingstone.

Salthouse, T. 1985. "Speed of behavior and its implications for cognition." In J.E. Birren and K.W. Schaie (eds) *Handbook of the psychology of aging* 2: 400–426. New York: Van Nostrand Reinhold.

Scheibel, A.B. 1996. "Structural and functional changes in the aging brain." In J.E. Birren and K.W. Schaie (eds) *Handbook of the psychology of aging* 4: 105–128. San Diego: Academic Press.

Schroots, J.J.F. and Birren, J.E. "Concepts of time and aging in science." 1990. In J.E. Birren and K.W. Schaie (Eds,) *Handbook of the psychology of aging*, 3rd edition 45–64. San Diego: Academic Press.

Schulz, R. 1985. "Emotion and affect." In J.E. Birren and K.W. Schaie (eds) *Handbook of the psychology of aging* 2: 531–543. New York: Academic Press.

Shaw, G.A. and Giambra, L.M. 1993. "Task-unrelated-thoughts of college students diagnosed as hyperactive in childhood." *Developmental Neuropsychology* 9: 17–30.

Shock, N.W., Greulich, R.C., Andres, R., Arenberg, D., Costa, P.T., Jr., Lakatta, E.G. and Tobin, J.D. 1984. *Normal Human Aging: The Baltimore Longitudinal Study of Aging* (NIH Publication No. 84–2450), National Institutes of Health, Bethesda, MD.

Singer, J.L. 1978. "Experimental studies of daydreaming and the stream of thought." In K.S. Pope and J.L. Singer (eds) *The stream of consciousness: Scientific investigations in the flow of human experience*, 187–223. New York: Plenum.

Singer, J.L. and Antrobus, J.S. 1970. *Manual for the Imaginal Processes Inventory.* Princeton, N.J.: Educational Testing Service.

Thomae, H. 1991. "Emotions and personality." In J.E. Birren, R.B. Sloane, and G.D. Cohen (eds) *Handbook of mental health and aging*, 2: 355–375. San Diego: Academic Press.

Thomae, H. 1992. "Personality and its attributes." In J.C. Brocklehurst, R.C. Tallis, and H.M. Fillit (eds) *Textbook of geriatric medicine and gerontology*, 4: 110–121. Edinburgh: Churchill Livingstone.

Wickelgren, I. 1996. "Is hippocampal cell death a myth?" *Science*, 271: 1229–1230.

Wigdor, B. 1980. "Drives and motivations with aging." In J.E. Birren and R.B. Sloane (eds) *Handbook of mental health and aging*, 245–261. Englewood Cliffs: Prentice-Hall.

Woodruff, D.S. 1985. "Arousal. sleep, and aging." In J.E. Birren and K.W. Schaie (Eds,) *Handbook of the psychology of aging*, 2nd edition, 261–295. New York: Van Nostrand Reinhold.

Part II

Individual Differences in Subconsciousness

Individual Differences in Subtle Awareness and Levels of Awareness

Olfaction as a Model System

Gary E.R. Schwartz
The University of Arizona

Introduction

The purpose of this chapter is to outline a theory of *Levels of Awareness* (Schwartz 1996), using olfaction as a model system, that begins with the seemingly paradoxical premise that all stimuli that activate neural receptors (or biological processes in general) have an inherent "consciousness" to them whether we are "aware" of this consciousness or not. The theory outlined in this chapter was stimulated by findings on EEG registration of subthreshold olfactory stimuli uncovering "subtle consciousness" of subliminal stimuli (Schwartz et al. 1994).

Just because a stimulus may be too weak in intensity to activate conscious awareness does not necessarily imply that the stimulus is too weak to activate receptors and be registered by the nervous system. A fundamental mystery in consciousness research is what determines the transition from so-called unconscious or non-conscious processing of stimuli to the conscious registration of stimuli. What makes it possible for us to experience stimuli consciously? Why is it that so many stimuli that are continuously monitored by the brain (e.g. chemoreceptors within the body) seem to be processed outside of conscious awareness? Is this information truly outside of awareness (the classic interpretation)? Or, is it possible that the information actually influences our awareness in subtle yet important ways, even though we are not aware that our awareness has been influenced?

This chapter begins by reviewing an experiment on EEG registration of subliminal olfaction (reported in Schwartz 1996). Unexpected evidence for what was called functional "blindsmell" (an olfactory analog of blindsight, Weiskrantz

1986) is described, and evidence suggesting that implicit perception may differ from implicit sensation in terms of higher frequency EEG registered in the frontal region is considered. Additional findings of "subtle awareness" to the subliminal odors are presented, and some implications for the hypothesis of "awareness without awareness" are put forth. Though individual differences in subtle olfaction are described in this chapter, the logic of the theory potentially applies to individual differences in subtle awareness in all sensory systems.

In this chapter the term awareness is operationalized as subjects' self-reported ratings of their perceptions. *Awareness without awareness is operationalized as subtle but systemic changes in subjects' ratings of their perceptions of subliminal stimuli where the changes are so subtle that subjects do not report being aware that their perceptions have changed systematically.*

From a systems perspective (Miller 1978), the concept of *Levels of Awareness* is proposed, where *Level I Awareness* is "pure awareness" (awareness without conscious awareness of the awareness — e.g. the "unconscious"), *Level II Awareness* is "awareness of awareness" (e.g. normal consciousness), and *Level III Awareness* is "awareness of awareness of awareness" (e.g. self-consciousness or reflective consciousness). Specific research directions are proposed.

As will become clear, the theory of Levels of Awareness meets three important criteria for proposing a new theory: (1) the theory incorporates previously published data, (2) the theory makes new predictions that can be confirmed or disconfirmed in future research, and (3) the theory integrates seemingly conflicting ideas and paradigms. It turns out that the theory of Levels of Awareness not only integrates concepts in modern science, but it also integrates some ancient spiritual ideas voiced by native peoples (e.g. Native Americans) with modern science.

EEG Registration of Subliminal Olfaction

Research from the Chemical Psychophysiology Laboratory at the University of Arizona has addressed the question of whether it is possible for the brain to register the presence of odors that are not experienced consciously (see Schwartz et al. 1994 for a review of these studies). The experimental paradigm is as follows:

Subjects were requested to smell pairs of bottles, one of which contains an odorant dissolved in a solvent, the other contains just the solvent, while EEG is continuously recorded. For example, one bottle might contain isoamyl acetate, an odorant that has a fruity smell, dissolved in non-odorous liquid silicone. Subjects were handed two bottles, and with their eyes closed, were requested to smell each bottle for two seconds. Each bottle was smelled twice. Then, subjects were instructed to open their eyes, guess which bottle contains the odor, rate the intensity of the odor (from 0 to 10) and the confidence of their guess (from 0 to 10). On half the trials, the odorant was placed in the right hand, on the other half of the trials, the odorant was placed in the left hand. In addition, on half the trials, subjects were instructed to initiate the smelling sequence with their right hand, on the other half of the trials, subjects were instructed to initiate the smelling sequence with their left hand. Hence, order was completely counterbalanced in a 2 X 2 factorial design.

If the concentration of the odorant was sufficiently high (supraliminal concentration), subjects would correctly guess which hand has the odorant on 100% of the trials. They would also rate the intensity of the odorant as fairly high and rate the confidence of their guess as high. However, if the concentration of the odorant was sufficiently low (subliminal concentration), subjects would correctly guess which hand had the odorant on only 50% of the trials (i.e. they would be truly guessing). Correspondingly, they would rate the intensity of the odorant and the confidence of their guess as very low.

EEG was spectral analyzed, and topographic EEG maps were created subtracting the EEG occurring during the smelling of the control bottles (solvent alone) from the EEG occurring during the smelling of the experimental bottles (odorant plus solvent). Subtraction was necessary to remove the effects of hand posture, breathing, attention, and registration of the control solvent, leaving just the effects of the registration of the odorant in the EEG.

In a series of studies, we found that when subjects smelled a subliminal concentration of isoamyl acetate, evidence of brain registration of the odorant is observed in the EEG (reviewed in Schwartz et al. 1994). Subjects showed relative decreases in alpha activity (8–12 Hz) in midcentral and posterior regions. When the concentration was high enough to be experienced consciously, relative decreases in alpha activity was also observed in anterior regions as well.

Summary subtraction EEG maps from a recent study are displayed in Figure 1. In this experiment, 19 channels of EEG were recorded from 86 college students. The subthreshold odors (isoamyl acetate dissolved in liquid silicone) were administered double-blind (neither the subjects nor the experimentors knew which were the experimental bottles and which were the control bottles). The number of subliminal isoamyl acetate trials was 16. EEG was spectral analyzed in 2-Hz bands, and analyses were performed on low-frequency theta (4–6 Hz), high-frequency theta (6–8 Hz), low frequency alpha (8–10 Hz), and high frequency alpha (10–12 Hz).

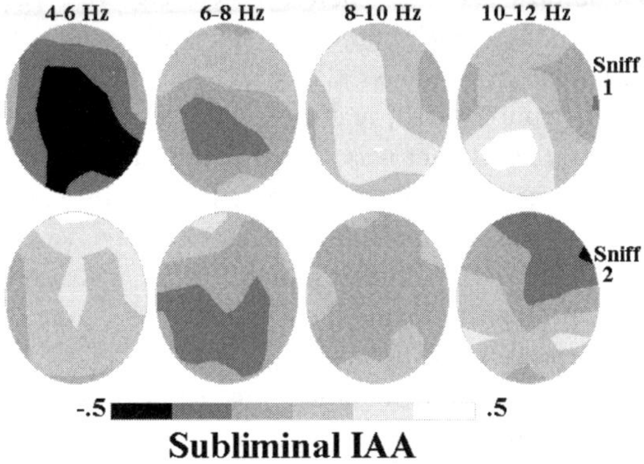

Figure 1. *Topographic EEG maps subtracting control bottles from the odor bottles for subthreshold isoamyl acetate trials (n=16) for 86 subjects. The top four maps reflect sniff one (the first sniff for the isoamyl acetate and control trials); the bottom four maps reflect sniff two (the second sniff for the isoamy acetate and control trials. The four EEG bands (4–6 hz, 6–8 hz, 8–10 hz, 10–12 hz) are all drawn on the same scale. Whites and light greys reflect increases in EEG, blacks and dark greys reflect comparable magnitude decreases in EEG. The top of each map reflects the front of the head; the bottom of each map reflects the back of the head.*

The top four subtraction maps reflect the data for sniff one averaged over the 16 trials; the bottom four subtraction maps reflect the data for sniff two. The four EEG bands are drawn on the same scale. Blacks and dark greys reflect increases in theta or alpha to the odorant (relative to the control), while light greys and whites reflect decreases in theta or alpha of a comparable magnitude. The top of each map is anterior (front of the head); the bottom of each map is posterior (back of the head).

It can be seen that for low-frequency theta (4–6 Hz), EEG registration of the subliminal odor occurred on the first sniff, especially in the central and posterior regions, more on the right side (the regions of the blacks and dark greys). For high-frequency theta (6–8 Hz), EEG registration of the subliminal odor occurred on both sniffs, again central and more posterior on the right side. For low-frequency alpha (8–10 Hz), some evidence for EEG registration was obtained, more central and right sided, somewhat for both sniffs. For high-frequency alpha (10–12 Hz), EEG registration was obtained especially for sniff two, and the effect was central and more anterior on the right side. These effects (and all future effects described in this chapter), were statistically significant at least a + $p < 0.05$.

Subjects' accuracy in guessing which bottle contained the subliminal concentration of isoamyl acetate was 48%. Subjects' mean rating of the odor's intensity was only 1.8 (of a possible 10) , and subjects' mean rating of the confidence of their guess was only 3.2 (of a possible 10). Hence, in terms of both performance and self-report, these low concentration isoamyl acetate trials were apparently "subliminal." Despite the fact that subjects did not appear to detect or perceive the odorant, the EEG showed compelling evidence that the odorant was detected by the nose and was registered by the central nervous system.

These subliminal olfaction findings, though theoretically interesting and important, are not especially surprising or controversial. However, when the data were analyzed more finely, a number of surprising and potentially controversial findings emerged. These findings led to the concept of functional "blindsmell", and ultimately, to the concept "awareness without awareness" and the theory of Levels of Awareness.

Functional "Blindsmell" and "Awareness without Awareness": Analyses of Individual Differences in Subtle Olfaction

Athough the average group performance in detecting the odor was 48% (50% is chance), individual subjects varied in the number of trials out of 16 that they correctly guessed the odorant. Some subjects did better than chance, and some subjects did worse than chance. Could it have been the case that the EEG effects described above occurred primarily in the subset of subjects whose performance was somewhat above chance? If their performance was above chance, did this mean that they were actually experiencing the odorant? And if they were experiencing the odorant, would this mean that the EEG effects were actually reflecting conscious processing of the odorant afterall?

To address this question, subjects were split into three performance subgroups (high n= 32; medium n=29; and low n=25). Their guessing performance is shown in Figure 2. It can be seen that the high group was somewhat better than chance (68%), and the low group was somewaht below chance (36%). The medium group was virtually at chance. If the performance of the high performance group reflected consciousness of the odorant, one would expect that their ratings of intensity (Figure 3) and confidence (Figure 4) would be somewhat higher than the other two groups. However, as seen in Figures 3 and 4, this was not the case. The high performance group rated intensity and confidence just as low as the medium and low performance groups. Hence, even though their "performance" was above chance, their "consciousness" was at chance.

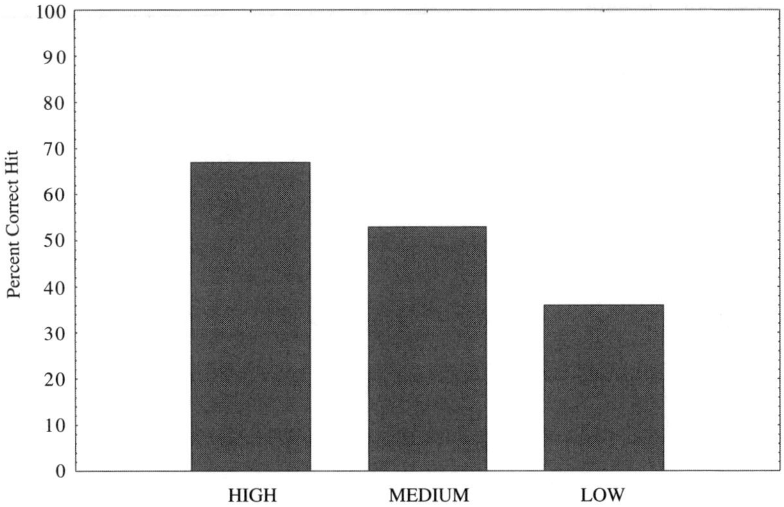

Figure 2. *Mean percent correct guessing for the subliminal isoamyl acetate trials separately for the high, medium and low performance subgroups. 50% is chance.*

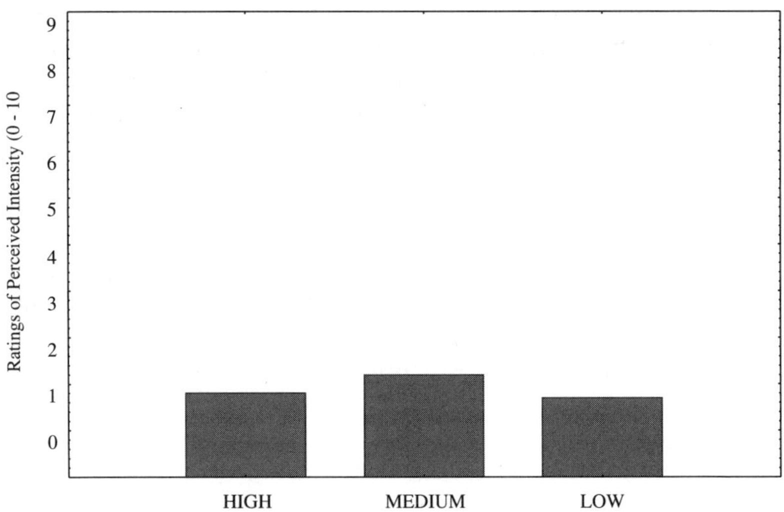

Figure 3. *Mean rating of perceived intensity (from 0 to 10) for the subliminal isoamyl acetate trials separately for the high, medium and low performance subgroups.*

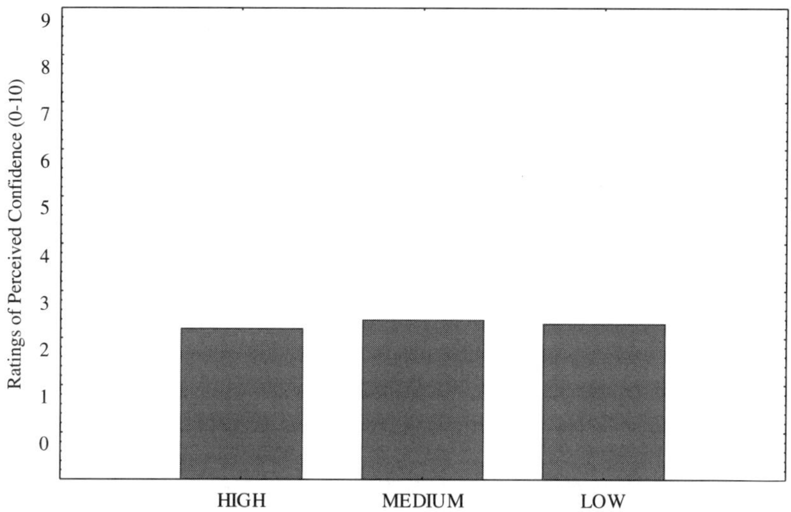

Figure 4. *Mean rating of perceived confidence of guessing (from 0 to 10) for the subliminal isoamyl acetate trials separately for the high, medium and low performance subgroups.*

One possible explanation is that their somewhat better performance simply represented "noise" due to a relatively small number of trials (n=16). However, another possibility is that the high performance subjects were actually more "sensitive" to the subliminal odorant. Their olfactory system (receptors and/or central nervous system) may have been better able to detect subtle concentrations of the odorant, even though they were not consciously aware that they were registering the odorant above chance.

Data suggesting that sensory performance can occur in the absence of conscious awareness has been reported for other senses. Research in vision has documented a phenomenon termed "blindsight" (Weiskrantz 1986) Patients who have received injuries to their primary visual cortex will report an absence of vision in corresponding regions of their visual field. However, they can be trained to detect above chance the presense of a visual stimulus presented in these regions, even though they continue to report seeing nothing. They may "intuit" that the stimulus is present, even though they do not "see it." Similiar reports have been made for "blindtouch." (Paillard, Michel, and Stelmach 1983).

In the present experiment, if the EEG indicated greater registration of the odorant in high performance subjects, these findings would suggest that "sensitive" subjects actually registered the subliminal odorant more strongly, enabling their performance to be better than chance, even if they were not aware that they were able to detect the odorant. Such findings would support the hypothesis of "blindsmell."

When the EEG data were analyzed as a function of performance, surprising results were obtained. Figure 5 displays EEG maps for low frequency theta (4–6 Hz). It can be seen that for low frequency theta (similar results were found for high frequency theta), EEG registration was observed in all three groups, again primarily in sniff one. Even in subjects whose performance was below chance, the odorant was clearly registered. However, the maps suggest that the effects are somewhat stronger as performance increases, and the effects become more anterior.

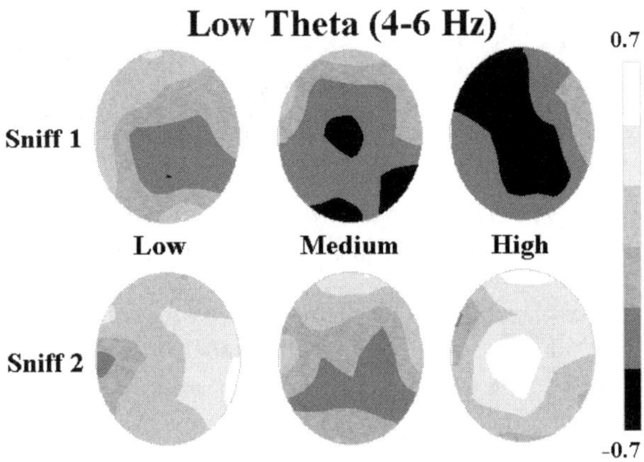

Figure 5. *Topographic EEG maps for low frequency theta (4–6 Hz) subtracting control bottles from the odor bottles for subthreshold isoamyl acetate trials (n=16) for high, medium and low performance subgroups. The top three maps reflect sniff one (the first sniff for the isoamyl acetate and control trials); the bottom three maps reflect sniff two (the second sniff for the isoamy acetate and control trials. The three subgroups are all drawn on the same scale. Whites and light greys reflect increases in EEG; blacks and dark greys reflect comparable magnitude decreases in EEG. The top of each map reflects the front of the head; the bottom of each map reflects the back of the head.*

Figure 6 displays EEG maps for high frequency alpha (10–12 Hz). It can been seen that for high frequency alpha (similar results were found for low frequency alpha), EEG registration was observed primarily in the high performance group, on sniff two.

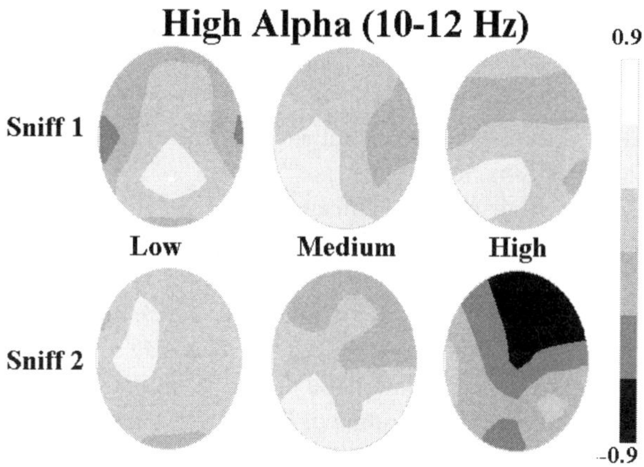

Figure 6. *Topographic EEG maps for high frequency alpha (10–12 Hz) subtracting control bottles from the odor bottles for subthreshold isoamyl acetate trials (n=16) for high, medium and low performance subgroups. The top three maps reflect sniff one (the first sniff for the isoamyl acetate and control trials); the bottom three maps reflect sniff two (the second sniff for the isoamy acetate and control trials. The three subgroups are all drawn on the same scale. Whites and light greys reflect increases in EEG; blacks and dark greys reflect comparable magnitude decreases in EEG. The top of each map reflects the front of the head; the bottom of each map reflects the back of the head.*

In other words, the high performance group showed clear evidence for greater EEG registration of the subliminal odorant in the higher EEG frequency (alpha). The lower EEG frequency (theta) seemed to immediately register the odorant (sniff one), even in subjects whose performance was below chance (e.g. implicit sensation). The higher EEG frequency (alpha) took time to register the odorant (sniff two), and primarily in subjects whose performance was above chance (e.g. implicit perception). Yet, these "sensitive" subjects showed no evidence of "experiencing" the odorants more strongly than less sensitive subjects. In a word, the high performance subjects showed evidence for functional "blindsmell."

The data became even more surprising and controversial when the data were analyzed more finely. By definition, when subjects were guessing (recall that the average accuracy for the sample as a whole was 48%), on some of the trials subjects would correctly guess which bottle contained the odorant (hits) and on other trials subjects would be incorrectly guess which bottle contained the odorant (misses). If the EEG was actually registering the presense of the subliminal odorant (and not simply the "belief" that the odorant was present), both hit and miss trials involving the odorant should show EEG registration. Given the large number of subjects in the present experiment (n=86), both the self-report and EEG data could be examined in terms of hits and misses for high, medium and low performance groups.

Figures 7 and 8 display the mean ratings of intensity and confidence separately for hit and miss trials for each of the three groups. First, it can be seen that there was a subtle, but consistent effect for intensity as a function of hit versus miss (Figure 7). Ratings of intensity were slightly but consistently higher for the hit trials than the miss trials. The size of the difference was approximately 2/10ths of one point! Though this effect is tiny, it was statistically significant for the three groups combined. Hence, even though the subjects were rating the subliminal odorant as very low in intensity, they somehow "sensed" the intensity slightly stronger on those trials when they happened to guess correctly than when they happened to guess incorrectly. It is highly improbable that they were "aware" that their "awareness" of the intensity of the odor was slightly higher for hit trials than miss trials!

For ratings of confidence, the picture is even more curious. The high performance group (i.e. the "sensitives") rated the confidence of their guesses significantly higher on hit trials compared to miss trials (Figure 8). Even though they seemed to be no more aware of the intensity of the odorant than the medium and low performance groups, they seemed better able to "sense" when they were guessing correctly. Recall that their overall confidence was no higher than the medium and low performance groups. In other words, in sensitive subjects, although their "awareness" of confidence was somewhat higher for hit trials than miss trials, they were apparently not "aware" that their awareness of confidence was slightly higher on the hit trials compared to the miss trials.

The EEG data complimented these subtle self-report differences, primarily for the higher frequencies. Figure 9 displays the high frequency alpha data for the three groups separately, for sniff one and sniff two, separately for hit and miss trials. First, it can be seen that for the low and medium groups, there were somewhat greater decreases in alpha during hit trials than miss trials (on both sniff one and sniff two). Second, it also can seen that for the high performance group, large EEG alpha decreases occurred, primarily for sniff two, and the *patterns* of the alpha decreases were different for the hit versus miss trials. When sensitive subjects guessed incorrectly (misses), the alpha decrease effects were more posterior and right hemispheric, whereas when the sensitive subjects guessed correctly (hits), the alpha decrease effects were more anterior and

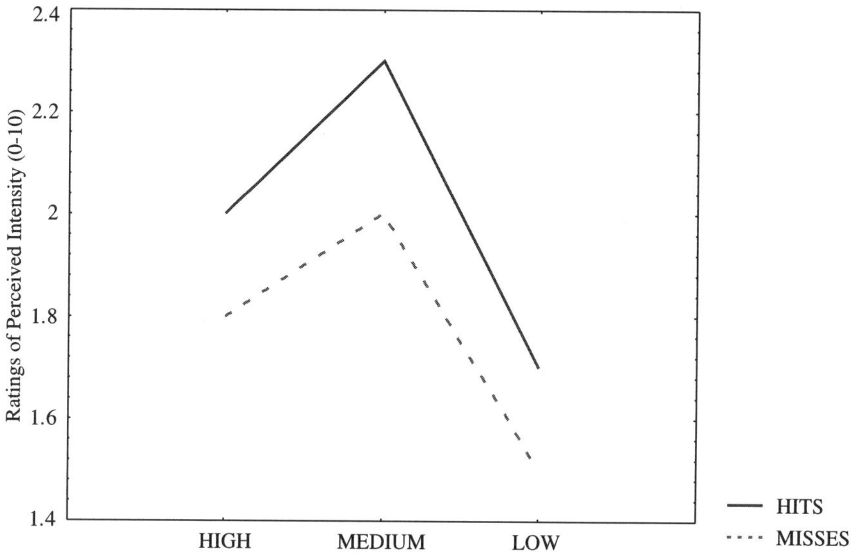

Figure 7. *Mean rating of perceived intensity (from 0 to 10) for the subliminal isoamyl acetate trials separately for hits and misses for the high, medium and low performance subgroups.*

included the left hemisphere. Note that the alpha decrease effects for the medium and low performance groups also involved the left hemisphere.

As mentioned above, when an odorant is perceived consciously, that is, the subject guesses above chance *and* rates the intensity of the odorant and the confidence of her/his guess appropriately high, alpha decreases are also observed in anterior regions, including the left hemisphere. The frontal cortex may play a special role in consciousness, especially the left frontal cortex (Natsoulas 1992).

The paradox posed by these unexpected hit/miss findings, especially for the sensitive subjects, can be stated simply: How can a subject's awareness of a stimulus (e.g. an odorant) be influenced by the stimulus when the subject is not aware that his awareness has been influenced? Since by definition, ratings of perceived intensity and confidence are measures of "awareness", the data suggest that "awareness" has been influenced in the absence of "awareness" (that is, the subjects were not aware that their awareness was different, since in this case, the stimuli were all "subliminal").

Continuing to label these effects as simply "subliminal" or "unconscious" begs the fundamental question. Subjects' "awareness" can change as a function

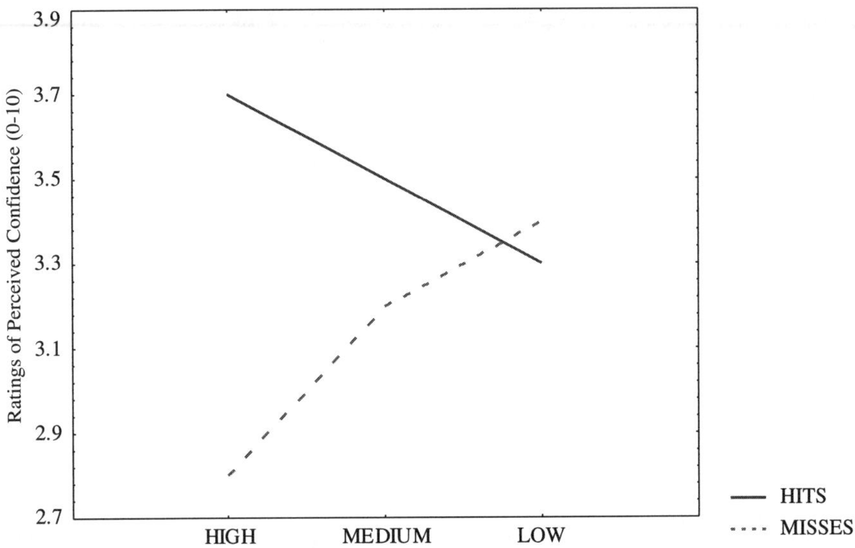

Figure 8. *Mean rating of perceived confidence of guessing (from 0 to 10) for the subliminal isoamyl acetate trials separately for hits and misses for the high, medium and low performance subgroups.*

of stimuli, even if subjects are not "aware" that their "awareness" is changing. How can we explain such effects? Must a stimulus have sufficient intensity and/or meaning to break into consciousness to be defined as "awareness"? Or, is it possible that all stimuli that activate biological processes have an inherent "awareness-ability" that can ultimately be measured, whether the subject is "aware" of this "awareness" or not? The hypothesis of "levels of awareness", formulated to explain the olfaction data described above, begins with the premise that all stimuli, by nature, are "pregnant with consciousness", and that some level of awareness is the rule, not the exception, in nature.

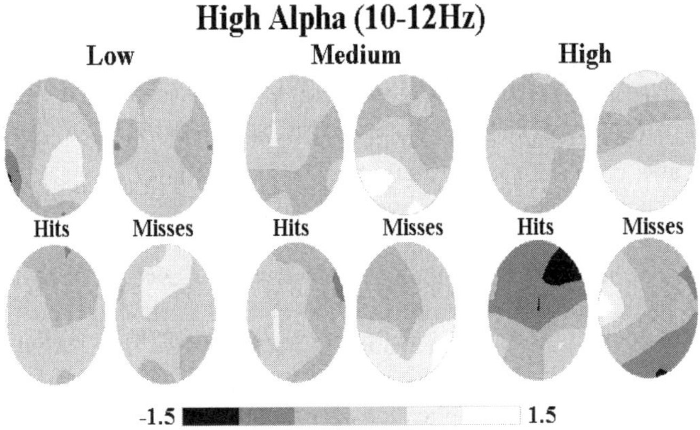

Figure 9. *Topographic EEG maps for high frequency alpha (10–12 Hz) subtracting control bottles from the odor bottles for subthreshold isoamyl acetate trials (n=16) separately for hits and misses for high, medium and low performance subgroups. The top six maps reflect sniff one (the first sniff for the isoamyl acetate and control trials); the bottom six maps reflect sniff two (the second sniff for the isoamy acetate and control trials. The three subgroups are all drawn on the same scale. Whites and light greys reflect increases in EEG; blacks and dark greys reflect comparable magnitude decreases in EEG. The top of each map reflects the front of the head; the bottom of each map reflects the back of the head.*

Levels of Awareness and "Awareness without Awareness"

If we begin with the premise that all stimuli that can activate biological processes have an inherent "awareness-ability" to them, we can create a theoretical framework that examines awareness in terms of hierarchical levels.

The core of the theory involves three general Levels of Awareness, termed Level I, Level II and Level III (Schwartz 1996). Consider Level II Awareness. This is what is typically thought of as "normal consciousness." When a subject says "I am aware of stimulus X" what she/he is actually saying is that "I — who is aware — is aware of the stimulus." Hence, implicit in normal consciousness is the notion of "awareness of awareness."

Level I Awareness can be thought of as pure awareness, the "awareness-ability" of any stimulus registered by a biological system. This awareness, per se, occurs in the absence of consciousness awareness (i.e. awareness of awareness, Level II). Level I Awareness traditionally has been referred to as the "unconscious", the "preconscious", the "subconscious" and/or the "nonconscious." It also includes what is currently refered to as "implicit" experience, be it implicit memory, implicit emotion, implicit perception, or implicit sensation.

Level III Awareness can be thought of "awareness of awareness of awareness". Level III awareness is an awareness of Level II awareness, just as Level II awareness is an awareness of Level I awareness. The idea of "self-concept" (i.e. being aware of self) is, by definition, a Level III (or higher) Awareness. Concepts of knowledge, understanding, and wisdom, reflect Level III (or higher) levels of awareness.

Space does not permit developing the concept of Levels of Awareness more extensively here. The particular organization of the Levels can be debated, and appropriately so, but precise organization is not important here. What is important here is the general concept of Levels of Awareness, beginning with Level I Awareness, and some of its implications for theory and research.

Predictions of Levels of Awareness Theory

At least three general predictions follow from the theory that can be confirmed or disconfirmed in future research. First, the theory requires that all stimuli registered by the brain should show evidence of subtle awareness (Level I Awareness) using appropriately sensitive paradigms as measures of self-reports and performance. Theoretically, if a stimulus is registered by the brain, it will be found to subtlely, yet reliably, influence measures of awareness (e.g. measures of perceived intensity) even though subjects will not be aware that their reports are linked to stimulus presentation. For example, chemoreception normally thought of as being "unconscious" (e.g. oxygen and carbon dioxide reception in the blood stream) should be found to show evidence of subtle awareness as measured by small but consistent changes in subjects' perceptions. The history of science can be thought of, in part, as the process of becoming increasingly aware of stimuli, processes, and orders that were here-to-fore outside of human consciousness. The concept of Level I Awareness is consistent with this vision of science.

A second prediction is that all stimuli registered by the brain can be transformed from Level I to Level II Awareness using appropriate training procedures and measurement techniques. If the apparatus that allows Level II Awareness is functional (e.g. the brain is healthy), theoretically, the information can be transformed with sufficient training. Everyday experience indicates that with training, people become aware of information of wich they previously were not aware. If awareness is the rule, not the exception, in nature, and the brain can access this awareness, then even if the intensity of the stimuli are very weak, "awareness" of the inherent "awareness" should be increaseable, at least to some degree. There are important clinical as well as basic science implications that follow from this prediction (e.g. patients with blindsight might be trained to regain some of their "vision").

A third prediction is that higher levels of awareness may involve higher EEG frequencies, more anterior cortical regions, and greater cortical integration. This prediction not only follows from the olfaction data. It logically follows that more complex systems will involve greater numbers of levels of information processing. Hence, higher rates of information exchange and greater system integration (e.g. coherence and the so-called "binding" problem) will be required as higher levels of awareness are acheived.

Becoming Aware of "Awareness Without Awareness"

The hypothesis that all stimuli have an inherent "awareness-ability" that is "experienced" as "awareness without awareness" has philosophical as well scientific implications. The hypothesis of Level I Awareness is implicit in the writings of Chalmers (1995). Chalmers proposes that consciousness is an inherent quality of matter. According to the double-aspect theory of information, information has two basic aspects: a physical aspect and a phenomenal (or experiential) aspect. If everything in nature has inherent "consciousness-ability", then theoretically human beings have the capability to access information normally thought of as non-existent (perhaps because it is normally experienced as outside of awareness). Future research may document that "subliminal" olfaction is the rule, not the exception, that "subliminal" registration of stimuli throughout the electromagnetic spectra occurs to varying degrees all the time (including internal sensations generated physiologically by organs such as the heart, e.g. Russek and Schwartz 1996), and that this information is expressed in our awareness to varying degrees, whether we are aware of this information or not.

Conceptual integrity requires that one follow predictions suggested by a theory, whether one likes the implications of the predictions or not. The concept of Level I Awareness turns out to have implications for controversal research that historically has not been part of main stream science, including parapsychology (e.g. Bem and Honorton 1994). If Level I Awareness is the rule, not the exception, in nature (including human nature), and people vary in their sensitivity to this fundamental level of information processing, it is conceivable that registration of subtle information, as documented in systematic research on parapsychology (Bem and Honorton 1994), may be more common than is generally recognized. What Native Americans in the Southwest and other native peoples have termed "spiritual awareness" may not only reflect higher levels of awareness, but may reflect a deep awareness of awareness of Level I awareness. Registration of subtle information and energy may find curious parallels to ancient ideas of "soul" and "spirit" (Schwartz 1997).

Philosophical issues aside, a fundamental challenge for the science of consciousness and individual differences in conciousness is to define awareness in such a way that it addresses all levels of awareness-ability. If the present chapter challenges the reader to reevaluate her/his concept of the "unconscious" and the nature of levels of conscious experience, then it will have acheived its goal.

Acknowledgments

Important contributions to the theory presented in this chapter were made by Geoffrey Ahern, Ziya Dikman, Mercedes Fernandez, John Kline, Ernest Polak, Linda Russek, and Lloyd Smith. Their suggestions and criticisms are warmly acknowledged. This chapter is a revised version of Schwartz (1996).

References

Bem, D. J. and Honorton, C. 1994. Does Psi exist? Replicable evidence for an anomalous process of information transfer. *Psychological Bulletin* 115: 4–18.

Chalmers, D. J. 1995. *Toward a Theory of Consciousness.* Cambridge, MA: MIT Press.

Miller, J. G. 1978. *Living Systems.* New York, NY: McGraw-Hill.

Natsoulas, T. 1992. Consciousness and Commisurotomy: Three hypothesized dimensions of deconnected left-hemisphere consciousness. *Journal of Mind and Behavior* 13: 37–67.

Paillard, J. F., Michel, F. and Stelmach, G. 1983. Localization with content: A tactile analogue of 'blindsight.' *Archives of Neurology* 40: 548–551.

Russek, L. G. and Schwartz, G. E. 1996. Energy Cardiology: A dynamical energy systems approach for integrating conventional and alternative medicine. *Advances: The Journal of Mind-Body Health* 2(4): 4–24.

Schwartz, G. E. 1996. Levels of awareness and "awareness without awareness": Data and Theory. In S. Hameroff, A. Kaszniak and A. Scott (eds). *Toward a Science of Consciousness. Contributions from the 1994 Tucson Conference.* Cambridge, MA., MIT Press.

Schwartz, G. E. 1997. Energy and Information: The soul and spirit of mind-body medicine. *Advances: The Journal of Mind-Body Health* 13(1): 75–77.

Schwartz, G. E., Bell, I. R., Dikman, Z. V., Fernandez, M., Kline, J. P., Peterson, J. M. and Wright, K. P. 1994. EEG responses to low level chemicals in normals and cacosmics. *Toxicology and Industrial Health* 10: 633–643.

Weiskrantz, L. 1986. *Blindsight: A Case Study and Implications.* Oxford, U. K.: Oxford University Press.

Individual Differences in Implicit Learning

Implications for the Evolution of Consciousness

Arthur S. Reber
Brooklyn College and The Graduate Center of the City University of New York

Rhianon Allen
Long Island University

Introduction

In this chapter we focus on the issue of individual differences in implicit learning (IL). We will treat the notion of individual differences in the standard fashion, referring to variations in the levels of performance exhibited by persons who make up an identifiable cohort. However, we will also find ourselves musing over some extensions of this canonical sense of the term by exploring the possibility that individuals from different populations (e.g., the very young, the aged, those with various disabilities) show distinct patterns of variation in performance with implicit tasks.

We will use the notion of implicit learning in similarly standard fashion, referring to the process by which knowledge about complex stimulus domains is acquired largely independent of conscious awareness of either the process or the products of acquisition. Implicit learning is ubiquitous in the real world, in fact so much so that it has often gone unnoticed — rather like that old joke about the fish being the last to discover water. However, it seems clear that such foundational processes as language acquisition and socialization which take place during infancy and early childhood are processes that are guided, in part, by implicit acquisition mechanisms. All of us emerge from our childhood inculcated with the social mores of our cultures and fluent in the languages of our communities — and virtually bereft of any introspectively available or reportable knowledge of the rich fabric of rules and conventions that form the bases of these epistemic systems. Moreover, the earliest acquisition of these complex skills takes place during developmental stages where the more commonly explored, top-down, conscious mechanisms are still relatively undeveloped (Piaget 1976).

Current research into implicit learning uses a variety of experimental paradigms, the most common of which are the sequential reaction time (SRT) task and artificial grammar (AG) learning. In the former, people are asked to respond as quickly as possible to a series of lights that flash at specific locations on a computer screen. Unbeknownst to the subjects, the order of locations is either dictated by a complex set of rules or is a repeating sequence. In both cases subjects show a gradual diminution in reaction times (TRs), indicating that have learned to exploit the sequence by anticipating the location of upcoming events. If the sequence is modified or the rules changed, the RTs immediately increase.

The AG learning procedure consists of two phases. During learning, people are asked to observe or memorize a series of symbol strings which have been constructed following an arbitrary but complex set of rules (the "artificial grammar"), again unbeknownst to them. Following the acquisition phase they are presented with a set of novel symbol strings, some of which follow the rules of the AG and some of which contain violations. Subjects display evidence of learning by being able to reliably distinguish between "grammatical" and "nongrammatical" strings. In these and various other procedures, people are typically unaware of the nature of the rules that control the structure of the displays and in many cases unaware of even the existence of the rules or that sequences repeated. Detailed discussions of these (and other) procedures can be found in any of several chapters in Stadler and Frensch (1998).

While we and a few others have been pursuing the study of these unconscious cognitive functions for some time (e.g., Allen & Reber 1980; Broadbent 1977; Brooks 1978; Reber 1967; Reber & Allen 1978), it is only recently that the issue has begun to attract widespread attention. Stimulated largely by the rediscovery of implicit memory and its neurocognitive underpinnings in the 1980's (Schacter 1987; Schacter & Graf 1986; Squire 1992), the past decade has witnessed a rather remarkable outpouring of work on the cognitive unconscious in general and implicit learning in particular. Since 1993 implicit learning has been the topic of three major theoretical books (Berry & Dienes 1993; Cleeremans 1993; Reber 1993), two comprehensive edited overview volumes (Berry 1997; Stadler & Frensch 1998), and two special issues of international journals (*Psychologia Belgica* and *Psychonomic Bulletin and Review*, both in 1997). While there is no need to go into detail here, it should come as no surprise that these works are replete with the theoretical disputes, empirical arguments, and philosophical give-and-take that mark a scientific field as it settles into shape.

However, what is relevant here is that, despite this wide-spread attention from so many quarters, the issue of individual differences in implicit learning has gone almost completely unexplored. With the sole exception of some entailments of the theory of implicit learning discussed in Reber (1993, 1997a), there is not a single reference in any of these recent works to the issue of individual differences in IL — a state of affairs that is going to make our contribution to this book a bit unorthodox.

Nevertheless, for reasons that will become clear, we feel that the issue of individual variation in implicit learning is of considerable theoretical and practical importance. What is missing to date has been a coherent framework within which to view it and a sensible theoretical basis for studying it — a conceptual lacuna we will try to remedy here. In what follows we will first present a series of arguments, largely theoretical in nature, concerning the patterns of interindividual variation in implicit learning. These arguments will turn on a model of the cognitive unconscious outlined in Reber (1992, 1993) which places the processes and underlying mechanisms of IL in an evolutionary framework. We will then have a short section in which we review the few relevant studies that have been published and attempt to get some sense of how well the theory is standing up to empirical test. As we go, we will issue from time to time invitations to our colleagues to involve themselves in this area by outlining a number of related problems that are in need of investigation. So, in this book on individual differences we are actually going to have very little to say about empirical individual differences. Our chapter is like an uncashed check — and it's likely to be some time before we know whether there are any funds to back it up.

The Theory: An Evolutionary Perspective on the Cognitive Unconscious

Before we get into the details of the theory, we need a little conceptual scaffolding and some understanding of how the theory came about, how we are applying principles borrowed from evolutionary biology, and why we feel that the theory provides a coherent perspective within which to view, not just implicit learning, but the full panoply of functions now understood to make up the cognitive unconscious (Kihlstrom 1990; Reber, Allen, & Reber 1999).

The original motivation for the development of the theory was a desire to embed contemporary cognitive science within a biologically coherent framework (Reber 1992). We have long been troubled by theories of cognitive function that fail to satisfy the requirements of biological coherence and ecological validity. We regard such modeling as suspect from the outset. Included here are such influential models of recent decades as the information processing framework within which complex, linearly arranged modules were presumed to operate by shuttling snippets of information about from metaphoric box to metaphoric box and the Chomsky-inspired nativistic theories of language functions in which a language acquisition device is assumed to have sprung up *de novo* to guide the acquisition of natural language.

All theories of human cognitive function necessarily have evolutionary entailments in that the hypothesized mechanisms that are recruited to do the cognitive work within the theory must be biologically and neurologically coherent — although this aspect of theory building is often ignored or perhaps simply unappreciated. For example, the degree of encapsulation of function required by the information processing metaphor is simply not to be found in cortical architecture and its linear nature is, moreover, in conflict with what we know about the massive parallelism of the brain. (See Feinberg & Farah 1997 for an historical overview.) In a similar fashion, the immensely complex and highly specific language acquisition device presumed by Chomsky's linguistic nativism is highly unlikely to have evolved in the short time frame required by the theory (Tomasello 1995; Winter & Reber 1994). There are other, even more flagrant violators of this doctrine, but our point, we hope, is made.

Framing the emergence of implicit and explicit cognitive function within the basic parameters of evolutionary biology was a conscious exercise in theory building that, hopefully, has resulted in a model that not only makes psychological sense but is biologically sensible. As we hope will become clear, the relationships between the implicit, unconscious cognitive functions (those that occur relatively independent of awareness and conscious control), and the explicit, conscious functions (those that take place within the spotlight of awareness and are subject to conscious control and modulation) become crystallized when the two systems are viewed as having evolved at very different times and because of very different evolutionary pressures.

Finally, before we get to the theory itself, we want to be clear about how we are using principles of evolutionary biology. Our approach is different in kind from that typically carried out under the rubrics of *evolutionary psychology* and *sociobiology*. That is, we are not hypothesizing about the various kinds of evolutionary scenarios that might have led to the emergence of implicit and/or explicit cognitive functions. This is not a "how the leopard got its spots" exercise. Rather, our point is to show how, when particular principles of evolutionary biology are taken into consideration, rather specific predictions about the dissociations between implicit and explicit cognitive functions can be made — and among these predictions will be several intriguing ones about the patterns of individual differences that should emerge when the implicit and the explicit are compared.

Some Simple Principles of Evolutionary Biology

There are several straightforward principles that form the conceptual foundation of evolutionary biology. These principles are not particular to one or another model of evolution. They pertain whether one is working within standard parameters of a Darwinian gradualism or the more recent saltationist models based on the principles of punctuated equilibrium. The precise temporal course of evolutionary change is not an issue.

The Principle of Hierarchical Structure

Novel forms do not emerge *de novo*. Instead, they build upon existing forms. The immediate entailment of this principle is that all evolutionary processes are pyramidal in nature in that there will be a large base of foundational forms of greater antiquity upon which more recently evolving forms will rest.

The Principle of Success

In the course of evolution, processes and structures that have proven their adaptive value tend not to be jettisoned. That is, only lethal or otherwise nonadaptive forms disappear from a population.

The Principle of Conservation

Following from the preceding, evolutionary processes are necessarily conservative. That is, once successful forms become fixed and begin to serve as the foundations for developing forms, their core features and properties are unlikely to be substantially modified by subsequent adaptational processes. To take a classic example, once the set of jaw bones in early fish underwent the appropriate modifications to enable them to transmit vibratory information, the structural and functional aspects of the inner ear were established. While there are minor variations on this basic theme (e.g., bats and dolphins have a far greater range of sensitivity than most other species), the foundational forms are conserved. The auditory system of every species that counts this fish as among its ancestors (including, of course, *Homo sapiens*) uses these three ancient bones in this general fashion.

The Principle of Stability

Again, following from the preceding, early appearing, successful, and well-maintained structures tend to be relatively invariant. Successful variations in forms and structures that emerged early in the evolutionary history of a species are rare; in fact, mutations to foundational forms are almost always lethal (e.g., mutations to the form and structure of the spine are devastating to any vertebrate species). However, modifications in forms and structures that are more recent are often viable (e.g., the shape of a bird's beak) and, of course, form the basis of both individual variation and the emergence of novel species. Thus, pyramidal structures are always broad (either literally or conceptually), stable and relatively invariant at the base, and allow for greater variation as they progress.

These four principles operate as a cluster of heuristics that form the foundation of modern evolutionary biology. They have a rich history and can be shown to be necessary consequences of particular models of evolution and cladistic classification systems. We will not, however, go into any more detail issues here. A more in-depth characterization of the model can be found in Reber (1993, Chapter 3), and a formal presentation can be found in Schank and Wimsatt (1987). Our point here is merely to lay these principles out and look at their logical entailments when we introduce a simple, hopefully uncontroversial axiom.

> **Axiom**: *Consciousness is a relatively late arrival on the evolutionary scene and was, perforce, preceded by sophisticated perceptual and cognitive functions that operated without its benefit.*

Before we explore the sequelae of this assumption, we need to be clear about the meaning of this term *consciousness*. In what follows, we are going to use the term in its folk psychology sense. That is, consciousness is that sense of selfness that James (1890) was so fond of. It is that cluster of cognitive functions that enables us to be aware of self (*cogito ergo sum*), to manipulate and modulate cognitive functions (see Baars 1997 for an extended compendium of these), and to capture the notion of experience (i.e., it *hurts* when I hit my thumb with a hammer). While primitive forms of consciousness may be as old as life itself (Reber 1997b) and species other than ourselves may possess viable and possibly familiar forms (Griffin 1981), these forms of consciousness of phylogenetic antiquity are not the kinds of intentional and controllable consciousness and cognizance that are of interest here.

So, if this consciousness of ours, characterized as it is by the rich array of functions that enables us to do all those wonderful cognitive things like prove mathematical theorems, play the stock market, reason through complex situations, hold lots of information in mind at once, read this chapter and know what its authors are talking about — if this consciousness, being the private domain of members of our species, is a late arrival on the evolutionary scene then it must have been preceded for a considerable amount of time (geologically speaking) by a clutch of cognitive functions that operated before it emerged. It must have been preceded by adaptive learning mechanisms that are not fully 'conscious.' That is, there must be a rich and effective implicit system that has functioned for eons in other species and continues to operate effectively in ours without benefit of top-down modulation or symbolic representation.

This simple statement, when looked at in the context of the basic principles discussed above, turns out to have a number of theoretically interesting entailments regarding the patterns of dissociation we expect to observe when we compare implicit (or unconscious) processes with explicit (or conscious) ones. First we will briefly discuss three of the predictions of the theory just to give some sense of the breadth of issues involved. Then we (finally) get to the predictions that speak directly to the issue of individual differences.

Some Predictions of the Model

Cross-Species Commonality

It goes almost without saying that the model predicts that implicit systems should show strong interspecies similarities. The degree of commonality is best seen when it is understood that the process of implicit learning is essentially the detection of covariations among components of stimulus displays. For example, what subjects acquire in experiments using the SRT task or artificial grammar learning is captured by the notion that they are learning which stimulus events "go with" or "are predictive of" other events. This process is, of course, the one that lies at the core of the Rescorla-Wagner model of conditioning and learning (see Rescorla 1988) which is the generally accepted theory of animal learning. It is also the process which is easily represented by connectionist models of learning that express complex learning as precisely the process of the detection of covariation among elements of complex stimulus displays (Cleeremans 1993; Elman, Bates et al. 1996). There might indeed be some inter-species variation in the amount or complexity of associations that can be learned, but the basic process of acquisition should be similar or identical. In contrast, explicit functions occur in only some (albeit most) of the species tested to date (Wynne 1998).

Age Independence

The functioning of implicit systems can also be expected to be relatively independent of age and developmental level. Such age independence differs dramatically from what we see in the core fields of developmental psychology and gerontology where the exploration of changes in function and behavior observed as individuals age lies at the heart of the disciplines. However, the functions and behaviors that are the focus of these fields of study tend to be those that *do* change — those that are top-down and modulated by consciousness. Overwhelmingly, the study of cognitive development examines the emergence and rate of change of reasoning, symbolic representation, problem solving, memory, logic and similar processes. Similarly, explorations of aging typically examine the degree and rate of cognitive loss in processes like memory, problem solving, planning functions and the like. The direct entailment of the evolutionary model is, of course, that we do not expect to see these kinds of ontological changes with *implicit* processes.

Clearly, there are two subtexts here — one dealing with the early years of life, one with the waning. From a simple, common sense perspective, the existence of implicit functioning during the early years is utterly obvious. As we noted earlier, infants and young children acquire stunning amounts of information about the causal nature of their world, the grammatical and pragmatic aspects of their native languages, the rich fabric of the social mores of their cultures, and they do so with little contribution from an adult-like top-down, modulating consciousness. Developmentally speaking, the implicit takes primacy over the explicit. In recent years direct empirical support for this picture has begun to appear. For example, Haith, Wentworth, and Canfield (1993) found that 3-month old infants learn to anticipate alternating and repeating visual patterns; Gomez and Gerken (in press) report that 12-month old infants can learn an artificial grammar implicitly; and Saffran and her colleagues (Saffran, Aslin, & Newport 1996; Saffran, Newport, & Aslin 1996) have shown that by 3 months of age infants can pick up arbitrary patterns of phonetic variation incidentally. Saffran et al.'s work is especially interesting in that a comparison group of adults showed no advantage over the infants in this task.

At the other end of the life span the empirical picture is less clear. A review of the literature by Shimamura (1990) found that implicit memory is more resistant to aging than explicit memory, and recent work by Light and her colleagues (see Light 1992) tends to support this view. The only systematic examinations of implicit learning in an aged population we are aware of have been carried out by Howard and Howard (1989, 1992, 1997). They report that both young and old adults show learning of a standard SRT task with second-order dependencies built into the sequence. However, there was evidence that the younger subjects (between 19 and 21 years old) learned better than the old (65 to 73 years) and the old-old (76–80 years). In Howard and Howard (1997), the advantage the younger subjects typically display was traced to their ability to pick up more higher order information in the time given. Younger subjects were also able to generate more appropriate sequences on their own in a later follow-up production task. Howard and Howard suggest that this latter result may be due to the elderly subject's diminished ability at voluntary retrieval and not necessarily a deficit in implicit learning.

In passing, we note that interpreting life-span findings is surely going to turn out to be a difficult task. The problem is that secondary factors such as attention and motivation are likely to be playing a role. Hence, as children age and their capacity to allocate and organize attentional resources improves or as distinct patterns of motivation emerge, increased performance on implicit tasks might be observed but not necessarily because of an improvement in implicit learning, per se. Shifts in the other direction in an aged population would, of course, result in the opposite pattern of results. More on this problem later.

Neurological Robustness

Implicit systems can also be expected to show greater robustness than explicit systems. Specifically, we expect to find that implicit functions that operate independently of consciousness will be relatively unaffected by dysfunctions and disorders that compromise explicit, conscious functions. By virtue of the pyramidal character of evolution, all functions that are mediated through systems of greater antiquity should display greater stability and resiliency than those mediated through more recently evolved systems.

Of the entailments we discuss here, this one has the strongest support and is particularly relevant to the notion of individual variation. There is, in fact, an enormous and growing body of psychological, psychiatric and neurological evidence that points to the conclusion that implicit (or "nondeclarative" as they are often called in this literature) functions survive physiological assaults that seriously compromise explicit (or "declarative") functions. For example, profoundly amnesic patients who have suffered widespread damage to their hippocampal structures display normal implicit memories (Schacter, Chiu, & Ochsner 1993) and implicit learning (Knowlton & Squire 1994, 1996); deeply psychotic patients display virtually normal behavior in an AG learning experiment although they are incapable of explicitly solving simple problems that cause non-patients little difficulty (Abrams & Reber 1988); blindsight patients reliably respond appropriately to visual displays despite being totally unaware of not only what stimuli were displayed but even that a display existed (Weiskrantz 1986). In short, the neurological structures that support the implicit systems show greater robustness than those that are part of the conscious representational system, possibly because they are more distributed than the latter (see Reber, Allen & Reber 1999).

On Individual Differences in Implicit Learning

The preceding demonstrates that people with identifiable neurological damage are not substantially different from non-patients in their abilities to form implicit representations, although admittedly they are in some cases somewhat slower to reach a criterion of learning. But the evolutionary model predicts not only diminished variance associated with neurological robustness, but also a relative lack of variation among intact individuals for processes mediated by evolutionarily old structures and functions. That is, the model makes predictions, not just about group differences in unconscious cognitive processing, but about the degree of interindividual variation that is expected when we directly compare implicit and explicit functions within the same population.

This is where we are faced with a paucity of research — in part because the issue has not been recognized by many as one of theoretical importance but also, in part, because of methodological problems. The main difficulty has been the lack of common tasks and metrics whereby explicit and implicit functions can be compared. Without such methodological consistencies, evaluating individual differences in explicit and implicit functions is like attempting to prove that there is less variation in visual acuity than there is in verbal fluency. Nevertheless, there have been studies which speak, in principle, to the issue. Specifically:

Covariation with other Cognitive Factors

One, somewhat inferential approach, is to look for covariation between a measure of implicit learning and either some measure of explicit learning or some other feature of functioning which is known to exhibit consistent individual differences with a high stability coefficient. This strategy rests on the entailment of the evolutionary model that the slight individual differences found in implicit learning might not be influenced by the same factors that influence explicit functions. Most of the speculation here has concerned the relationship between implicit functions and IQ. If the evolutionary model is correct, then implicit cognitive functions should display little concordance with standard psychometric measures of "intelligence." This relatively straightforward prediction rests on the observation that contemporary instruments for measuring intelligence are based virtually entirely on explicit cognitive functions, although this assumption has been challenged by some (e.g., Carpenter, Just & Shell 1990).

While we appreciate that this strategy is less than satisfactory because it relies on the questionable search for patterns rather than on direct examination of individual differences in implicit and explicit functioning, it has produced some interesting findings. For example, Maybery, Taylor, and O'Brien-Malone (1995) found that performance on an implicit contingency detection task was not related to IQ (*r*'s= .02 and .04 for children in Grades 1–2 and 6–7 respectively), but that performance on a similar explicit task was (*r*'s = .37 and .56). Further, the children in these studies showed no association between their success on the implicit task and actual verbalized knowledge of the contingency tested (*r*'s = .05 for both groups), whereas verbalized knowledge was associated with success on the explicit task (*r*'s = .47 and .80 for Grades 1–2 and 6–7 respectively). Interestingly, the low correlations between implicit learning and explicit measures were *not* due to lack of variation in implicit functioning. That is, there *were* individual differences in implicit learning, but these were not related to the differences obtained on explicit measures. Also of interest here is the fact that performance on both the explicit and implicit tasks increased systematically with age — a point we will discuss briefly at a later point.

Reber, Walkenfeld and Hernstadt (1991) also found performance on an explicit problem-solving task to be related to tested IQ in adults (r =. 69). In contrast, IQ was not related to performance on an AG learning task (r=.25), and, as with Maybery et al. (1995), there was no significant correlation between implicit and explicit learning (r=.32) — although there is little doubt these latter two correlations would become significant with larger subject populations. These nonsignificant correlations between implicit and explicit functions found by Reber et al. (1991) might be higher than those obtained by Maybery et al. (1995) because Reber et al. (1991) noted that some of their participants were engaging in some explicit learning during the AG task. As with Maybery et al. (1995), Reber et al. (1991) found some individual variation in success on the implicit task.

Recently, McGeorge, Crawford and Kelly (1997) extended some of these findings in interesting ways. First, a factor analysis showed that while the correlation between performance on the implicit task and overall IQ was not significant (r = .12), there was a small but statistically real loading on the

Perceptual Organization factor ($r=.19$). Interestingly, this factor is the one most clearly associated with fluid intelligence. The explicit task, on the other hand, showed strong correlations with overall IQ ($r=.67$) and with both the Perceptual Organizational and Attention-Concentration factors (r's$=.65$ and 53, respectively). And relevant to our earlier discussion, since McGeorge et al. ran subjects whose ages ranged from 18 to 77 years, they were also able to test the age-independence prediction of the evolutionary model. The results fit neatly with prediction. There were no differences in performance on the implicit task with increasing age but a significant drop off in performance was observed in the explicit series completion task.

Returning to our discussion of covariation with performance on IQ tests, Ellis and his colleagues have also found that individuals identified as retarded often display intact incidental learning. (Incidental learning is not identical to implicit rule or pattern learning, but is similar in the sense that it is unintentional and uncontrolled.) In the first of these studies, Ellis, Katz and Williams (1987) found that mildly retarded adolescents, normal children and normal adults were all equivalent in incidental learning of location. As with the studies discussed above, individual differences were obtained, but were unrelated to gross measures of high-level cognitive function. Furthermore, relevant to a point we will discuss later, the standard deviations on Ellis et al.'s (1987) incidental and intentional tasks appear to be equivalent.

Ellis and Allison (1988) painted a more complex picture. Incidental learning of frequency of occurrence was equivalent for mildly retarded adolescents and college students, but only for pictorial (visual) information. While many individuals with a diagnosis of retardation displayed normal incidental learning of verbal-semantic material, several such individuals did not. These findings suggest that uncontrolled, unintentional learning processes show little age and IQ variation when we are examining visual-spatial or noncomplex material, but that individual differences might emerge in processing of verbal or complex material. Such an outcome is consistent with Schultz's (1983) proposition that persons with intellectual disabilities experience difficulty with materials and tasks that require greater depth of processing — a feature of much explicit processing. Anderson (1998) has recently reviewed research into related phenomena, arguing that variation in IQ is associated primarily with variation in mechanisms that are amenable to conscious control and reflection.

In all the above studies, however, we note that individual variation does seem to occur in unintentional, uncontrolled processes, and that it generally seems to be of the same degree as that found in intentional, controlled processes. In no case, however, is performance on these two sets of tasks correlated when the material does not need to be processed deeply. Hence, although the literature is somewhat sparse, there seem to be measurable differences in both implicit rule learning and more simple incidental learning. However, the suggestion is that success on implicit tasks is likely *not* associated with performance on standardized IQ tests. Whether the individual differences observed are stable has not been assessed.

Covariation with Non-Cognitive Factors

Few factors other than explicit cognitive function have been examined for their relationship to implicit learning in intact adults. However, anxiety and depression — two semi-stable emotional factors known to affect some facets of explicit cognitive performance — have been studied. Rathus, Reber, Manza and Kushner (1994) found that reported test anxiety interfered with time to memorize learning strings during the memorization phase of an AG task, but not with grammaticality judgments in a later phase. Thus, anxiety disrupted explicit memory, but not the formation of implicit knowledge about the rule structure.

The tale is a bit more complicated with depression. There is a substantial body of research suggesting that depression interferes with effort expended on a task, and hence interferes with explicit memory and explicit cognitive operations (see Cohen, Weingartner, Smallberg, Pickar & Murphy 1982; Johnson & Magaro 1987). More recently, the work of Williams, Watts, MacLeod and Mathews (1988) suggests that clinical depression interferes with the formation of explicit, episodic and autobiographical memory while it enhances implicit memory of negative events. That is, depression might be associated with automatized encoding biases. However, little work has been done on the effects of depression on implicit rule or contingency learning. Rathus et al. (1994) administered an AG task and the Beck Depression Inventory to a large sample of college students. Using a variety of criteria to separate depressed from non-depressed students, they found that the two groups were statistically indistinguishable on explicit memorization during learning, accuracy on the (implicit) well-formedness task, speed of decision making on the latter task, and confidence in decisions made. Thus, differences in the range of depressive symptoms reported by non-clinical participants do not seem to be associated either with explicit short-term memory or with implicit learning of structure.

There is, so far as we know, only one study of implicit learning that examined associations between implicit learning and non-affective features of personality. Kassin and Reber (1979) examined the factor of locus of control and reported that participants who were high on the "internal" scale tended to be better at implicit learning than those who were more "external". However, as with the aging data, it is not clear whether to attribute this result to true differences in implicit learning ability or to differences in motivation and/or attention which are known to covary with internality/externality.

Thus, the story about the relationship between implicit learning and non-cognitive factors is clearly far from complete. Implicit learning seems to be robust against the onslaughts of test anxiety, and probably those associated with depression. But truth is there has been little in the way of careful empirical exploration of this issue. Much work needs to be done using a variety of personality and affective factors, in both clinical and non-clinical populations, and using implicit and explicit tasks of greater cognitive complexity.

Different Instructional Sets

A more direct way of assessing implicit and explicit processing is to use the same stimulus display but manipulate instructional set. While this won't guarantee deployment of a single learning type, an explicit problem-solving cognitive set should be induced by instructions to look for rules and regularities in a series of stimuli. Behavior under such conditions can be compared with the neutral instructional set typically used. There are, in fact, two early studies with an AG learning task that used just such instructional sets (Reber 1976; Reber, Kassin, Lewis & Cantor 1980). While no measure of variability was presented in these papers, we were able to retrieve the original data and calculate standard deviations for proportion of correct well-formedness judgments. The results are not simple. Combining across both studies for the typical (unorganized) learning displays, the interindividual variability in performance did *not* differ as a function of instructional set, $F_{max}(14, 14) = 1.5, p > .05$. That is, approximately the same degree of interindividual variability was found in implicit and explicit processing of an AG.

Maybery, et al. (1995) carried out the only other study we are aware of where this instructional variable entered in — although as with the above, it was not the primary focus of their work. They provided a large group of children with an implicit learning contingency task and a similar explicit task. The resultant obtained standard deviations on the two tasks appear to be roughly commensurate relative to their means, although the standard deviations for the explicit task might be somewhat larger. However, since the two tasks were not precisely analogous, and the means and potential maxima on the two tasks differed, it is impossible to come to firm conclusions.

Despite these two less than convincing outcomes, the use of different instructional sets does provide, in principle, a set of conditions under which the hypothesis about interindividual variation can be tested. We invite any interested readers to get involved.

Establishing a Common Metric

This last discussion highlights the point that, if we are to come to some conclusions about inter-individual differences in implicit learning, we need to examine individual performances on implicit and explicit tasks which use a common metric. This is not an easy endeavor. In order to compare measures of individual variation (e.g., standard deviations) on two different tasks, one must construct two tasks which have the same possible minima and maxima, and upon which average learners obtain the same mean score. Ideally, the two tasks should be superficially similar and engage the same level of attention and motivation, but recruit different processes.

To date we know of only two studies that attempted to establish this kind of common metric. Reber et al. (1991) ran subjects through both an AG task and an explicit problem-solving task in which participants had to discover the patterns in letter series in order to continue the series. In both cases, responses during testing were converted to percentage correct in order to convert the two tasks to a common metric. Since the obtained means on these two tasks were virtually identical, direct comparison of the obtained variances and ranges could be carried out. Both the range and variance were larger on the explicit task, with the range of obtained percent correct being over twice as large for the explicit task, and the obtained variance over four times greater. This basic finding was replicated by McGeorge, et al. (1997).

Summary

In this chapter we have tried to come to grips with the question of whether there are distinct patterns of individual variation in implicit, unconscious cognitive functions when compared with those functions normally carried out under the spotlight of consciousness. The presentation has been couched in a general theory of the cognitive unconscious which emerged from some basic considerations of evolutionary biology. Overall, the conceptual landscape we have surveyed appears to be a bit rocky although there were a few discernable landmarks. The evolutionary framework within which our approach to implicit learning is tucked appears to have fairly strong support in many of its predictions. However, the issue that is the central focus of this chapter, individual differences, is where matters are least clear. Specifically, while we find little variation in implicit learning associated with neurological factors, performance on some aspects of IQ tests, or high levels of anxiety, the data are less clear when it comes to aging, depression, and the impact of instructional set.

It is our sense that individual differences in implicit functioning do exist. The question is whether such interindividual variation is distinguishable from what we commonly see in consciously modulated, top-down cognitive processing. The key issues are whether the observed differences are: (a) traceable to stable and intrinsic interindividual variation in implicit processing per se, or whether they are due primarily to secondary factors such as attention, motivation, sensorimotor skills and the like, and (b) uniformly smaller than those associated with comparable tasks that tap primarily explicit, top-down cognitive functions. For example, did Kassin and Reber (1979) find differences between high internalizers and externalizers because such distinct personality types *are* associated with differences in implicit processing or because high internalizers tend to pay more attention to the patterns of covariation in the stimulus display? Did Maybery et al. (1995) obtain age effects because there *are* age effects in implicit contingency learning, or because younger children do not attend to left-right location or have difficulty encoding left-right location, even implicitly? Similarly, it will be impossible to establish age invariance unless experimental procedures are devised that are equally appealing to all ages and are capable of sustaining the attention and motivation of infants, children, young adults and the elderly.

And, just to take one last example to show how complex these issues are likely to turn out to be — even when looking at simple, noncognitive domains. In a series of recent papers, Masters and his colleagues have drawn specific parallels between a variety of sensorimotor skills (like putting a golf ball) and the cognitive implicit/explicit distinctions we have been developing in this chapter. For example, Masters (1992) showed that when placed under pressure to perform, an implicitly acquired sensorimotor skill is less likely to become degraded than one acquired explicitly. However, individual differences were observed in the implicit group. A follow-up study (Masters, Polman & Hammond 1993) traced these differences to a personality factor which has been dubbed "reinvestment" or the extent to which individuals focus attention back on their own bodies when under pressure to perform skilled movements.

This result, when placed in context of other findings from the implicit learning literature and the study of sensorimotor skills, hints at several complications. Specifically, Hsiao and Reber (1998) have made it abundantly clear that most implicit learning is demanding of attentional resources, and Wulf and her colleagues (Wulf, Lee, & Schmidt 1994; Wulf, & Schmidt 1997) have produced dramatic differences in performance on simple sensorimotor tasks (like those Masters has used) simply by having subjects alter the focus of their attention. For example, in one study Wulf, Höss, and Prinz (1997) had subjects attempt to control a balance beam with their feet. Subjects who focused on their feet did more poorly than subjects who focused on a tiny red dot which they placed their feet next to. Hence, factors such as internal vs. external focus, attention, personality, and method of training all interact in ways yet not understood.

Unpacking exactly how implicit and or explicit processes are mapping themselves into these kinds of behaviors and just which factors are going to turn out to be responsible for the patterns of individual differences observed is certainly going to be challenging. As we noted at the outset, we have no feelings of possessiveness over these ideas. We are in a 'give it away' mode here and hope that readers find some of the questions raised by this research sufficiently intriguing that they join us in that ongoing struggle to understand.

References

Abrams, M. and Reber, A. S. 1988. Implicit learning: Robustness in the face of psychiatric disorders. *Journal of Psycholinguistic Research* 17: 425–439.

Allen, R. and Reber, A. S. 1980. Very long term memory for tacit knowledge. *Cognition* 8: 175–185.

Anderson, M. 1998. Individual differences in intelligence. In K. Kirsner, C. Speelman, M. Maybery, A. O'Brien-Malone, M. Anderson and C. MacLeod (eds) *Implicit and explicit mental processes*, 171–185. Mahwah, NJ: Erlbaum.

Baars, B. J. 1997. *In the theater of consciousness: The workspace of the mind.* NY: Oxford University Press.

Berry, D. C. (ed.) 1997. *How implicit is implicit learning?* NY: Oxford University Press.

Berry, D. C. and Dienes, Z. 1993. *Implicit learning: Theoretical and empirical issues.* Hillsdale, NJ: Erlbaum.

Broadbent, D. E. 1977. Levels, hierarchies, and the locus of control. *Quarterly Journal of Experimental Psychology* 29: 181–201.

Brooks, L. R. 1978. Nonanalytic concept formation and memory for instances. In E. Rosch and B. B. Lloyd (eds). *Cognition and categorization.* 170–211 NY: Wiley.

Carpenter, P. A., Just, M. A. and Shell, P. 1990. What one intelligence test measures: A theoretical account of the processing of the Raven Progressive Matrices test. *Psychological Review* 97: 404–431.

Cleeremans, A. 1993. *Mechanisms of implicit learning: Connectionist models of sequence processing.* Cambridge, MA: MIT Press.

Cohen, R. M., Weingartner, H., Smallberg, S. A., Pickar, D. and Murphy, D. L. 1982. Effort and cognition in depression. *Archives of General Psychiatry* 39: 593–597.

Ellis, N. R. and Allison, P. 1988. Memory for frequency of occurrence in retarded and nonretarded persons. *Intelligence* 12: 61–75.

Ellis, N. R., Katz, E. and Williams, J. E. 1987. Developmental aspects of memory for spatial location. *Journal of Experimental Child Psychology* 44: 401–412.

Elman, J. L., Bates, E. A., Johnson, M. H., Karmiloff-Smith, A., Parisi, D. and Plunkett, K. 1996. *Rethinking innateness: A connectionist perspective on development.* Cambridge, MA: MIT Press.

Feinberg, T. E. and Farah, M. J. 1997. The development of modern behavioral neurology. In T. E. Feinberg and M. J. Farah (eds). *Behavioral neurology and neuropsychology*, 3–24. NY: McGraw-Hill.

Gomez, R. L. and Gerken, L. A. (in press). Artificial grammar learning in one-year-olds: Evidence for generalization to new structure. In *Proceedings of the 21st Boston University Conference on Language Development.* Boston, MA: Cascadilla Press.

Griffin, D. R. 1981. *The question of animal awareness: Evolutionary continuity of mental experience.* NY: Rockefeller University Press.

Haith, M., Wentworth, N. and Canfield, R. L. 1993. The formation of expectations in early infancy. In C. Rovee-Collier and L. Lipsett (eds). *Advances in infancy research.* NJ: Ablex.

Howard, D. V. and Howard, J. H. Jr. 1989. Age differences in learning serial patterns: Direct versus indirect measures. *Psychology and Aging* 4: 357–364.

Howard, D. V. and Howard, J. H. Jr. 1992. Adult age differences in the rate of learning serial pattern: Evidence from direct and indirect tests. *Psychology and Aging* 7: 232–241.

Howard, J. H. Jr. and Howard, D. V. 1997. Age differences in implicit learning of higher order dependencies in serial patterns. *Psychology and Aging* 12: 634–656.

Hsiao, A. and Reber, A. S. 1998. The role of attention in sequence learning: Theories, findings, and methodological issues. In M.S. Stadler and Frensch (eds.). *Handbook of Implicit Learning*. 471–494. Thousand Oaks, CA: Sage.

James, W. 1890. *Principles of psychology*. NY: Holt.

Johnson, M. H. and Magaro, P. A. 1987. Effects of mood and severity on memory processes in depression and mania. *Psychological Bulletin* 101: 28–40.

Kassin, S. and Reber, A. S. 1979. Locus of control and the learning of an artificial language. *Journal of Research in Personality* 13: 111–118.

Kihlstrom, J. F. 1990. The psychological unconscious. In L. Pervin (ed.), *Handbook of personality: Theory and research.* 445–464. NY: Guilford.

Knowlton, B. J. and Squire, L. R. 1994. The information acquired during artificial grammar learning. *Journal of Experimental Psychology: Learning, Memory, and Cognition* 20: 79–91.

Knowlton, B. J. and Squire, L. R. 1996. Artificial grammar learning depends on implicit acquisition of both abstract and exemplar-specific information. *Journal of Experimental Psychology: Learning, Memory, and Cognition* 22: 169–181.

Light, L. L. 1992. The organization of memory in old age. In R. I. M. Craik and T. A. Salthouse (eds). *The handbook of aging and cognition.* 111–166. Hillsdale, NJ: Erlbaum Press.

Masters, R. S. W. 1992. Knowledge, knerves and know-how: The role of explicit versus implicit knowledge in the breakdown of a complex motor skill under pressure. *British Journal of Psychology* 83: 343–358.

Masters, R. S. W., Polman, R. C. J. and Hammond, N. V. 1993. 'Reinvestment': A dimension of personality implicated in skill breakdown under pressure. *Personality and Individual Differences* 14: 655–666.

Maybery, M., Taylor, M. and O'Brien-Malone, A. 1995. Implicit learning: Sensitive to age but not IQ. *Australian Journal of Psychology* 47: 8–17.

McGeorge, P., Crawford, J. R. and Kelly, S. W. 1997. The relationships between psychometric intelligence and learning in an explicit and an implicit task. *Journal of Experimental Psychology: Learning, Memory, and Cognition* 23: 239–245.

Piaget, J. 1976. *The grasp of consciousness: Action and concept in the young child.* Cambridge, MA: Harvard University Press.

Rathus, J. H., Reber, A. S., Manza, L. and Kushner, M. 1994. Implicit and explicit learning: Differential effects of affective states. *Perceptual and Motor Skills* 79: 163–184.

Reber, A. S. 1967. Implicit learning of artificial grammars. *Journal of Verbal Learning and Verbal Behavior* 6: 317–327.

Reber, A. S. 1976. Implicit learning of synthetic languages: The role of instructional set. *Journal of Experimental Psychology: Human Learning and Memory* 2: 88–94.

Reber, A. S. 1992. The cognitive unconscious: An evolutionary perspective. *Consciousness and Cognition* 1: 93–133.

Reber, A. S. 1993. *Implicit learning and tacit knowledge: An essay on the cognitive unconscious.* NY: Oxford University Press.

Reber, A. S. 1997a. Implicit ruminations. *Psychonomic Bulletin and Review* 4: 49–55.

Reber, A. S. 1997b. Caterpillars and consciousness. *Philosophical Psychology* 10: 437–450.

Reber, A. S. and Allen, R. 1978. Analogy and abstraction strategies in synthetic grammar learning: A functionalist interpretation. *Cognition* 6: 189–221.

Reber, A. S., Allen, R. and Reber, P. J. (1999). Implicit vs. explicit learning. In R. J. Sternberg (ed.). *The nature of cognition.* 475–514. Cambridge, MA: MIT Press.

Reber, A. S., Kassin, S. M., Lewis, S. and Cantor, G. W. 1980. On the relationship between implicit and explicit modes in the learning of a complex rule structure. *Journal of Experimental Psychology: Human Learning and Memory* 6: 492–502.

Reber, A. S., Walkenfeld, F. F. and Hernstadt, R. 1991. Implicit and explicit learning: Individual differences and IQ. *Journal of Experimental Psychology: Learning, Memory and Cognition* 17: 888–896.

Rescorla, R. A. 1988. Pavlovian conditioning: It's not what you think it is. *American Psychologist* 43: 151–160.

Saffran, J. R., Aslin, R. N. and Newport, E. L. 1996, Statistical learning by 8-month old infants. *Science* 274: 1926–1928.

Saffran, J. R., Newport, E. L. and Aslin, R. N. 1996. Word segmentation: The role of distributional cues. *Journal of Memory and Language* 35: 606–621.

Schacter, D. L. 1987. Implicit memory: History and current status. *Journal of Experimental Psychology: Learning, Memory, and Cognition* 13: 501–518.

Schacter, D. L., Chiu, C.-Y. P. and Ochsner, K. N. 1993. Implicit memory: A selective review. *Annual Review of Neuroscience* 16: 159–182.

Schacter, D. L. and Graf, P. 1986. Preserved memory in amnesic patients: Perspectives from research on direct priming. *Journal of Clinical and Experimental Neuropsychology* 8: 727–743.

Schank, J. C. and Wimsatt, W. C. 1987. Generative entrenchment and evolution. In A. Fine and P. Machamer (eds). *PSA 1986: Proceedings of the meetings of the Philosophy of Science Association* 7: 33–60. East Lansing, MI: Philosophy of Science Association.

Schultz, E. E. 1983. Depth of processing by mentally retarded and MA-matched non-retarded individuals. *American Journal of Mental Deficiency* 88: 307–313.

Shimamura, A. P. 1990. Aging and memory disorders: A neuropsychological analysis. In M. J. Stones, and C. J. Brainerd (eds.). *Cognitive and behavioral performance factors in atypical aging*. New York: Springer-Verlag.

Squire, L. R. 1992. Memory and the hippocampus: A synthesis of findings with rats, monkeys and humans. *Psychological Review* 99: 195–231.

Stadler, M. A. and Frensch, P. A. (eds) 1998. *Handbook of implicit learning.* Thousand Oaks, CA: Sage Publications.

Tomasello, M. 1995. Language is not an instinct. (Review of Pinker, *The language instinct*) *Cognitive Development* 10: 131–156.

Weiskrantz, L. 1986. *Blindsight.* NY: Oxford University Press.

Williams, J. M. G., Watts, F. N., MacLeod, C. and Mathews, A. 1988. *Cognitive psychology and the emotional disorders.* Chichester, England: Wiley.

Winter, B. and Reber, A. S. 1994. Implicit learning and natural language acquisition. In N. C. Ellis (ed.). *Implicit and explicit learning of languages*, 115–146. London: Academic Press.

Wulf, G., Höss, M. and Prinz, W. 1997. *Effects of internal versus external focus of attention on motor learning.* Paper presented at the 38th meeting of the Psychonomic Society, Philadelphia, PA. November, 1997.

Wulf, G., Lee, T. D. and Schmidt, R. A. 1994. Reducing knowledge of results about relative versus absolute timing: Differential effects on learning. *Journal of Motor Behavior* 26: 362–369.

Wulf, G. and Schmidt, R. A. 1997. Variability of practice and implicit motor learning. *Journal of Experimental Psychology: Learning, Memory, and Cognition* 23: 987–1006.

Wynne, C. D. L. 1998. A natural history of explicit learning and memory. In K. Kirsner, C. Speelman, M. Maybery, A. O'Brien-Malone, M. Anderson and C. MacLeod (eds) *Implicit and explicit mental processes*, 255–269. Mahwah, NJ: Erlbaum.

Part III

Individual Differences in Self-Consciousness

Thought People and Dream People

Individual Differences On the Waking to Dreaming Continuum

Ernest Hartmann
Tufts University School of Medicine

We are not all the same. Human beings obviously differ tremendously from one another and one of the most interesting ways we differ is in the extent and way in which our minds produce dreams, daydreams and related processes. I believe that examining dreaming is especially important since dreaming is in some ways our purest state of mental functioning. It represents the functioning of our neural nets without the constraints of sensory input, the requirements for organizing motor output, or the constraints we put on our networks when we are engaged in a focused waking task such as doing arithmetic.

What I will do here is not demonstrate the diversity of dreaming experience, which is well known, but rather provide a framework for organizing it. I will present the concept of *boundaries in the mind*, a personality dimension running from thick to thin boundaries and show that this has a great deal to do with quantitative and qualitative dream and daydream experience. I will then propose that the "trait continuum," describing individual differences, running from thick boundaries at one end to thin boundaries at the other is actually the same continuum or very similar to the "state continuum" running from focused waking thought at one end to dreaming at the other. I will consider how this state/trait continuum can be understood in terms of the functioning of a simple network model of the mind, and I will suggest that the thick boundary/focused waking end of the continuum corresponds to efficient functioning within a subsystem with little communication between subsystems while the thin boundary/dreaming end of the continuum may involve less activity within a subsystem but more activity between subsystems.

Boundaries in the Mind

Thickness versus thinness of boundaries is a dimension of personality, measured by the Boundary Questionnaire. Boundaries (Boundaries in the Mind) is a broad psychological term referring to a large number of boundaries (Table 1) all to some extent interrelated. We can speak of the contents of our minds in many different ways. Laypeople often speak in terms of thoughts, feelings, memories, etc. Psychoanalysts speak of ego, id, superego, drives, defenses. Cognitive scientists may speak of perceptual processes, memory processes, linguistic or semantic processing modules and so on. No matter what terms we use to describe the mind, we are speaking of regions, functions or processes which are separate from one another, yet obviously connected. Thick boundaries refers to the extent to which these entities or processes are kept separate or distinct, while thin boundaries refers to the closeness or communication between them.

As a rough overview, people with very thick boundaries tend to focus exclusively on one thing at a time; differentiate clearly between thoughts and feelings, between reality and fantasy and so on. They have a clear and sharp boundary between themselves and others, between men and women, between different groups. Someone with thick boundaries says, "I am a man, you are a woman. Vive la difference!" These persons keep their memories well organized with a clear sense of exactly what happened when. They maintain their identity in a relationship, never losing their sense of self. They prefer well-demarcated social structures and overall tend to see the world in terms of black and white.

On the other hand, those with very thin boundaries allow many things into their perceptual field at once and may have difficulty focusing on one thing at a time. They may experience synesthesia and often experience the merging of thoughts with feelings, "I cannot imagine having a thought without a feeling." They often have a rich fantasy life, and sometimes become lost in fantasy, not distinguishing it clearly from waking reality. They have a less definite sense of personal space and they make less use of protective psychological defenses. They have a tendency to become lost in relationships and they tend to emphasize similarities rather than differences between themselves and others, between groups, between genders ("I am a man, but I can see a lot of feminine things in myself as well.") They see the world in shades of gray. These descriptions of course refer to the extremes. Most of us fall somewhere in between and may have different boundaries in different realms of experience.

The 138-item Boundary Questionnaire has been developed to measure differences in boundaries. It includes items chosen from all of the above areas of boundary functioning, organized originally into twelve categories of boundaries from sleep, wake, dreaming to opinions on truth and beauty. Table 2 represents items representative of each of these categories in the Boundary Questionnaire.

Scores on the Boundary Questionnaire (BQ) demonstrated a number of interesting relationships with other variables. For instance, in terms of occupation, naval officers (male and female) scored significantly "thicker" than average on the BQ, as did lawyers and salesmen. Several groups of music and art students scored very "thin" on the BQ, though this was not true of established artists (Hartmann 1991). Persons identifying themselves as "channellers" or followers of channellers, scored very thin on the BQ (Krippner, et a. 1998), as did persons identifying themselves as "spiritualists" or spiritual healers. (Laria 1998).

Although the questionnaire is a personality measure and not designed as an indicator of illness, nonetheless some relationships with psychopathology have emerged, most clearly with personality disorders. Persons diagnosed Obsessive-Compulsive Personality Disorder score unusually thick, while those diagnosed with either Schizotypal or Borderline Personality Disorder scored much thinner than average.

There are investigations relating the BQ with numerous other personality measures. On the most widely used personality measure, the MMPI, high scores on the BQ (thinness) show a correlation of .41 with Pa; and .40 with Mf (in males only). This is according to expectations since Pa in normal subjects relates not so much to actual paranoia as to sensitivity; Mf measures the noticing of "feminine" aspects of themselves — in males only (Hartmann 1991). Thinness on the BQ correlates −.37 with K, which is generally thought to measure defensiveness. Again this relationship is, as we predicted; some of the psychological defenses themselves — such as repression or intellectualization — can be thought of as boundaries, and the overall defensive attitude of "none of your business, get out of my space," is clearly an aspect of thick boundaries. Thinness on the BQ is also positively correlated with Absorption (Tellegen and Atkinson 1974) and several other measures related to hypnotizability (Barrett 1989).

High scores (thinness) on the BQ are correlated to some extent with the Intuition and Feeling subscales on the Myers-Briggs Type Indicator (Ehrman 1993). There is a highly significant correlation (r = .70) between thinness of boundaries and Openness to Experience, one of Costa and McRae's five basic dimensions of personality (McCrae 1994). However Openness to Experience is related especially to the positive side of thin boundaries; openness, empathy, flexibility and so on, but not to the more vulnerable or sometimes pathological side ("I get too involved in relationships, I'm afraid I may fall apart").

Boundaries and Dreaming

There is considerable evidence of the relationship between boundary structure, as measured by the BQ, and dreaming. First of all, in 800 subjects there was a strong positive correlation ($r = .40$, $p < .0001$) between boundary score (thinness) and answers to the simple question "How many dreams do you recall per week?" (Hartmann et al. 1991). The relationship was even higher ($r = .58$) in a group of subjects who were members of the Association of the Study of Dreams ($N = 42$) and were more interested in and aware of their dreaming than most people. Since the questionnaire contains some items relating to dreaming, daydreaming and fantasy, the correlation was therefore recalculated omitting any items remotely related to sleep, dreaming, daydreaming or fantasy. This had little effect on the overall correlation (reducing it from $r = .40$ to $r = .37$, $p < .0001$). Schredl et al. (1996) confirmed the relationship between boundaries and dream recall using a German translation of the Boundary Questionnaire, and using dream diaries to assess dream recall.

A sample of frequent dreamers ($N = 64$) has been compared with a sample of non-dream recallers ($N = 69$), from our larger population. The frequent dreamers (reporting seven or more dreams per week) scored significantly higher not only on the overall boundary score, but on each of the twelve content categories of the Boundary Questionnaire (Table 3) (Hartmann 1991).

Thin boundaries also show a positive correlation with such measures as nightmare frequency, reports of recurrent dreams, and reports of "unusual events at night" (Zborowski et al. 1998). On interview, "unusual events" refers usually to hypnogogic or half-asleep phenomena. The relationship of Boundary scores to daydreaming has not been addressed in an actual study, but some of the items on the Boundary Questionnaire itself as well as numerous interviews with persons with very thin or thick boundaries make it certain that there would be a positive relationship between thinness of boundaries and daydream recall or amount of daydreaming as well.

Several studies have addressed the relationship of boundaries to dream content. First of all, having thin boundaries is related to reporting longer dreams (Hartmann et al. 1991; Schredl et al. 1996; Hartmann et al. 1998). Thinness of boundaries has also shown a positive correlation with measures of vividness, detail, dreamlikeness, emotionality, interaction between characters, and bizarreness. Those with thin boundaries are also likely to have more, and more intense *contextualizing images* in their dreams. A contextualizing image is a powerful, intense image in a dream which can often be seen as picturing (contextualizing) an emotion or emotional concern. For instance, in the clearest case, we have found that people who have just experienced a serious trauma of any kind often dream of being overwhelmed by a tidal wave. The tidal wave has nothing to do with what actually happened to them, rather it contextualizes the emotional state, "I am terrified, I am overwhelmed." Contextualizing images scored on a blind basis have been found to be more frequent after trauma (Hartmann et al. 1998), and more frequent in dreams than in daydreams (Kunzendorf et al. 1997).

In some sense it would appear that having thin boundaries is related to having "more of everything" in one's dreams, but this may not be entirely true. Thinness of boundaries rather seems related to one large factor in dream recall which includes vividness, detail, emotions, etc. while thinness is not related to other weaker factors involving such material as sexual interaction or aggressive interaction in dreams (Hartmann et al. 1998).

We have also attempted to relate boundaries to the physiological aspects of sleep. It appears there is no clear difference in amount of REM-sleep or other sleep states related to thinness of boundaries. There is no definite evidence that those who have thin boundaries awaken more during REM-sleep, which would lead to more dream recall. However, preliminary data suggest that thin boundaries may be related to more "in-between states" not clearly scorable as REM or non-REM as opposed to those with thick boundaries who have very clear demarcations between the physiological states. Thus, it may be possible to explain the relationship with dreaming to some extent on the basis that perhaps the states of waking and REM-sleep are "not as different" in those with thin boundaries. This has not been studied directly in persons with thin or thick boundaries, but this explanation would be consistent with some recent work showing that dream recall was associated with less change on certain EEG measures between REM sleep and subsequent awaking (Rochlen, Hoffman and Armitage 1998). That is also consistent with work by Koukkou and Lehmann (1993) on organization of brain states in dreaming and waking.

In any case there is no question that the dimension Thick vs. Thin Boundaries relates to dreaming and other aspects of conscious experience. The thick boundary end of the continuum is associated quantitatively with less fantasy life, less reverie, daydreaming, and dreaming and qualitatively it is associated with less merging, sharper maintenance of distinction between categories. People who score at the thin end of the boundary questionnaire have more vivid, complex dreams and a richer fantasy life. They repeatedly describe experiencing several things at once, synesthetic experiences, having thoughts almost always with a feeling tone attached, and experiencing fantasy, reverie, daydreams or dreams which appear very "real" and are sometimes difficult to distinguish from waking activity.

A "State Continuum" Running from Focused Waking to Dreaming

Although we like to believe, following Aristotle, that "man is a rational animal," it is quite clear from examining our own experiences, as well as from a number of lines of recent research, that we do not spend a majority of our time engaging in clear logical rational thought. For instance the richness and varieties of our daydream experiences are attested to by Singer (1975) and Klinger (1990). Antrobus has demonstrated that mental activity during relaxed wakefulness often cannot be reliably distinguished from dreaming by blind scorers (Antrobus and Bertini 1992). There is an especially close similarity between mental activity at sleep onset and mental activity of dreaming (Foulkes and Vogel 1965). Clearly there is considerable overlap between various forms of conscious mental activity.

I suggest it may be useful to consider a continuum running from focused waking thought at one end to dreaming at the other (Figure 1). Focused waking thought at the left end of the continuum refers to such things as performing arithmetic problems or mentally plotting the trajectory of an approaching fly ball and moving the body in order to catch the ball. Of course, in these activities a great deal also occurs below the level of consciousness. Insofar as these processes are conscious they may involve such things as mathematical symbols, signs, words, etc.; there is a continuous line of thought — A leads to B leads to C. There is a clearly defined logical relationship: "All men are mortal, Socrates is a man, therefore Socrates is mortal." Attention at this end of the continuum is highly focused and there is a high degree of self-reflectiveness. And in these situations we tend to categorize: this fact is relevant, this one is not; this is black, this is white, etc. All of these characteristics become less distinct as we move to the right on the continuum. In daydreaming and dreaming attention is less focused, and imagery becomes far more dominant than words or mathematical symbols. We give up the strict linear A to B to C reasoning and instead appear to be influenced by many things at once. And we are not self-reflective.

I believe it may be convenient to consider such a continuum although I realize it is not conceptually pure. The continuum is composed of a number of separate strands as we have seen which will not always flow together. For instance, prevalence of imagery across subjects is distinct from vividness of imagery, though they show a modest positive correlation (Kunzendorf 1982). For instance, the *word vs. imagery* thread can sometimes be dissociated from the others. It is certainly possible to be in an intense, focused waking mode and yet to be concentrated on a visual image rather than on words or mathematical symbols. This might happen, for instance, when one is intently examining a map, and planning a military campaign. Likewise, it is possible to have a logical argument in dreams, or to write something in a dream, though in fact I have shown this is extremely rare — we almost never engage in reading, writing or arithmetic in dreams (see below). And there are special situations, for instance lucid dreams when the usual voluntary focused processes of wakefulness are superimposed onto a dream. But all of these are unusual. Generally there is a surprising tendency for these processes to move together.

If we want to think biologically, the left hand end of the continuum can certainly be intensified chemically by the use of caffeine or other stimulants. The amphetamines, or methylphenidate, will move one towards the left and intensify the voluntarily, reflective, intensely focused frame of mind. The other end of the continuum is favored by sleepiness and to a varying extent by many "psychedelic" drugs.

It seems to me that a rough continuum of this sort is obvious and does not exactly need proof and overall proof would of course be difficult to come by. This is a framework rather than a rigid description, the question is more whether this is useful rather than if it is absolutely true. There are certainly times when thinking in terms of one broad continuum of this kind can be useful, and at other times when it is useful to pick up the separate strands.

Some bits of research are relevant in establishing this sort of continuum. For instance there is a widespread view that "anything can occur in a dream" and indeed I do believe in general that dreaming makes connections more broadly than waking and thus a broader range of "things" may happen in dreams (Hartmann 1998). However, as I stated before, the focused activities of the left hand end of the continuum are very rare in dreams. I have shown in a study (Hartmann 1996) that we do remarkably little reading, writing or arithmetic in our dreams. A group of 240 respondents to a questionnaire reported in most cases that they either "never" or "rarely" did any word-by-word reading, writing, or any arithmetic in their dreams, even though they spent an average of six hours per day engaged in these activities in their waking lives. The respondents were also asked to rate six activities as to their relative prominence in their waking and dreaming lives. Each activity was rated on a seven-point scale from 1 ("much more prominent in my waking life, hardly ever occurs in dreaming") to 7 ("much more prominent during dreaming"). The results show that the six activities fell neatly into two groups. Reading, writing, and typing received very low scores ("much more prominent in waking") whereas the other group (walking, talking with friends, and sexual activity) despite the disparate nature of the group, all scored between 3 and 4 ("equally common, or slightly more common during waking and dreaming").

The State Continuum (Focused Waking to Dreaming) is Very Similar to the Trait Continuum (Thick vs. Thin Boundaries)

We can consider a continuum in mental functioning running from the most focused waking thought (doing arithmetic problems for instance) to looser thought, reverie or daydreaming and then to dreaming. We suggest that this "state continuum" is in many ways similar to the "trait continuum" running from very thick boundaries to very thin boundaries. In this sense, when awake we are engaging in relatively "thick boundary" functioning (making categories, making distinctions, etc.). In dreams we give up these categories and distinctions; images, thoughts, feelings come together more readily; we are in a merging mode. Dreaming can be considered a relatively "thin boundary" state. In fact the first and most important factor that emerges from the Principal Components Analysis of the Boundary Questionnaire was labeled "primary process thinking" including "imagery so vivid that it is hard to distinguish from reality" (Harrison et al. 1989; Hartmann 1991, p. 64). This definitely has a dreamlike sound; and more specifically this first factor has similar characteristics to the first factor that emerged in another study from the dream content variables — including vivid imagery and emotionality (Hartmann et al. 1998).

Based on these continua, we suggest that a person who has thin boundaries overall will generally tend, even when awake, to be functioning further towards the right on the continuum (Figure 1) towards daydreaming and dreaming, compared to an average person or a person with thick boundaries. This "thin-boundary" person can be thought of as functioning in a more "dreamlike" fashion even while awake, relative to the solid, serial, well-delineated, focused waking thought of the person with thick boundaries. For instance we have just completed a study comparing dreams and daydreams in a group of college students. Dream and daydream material was rated on a blind basis on well-established global measures of "dreamlikeness" and "bizarreness." Overall, as expected, dreams were rated significantly more dreamlike and more bizarre than daydreams. In addition, however, the material from students who scored "thin" on the BQ was rated significantly more dreamlike and bizarre than material from the "thick" students. In fact the results showed that daydreams from the "thin" students were scored almost identical to dreams from the "thick" group on bizarreness and dreamlikeness (Kunzendorf et al. 1997).

In these senses we suggest that the thick to thin boundary (trait) continuum and the focused waking to dreaming (state) continuum are quite similar and involve the same broad aspect of mental functioning. In terms of neural nets in the cerebral cortex, the thick boundary/focused waking end of the continuum may correspond to efficient functioning within a subsystem, with little communication (spread of excitation) between subsystems; while the thin boundary/dreaming end of the continuum may involve less activity within a subsystem but more communication between subsystems.

We can think of certain portions of our nets as more "tightly woven" than others (Figure 2). This would involve portions trained to do certain tasks — reading, writing, arithmetic, plotting trajectories, guiding movements to catch a fly ball, etc.. We can visualize the nets of the mind as involving a number of such tightly woven regions, and then more loosely woven regions between them. Anatomically this is oversimplified, of course. Imaging studies show that regions devoted to one task may be very widespread in the cortex. In this model we suggest that focused waking thought can be described as functioning more within the tightly woven regions and less between them whereas daydreaming and finally dreaming involve more activity in between these regions. Likewise persons with very thick boundaries will tend to have activation of the neural nets chiefly within tightly woven regions with less in between, whereas those with thin boundaries would have less activation or functioning within these regions and more between them.

We have spoken above in an oversimplified matter of quasi-anatomical "regions." It might also be useful to think in terms of modes of processing. Connectionist nets have been divided roughly into two types (Figure 3): feed-forward nets, in which activation or "computation" moves forward from one layer of units to another and produces an "output" at the end, and autoassociative nets, where there is no uni-directional movement towards a given output. In an autoassociative net, output can be read as the connectivity strength between all units at a given moment.

In this sort of model, the left-hand end of our continuum (both the state and the trait continuum) would correspond to the net functioning as a feed-forward net, whereas the right-hand of the continuum would correspond more to an autoassociative net. In other words we could say that when we are performing focused waking activities our nets are constrained into acting as feed-forward nets — this occurs especially often and prominently in persons with thick boundaries. On the other hand, when we are in a dreaming mode — or to some extent a daydreaming mode — our nets are less so constrained and function relatively more in an autoassociative manner, which is where people with very thin boundaries function much of the time.

Modeling our mental functioning along these lines should allow a great deal of the mathematics developed for neural nets and connectionist nets to be applied to our continuum of mental processing.

Table 1. *Types of Boundaries*

- Perceptual boundaries
  - Between sensory inputs
  - Sensory focus or "bandwidth"
  - Around perceptual entities
- Boundaries related to thoughts and feelings
  - Between two thoughts or two feelings
  - Between thought and feeling
  - Around thoughts and feelings (free association)
- Boundaries between states of awareness or states of consciousness
- Sleep-dream-wake boundaries
  - Between sleep and waking
  - Between dreaming and waking
  - In and around the dream
  - In and around daydreaming
- Boundaries related to play
- Boundaries related to memory
  - Early memories
  - Recent memories and memory organization
  - Personal past
  - Future plans
- Boundaries around oneself (body boundaries)
  - Barriers against stimuli
  - The skin as a boundary
  - Posture and musculature as boundaries
  - Personal space
- Interpersonal boundaries
- Boundaries between conscious and unconscious and between id, ego, and superego
- Defense mechanisms as boundaries
- Boundaries related to identity
  - Sexual identity
  - Age identity: Between adult and child
  - Constancy of identity
- Group boundaries
- Boundaries in organizing one's life
- Boundaries in environmental preferences
- Boundaries in opinion and judgments

Table 2. *Boundary Questionnaire: Examples of Questions. Each question is scored from 0 (not at all true of me) to 4 (definitely true).*

Category 1: Sleep/Dream/Waking	
1.	When I awake in the morning, I am not sure whether I am really awake for a few minutes.
37.	I spend a lot of time daydreaming, fantasizing, or in reverie.
Category 2: Unusual Experiences	
61.	At times I have felt as if I were coming apart.
100.	I have had déjà vu experiences.
Category 3: Thoughts/Feelings/Moods	
15.	Sometimes I don't know whether I am thinking or feeling.
74.	I can easily imagine myself to be an animal or what it might be like to be an animal.
Category 4: Childhood/Adolescence/Adult	
4	I am very close to my childhood feelings.
40.	I have definite plans for my future. I can lay out pretty well what I expect year by year for the next few years.
Category 5: Interpersonal	
53.	When I get involved with someone, we sometimes get too close.
103.	I am a very open person.
Category 6: Sensitivity	
6.	I am very sensitive to other people's feelings.
42.	I am unusually sensitive to loud noises and bright lights.
Category 7: Neat/Exact/Precise	
19.	I keep my desk and work table neat and well organized.
43.	I am good at keeping accounts and keeping track of my money.
Category 8: Edges/Lines/Clothing	
32.	I like heavy, solid clothing.
44.	I like stories that have a definite beginning, middle, and end.
Category 9: Opinions re Children, etc.	
33.	Children and adults have a lot in common. They should give themselves a chance to be together without any strict roles.
56.	I think a good teacher must remain in part a child.

Category 10: Organizations

10. In an organization, everyone should have a definite place and a specific role.

58. A good relationship is one in which everything is clearly deefined and spelled out.

Category 11: Peoples/Nations/Groups

11. People of different nations are basically very much alike.

105. There are no sharp dividing lines between normal people, people with problems, and people who are considered psychotic or crazy.

Category 12: Beauty/Truth

36. Either you are telling the truth or you are lying; that's all there is to it.

76. When I am in a new situation, I try to find out precisely what is going on and what the rules are as soon as possible.

Table 3. *A Comparison of Frequent Dreamers (Seven or More Dreams per Week) and Nondreamers*

	Frequent Dreamers (N = 64)	Nondreamers (N = 69)	*t*	*p*
SumBound Total	314 ± 60	232 ± 40	9.2	< .0001
Personal Total	208 ± 48	142 ± 32	9.2	< .0001
World Total	106 ± 17	89 ± 17	5.6	< .0001
Sleep-Dream-Wake	23 ± 13	8 ± 7	8.6	< .0001
Unusual Experiences	34 ± 13	15 ± 9	9.5	< .0001
Thoughts, Feelings, Moods	33 ± 11	24 ± 9	5.7	< .0001
Child, Adol, Adult	13 ± 4	10 ± 4	3.3	< .01
Interpersonal	27 ± 6	23 ± 6	3.7	< .001
Sensitivity	15 ± 3	12 ± 4	4.2	< .0001
Neat, Exact, Precise	21 ± 7	18 ± 6	3.4	< .001
Edges, Lines, Clothing	41 ± 8	33 ± 8	6.3	< .0001
Opinions about Children	23 ± 5	20 ± 5	3.8	< .001
Opinions about Organizations	26 ± 6	22 ± 6	4.4	< .0001
People, Nations, Groups	38 ± 7	32 ± 8	4.5	< .0001
Beauty, Truth	19 ± 4	16 ± 4	4.1	< .0001

	Focused Waking thought	Looser, Less-structured Waking thought	Reverie free association daydreaming	Dreaming
What dealt with imagery	Percepts: Math symbols signs, words	fewer words, signs, more visual-spatial imagery		almost pure imagery
How	logical relationship — If A then B	less logic, more noting or picturing of similarities, more metaphor		almost pure picture - metaphor
Self-reflection:	highly self-reflective — "I know I am sitting here reading."	less self-reflective, more "caught up" in the process, the imagery		in "typical dreams" total *thereness,* no self-reflection
Boundaries:	solid divisions, categorizations, thick boundaries	less rigid categorization, thinner boundaries		merging condensation loosening of categories, thin boundaries

Sequence of ideas or images:

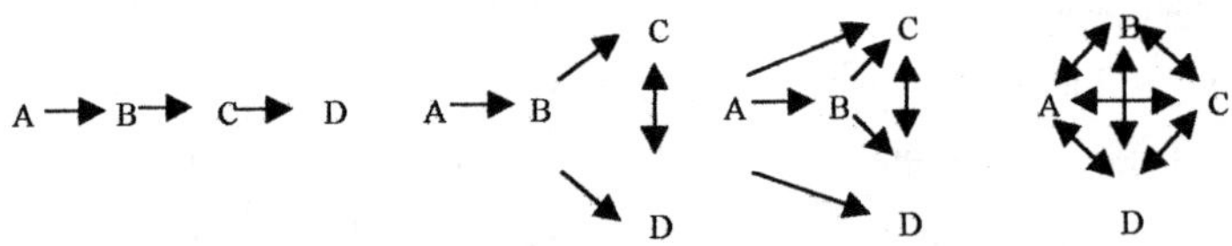

	Focused Waking thought	Looser, Less-structured Waking thought	Reverie free association daydreaming	Dreaming
Processing:	relatively serial; net functions chiefly as a feed-forward net.		net functions more as an auto-associative net.	
Subsystems:	activity chiefly *within* structured subsystems		activity less *within,* and more *across* or *outside* of structured subsystems	

Figure 1. *A continuum running from focused waking mental activity through reverie and daydreaming, to dreaming*

Reprinted with permission from Hartmann, E. (1998) Dreams and Nightmares: The New Theory on the Origin and Meaning of Dreams. *New York: Plenum Press.*

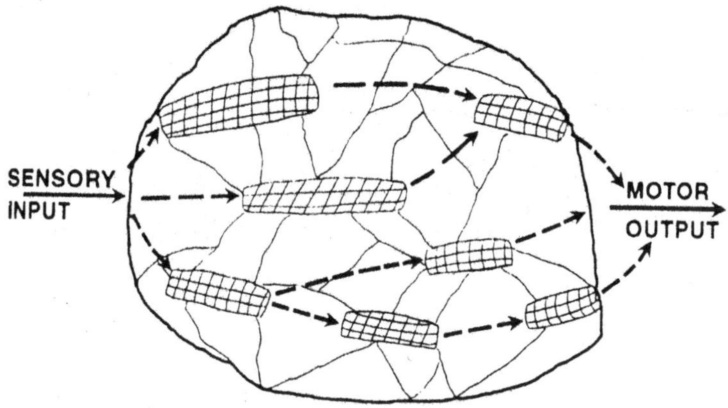

Figure 2. *This Figure represents schematically a portion of the nets of the mind in the human cortex, showing a few tightly-woven regions corresponding to well-learned, rapid-processing abilities and functions, surrounded by more loosely woven regions. In this figure, focused waking thought involves a relatively rapid movement from input to output, using the tightly woven regions as indicated by the arrows, whereas dreaming involves the more loosely woven regions. This is of course oversimplified in many ways. There is likely to be a gradation, rather than simply two types of regions.*

Reprinted with permission from Hartmann, E. (1998). Dreams and Nightmares: The New Theory on the Origin and Meaning of Dreams. *New York: Plenum Press.*

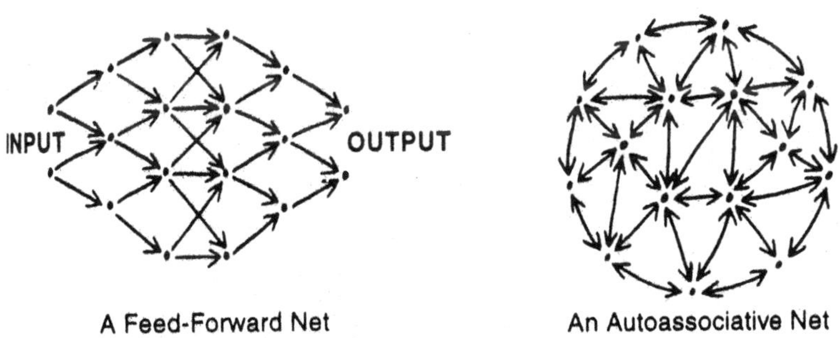

Figure 3. *Two basic types of connectionist nets. The idea is that our neural nets can assume both of these forms. The net is constrained into acting relatively more as a feed-forward net in focused waking, and acts more as an auto-associative net in dreaming.*
Reprinted with permission from Hartmann, E. (1996). Outline for a Theory on the Nature and Functions of Dreaming. *In* Dreaming, *6:147–170.*

References

Antrobus, J. and Bertini, M. (eds.) 1992.*The Neuropsychology of Sleep and Dreaming*. Hillsdale, NJ: Lawrence Erlbaum Associates.

Barrett, D. 1989. "The relationship of thin vs. thick boundaries to hypnotic susceptibility". Paper presented at a meeting of the Eastern Psychological Association, Boston, MA.

Ehrman, M. 1993. "Ego boundaries revisited: Toward a model of personality and learning". In J.E. Alatis (ed), *Strategic Interaction and Language Acquisition: Theory, Practice, and Research*. Washington, D.C.: Georgetown University Press.

Foulkes D. and Vogel, G. 1965. "Mental activity of sleep onset". *Journal of Abnorma Psychology* 70: 231–243.

Harrison, R., Hartmann, E. and Bevis, J. 1989. "The Hartmann Boundary Question: A measure of thin and thick boundaries". Presented in part to a meeting of the Eastern Psychological Association, Boston, MA.

Hartmann E. 1991. *Boundaries in the Mind: A New Psychology of Personality*. New York: Basic Books.

Hartmann, E. 1996. "We do not dream of the Three R's: a study and implications". *Sleep Research* 25: 136.

Hartmann, E. 1998. *Dreams and Nightmares: The New Theory on the Origin and Meaning of Dreams*. New York: Plenum.

Hartmann, E., Elkin, R., Garg, M. 1991. "Personality and dreaming: the dreams of people with very thick or very thin boundaries". *Dreaming* 1: 311–24.

Hartmann, E., Rosen, R., Rand, W. 1998. "Contextualizing Images in Dreams: More Frequent and More Intense After Trauma". *Sleep* 21S: 284.

Klinger, E. 1990. *Daydreaming*. Los Angeles, CA: Jeremy P. Tarcher.

Koukkou, M. and Lehmann, D. 1993. "A Model of Dreaming and Its Functional Significance: the State-Shift Hypothesis". In A. Moffit, M. Kramer, R. Hoffman (eds), *The Functions of Dreaming*. New York: State University of New York Press.

Krippner, S., Wickramasekera, I. Wickramasekera, J., Winstead, C. 1998. "The Ramtha Phenomenon: Psychological, Phenomenological, and Geomagnetic Data". *The Journal of the American Society for Psychical Research* 92: 1–24.

Kunzendorf, R. 1982. "Mental images, appreciation of grammatical patterns, and creativity". *Journal of Mental Imagery* 6: 183–202.

Kunzendorf, R. Hartmann, E., Cohen, R., Cutler, J. 1997. "Bizarreness of the Dreams and Daydreams Reported by Individuals with Thin and Thick Boundaries". *Dreaming* 265–271.

Laria, A. 1998. "Dissociative Experiences Among Cuban Spiritist Mediums and Mental Health Patients". Ph.D. Dissertation, Department of Psychology, University of Massachusetts Boston.

McCrae, R. 1994. "Openness to experience: expanding the boundaries of factor V". *European Journal of Personality* 8: 251–272.

Schredl, M., Kleinferchner, P., Gell, T. 1996. "Dreaming and personality: thick vs. thin boundaries". *Dreaming* 6: 219–223.

Rochlen, A., Hoffmann, R., Armitage, R. 1998. "EEG Correlates of Dream Recall in Depressed Outpatients and Healthy Controls". *Dreaming* 8(2): 109–123.

Singer, J. L. 1975. *The Inner World of Daydreaming*. New York: Harper and Row.

Tellegen, A. and Atkinson, G. 1974. "Openness to absorbing and self-altering experiences ("apsorption"): A trait related to hypnotic susceptibility". *Journal of Abnormal Psychology* 83: 268–277.

Zborowski, M., McNamara, P., Hartmann, E., Murphy, M., Mattle, L. 1998. "Boundary Structure Related to Sleep Measures and to Dream Content. *Sleep* 21 (supplement): 474.

Varieties of Lucid Dreaming Experience

Stephen LaBerge
The Lucidity Institute

Donald J. DeGracia
Wayne State University

1. Introduction

> Realization that one is dreaming brings a wonderful sense of freedom — freedom to try anything in the extended range of experience. … The nature of lucid dream experience may range up to the mystical, *whilst there seems to be an inherent resistance to anything erotic*. (McCreery 1973: 114)

> When lucid dreams endure beyond a certain point, at least for me, orgasm is almost inevitable… *in fully two-thirds of my lucid dreams, I feel the flow of sexual energy; this arousal culminates in an orgasmic burst on about half of these occasions.* (Garfield 1979: 134–35)

What can we conclude from the above quotations? Certainly nothing regarding the nature of eroticism in the lucid dream state. Rather, they illustrate that the experience of lucid dreaming is subject to individual variation. This should not be surprising since lucid dreaming, like all forms of conscious experience, is comprised of a flow of subjective events created by brain processes using input from sensory-perceptual modalities, internal algorithms or schemata and, perhaps, poorly understood neuronal activity associated with central nervous system homeostatic maintenance. Variability in individual experience is inherent at all levels: anatomical in the form of limitations imposed by breath and sensory system development, physiological as sleep and REM sleep needs, inborn activation and damping tendencies, and psychological variation caused by recent and long-term experiences, the development of habits of interaction with the environment, and assumptions about the way the world works.

The range of subjective experiences reported to occur during dreaming appears wider and more variable than those typical of waking. In this chapter we will focus on the nature of experience in lucid dreams. We begin by showing that lucidity in dreams is not a discrete phenomenon, but that reflective consciousness exists in all dreams and can be measured on a continuum with "lucidity" and "non-lucidity" representing two ends of the spectrum. The remainder of the chapter will explore the substantial individual variation in lucid dreams, illustrated with examples derived from the authors' experiences. The discussion will focus on two primary themes: the role played by belief systems and learning in shaping lucid dream experiences, and the role played by factors which appear to be independent of the dreamer's beliefs and learning.

2. The Meaning of "Lucid Dreaming"

The distinction between nonlucid and lucid dreams represents perhaps the broadest level of variation in dream experiences presently recognized. The contemporary notion of a lucid dream is a "dream in which one knows one is dreaming" (Green 1968). This is in contrast to the nonlucid dream, in which dreamers are not aware of being in the dream state. Some dream theorists treat the lucid/nonlucid distinction in a way we consider too rigid, arguing these are two completely distinct types of phenomena (Hobson 1988, 1994; Tart 1984; Tholey 1988). In our view, the distinction between lucid and nonlucid dreams is not as clear-cut as the definition suggests and fails to do justice to the subtlety of the actual experience. We feel the contemporary distinction has misplaced focus away from what we consider the essential variations in dream cognition underlying dream lucidity.

We have recently developed a psychological model that we believe captures the *experiential essence* of the differences between lucid and nonlucid dreams (DeGracia and LaBerge 1998) In brief, our model hinges on the relationship of the waking self and the identity of the dreamer, and addresses the question: at what psychological levels do changes in self-awareness in the dream state occur that correspond to the onset of dream lucidity? Or stated somewhat differently, what exactly *is* dream lucidity?

Our basis for answering this question involved a systematic comparison of waking, lucid and nonlucid dreaming within the framework of the Global Workspace (GW) model of consciousness developed by Bernard Baars (1988). Recognizing that dreams in general are an expression of consciousness during sleep, the critical feature of Baars's GW model we used was his formulation that conscious processes are molded and framed by unconscious processes. Baars formulates unconscious processes as *contexts*. Contexts are operationally defined as "a system (or set of systems) that constrains conscious contents without itself being conscious" (Baars 1988: 372). Accordingly, we compared the unconscious contextual structures underlying waking, nonlucid and lucid dream consciousness.

2.1 *Waking*

Baars' GW model provides a model of waking consciousness. The GW model posits that waking consciousness is framed by a nested hierarchy of *unconscious* elements which Baars terms a *context hierarchy*. The context hierarchy is a relatively stable global construct that transforms through time as a function of learning and experience. The context hierarchy of the waking personality is composed of many relatively distinct contexts which correspond to, or are a computational way to model, the sensory, perceptual, attentional, mnemonic, cognitive, metacognitive, goal and effector operations carried out unconsciously by the nervous system, but which in turn condition conscious experience. Contexts can be relatively more innate (such as the topographic organization of conscious perceptions) or relatively more learned (such as language and culture).

A context strongly dependent on learning can involve *situation-dependent* forms of cognition, in which the context remains latent until external circumstances dictate its full expression. An example of a situation-dependent context would be the knowledge and skills associated with piano playing. The full expression of a "piano playing context" is situationally dependent on the presence of an actual piano. When confronted with a piano, the "piano playing context" expresses itself as a nested hierarchy of effectors: the desire (or goal) to play triggers the necessary declarative knowledge (of notes and music, etc.) which in turn triggers the necessary motor effectors (eye motions for reading music, hand motions for striking keys) resulting in the act of playing the piano. According to Baars, context formation initially requires conscious participation. But, once established, contexts are unconscious factors framing conscious experience. Many such contexts accumulate within the waking personality as a function of learning and life experiences, and mold and frame the conscious aspects of waking.

2.2 *Nonlucid Dreams*

During nonlucid dreams, the consciousness of the dreamer is similarly constrained by unconscious contextual elements. These elements combine to form relatively *transient* global contexts that last only for a dream's duration, or possibly through a series of sequential dreams. The transience of global contextual structures in dreams contrasts to the relatively stable context hierarchy framing waking consciousness. One factor contributing to the transient quality of dream contexts involves the dreamer operating "in the moment" in response to the dream context with no conscious memory of precedents or antecedents to the events occurring in the dream. The unconscious global context framing nonlucid dream consciousness may or may not use elements from the waking context hierarchy. Typically, dream contextual elements related to explicit memories do not necessarily correlate to elements of the waking personality, while contexts related to non-explicit memories do. For example, the dreamer's sense of identity (a declarative context) may be significantly different from the waking sense of identity (LaBerge 1985). Likewise, the conceptual situation of the nonlucid dream (e.g. the "dream plot") may have little to do with the episodic experiences of the waking personality. This "incongruency of contexts" between waking and nonlucid dreaming perhaps contributes to the view of some theorists that the nonlucid dream state is akin to madness (Hobson 1994). However, contexts defining non-explicit behaviors, when expressed in nonlucid dreams, are closely similar to waking. Such non-explicit behaviors include, for example, conscious perceptual representation (DeGracia and LaBerge 1998), speech production (Salzarulo and Cipolli 1974), or metacognitive monitoring (Kahan and LaBerge 1994).

The carry over of waking habits of metacognitive monitoring has a particular significance in nonlucid dreams. We typically do not metacognitively monitor our state of consciousness when awake. The general set of expectancies guiding our ordinary waking experience also governs our ordinary dream state. Since we tacitly assume, in both cases, that we are awake, our cognition during dreaming is distorted to fit the assumption that we are awake. When bizarre dream events occur, as they frequently do during REM sleep, they are simply assimilated into the contextual structure of the dream in a consistent fashion (DeGracia and LaBerge 1998). Again, some theorists have used this assimilation by the dreamer of unusual dream events as evidence that dreaming cognition is akin to madness. From our view, however, we are simply observing the adoption of the waking self's habitual form of metacognitive monitoring by the dreamer.

Importantly, the contextual structures and conscious experiences of nonlucid dreams tend not to contribute episodic memories to the waking personality; a condition recognized as dream amnesia (Hobson 1988). Although it is common to recall fragments of dreams upon awakening, it is likely that the great majority of our nightly dreams are not remembered at all (Diamond 1963). For most individuals there is only a piecemeal conscious recollection of dream experiences. However, as stated above, the nonlucid dreamer can access both explicit and non-explicit memories of waking experience. Nonlucid dreaming therefore tends to be a one-way street with respect to memory transfer between states: from waking to dreaming, but not the reverse. The result of this relatively one-sided transfer of memories between states means that elements of the waking personality can contribute to the identity of the dreamer as building blocks in the global (albeit temporary) contextual structure of the dream. But, dreams rarely contribute to the consciously accessible memories of the waking personality.

Because of the transient nature of the global contexts in nonlucid dreams, we suggest nonlucid dreams may function, among other things, to recombine unconscious elements within consciousness on a temporary basis. We call this process "mental recombination" (cf. Hunt 1989) by analogy with genetic recombination. From the viewpoint of biocomputation, mental recombination likely contributes to maintaining an optimal information processing flexibility in brain neuronal networks. This notion is practically identical with Greenberg and Pearlman's (1974) conclusion that the evolutionary development of the dream state "has made possible the increasingly flexible use of information in the mammalian family". The notion of dreaming as mental recombination is also consistent with the role of REM sleep in learning and assimilation of new knowledge (reviewed in LaBerge 1985).

2.3 *Lucid Dreams*

Lucid dream consciousness, like waking and nonlucid dreams, is also framed by unconscious contextual elements. To understand the contextual structure of lucid dreams, we must look at the role played by consciously accessible memory across lucid dreams and waking. Lucid dreamers are able to freely recall details of waking life, to a greater or lesser extent, while within a lucid dream (LaBerge 1985). Just as important, lucid dreams are remembered after awakening with a much higher frequency than nonlucid dreams, probably due to the presence of a *mental set to remember* in lucid dreams. Although it would be difficult to empirically ascertain, the anecdotal evidence suggests that at least some lucid dreamers remember their lucid dreams during waking at least as well as their waking experiences (LaBerge 1985). In other words, lucid dreams contribute to the episodic memories of the waking personality. Therefore, in contrast to nonlucid dreams, there is a two-way transfer of consciously accessible memory between waking and lucid dream experiences. Thus, *there is a relative continuity of consciously accessible memory linking lucid dreams and waking experience*.

With repeated experiences of lucid dreaming, the associated memories of these experiences contribute to the formation of a stable and cumulative contextual structure in the mind of the waking self. This stable contextual structure we call the *lucid dream context*. The lucid dream context serves two complementary roles: (1) it serves as the global contextual structure framing lucid dream consciousness providing both precedent and antecedent structure to lucid dreams, and (2) it forms a situationally-dependent context within the waking personality. Regarding this latter point, lucid dreaming is a learnable skill (Moffitt, Hoffmann et al. 1988; LaBerge 1980, 1985; LaBerge and Rheingold 1990). The full expression of this skill is dependent upon its occurrence during sleep, and is in this sense a form of situational cognition. The skill, however, belongs to the waking personality and shares features with other learned skills, particularly that it can be improved upon by learning and practice (LaBerge 1980).

Thus, our distinction between lucid and nonlucid dreams is based on the contextual structure underlying dream consciousness: nonlucid dreams can be characterized by the formation of transient global contexts different from dream to dream, but lucid dreams are characterized by the presence of a distinct and persistent context, the lucid dream context. This lucid dream context belongs to both the waking personality and the lucid dreamer identity, serving as a bridge between them, and will continue to frame all future lucid dreams. The lucid dream context is susceptible to modification by learning and experience acquired in either the waking or lucid dream states.

There appear to be at least three essential components to the lucid dream context, each operating at a specific psychological level: (1) a "reference to state" operating as a metacognitive context, (2) a semantic contextual framework operating at the level of declarative knowledge, expectation and belief, and (3) a goal-option framework operating at the level of effector action.

2.3.1 *The Reference to State*

When a lucid dreamer thinks "I am dreaming" there are at least two levels of cognitive activity at work in this thought: a direct experiential realization of, and self-reflection on, ones condition ("I am…"), and an interpretation of the nature of that condition ("…dreaming"). The former is a metacognitive act, the latter a semantic interpretation. The notion of "reference to state" indicates the metacognitive component of the lucid dream context. The reference of subjects to their state of being is not merely declarative knowledge, it is a direct apprehension of their immediate experience. Metacognition is not unique to lucid dreams but also occurs in nonlucid dreams (Kahan and LaBerge 1994). However, in nonlucid dreams, "reflection during dreaming involves an awareness of conditions within the dream" (ibid., p. 250). That is to say, reflection on events in nonlucid dreams is confined to the contextual scope of the nonlucid dream (typically limited by the absence of the habit of metacognitively checking one's state). Metacognition during lucid dreams is not confined to events occurring in the dream, but references, either explicitly or implicitly, waking experience as well (DeGracia and LaBerge 1998). The reference to state in a lucid dream is framed by access to memories of waking experience, allowing a *contrast* between one's current situation and the knowledge of waking life. This contrast provides the contextual structure for the metacognitive recognition that the current experience is not a normal waking experience. Hence, lucidity in the context of dreaming, implies metacognition framed by consciously accessible memories of waking experience.

2.3.2 *The Semantic Framework*

Individuals who experience lucid dreaming develop a framework of knowledge by which to conceptualize and give meaning to their experiences. These semantic frameworks affect the consciousness of lucid dreamers in a contextual fashion by providing assumptions, expectations and beliefs upon which the lucid dreamers interpret their experiences and acts. Because there is a large diversity of perceptual experience in lucid dreams (to be outlined below), an equally wide variety of semantic frameworks have developed to give meaning to these experiences. The knowledge framework used by a given individual does *not* require that the experiences be conceptualized by that individual as "a lucid dream". The semantic framework itself does not even have to be true. How lucid dreamers conceptualize their "non-waking experience" is a function of their general knowledge. Alternative modes of conceptualizing the lucid dream experience include the notions that one is undergoing an "out of body experience" (OBE) or an "astral projection" (reviewed in DeGracia 1997). The forms taken by one's reference to state depend on one's semantic framework. So, the semantic component of the statement "I am dreaming" reflects a knowledge structure conceptualizing the experience as a form of dreaming. A reference to state can just as easily take the forms "I am having an OBE" or "I am having an astral projection". As one of us stated previously: "...lucid dreams and OBEs [and we will add here, astral projections] are necessarily distinguished by only one essential feature: how the person interprets the experience at the time" (LaBerge 1985, p. 234) In other words, these are not phenomenologically distinct categories of experience but are alternative conceptualizations of the intrinsic variety present in lucid dream experiences.

Because dream experience is not constrained by sensory input or other limits of waking experience (such as the law of gravity, for example) beliefs and expectations play a key role in determining the form of and behavior occurring within a lucid dream. As we stated in the Introduction, we are interested in ascertaining which features of lucid dream variability are belief-dependent and which are not. By "belief-dependent" we are referring precisely to the role played by a semantic framework in conditioning an individual's lucid dream experiences. The semantic framework, because it is a declarative framework of knowledge, is susceptible to modification by learning and experience, and therefore is a crucial dynamic element in an individual's lucid dream context.

2.3.3 *The Goal-Options Context*

Lucid dreaming includes a set of intentional actions that, taken as a whole, we call a goal-options context. As the semantic framework is the declarative component of the lucid dream context, the goal-options context includes the procedural aspects of lucid dreaming related to effector actions. A lucid dreamer's goal-option context includes both lucid dream initiation techniques and the range of behaviors expressed in an individual's lucid dreams. Examples of characteristic goal-option behaviors include making voluntary choices in lucid dreams, making a habit of metacognitively checking one's state of consciousness, and making a habit of remembering lucid dream experiences. The goal-option context is also a dynamic element of the lucid dream context which undergoes refinement concomitant with the accumulation of direct experience in the lucid dream state. The semantic framework has a direct effect on the goal-options available to the lucid dreamer by limiting what the dreamer believes is and is not possible to do in the lucid dream state.

2.3.4 *The Relationship Between Nonlucid and Lucid Dreams*

Let us summarize the discussion thus far. Dream lucidity involves specific unconscious contextual structures operating at metacognitive, semantic and effector levels that frame the consciousness of the lucid dreamer: together these form a lucid dream context. A lucid dream context develops from a two-way, consciously accessible memory transfer between the lucid dreamer and waking self, represents learned skills, and is a stable facet of the waking personality which grows with experience. In contrast, nonlucid dreams are characterized by the transient formation of dream contexts which draw, to a variable extent, on elements of the waking personality, and do not contribute substantially to the consciously accessible memory structure of the waking personality.

Although this model appears to provide a clear-cut distinction between lucid and nonlucid dreams, it is not the main intention of this model to rigidly distinguish these experiences. We stated above our dissatisfaction with the current dichotomous notions of nonlucid and lucid dreams in this regard. This dissatisfaction derives from the inability of contemporary notions to adequately capture the lucid dreamer's experience, which can display subtle variations in cognition that are difficult to conceptualize. These variations seem to span the distinction between lucidity and non-lucidity as presented above so that our model is really intended to provide a basis for conceptualizing the subtle array of differences present in lucid dream experiences. Thus, the final step in our model is to develop how lucid and nonlucid forms of cognition can *interact* with one another.

To do so, we must turn again to notions introduced by Baars in the GW system. Baars defines the processes of *cooperation* and *competition*; these are mechanisms by which contexts interact. Cooperation refers to how contextual elements can form symbiotic linkages and mutually support each other in framing conscious processes. For example, the association of the metacognitive reference to state, semantic framework and goal-options context within the lucid dream context is an example of the cooperation of contextual elements. Competition is the opposite process whereby contextual elements displace one another in their effects on conscious processes. A waking example of competition can be found in the Stroop test, where one reads colored words of the names of colors flashed briefly on a monitor. People tend to mistakenly say the color of the word, instead of reading the word itself. Here, unconscious color recognition processes compete with unconscious word recognition for control of the contents of consciousness.

We showed that cooperation and competition of contextual elements can be observed in both nonlucid and lucid dreams (DeGracia and LaBerge 1998). We also showed that *the tendency of nonlucid dreams to form transient global contexts is present during lucid dreams*. Characters and situations encountered unintentionally in lucid dreams can serve as factors around which may nucleate a nonlucid dream context. These factors can *compete* with the lucid dream context for access to the dreamer's intentions. If the lucid dreamer does not make a conscious effort to maintain the lucid dream context, it is possible for these distractions to absorb the attention of the lucid dreamer and draw the dreamer into a situation that unfolds independent of the dreamer's volition. At the extreme, a newly generated dream context can displace the lucid dream context resulting in a loss of lucidity and the transformation of the lucid dream into a nonlucid dream. In practice, however, subtler forms of competition will allow the lucid dream context to co-exist with competing dream elements that are not contained in the lucid dream context, resulting in modifications of the cognition of the lucid dreamer which affect memory access, thinking and behavior. In such situations, the dreamer appears to phase in and out of lucidity to various degrees.

Thus, because of competitive processes, the degree of lucidity can itself vary within a single lucid dream. These notions will form part of our basis for discussing variations in lucid dream cognition in following sections.

3. Variations in Lucid Dream Experiences

Having presented a way of looking at the distinction between lucid and nonlucid dreams, we will now turn our attention to outlining the degree of variety that exists in lucid dream experiences. Because lucid dream experiences tend to be remembered nearly as well as waking experiences, and because lucid dreams are cumulative experiences, lucid dream reports can provide highly detailed and descriptive accounts of lucid dream phenomenology. We will draw on such reports below to illustrate the range of variation in lucid dreams. Our survey of lucid dream variations will parallel the general temporal course of lucid dreams, discussing in turn, lucidity initiation, variations in perception, emotion, cognition and action within lucid dreams, and finally, the termination of lucid dreams.

3.1 *Variations in Lucid Dream Initiation*

Since the lucid dream context bridges the waking and dream states, logic suggests that lucid dreams could be initiated either from the nonlucid dream state (a dream-initiated lucid dream, or DILD) or from the waking state (a wake-initiated lucid dream, or WILD) (LaBerge 1980). Because transitions directly from the waking state to the REM sleep state are very rare, one would expect WILDs to occur with a lower frequency than DILDs — just what the data shows.

3.1.1 *Dream-Initiated Lucid Dreams*

More than 80% of lucid dreams are initiated when a nonlucid dream transforms into a lucid dream (LaBerge, Nagel, Dement, and Zarcone 1981). This process involves the lucid dream context displacing the current nonlucid dream context. The form of this displacement is dependent upon the individual's specific training in lucidity induction techniques and degree of lucid dreaming experience.

For inexperienced lucid dreamers, lucidity is perhaps most likely to arise from a nightmare or anxiety dream. LaBerge (1985) argues that there is an evolutionary-biological basis for anxiety stimulating reflective consciousness. Not all novice lucid dreamers experience anxiety-triggered lucidity; specifically, for example, DLD reports none, while SLB reports his percentage of anxiety-triggered lucid dreams recognized in years 1–3 respectively were 36%, 19%, and 5%. The decrease in proportion (and frequency) of anxiety-initiated lucid dreams with time was probably due to the psychotherapeutic techniques SLB was practicing (LaBerge 1985; see also Tholey 1988) as the following example illustrates:

> (SLB106) I was in the middle of a riot in a classroom; a furious mob was raging about, throwing chairs and fighting with each other. A huge repulsive barbarian with a pock-marked face, the Goliath among them, had me hopelessly locked in an iron grip from which I was desperately trying to free myself. At this point, I recognized that I was dreaming, and remembering what I had learned from handling similar situations previously, I immediately gave up my struggle … and tried to feel loving as I stood face to face with my ogre.
>
> At first, I failed utterly, feeling only repulsion and disgust for the ogre. He was simple *too ugly* to love: thus spoke my visceral reactions. But I tried to ignore the image and seek love within my own heart. Finding it, I looked my ogre in the eyes, trusting my intuition to supply the right things to say. Beautiful words of acceptance flowed out of me, and as they did, he melted into me. As for the riot, it had vanished without a trace; the dream was over and I awoke, feeling wonderfully calm.

Other intense emotions such as embarrassment or delight can also initiate lucidity. Such lucid dreams are typically spontaneous and brief, and lucidity onset is quickly followed by awakening. Survey data suggest that most people have experienced a nominally lucid dream at least once in their lifetime (Snyder and Gackenbach 1988). A spontaneously experienced lucid dream can serve as a nucleation event for the development of a lucid dream context, if there is follow-through on the part of the individual to cultivate these experiences.

A number of methods exist for the individual to intentionally cultivate the onset of lucidity from within nonlucid dreams (LaBerge 1981, 1985; LaBerge and Rheingold 1990; Rogo 1983). The learning of these methods occurs during waking and adds to both the semantic and goal-option components of an individual's lucid dream context. The essence of methods to initiate lucidity during nonlucid dreams is to condition dreamers to recognize that they are dreaming through some form of *state testing* (also called "reality testing"). Some approaches to state testing are:

a. *Anomaly recognition* – Here dreamers condition themselves to use the recognition of bizarre dream events as a cue for lucidity onset. This approach is not limited to observing events in the dream but can be based on self-observation as well, so that, if they perceive their behavior as unusual (not typical of waking) this may induce lucidity.

> (SLB351)[1] "I'm walking through a field that is fantastically animated with extravagant life: Magic Mushrooms (*Psilocybe cubensis*) popping up everywhere and growing to gigantic proportions. I realize the fantasy element of this scene: I must be dreaming. I do two all up eye movement signals, but this causes the dream to begin to fade. I try to press the micro-switch, and I seem to have succeeded, but it feel like I'm already awake…"

The anomalies that serve as lucidity cues, or "dreamsigns" (LaBerge and Rheingold 1989) can be very subtle indeed as the following account from von Moers-Messmer (1938) illustrates:

> From the top of a rather low and unfamiliar hill, I look out across a wide plain towards the horizon. It crosses my mind that I have no idea what time of year it is. I check the sun's position. It appears almost straight above me with its usual brightness. This is surprising, as it occurs to me that it is now autumn, and the sun was much lower only a short time ago. I think it over: the sun is now perpendicular to the equator, so here it has to appear at an angle of approximately 45 degrees. So if my shadow does not correspond to my own height, I must be dreaming. I examine it: it is about 30 centimeters long. It takes considerable effort for me to believe this almost blindingly bright landscape and all of its features to be only an illusion. [Translation from LaBerge 1985, pp. 38–39.]

b. *Programmed behaviors* – Here dreamers condition themselves to perform an act that will tend to produce distinguishable results when performed during either waking or dreaming. For example, attempting to fly in a dream will tend to lead to the experience of flying; if the individual actually "lifts off" then this is a strong indication that the experience is a dream (as in the following example). Another behavior that can result in lucidity initiation is attempting to read and reread text; if the text changes, then this is used as a lucidity cue. This approach can be simplified to the point of simply looking at one's hands as a cue for lucidity onset.

> (SLB1032) "At a movie theatre, I am running down a flight of stairs, skipping more and more steps, until I notice that I seem to be able to skip as many as I like! Wait a minute! That makes this a *dream*. But it doesn't seem at all like it. So I step into the air to convince myself. It is indeed! As I float upward close to the wall, the scene begins to fade. I decide to test rubbing hands together instead of spinning. I vividly feel the sensation and then also the wall at my back. I keep rubbing for perhaps 15 seconds, and then I feel a closet door, which I open. At first the closet contains only vague images, but they

> finally become vivid. I am now in a bedroom. L is on the bed, "talking in her sleep." She says something unintelligible. I ask her to repeat it: She says "Wisdom is being given out …mumble, mumble." While wondering what she means, the dream fades and I awaken."

c. *Déjà rêvé* – Lucidity can sometimes be initiated when lucid dreamers have an apparent or actual recognition that they have had a similar dream before as in the following example:

> (SLB31) "I am walking with my friend, M, when I recognize that we are in a place I have dreamed of before — 'The Museum of Uninvented Inventions' — and that *this* therefore, is a dream. I reflect how the real M. would like to have lucid dreams, knowing quite explicitly that this is 'M', a dream figure. Nevertheless, I suggest to him that even though he is only a dream character, perhaps he could realize that he is dreaming. Maybe he does, for *I* wake up."
> With increasing experience, DILD techniques become habitual. After a certain degree of experience, the individuals may simply recognize that they are dreaming without any apparent state testing or lucidity onset cue. Frequently dreamers question their state and decide they are awake and not dreaming. A dream in which the dreamer has at one point raised this question without arriving at the correct conclusion is commonly termed "pre-lucid" (Green 1968). Pre-lucid dreams can be interpreted as a failed attempt by the lucid dream context to gain full access to framing dream consciousness.

3.1.2 *Wake-Initiated Lucid Dreams*

It is possible to maintain continuous reflective consciousness while falling asleep and hence to enter a lucid dream directly from the waking state. As with DILDs, this form of lucid dream initiation is a skill that improves with motivation and practice. Its cultivation has been described by Tibetan yogis, and several modern sources (LaBerge 1985; LaBerge and Rheingold 1990; Ouspensky 1960; Rogo 1983). WILDs are most likely to occur after awakening in the morning or during afternoon naps (LaBerge 1980). While falling asleep, the subject's mind is kept focused and lucid through the transition from waking to dreaming. Experiences of visual and auditory hypnagogic imagery are common during this transition. Unusual somesthetic imagery may also occur; subjects may feel themselves "float" or "sink out of their body". There may (e.g. SLB561) or may not (e.g. SLB37) be a momentary break in subjects' consciousness. Then the subjects will find themselves fully in a dream scene and lucid. Once in the dream-state, the lucid dream continues exactly like those initiated directly from the dream state. Some examples from the authors' personal experiences illustrate the fascination of this transition:

(DJD55) "I went back and laid on my bed hoping to project some more. I laid there and hypnagogic images came and went: city scenes, people sitting at a bar, a friend sitting on a stool behind an open door with a beautiful girl standing next to him. I could feel myself sinking deeper and deeper. Finally, I felt myself sink very deep and simultaneously my visual field locked into a stable scene and I felt a strong wind blowing over me. I could hear loud "whooshing" and wind sounds. Next I knew, the "wind" grabbed me and was pulling me along. It seemed to be pulling me forward but what I saw was me passing through fuzzy but identifiable frames of my bedroom."

(DJD48) "I woke from sleep. Had fleeting glimpses of my dream memories, then they were gone. I shut my eyes and could see hypnagogic images. A few scenes formed and faded but I don't recall what they were. The scene of a street formed vividly in front of my closed eyes. There was a river off to my left, 50–100 yards from the road. On the left seemed to be a construction site. There were buildings on my right. I was trying to observe details and I felt my foot step forward! This surprised me! Next thing I knew, I was walking along the street."

(SLB561) "I have just awakened from a dream in the sleep lab and am worrying about how the night is almost over and I *still* haven't succeeded in having a lucid dream. Suddenly, I find myself flying hundreds of feet above a field of wildflowers: I realize at once, with great excitement, that *this* is a dream and carry out the pre-planned protocol, making an eye-movement signal and singing 'Row, row, row your boat/ Gently down the stream/ Merrily, merrily, merrily/ Life is but a dream!' Then I make another signal and estimate 10 seconds by counting 'One thousand-one, ... 1000–10' and signal again. When I finish this sequence, I am overjoyed and do a virtual cartwheel in the air. After a few seconds, the dream begins to fade...."

(SLB37) "I was lying awake in bed late in the morning listening to the sound of running water in the adjoining bathroom. Presently, an image of the ocean appeared, dim at first like my usual waking imagery. But its vividness rapidly increased while, at the same time, the sound level of the running water decreased; the intensity of the internal image and external sound seemed to alter inversely (as if one changed a stereo balance control from one channel to the other). In a few seconds, I found myself at the seashore standing between my mother an a girl who seemed somehow familiar. I could no longer hear the sound of the bath water, but only the roar of the dream sea...."

Differences in styles of lucid dreaming give rise to individual differences in DILD and WILD frequency. Although quantification of such differences has not been attempted in a large sample of lucid dreamers, to illustrate such stylistic differences, a comparison of lucid dream initiation frequencies of the authors is here presented. DJD has 114 recorded lucid dreams of which 43% were WILDs and 56% were DILDs. In contrast, only 8% of SLB's dissertation sample of 388 recorded lucid dreams were WILDs, a significantly lower proportion.

3.1.3 *Ambiguities in Lucidity Induction*

With increasing experience, some facets of lucid dreaming become habitual, making the classification of dream lucidity more ambiguous. Consider the following example:

> (DJD74) "My (nonlucid) dream involved me, X and a bunch of other people. We were all roommates in a big house. I was unaware that I was dreaming. There was a party going on or something. We were down in the basement hanging out. However, at some point in the dream I looked at X and told him I'd be back in a little bit because I was going to go up to my room and try to project! I went up to my bedroom in this dream house. Again, at this point I thought everything was normal and had no idea I was dreaming. I laid down on my bed and started concentrating to leave just exactly like I always do on the physical plane....[text omitted of a 1400 word lucid dream report]
>
> ...I decided I was done for the time being, so I got up out of bed. I was still in the dream house and still unaware that I was dreaming. I went looking for some paper to record my experience. I ended up going back into the basement where everyone was still hanging out. X was there and the others and I told them all about the projection I had just had. Meanwhile, I'm getting very concerned that I can't find any paper. Then I woke up for real. For a moment I was totally disoriented."

In this example, DJD, in the midst of a nonlucid dream, performs his habitual techniques for achieving a WILD. He then experienced what was, for all practical purposes, a typical lucid dream. Following this, he "awakes" in the exact same nonlucid dream setting and seeks paper to record his lucid dream, which is also a habitual behavior. Shortly thereafter, DJD truly wakes up in a momentarily disoriented state.

How is one to classify such an experience? What we see here is a lucid dream nested perfectly inside of a nonlucid dream. One could argue that DJD merely *dreamt* that he was lucid dreaming, but this clarifies nothing. The characteristics of the lucid dream (the omitted text) were identical in general features to all of his other lucid dreams. What we believe this particular sequence represents is the *cooperation* between the global nonlucid dream context and DJD's lucid dream context. In this particular instance, the global nonlucid dream context provided perfectly for the full expression of the lucid dream context because the subject dreamt all of the requisite details needed for activation of his lucid dream context. After completion of the lucid dream, the lucid dream context returned control of access to the dreamer's consciousness to the previous nonlucid dream context. This kind of situation could only result because the subject possessed a well-defined lucid dream context that could clearly demarcate itself from the global nonlucid dream context.

This is an extreme example of the mixing of nonlucid and lucid dream elements. However, it is not uncharacteristic of the kind of subtleties and ambiguities encountered when attempting to characterize dream consciousness and what does and does not constitute dream lucidity. A related issue is the characterization of intentionality in lucidity induction. It is not always easy to draw a clear distinction between a lucid dream that is "spontaneous" and one that is "deliberately" induced. In fact, the characterization of such factors is critically dependent upon the subject's degree of experience, and the relative maturity of the lucid dream context. As the lucid dream context matures, and hence, becomes more habitual, the likelihood of unintended lucid dreams increases and the ambiguity of what constitutes dream lucidity also increases. WILDs are typically intentional by nature. However, it is possible, for example, for an experienced lucid dreamer to lie down and nap with the intention to merely rest, and have an unintended WILD. In the case of DILDs, the issue of intention becomes even more ambiguous because the experienced subject may simply come to learn to recognize that he or she is dreaming, with no cause other than sheer familiarity with the state; in such a case, there may be no explicit onset of lucidity (e.g. no reality testing, no statement "I am dreaming").

Alternatively, experienced lucid dreamers may have a nonlucid dream in which they access elements of their lucid dream context incompletely and never achieve full lucidity. These types of considerations are important because they indicate that the subject's degree of experience can profoundly affect how dream lucidity manifests itself, and clearly indicate that lucidity induction is not homogeneous across subjects. What constitutes dream lucidity may be more subtle and ambiguous to identify for experienced subjects who have programmed aspects of lucidity induction and manifestation to be habitual.

3.2 *Perceptual Variations in Lucid Dreams*

The examples listed above begin to illustrate the diversity of perceptions that can occur in lucid dreams. By "perception" we are referring to the *hallucinated* sensory modalities characteristic of dream consciousness. Because afferent input from peripheral senses is attenuated during dreaming (LaBerge 1985), it should be understood that the use of the term "perception" in the following discussion refers to the hallucinated analogs of the sensory modalities. Dreams are, in general, highly perceptual experiences expressing all the dream analogs of waking sensory modalities. Dream perceptions are typically characterized as "bizarre" (Hobson 1988). Examples of perceptual bizarreness in dreams may include dream characters or environments transforming abruptly (discontinuities), or the perception of physically impossible scenes and events. Perceptual bizarreness occurs in lucid dreams just as it occurs in nonlucid dreams (Gackenbach 1988). However, bizarreness in perception is often recognized as such by lucid dreamers, and can be described by them in vivid detail, providing us with a clear window into the perceptual qualities of lucid dreams.

To understand the perceptual diversity of lucid dreams we need to introduce the notion of *perceptual environment*. This is the complete hallucinated sensorium of the dreamer including all the sensory modalities: vision, audition, somatosensation, gustation, olfaction and the submodalities therein. These hallucinated sensory perceptions combine to form the dreamer's body image (if present), and the allocentric space perceived by the dreamer. The dreamer can be either immersed within the dream environment or observing it from without. For both authors, our lucid dreams are associated with immersion in the perceptual environment, which seems to hold true in general; reports of lucid dreamers as pure observers are rare (LaBerge 1985). The vividness and richness of the perceptual environment ranges from the "minimal" in which most or all sensory qualities are absent or greatly attenuated, through the "typical" much like everyday experience, to the "surreal" in which the environment is vibrantly, psychedelically alive with fantastic, extravagant detail.

3.2.1 *Typical Perceptual Environments*

A "typical" perceptual environment is experienced as immersion within or observation of a rich sensory environment containing all sensory modalities. Typical perceptual environments are characteristic of both nonlucid and lucid dreams. These environments generally contain the same elements that waking environments do such as landscapes, city streets, trees, buildings, driving in cars, etc., and are readily comprehensible by the dreamer, although bizarreness is frequent.

Within lucid dreams, typical perceptual environments display a large variety of perceptual qualities. In some the scene is dimly lit or vaguely delineated; others overwhelm the lucid dreamer with their intense beauty and extravagant detail. Some seem, indeed, "more real than real". In general, the average lucid dream is more perceptually vivid than the average nonlucid dream. This conclusion is supported by relatively intense brain activation during lucid dreaming which may correlate with increased perceptual vividness (LaBerge 1981).

3.2.2 *Surreal Perceptual Environments*

A surreal perceptual environment is characterized by the presence of at least some sensory modalities displaying rich perceptual content. However, surreal environments have no counterpart in normal waking experience; they are often abstract spaces of color, shape, and motion within which the dreamer is immersed. These environments are abstract, and typically are not comprehendible by the dreamer. Surreal perceptual environments occur very rarely in nonlucid dreams (Hall and Van de Castle 1966), although Hunt (1989) has discussed them in the context of activated dreams. A clear distinction should be drawn between surreal environments and bizarreness perceived in typical environments. Some forms of hypnagogic imagery and psychedelic drug-induced hallucinations (e.g. described in Mavromatis 1987; and Aaronson and Osmond 1970, respectively) resemble surreal perceptual environments, but in lucid dreams, there is a definite sense of somatic immersion in the environment. The following are examples of surreal perceptual environments; the lucid dreamer's lack of comprehension of his perceptions are apparent:

> (DJD75) "But I managed to turn around and what I saw was unbelievable and utterly amazing. I don't even really know how to describe it! When, after great effort, I turned myself around, I was no longer seeing the forest. Instead I was looking onto this unbelievable colored field and there were three spheres ahead of me and they had something that looked like butterflies dancing in each of them. But they were not butterflies, though they looked a little like them. Whatever they were, there was one each inside of the three spheres and these "butterflies" were spinning and rotating within the sphere and constantly changing color. The way they changed color was strange, it was as if colors were welling into them from somewhere I could not see, like a liquid, and flowing around inside of these butterfly creatures. I was both awed and confused; confused that the forest was gone, and confused at what I was looking at, awed because whatever I was looking at was very, very beautiful."

> (DJD70) "I got the idea to shut my eyes, spin around rapidly, and pretend that I was shrinking. When I did this and opened my eyes up I was quite surprised to see that I was actually somewhere else! And what I saw when I opened my eyes was amazing. I was in the midst of a spectacular panorama of swirling activity and spiraling colors. The scene was staggering in its complexity. I was floating amongst the images, floating surrounded by these moving color patterns. I remember that I was amazed, but baffled, and didn't understand in the least what I was looking at, other than that it was very beautiful and moving around too much to make out any definite structure."

What these surreal perceptions represent is currently unknown. It is intriguing, however, to speculate that lucid dreamers perceiving such imagery may be in fact perceiving the lower level neurological processes that underlie normal conscious sensory perceptions, as has been suggested for LSD-induced hallucinations (Mavromatis 1983).

3.2.3 *Minimal Perceptual Environments*

Minimal perceptual environments are characterized by immersion in an environment containing a minimum of sensory perception. Again, these appear to occur frequently in lucid dreams, but rarely in nonlucid dreams. This is a relatively neglected area in the literature with the exception of Gillespie (1988), who has experimented extensively with deliberately eliminating sensory content from his lucid dreams.

It is not uncommon for lucid dreamers to involuntarily "fade" from a lucid dream to the waking state with no break in consciousness (LaBerge, DeGracia et al. 1998). Prior to and during the fading process, lucid dreamers perceive their sensorium as "unstable". In general, lucid dreamers learn to perceive their sensorium as more or less stable; this is a perception with no counterpart during waking. When a lucid dream is "stable", all perceptions of the dream environment appear normal. When a lucid dream is "unstable", there may be a "blinking on and off" of the visual field, as if one is phasing in and out of blindness. The visual field may also become cartoon-like or pale in color. Somatic sensations may feel as if they are fading in and out. Although the basis of this fading process is not currently understood, techniques exist to stabilize one's sensorium in the event that it is perceived to be fading (LaBerge, DeGracia et al. 1998). The degree to which lucid dreamers experience instability events seems to be quite variable both between and within subjects. We know of no waking counterparts for the perception and sensations associated with fading and stability. These are wholly experienced and learned in the lucid dream state. Even in nonlucid dreams the experience of fading appears confined to the transition to waking. However, in lucid dreams, variations in one's "stability" can occur at any time during a lucid dream, for a greater or lesser duration.

Minimal perceptual environments are related to perceptions of fading and stability. Some individual lucid dreamers do not awaken when they experience a complete loss of stability and fade from their lucid dreams. Instead they find themselves in minimal perceptual environments. Minimal perceptual environments are characterized by a loss of the rich sensory modalities typical of dreaming; such experiences may be perceived by the lucid dreamer as being in a "void" or in "darkness". However, lucidity is preserved; internal speech, affect and cognitive function remain intact within this minimal environment. Some sensory modalities are also preserved; kinesthetic sensations may be present (so that the subject seems to be "moving") although somesthetic sensations (sense of body image) typically are absent. There are perceptions of visual depth (e.g. the "darkness" has a sense of depth and size to it), but typically not visual perceptions of color or form. The "darkness" can sometimes appear to have visual motion; it may "swirl" or "bellow".

Because some lucid dreamers can undergo a loss of stability and appear in a minimal perceptual environment instead of awakening, it is possible for a lucid dream experience to consist of a string of lucid dreams occurring in typical or surreal environments punctuated by minimal environments (a multi-part lucid dream). That is, the lucid dreamer will be in a typical lucid dream, lose stability and fade from the dream into a minimal environment. Techniques similar to those used to prevent lucid dream fading, such as spinning in place or inducing somatic sensations, can also be used to cause a sensorium to re-form around the lucid dreamer, giving rise to the second lucid dream. The second lucid dream environment may or may not be the same as the first. The cycle can then repeat. It is possible for a single lucid dream session to consist of perhaps six or more lucid dreams in typical or surreal environments punctuated by fadings or minimal experiences.

The following are accounts of minimal sensory environments from the authors' records.

> (DJD16) "Found myself in the void. My mind was wandering in all kinds of thoughts. Then I noticed that I could 'leave' my body. I flew off through the void. Everything was dark, kind of somber, and I didn't have a body. I had the desire to be somewhere. Soon a large, what appeared to be wooden fort appeared in the mist. It was still quite dark but I could 'see' now."

> (DJD31b) "Though I was in the void, I was still being pulled along by this mysterious wind force. As I was being pulled along, a very beautiful rainbow colored sphere came rolling past me and it was very clear and well defined in appearance. I was very surprised because this is the first time I had ever actually seen an object in the void and I began to wonder what was going on. I quickly noticed that I was surrounded by subtle arrays of colored patterns. It was very subtle because the darkness of the void seemed to be covering over these color patterns, the patterns seemed to be behind the darkness. The colors and patterns were very intricate and I have no words to describe what I was seeing."

> (DJD61) "In my imagination, I imagined flying off, but got pulled back again. This happened twice. Then, I dove off my bed straight downwards. I was moving straight downwards in the void. Far below me in the darkness I saw a square floating. In the square I could see colors, like a scene was inside the

square. I stretched to grab this square and my arms stretched far below me like Plastic Man, and I grabbed the floating square. I pulled it up over me like putting on a pair of pants, and was thinking to myself, 'I'm not gonna let this one go!' I stepped into this square and was all of a sudden somewhere! I was very surprised. I was in what looked like a high school hallway standing in line with people going into a room."

(SLB56) "Found myself in the void. My mind was wandering in all kinds of thoughts. Then I noticed that I could 'leave' my body. I flew off through the void. Everything was dark, kind of somber, and I didn't have a body. I had the desire to be somewhere. Soon a large, what appeared to be wooden fort appeared in the mist. It was still quite dark but I could 'see' now."

It is of interest to note that the lucid dreamer can "fade out" from both typical and surreal environments into minimal environments, and conversely, can "materialize" out of a minimal environment into typical or surreal environments (as DJD61). As (DJD31b) indicates, the dreamer perceived "the darkness of the void seemed to be covering over these color patterns, the patterns seemed to be behind the darkness". It is almost as if the lucid dreamer's sensorium is tuning in and out of stable patterns of perceptions, akin to tuning a radio to a radio station. The following journal entry illustrates clearly how surreal and minimal environments can fuse, and fade into typical environments. This example suggests that clues to understanding sensory consciousness may be found in the phenomenology of lucid dream perceptions:

(DJD64) "I seemed to now be floating in the void. However, there were what seemed to be colored triangles moving around, crossing and spinning over one another making distinctly geometric patterns in front of me. The colors were mainly a yellowish green with red, orange and pink hues and they had the texture of clear and smoky, but smooth glass. 'This is a weird view of the void,' I thought to myself. I stared at these patterns wondering what the hell I was looking at. I began to focus harder and harder on these patterns, trying to discern some detail in them. Then, as I was focusing, the most incredible thing happened. I watched these patterns 'solidify' and transform into the scene on the dance floor of the club I had just faded from. The spinning triangles were actually the dancing people in the club! I was amazed. I relaxed my focus and the scene faded back to the spinning triangles. I was thinking, 'Wow! This is amazing!' I tightened my focus again and the triangles again transformed into the dancers on the dance floor. This time I tightened my focus so much that the entire bar scene faded in around me! I was back in the bar again!"

What minimal lucid dream environments correspond to in physiological terms is unknown. It is tempting to speculate that minimal, surreal and typical perceptual environments correspond with lesser to greater degrees of brain activation, respectively, during REM sleep. Minimal environments superficially resemble the "thought-like" character of non-REM subjective experience (Hobson 1988). However, given the fact that it is more or less easy to re-establish a typical or surreal environment from a minimal environment, the minimal environment may correlate with tonic REM. The time after REM onset may also be an important variable affecting perceptual qualities of lucid dreams. The interrelated phenomena of stability, fading, and minimal perceptual environments during lucid dreams has interesting implications for our understanding of conscious processes. Clearly, in these experiences, higher level cognitive functions of consciousness continue to operate in the relative absence of conscious sensory modalities. We are observing in these phenomena some type of dissociation, or perhaps lack of binding, of the contents of consciousness. Psychophysiological characterization of this phenomena would be of great interest.

No previous studies have presented data regarding the frequency with which lucid dreamers as a population or individual lucid dreamers experience the three perceptual environments we have identified here. Published dream reports indicate that typical environments predominate lucid dreamers' perceptions, although we have encountered cases where this is not true for single individuals, and it seems likely that individuals will have characteristic distributions of environment type. For example, 52%, 96%, and 17% of DJD's lucid dreams had at least one scene with minimal, normal, and surreal environments, respectively; the figures for SLB are 16%, 92%, and 5%. Although the great majority of both authors' lucid dreams take place in normal environments, DJD's were significantly more likely to have minimal and surreal environments as well. The differences in frequency are even more striking if we consider the extreme case of minimal environments, the void, without any content at all; DJD, 32% vs. SLB, 3%.

3.2.4 *Perceptual Variation in Specific Sensory Modalities*

Within the context of one of the three varieties of perceptual environment just reviewed, the specific contents of consciousness in different sensory modalities can vary from the normal to the bizarre. Thus, for example, a particular lucid dream may take place in an environment that is almost entirely normal, with the exception of a single element of the sensory array. Or everything may appear perfectly normal if considered individually, but quite anomalous when considered in context. For example, van Eeden (1913) describes experimenting with breaking a claret-glass in a lucid dream: "It broke all right, but a little too late, like an actor who misses his cue. This gave me a very curious impression of being in a fake-world, cleverly imitated, but with small failures."

The factors affecting the variations in lucid dream perceptual bizarreness and their frequency of occurrence have yet to be investigated. Here we will very briefly review some of the variations in perceptual experience and bizarreness in several sensory modalities.

a. Vision. Although the visual contents of most lucid dreams seem quite normal, there are some aspects of the visual experience that do not operate in the same way as in waking perception. For example, the Marquis de Saint-Denys observed that he was often unable to alter the level of illumination in his lucid dreams (see LaBerge 1985), an effect termed the "Light-Switch" phenomenon by Hearne (1987).

> (SLB1029) "...[in a lucid dream] I remember the light task and look around for a switch. I find a table lamp and flick it's switch on: it dimly illuminates. I switch it off and it goes off. I try willing it to light, focussing my willpower on the bulb, but no luck. Then I try another lamp, a halogen desk lamp. I turn the on knob and it dimly lights (about as bright as in waking imagination). Twist off and off it goes. Magical will power has no effect, again.."

Visual bizarreness in the geometry of the dream environment (allocentric space) is described clearly by lucid dreamers, as the following two examples illustrate:

> (DJD20) "It didn't strike me at the time, but what was weird was how the ghoul was positioned in my backyard and the angle I was viewing him from out my window. He was standing at the corner of my room on the outside, with its side facing in my direction and its front facing towards the street and its back facing into the backyard. What I didn't realize until I woke up and wrote this is that there is no way I could see someone if they were standing in this position physically. After waking, I tried to look out my window from where I was standing in my room in the lucid dream, and you simply can't see that corner of the house. I had to put my face right up to the window and turn my head to see that position from my window. But in the lucid dream I could see that position perfectly standing back a few feet from the window."
>
> (DJD43) "I looked up at the ceiling and got a nice visual surprise. The hallway seemed to repeat itself upward and curving out of sight, like the effect of two mirrors up against each other, except there were no mirrors."

The visual texture of objects is highly variable in lucid dreams. Scenes can take on appearances ranging from highly realistic to "cartoon-like". Lucid dreamers frequently report that dream objects appear to be "glowing" as if self-illuminated. The visual texture of whole dream environments can take on drastically different appearances in lucid dreams, usually accompanied by distinctive affect, as the following examples indicate:

> (DJD76) "Standing on the lawn I saw a white picket fence running up the walk to the front door. Across the street was a lake and beyond the lake an amazing horizon of sun and colors. Everything seemed to have a pinkish red tint to it. The colors were like soft delicate pastels. A warm breeze was blowing. My movements were like slow motion as I walked through the front yard (not the slow motion kind of movement that makes it difficult to move, but a slow motion in the sense of being very dream like). My thoughts seemed very removed from my situation. The whole thing seemed to be beautifully unreal...."

> (SLB355) "...I find myself on a street (not at first aware that I'm dreaming). Then after a few seconds I realize that I am dreaming again. I fly up into the warm air towards the sun. But it always seems out of reach. I fly over mountains and then the sea and, as I continue to try for the sun, weird volcanic-organic forms sprout up from the ocean. Gradually this bizarre fractal-coral creature's transformations dominates the scene and the sun is above my field of vision. I find myself sinking into the water. I no longer seem to be able to fly and feel continuously more constrained by the dream...."

As in nonlucid dreams, visual aspects of dream characters, objects and environments in lucid dreams can transform visual appearance. In some cases, the effect of such transformations is similar to the familiar morphing process popular in computer graphics (DJD61), in other cases, the transformation is more abrupt, a discontinuity (DJD18). Often, discontinuities of perceptual environments involve a change in the visual setting of the dream contrary to the dreamer's expectation (DJD18):

> (DJD61) "...I was glad to have gotten her attention. But then I noticed as I was staring at her face, that her features kept shifting from that of an old lady to that of a beautiful young woman."

> (DJD18) "Through the window I saw that it was raining outside. I desired to experience this astral rain. I tried to pass through the wall to get outside but I couldn't. The window was open, but there was a screen blocking my way. I tried to open the screen but couldn't, so I decided to tear the window out. I smashed through it but the hole was too small to crawl through, so I tore away the wall around the window. But the hole was still too small to pass through! So I tore down the whole kitchen wall! Now the hole was big enough to climb through and I jumped through it. But I wasn't outside! Instead, I was in a strange and unfamiliar hallway. I turned around and the kitchen with the hole in the wall was gone! I was in some kind of hallway that looked like an apartment building."

Lucid dreamers report that reading, and especially re-reading, of text in lucid dreams can present challenges. Here is Oliver Fox's description: "...reading [in lucid dreams] is a very difficult matter. The print seems clear enough until one tries to read it: then the letters become blurred or run together, or fade away, or change to others" (1962, p. 46). If comprehended initially, the text, upon rereading, can change in either form, lexical structure, semantic structure, or based on rhyme and alliteration (LaBerge 1996). Here are some examples:

> (DJD53) "I saw a bulletin board and went and tried to read it. I managed to read, with great difficulty, one line of what looked like a flyer announcing a party. I tried to reread the line so as to memorize it, but it now read something completely different. Familiar with this kind of thing, I gave up trying to read."

> (DJD13) "I noticed a sign in front of a building and got the idea to go try to read it... The sign was on some steps leading into a building and I got the sense that it was some kind of official sign. I tried to read it but had a very difficult time. I could not get it into focus that easily. All I could make out were the letters 'OR', which for some reason I interpreted to mean Oregon, and, with difficulty I read the statement 'Cheyan Country'. At that moment I thought to myself 'This sign is senseless.' I gave up my attempt to read the sign and walked back down the steps somewhat shaken up."

There are other occasions in which lucid dreamers read dream material that is coherent and even especially meaningful as in the following example:

> (SLB592) "Exploring around a grand old hotel that for some reason I take to be 'Freud's Hotel'. Fully lucid, I find a piece of paper that appears at first to be a prescription, but upon closer inspection now seems the will or legacy of Anna Freud. On the paper I read the words:
>
> TO DUST, WE MUST;
> TO LIGHT, WE MIGHT."

Variations in dream reading presumably occur because the brain creates dreamed text without any external source of visual information, resulting in unstable perceptions of dream text. The relative roles of individual differences versus expectation in the variations of dream reading has yet to be determined.

b. Audition. Sound may be experienced during WILDs, in the transition from waking to sleep, in the form of cracking, hissing, twinkling, or similar sounds, sometimes reported as "haunted house" sounds. These are auditory forms of hypnagogia. Lucid dreamers have reported hearing songs during lucid dreams, as if a radio was playing, when in fact, there was no other source of the perception of music using other modalities. Subjects experiencing sleep paralysis have reported hearing voices, sometimes of a threatening or terrifying nature, reminiscent of the auditory hallucinations of schizophrenics. Lucid dreamers also frequently experience playing music:

> (SLB270) "In a 'high-school dream' that has become lucid, I walk up to the teacher who is demonstrating something on the piano as if I am an expected guest artist and sit down to play. I think of playing something from a book, but find that my vision is too weak. So I improvise a Fantasy in F#m, starting out prosaically enough, but building up gradually to a terrific climax. The dream fades with the last chord...."

There are infrequent reports reminiscent of fluent aphasia by lucid dreamers.

> (DJD76) "He said something about getting into a fight with his Dad. I asked him where he was from and he said 'the Land-O-Lakes, from Idaho.' I asked for his address but he mumbled nonsense. He told me his name but I can't remember it now."

However, reports containing aphasic qualities are rare, and even in (DJD76) word comprehension was mixed with incomprehension. Generally, auditory conversation with dream characters is marked by lexical, syntactical and pragmatic accuracy (Meier 1993).

c. Somatosensation. There is strong variability in somatosensation during lucid dreams. Variations in somatosensation are prevalent during initiation of WILDs where, during the transition from waking to lucid dreaming, the person may experience any of the following somatic sensations: vibrations, tingles, waves of warmth, a sense of melting, floating, peeling, flipping over, flopping, slipping, and sinking. Once in a lucid dream, there may be variations in perceptions of a body image, ranging from being a disembodied point or freely moving center of awareness (but still immersed in the perceptual environment), to perceiving in full detail that one is in a body and fully immersed in one of the varieties of perceptual environments. Autoscopy is reported in which the lucid dreamer may see his or her body as if looking at it from the outside. All of these variations in somatosensation have been proposed, at one time or another, as criteria to distinguish out-of-body experiences from lucid dreams (e.g. Gabbard and Twemlow 1984; Irwin 1988). There is little justification for this distinction (Levitan and LaBerge 1991) and it seems most reasonable to simply recognize that there is a wide variability of somatic sensations associated with lucid dreaming. Some of these embodiments can seem very strange indeed as in the following two cases:

> (SLB308) "I have been telling an improvised version of the story of *Fatima the Spinner and the Tent.* Through a forgotten transition, my awareness has come to rest within a collection of porcelain plates and china. Queen Fatima is walking through the gallery and I begin to communicate with here by rattling my plates. All the while I am fully aware that I'm dreaming. The courtiers try to stop the rattling, believing an earthquake to be taking place...Then I believe I have awakened during — an earthquake! I find the apparent incorporation of the earthquake in my dream interesting until I actually awaken a few moments later."

> (SLB880) "After lying on my back for a long while, still seemingly awake, I suddenly feel as if I've turned into a bluish gas: actually a cloud of coarse blue spheres in the general form of my body that floats above the bed..."

Tholey (1988) describes a very interesting phenomenon in which the lucid dreamer's "ego" leaves his dream body and "enters into another dreamer figure". The result can be a more complete degree of interpersonal understanding than usually results from such techniques as dialoguing with dream figures. Tholey reports that it is also possible to "slip into different dream figures, one after the other, during lucid dreaming, *and* to conduct a dialogue with a dream figure that one has left with the ego consciousness" (p. 284).

A particular kinesthetic sensation is reported by lucid dreamers but not nonlucid dreamers: this is a sensation of being uncontrollably dragged or whisked along by a "force", sometimes described as a "strong wind", which carries the lucid dreamer through the dream environment:

> (DJD31a) "I floated up through the roof to the outside. Suddenly, I lost my ability to fly, and I began to be pulled along by a strong force, that was like a strong wind gust. This force pulled me violently towards the house next door and I shut my eyes in fright, fearing that I was going to smash into the wall. But then, I just passed smoothly through the wall as the wind force continued to pull me along. I had a momentary glimpse of the inside of the house before I was pulled up through the roof of this house."

Hobson and coworkers have suggested a motor-control theory of dreams in which PGO-initiated stimulation of vestibular and motor pathways generates dreamed motion in a random fashion (Hobson 1988). Such phasic REM events are a potential explanation of the uncontrolled kinesthesia experienced in lucid dreams described here. However, lucid dreamers, to our knowledge, do *not* report autonomic sensations associated with vestibular activation in lucid dreams. For example, spinning is quite common for lucid dreamers (used as a technique to stabilize the dream sensorium) but this does not typically produce sensations of vertigo. Thus, it may be that vestibular pathways do not directly affect dream consciousness, and somatic sensations are generated at the level of sensorimotor cortex.

Sleep paralysis is commonly reported both by nonlucid and lucid dreamers. Sleep paralysis involves the intrusion of peripheral somatosensory input associated with REM atonia into the dreamer's consciousness. Closely related to sleep paralysis is the commonly reported feature of the difficulty of moving or talking in dreams, often when the dreamer is subject to a threat. This feature is also reported by lucid dreamers, and again suggests intrusion of peripheral somatosensory afferent information into dream consciousness.

d. Other senses. Lucid dreams can contain content in every sensory modality, including temperature, pain, olfaction, and gustation. Most of these modalities are somewhat rare in lucid dreams, just as they are rare in waking life; but all are possible. Here is an example from van Eeden (1913):

> On Sept. 9, 1904; I dreamt that I stood at a table before a window. On the table were different objects. I was perfectly well aware that I was dreaming and I considered what sorts of experiments I could make. ... Then I saw a decanter with claret and tasted it, and noted with perfect clearness of mind: "Well, we can also have voluntary impressions of taste in this dream-world; this has quite the taste of wine."

According to folk-lore, a dream pinch is supposed to be painless. LaBerge and Levitan (1998) tested this idea by asking lucid dreamers to induce several somatosensory experiences (pain, pressure and light touch) through dream actions and then awaken and rate the results on a seven-point scale for intensity, discomfort, and pleasure. The same procedure was also followed in waking and in imagination. The results showed a notable deficiency in the reproducibility of the conscious experience of pain on demand in lucid dreams (mean discomfort 1.5 in dreams vs. 3.9 in waking; $p < .05$). The subjects had much better success at eliciting lucid dream sensations of pressure (means of 2.9 in dreams, 3.7 in waking) and light touch (mean=3.2 in dreams, 3.0 in waking). These findings suggest that, while some sensory experiences are well modeled by the brain in the absence of primary sensory input, pain may be a special case. To experience convincing realistic pain in dreams, the brain may require some peripheral somatosensory input that may be interpreted as pain. Lest this study be misunderstood to suggest that one cannot experience pain in dreams, here is the testimony of one of the subjects to the contrary:

> (C. S.) However, as soon as I knew I was dreaming, I remembered the experiment... so I stopped and pinched my left forearm with my right hand. At first, I didn't feel anything but the touch. So, I pinched myself as hard as

> possible. The pain was so extreme that I yelled out "Oh my God!" … the sensation of pain [was] so severe … that I woke up.

On the other hand, the finding that it is easier to experience pleasure than pain in dreams is an intriguing result demanding explanation, and in any case, good news for lucid dreamers.

3.3 *Emotions*

Emotion in lucid dreams, while generally positive or relatively neutral, can vary over the entire range of human emotions from agony (mitigated by the realization that "it is only a dream") to the unmitigated ecstasy of sexual or religious bliss. The realization that one is dreaming is frequently accompanied by an unmistakable sense of excitement and delight. For Rapport (1948), the emergence of lucidity "instantly" transformed his dream into "an incommunicably beautiful vision." Fox (1962), described the onset of his first experience of lucidity: "instantly, the vividness of life increased a hundredfold…never had I felt so absolutely well, so clear brained, so divinely powerful, so inexpressibly *free*!" Not surprisingly, the emotions felt in lucid dreams often carry over into the waking state as in the following example:

> (SLB1027) I had somehow gotten myself out on a limb as it were: at the end of a girder high above the street below. I was trying to choose between walking or crawling. Both seemed too risky and I looked around for other alternatives. I observe that behind me is another way I can escape. I climb off the end of the girder onto another ledge and start to work my way through cobwebs in another passageway. I believe I was partially lucid during this because I have a false awakening in which I am telling someone about the preceding dream. I describe letting go of my mental set of going back on the beam the way I came. At the words "letting go" I realize that I'm dreaming again and that the real solution is to trust and *let go.* As I do so, leaping into the beautiful sunrise sky, I am overwhelmed with feeling and awaken with tears of joy.

Emotional arousal, whether associated with the excitement of lucidity onset or for any other reason, presents lucid dreamers with a problem: Experience of strong emotion within a lucid dream may increase sensations of instability and lead to fading from the lucid dream. Thus, prolonging the lucid dream state requires a degree of emotional control. According to Celia Green (1968: 99), "Habitual lucid dreamers almost unanimously stress the importance of emotional detachment in prolonging the experience and retaining a high degree of lucidity."

A second problem of emotional involvement is that the lucid dreamer's consciousness may be reabsorbed by the dream, and as the lucid dreamer becomes emotionally absorbed, re-identify with the dream role. This amounts to a displacement of the lucid dream context by a nonlucid dream context. This is a problem more often encountered by beginners than experienced lucid dreamers, and through practice and experience, one can learn to maintain lucidity in spite of intense and emotional involvement with the dream.

3.4 *Cognitive Functions*

Characterizing variations in cognition during lucid dreaming is both subtle and complex. Not only can variations in cognition occur amongst lucid dreamers, cognition can also vary for a single individual from lucid dream to lucid dream, or within the same lucid dream. Because lucid dreaming is a cumulative skill modified by experience and practice, this means there will always be at least some degree of continuous variation underlying the cognition of lucid dreamers, reflecting changes in the psychological development of that individual both with respect to lucid dreaming, and in general. Nonetheless, variations in cognition within lucid dreaming can be due to other factors including the subject's semantic framework and contextual competition, affecting in particular memory access and thinking.

3.4.1 *Variations in Memory*

Access to memories of waking experience can vary, in spite of the lucid dreamer's intention to access those memories. For example, a lucid dreamer may be unable to recall one's phone number, or the date, or even one's name, in a given lucid dream, although such memories may have been accessed in other lucid dreams. On the other hand, sleep laboratory subjects can remember to perform complex tasks during lucid dreams, tasks which had been previously planned and/or rehearsed during waking. Thus, variations in voluntary access to waking memory may be partly due to intrinsic factors, such as the degree of cortical activation in a given lucid dream or the degree of competition from elements outside the lucid dream context, and partly due to prior preparation and priming of memory.

Levitan and LaBerge (1993) tested memory for four different tasks in a group of 20 lucid dreamers. The tasks and percent of successful recall were: where one is sleeping (95%), the current date (94%), and arbitrary word learned before bed (100%), and a fact that one could not remember previously while awake despite multiple efforts (19%).

3.4.2 *Variations in Thinking*

The thoughts, conceptions, metacognitive reflections and expectations of lucid dreamers are strongly conditioned by the dreamers' semantic framework. Within a given semantic framework, the quality of lucid dreamers' thinking tends to be consistent. However, the use of different semantic frameworks results in more or less accurate conceptions of the lucid dream experience. For example, lucid dreamers who conceptualize their lucid dreams as out-of-body experiences (OBEs) may tend to confuse physical and dream objects, and may operate under the assumption that what they perceive in their lucid dreams corresponds to physical reality (LaBerge 1985). People who conceive of their lucid dreams as astral projections may come to similarly flawed conclusions. Within the astral projection lore, it is commonly taught that characters encountered during astral projections are the souls of the deceased (Leadbeater 1895; Fox 1962; Monroe 1985). Thus, the astral projector may act as if dream characters are "real" and not mental representations. These examples illustrate that what could be mistakenly taken for a flaw in thinking during a lucid dream is not necessarily a defect in thought per se, but a consequence of the lucid dreamer operating in a specific semantic framework. In such cases, it is the semantic framework that is flawed, not the dreamer's ability to think or reason. Because of the tremendous perceptual diversity of lucid dreams, the variations on this theme are boundless. Considerations of an individual's semantic framework also apply to near-death experiences (NDEs), which have phenomenological overlap with lucid dreams. NDEs are characterized by autoscopy, lucidity, and surreal perceptual environments such as the experiences of perceiving white light, or moving through a tunnel (Greyson 1993). NDEs are often interpreted in a religious context as proof of life after death (Reader 1995). Again, the emphasis here is that individuals' semantic frameworks will affect their interpretation of events and behavior in lucid dreams and phenomenologically similar states.

The semantic frameworks used by individuals is not confined to their lucid dream experiences but also has consequences for their waking life. Because lucid dreams are not widely understood in our society, and because of the variety of semantic frameworks available, some peoples' responses to their lucid dream experiences may alter the course of their waking lives. Furthermore, these individuals can influence the beliefs of others and thereby replicate their semantic framework within the wider culture. The elaboration of these notions involves the study of biographies of individuals who have undergone lucid dreaming but interpreted these as something else. This topic is beyond the scope of this chapter, but the interested reader can find sources illustrating these points (e.g. Lutyens 1975; Monroe 1985; Tillett 1982).

On the other hand, lucid dreamers can display alterations in thinking that are not in any obvious way the direct result of operating under a specific semantic framework (Barrett 1992; Levitan 1994). These alterations in thinking resemble minor lapses in rationality, unclear thinking, and drawing absurd conclusions. Several factors can account for these belief-independent variations in thinking: (1) the lucid dreamer's degree of experience is such that the lucid dreamer has not yet learned what is and is not appropriate behavior in a given dreamed circumstance, (2) competition from nonlucid dream contexts provided distractions that absorb the dreamer into a dream narrative, and influence the dreamer's thought processes toward this narrative, and (3) variations in brain activity during the course of the lucid dream could alter the performance of higher level cognitive tasks such as comprehending situations and formulating responses.

There is sometimes no obvious difference between belief-dependent and belief-independent variations in thinking when viewing isolated dream reports. Ascertaining these requires knowing a lucid dreamer's semantic framework and taking this into account when judging the quality of the thinking reported during lucid dreams.

3.5 *Volition and Action*

There is more voluntary choice available to lucid dreamers than to nonlucid dreamers. The experienced lucid dreamer seems capable of exercising at least as much free choice while dreaming as waking. However, waking volition is constrained by general knowledge and past experience. Likewise, volition during lucid dreams is constrained by the dreamer's semantic framework and past lucid dream experience. These factors together define to the lucid dreamer what is and is not possible, and therefore, what voluntary choices are available. The set of these possible choices are contained in the lucid dreamer's goal-options context.

The actions of lucid dreamers vary from simple to complex. A lucid dreamer's actions may be *reflexive*, as when walking in a lucid dream without losing balance. Others are *instinctive*, such as attempting to avoid threatening situations. Still others are *habitual*, such as speaking or driving a car or performing other procedural tasks in a dream. Finally, some of the actions are *deliberate* and based on volitional choice. Volitional actions are initiated by the lucid dreamer for any number of reasons: curiosity, desire, etc.

The actions of lucid dreamers are not constrained by the real world either physically or socially. Hence, lucid dreamers routinely fly, pass through walls or perform other actions impossible in the physical world as the following passage indicates:

> (DJD54) "I stared up at the big window before me and there was nothing on it indicating that I could open it. So then I did a very interesting trick to get out through the window. I stared at the window and "bent" my perspective on the window so that there was now a gap between the window and the wall that was large enough for me to climb through. I hovered up out of the chair, ignoring the nurse, and pulled myself through the opening I had just created. I was wiggling through the hole wondering what the nurse and other people in the room were thinking."

Lucid dreamers can also freely violate social mores, and behave in highly uninhibited fashions. This can provide a form of therapy to lucid dreamers in terms of overcoming anxiety, recognizing habitual patterns of social interaction, and developing self-knowledge, as well as simply providing a form of pleasure and entertainment (LaBerge and Rheingold 1990).

The characterization of the actions of lucid dreamers is subsumed under the notion of "dream control". A distinction can be drawn between two kinds of dream control (LaBerge 1985). One type involves magical manipulation of the dream environment or of dream characters other than the dream actor. The manipulation of the window in (DJD54) is an example of magical manipulation of the dream environment. The other kind of control open to lucid dreamers is *self*-control, exercised over one's own actions and reactions to events occurring in the lucid dream.

Contrary to some descriptions of lucid dreaming, lucid dreamers typically do not have complete volitional control over their lucid dreams. The most important factor in this regard is that lucid dreamers do not necessarily have control over the perceptual environment in which they find themselves. Like nonlucid dreams, lucid dreamers often find themselves in novel and completely unfamiliar environments which they had no intentional control over creating. This is particularly true of surreal lucid dream environments; here lucid dreamers often cannot even comprehend what they are experiencing (as in DJD75 and DJD70 above). Likewise, lucid dreamers do not intentionally desire to appear in minimal sensory environments, and often have no control over this happening. Thus, lucid dreaming is less like a fantasy experience and more like an exploratory experience.

There are also limits to the actions of lucid dreamers, particularly with respect to magical manipulations. For example, the attempt to fly during any given lucid dream may be met with varying degrees of success. The lucid dreamer may fly readily, merely hover, or not be able to fly at all. Likewise, a lucid dreamer may not always be able to pass through walls (as illustrated in DJD61). Thus, because the lucid dreamer may have performed such acts in previous lucid dreams, the inability to perform such an act will often be met with confusion. This variability in performance of actions from lucid dream to lucid dream appears to be belief-independent because, for example, a lucid dreamer may remember that he has flown before, and will expect to fly, but then cannot fly in the current lucid dream. It is reasonable to hypothesize that variations in performance of actions during lucid dreams reflects underlying variations in REM brain activity.

There are also situations where the dream environment itself imposes actions on the lucid dreamer completely outside the dreamer's intentions or expectations. We have presented examples of this in preceding sections: the need to maintain stability is perhaps the most general non-volitional action with which lucid dreamers are faced. Here, lucid dreamers must control their emotions, and often take steps to stabilize themselves (through spinning or other techniques) in order to prolong their lucid dreams. The kinesthesia experienced as being carried by a strong wind (DJD55 and DJD31a,b above) also occurs outside the will and intention of the lucid dreamer. Often, perceptual discontinuities, such as illustrated in (DJD61) will occur in spite of the lucid dreamer's intention and are often met with surprise by the lucid dreamer.

To suggest that the lucid dreamer "unconsciously" desires or wills experiences that are outside the dreamer's conscious intentions does not offer a credible explanation of these forms of lucid dream variability. It would appear that events and actions occurring in lucid dreams are a combination of: (1) those intentionally generated by the lucid dreamer, limited by the dreamer's experience and knowledge and (2) those generated by the dream environment outside of the conscious knowledge and intention of the lucid dreamer.

With respect to unintended actions generated by the dream environment, these events and actions must in some way be related to the occurrence of physiological phenomena in the sleeping brain. This is clearly the case with sleep paralysis in which peripheral atonia intrudes into the dreamer's consciousness unintentionally. A second example, the sensation of being uncontrollably whisked along by a "wind force" may be a subjective correlate of localized miniature seizure activity in somatosensory cortex, which itself may be grounded in the random brainstem neurotransmission so actively advocated by Hobson and his followers as a basis for dream generation. Another example highly suggestive of the involvement of neurophysiological processes is when a lucid dreamer "fades" from a lucid dream: there is a relatively stereotyped loss of conscious sensory modalities (LaBerge, DeGracia et al. 1998). These fade in the order of vision followed by somatosensation and audition. This suggests a pattern of cortical deactivation from occipital cortex followed by a medial to lateral and caudal to rostral deactivation in the temporal and parietal cortices, respectively. Together, these examples indicate that unconscious brain physiology can intrude into the consciousness of lucid dreamers, forcing unintended actions on the lucid dreamer.

There are Tibetan traditions of lucid dreaming dating from the Ninth Century which claim that a person can achieve complete control of the dream environment (LaBerge 1985); similar claims are commonplace in Western occult lore (e.g. Leadbeater, 1895). However, no one in the modern era has demonstrated this capability. It is perhaps reasonable, given the evidence at our disposal, to recognize that actions and events occurring in lucid dreams are due to a complex combination of psychological and neurological factors. This, of course, does not preclude testing the limits of possibility in lucid dreams. Indeed, teasing apart the relative roles of neurology and psychology in lucid dream experiences could provide significant insight into the workings of the mind and brain and further our understanding of the relationship between subjective experience and neurological events.

3.6 *Termination of Lucid Dreams*

Sooner or later, all things end, and lucid dreams are no exception. There are two general possibilities for terminating lucid dreams: lucidity is lost while the dream continues, or the lucid dream ends with an awakening. The first mode we have discussed above and involves displacement of the lucid dream context by a nonlucid dream context. Novice lucid dreamers are particularly susceptible to loss of lucidity and may need to explicitly remind themselves that they are dreaming (LaBerge and Rheingold 1989). With experience, some lucid dreamers learn to maintain lucidity without any special effort (e.g., SLB; The percentage of lucid dreams in which lucidity was lost in years 1–3 respectively were 18%, 1%, and 0.4% for SLB, and 17%, 21%, and 40% for DGD, and, a significantly different pattern).

For more experienced lucid dreamers, lucid dreams are more likely to terminate by awakening than by loss of lucidity. Termination by awakening typically involves the "fading out" sensations discussed above. Ordinarily there is a high degree of continuity of consciousness during this transition. In contrast, there is usually a moment of confusion when dreamers wake from a nonlucid dream, as they make the transition from the nonlucid dreamer to the waking self.

There are two other possible ways in which lucid dreams can come to an end. In one case, the lucid dreamer enters non-REM sleep and ceases dreaming. Typically, if awakened at this point, the dreamer would recall nothing. In the other case, lucidity is lost, and REM sleep continues, with the person *dreaming* that he or she has awakened. These dreams are usually called “false awakenings” (Green 1968) and are very commonly reported concomitants of lucid dreams. Sometimes, false awakenings occur repeatedly with the lucid dreamer seeming to awake again and again only to discover each time that he or she is still dreaming. In some cases, lucid dreamers have reported enduring literally *dozens* of false awakenings before they finally wake up “for real”. False awakenings tend to increase in frequency with experience in lucid dreaming. For example, here are the percentage of lucid dreams with false awakenings in years 1–3 respectively were 9%, 13%, and 24% for DGD, and 16%, 31%, and 39% for SLB. The reason for the increase frequency of false awakenings is probably that more experience with lucid dreams leads to the greater expectation that as a lucid dream is about to end that one is about to wake up. Thus the expectation of awakening leads to the dream content of the false awakening. Increased familiarity leads to increased likelihood of recognizing that one is dreaming during a false awakening. The percentage of false awakenings recognized in years 1–3 respectively were 4%, 8%, and 20% for DGD, and 0%, 3%, and 26% for SLB.

4. Conclusions

Dream experience is innately complex and the waking personality can choose to explore this complexity with a greater or lesser degree of involvement. When there is more involvement of the waking self with one’s dream life, one’s dreams partake more of lucidity. When lucid dreams are explored, significant variation is discovered, and individual factors underlie a great deal of this variation. Much of the phenomenology we have described above is not understood in either psychological or neurological terms, but it offers intriguing glimpses into the processes underlying conscious experience, and the relationship between subjective experience and neurological processes. A deeper understanding of the variety of lucid dream perceptual environments may shed light on sensory representations in waking. An understanding of the effects of semantic structures on lucid dream experience underscores the role of belief in subjective perception and behavior. Finally, study of the unintentional aspects of lucid dream action may bring us closer to understanding the generation of dreams, and the relationship between subjective experience and neurological events. We hope this chapter will inspire more comprehensive research on the phenomenology of lucid dreaming experience.

Notes

1. Examples are coded by author's initials and sequence number of lucid dream.

References

Aaronson, B. and Osmond, H. (eds.). 1970. *Psychedelics*. New York: Doubleday & Co. Inc.

Baars, B. 1988. *A Cognitive Theory Of Consciousness*. Cambridge: Cambridge University Press.

Barrett, D. 1992. "Just how lucid are lucid dreams?" *Dreaming* 2: 221–228.

DeGracia, D. J. 1997. "Les paradigmes de la conscience dans le sommeil (Paradigms of consciousness during sleep)". *Rêver* 1(3): 26–35. Online: http://www.users.imaginet.fr /~ghibelli/dondega.html.

DeGracia, D. J. and LaBerge, S. 1998. "In the theater of dreams: global workspace theory, dreaming, and consciousness". *Consciousness and Cognition*. In submission.

Diamond, E. 1963. *The Science of Dreams*. New York, NY: Macfadden Books.

Fox, O. 1962. *Astral Projection: a Record of Out-of-the-body Experiences*. New Hyde Park, NY: University books.

Gabbard, G. O. and Twemlow, S. W. 1984. *With the Eyes of the Mind*. New York: Praeger.

Gackenbach, J. 1988. "The psychological content of lucid versus nonlucid dreams". In J. Gackenbach and S. LaBerge (eds.), *Conscious Mind, Sleeping Brain*, 181–220. New York: Plenum.

Gackenbach, J. and LaBerge, S. (eds.), 1988. *Conscious mind, sleeping brain: Perspectives on lucid dreaming*. New York: Plenum.

Garfield, P. 1979. *Creative Dreaming*. New York: Ballantine.

Gillespie, G. 1988a. "Lucid dreams in Tibetan Buddhism". In J. Gackenbach and S. LaBerge (eds.), *Conscious Mind, Sleeping Brain*, 27–35. Plenum, New York.

Gillespie, G. 1988b. "Without a Guru: An account of my lucid dreaming". In J. Gackenbach and S. LaBerge (eds.), *Conscious Mind, Sleeping Brain*, 343–350. Plenum, New York.

Green, C. 1968. *Lucid Dreams*. Oxford: Institute for Psychical Research.

Greenberg, R. and Pearlman, C. 1974. "Cutting the REM nerve: an approach to the adaptive role of REM sleep". *Perspectives in Biology and Medicine* 17: 513–21.

Greyson, B. 1993. "Varieties of near-death experience". *Psychiatry* (56): 390–99. Hall, C. and Van de Castle, R. 1966. *The Content Analysis of Dreams*. New York: Appelton-Century-Crofts.

Hearne, K. 1987. "A new perspective on dream imagery." *Journal of Mental Imagery* 11(2): 75–82.

Hobson, J. A. 1988. *The Dreaming Brain*. New York: Basic Books.

Hobson, J. A. 1994. *The Chemistry of Consciousness*. Boston: Little Brown and Co.

Hunt, H. 1989. *The Multiplicity of Dreams*. New Haven: Yale University Press.

Irwin, H. 1988. "Out-of-the-body experiences and dream lucidity". In J. Gackenbach and S. LaBerge (eds.), *Conscious Mind, Sleeping Brain*, 353–371. New York: Plenum.

Kahan, T. and LaBerge, S. 1994. "Lucid dreaming as metacognition: implications for cognitive science". *Consciousness and Cognition* 3: 246–264.

Kahan, T.L., LaBerge, S., Levitan, L. and Zimbardo, P.G. 1997. Similarities and differences between dreaming and waking: An exploratory study. *Consciousness and Cognition* 6: 132–147.

LaBerge, S. 1980. "Lucid dreaming as a learnable skill: a case study". *Perceptual and Motor Skills* 51: 1039–1042.

LaBerge, S. 1985. *Lucid Dreaming*. New York: Ballantine Books.

LaBerge, S. 1988. The psychophysiology of lucid dreaming. In J. Gackenbach and S. LaBerge (eds), *Conscious mind, sleeping brain: Perspectives on lucid dreaming*, 135–153. New York: Plenum.

LaBerge, S. 1990. Lucid dreaming: Psychophysiological studies of consciousness during REM sleep. In R.R. Bootsen, J.F. Kihlstrom, and D.L. Schacter (eds), *Sleep and Cognition*, 109–126. Washington, D.C.: American Psychological Association Press.

LaBerge, S. 1993. Physiological studies of lucid dreaming. In J. Antrobus and M. Bertini (eds) *The neuropsychology of dreaming sleep*, 289–303. Hillsdale, NJ: Erlbaum.

LaBerge, S. 1994. The stuff of dreams. *Anthropology of Consciousness* 5: 28–30.

LaBerge, S. 1996. "To sleep, perchance to read" *Nightlight* 3(2): 17–21. LaBerge, S. 1998. Dreaming and consciousness. In S. Hameroff, A. Kaszniak, and A. Scott (eds), *Toward a science of consciousness II*, 495–504. Boston: MIT Press.

LaBerge, S., DeGracia, DJ. and Zimbardo, P. 1998. "Prolonging lucid dreams". In preparation.

LaBerge, S. and Gackenbach, J. 1986. Lucid dreaming. In B. Wolman and M. Ullman (eds), *Handbook of states of consciousness*, 159–198. New York: Van Nostrand Reinhold.

LaBerge, S. and Gackenbach, J.I. (in press). Lucid dreaming as anomalous experience. In S. Krippner and E. Cardeña (eds), *Varieties of anomalous experience: Phenomenological and scientific foundations*. Washington, D.C.: American Psychological Association Press.

LaBerge, S. and Levitan, L. (November, 1998). *Does the subjective experience of pain require neuronal activity below the level of the brain? A study of pain in lucid dreams*. Paper presented at the 17th annual meeting of the American Pain Association, San Diego, California.

LaBerge, S., Nagel, L., Dement, W. and Zarcone, V. 1981. Lucid dreaming verified by volitional communication during REM sleep. *Perceptual and Motor Skills* 52: 727–732.

LaBerge, S. and Rheingold, H. 1990. *Exploring the World of Lucid Dreaming*. New York: Ballantine Books.

Leadbeater, C.W. 1895. (12th reprint, 1984). *The Astral Plane*. Madras: Vasanta Press.

Levitan, L. 1994. "A fool's guide to lucid dreaming". *Nightlight* 6(2): 1–5. Online: http://www.lucidity.com/NL62.FoolsGuide.html

Levitan, L. and LaBerge, S. 1991. "Other worlds: out-of-body experiences and lucid dreams". *Nightlight* 3(2): 1–5. Online: http://www.lucidity.com/NL32.OBEandLD.html.

Levitan, L. and LaBerge, S. 1993. "Dream times and remembrances." *NightLight* 5(4): 9–14.

Lutyens, M. 1975. *Krishnamurti: The Years Of Awakening*. London: John Murray.

Mavromatis, A. 1987. *Hypnogogia*. London: Routledge & Kegan Paul.

McCreery, C. 1973. *Psychical Phenomena and the Physical World*. London: Hamish Hamilton.

Meier, B. 1993. "Speech and thinking in dreams". In C. Cavallero and D. Foulkes (eds.) *Dreaming As Cognition*. New York: Harvester Wheatsheaf, 58–76.

Moers-Messmer, H. von, 1938. *Traüme mit der gleichzeitigen Erkenntnis des Traumzustandes [Dreams with simultaneous cognizance of the dream state], Archiv für Psychologie* 102: 291–318.

Moffitt, A., Hoffmann, R., Mullington, J., Purcell, S., Pigeau, R. and Wells, R. 1988. "Dream psychology: operating in the dark". In J. Gackenbach and S. LaBerge (eds.), *Conscious Mind, Sleeping Brain*, 429–439. New York: Plenum.

Monroe, R. 1985. *Far Journeys*. New York: Doubleday.

Ouspensky, P. 1960. *A New Model of the Universe*. London: Routledge & Kegan Paul.

Rapport, N. 1948. "Pleasant dreams!" *Psychiatric Quarterly* 22: 309–17.

Reader, A. L. 1995. "The internal mystery plays: the role and physiology of the visual system in contemplative practices." *Alternative Therapies* 1(4): 54–63.

Rogo, D. S. 1986. *Leaving The Body*. New York: Prentice Hall.

Salzarulo, P. and Cipolli, C. 1974. "Spontaneously recalled verbal material and its linguistic organization in relation to different stages of sleep". *Biological Psychology* 2: 47–57.

Snyder, T. and Gackenbach, J. 1988. "Individual differences associated with lucid dreaming". In J. Gackenbach and S. LaBerge (eds.), *Conscious Mind, Sleeping Brain*, 221–259. New York: Plenum.

Tart, C. 1984. "Terminology in lucid dream research" *Lucidity Letter* 3: 4–6.

Tholey, P. 1988. "A model for lucidity training as a means of self-healing and psychological growth". In J. Gackenbach and S. LaBerge (eds.), *Conscious Mind, Sleeping Brain*, 263–287. New York: Plenum.

Tillett, G. 1982. *The Elder Brother A Biography Of Charles Webster Leadbeater*. London: Routledge & Kegan Paul.

van Eeden, F. 1913. A study of dreams. *Proceedings of the Society for Psychical Research* 26: 431–461.

Individual Differences in Patterns of Hypnotic Experience Across Low and High Hypnotically Susceptible Individuals

Ronald J. Pekala
Coatesville V.A. Medical Center

V.K. Kumar
West Chester University of Pennsylvania

The present chapter will (a) review several theoretical approaches for understanding consciousness and its various states, (b) briefly describe the research on parallel distributed processing (PDP) models of cognition; (c) report on a phenomenological methodology for quantifying, statistically assessing, and diagraming patterns of subjective experience congruent with the theorizing described in (a) and (b); (d) review previous hypnosis research which found significant phenomenological pattern effects as a function of individual differences, and (e) present a phenomenological pattern approach for understanding the information processing underlying hypnotic effects, particularly in reference to individual differences.

Consciousness, Information Processing, and Hypnosis

The study of information processing and its role in consciousness and conscious experience has become a legitimate scientific research area within the last decade (Baars 1988, 1997; Mandler 1985). Conferences on consciousness and it's involvement within cognitive science and psychology, neuroscience, philosophy, physics and mathematics, and biology are now in vogue (Laukes 1997). The study of the phenomenological aspects of hypnosis (Orne 1977; Sheehan & McConkey 1996; Sheehan & Perry 1976) appears quite consistent with this revival of interest in consciousness. Although hypnosis has always intrigued mental health professionals and individuals interested in consciousness, researchers in hypnosis have generally been reluctant to embrace a quantitative phenomenological perspective (Pekala 1991a). Yet a comprehensive assessment of hypnotic phenomenological effects as a function of individual differences may lead to an increased understanding of the nature of information processing underlying the production of hypnotic effects and their relationship to ordinary, waking consciousness.

For example, an important question in hypnosis research in the 1960's was: to what extent is a hypnotic induction a necessary condition for hypnotic effects? At that time some theorists (Hilgard & Tart 1966) regarded a hypnotic induction as adding significant effects to the hypnotic experience, but others (e.g., Barber & Calverley 1962; Barber, Spanos, & Chaves 1974) suggested that an induction was superfluous and task-motivation instructions, or even no induction at all (for some individuals), could be associated with hypnotic effects as classically-defined (Wilson & Barber 1983). Although some of these controversies have been adequately addressed since, several others have also resurfaced in somewhat different form in the 1990's (Kirsch & Lynn 1995). One of these concerns the fact that researchers have failed to find consistent physiological "markers" of the hypnotic state (Dixon & Laurence 1992; Kirsch & Lynn 1995). The possibility exists that an empirical phenomenological approach may provide a means to help define "markers" of the hypnotic state that has heretofore eluded physiological efforts.

If a comprehensive phenomenological methodology can generate data which illuminate the nature of the cognitive processes associated with hypnotic effects, it may help to further understand who can and cannot be hypnotized. It may also shed light on the extent to which hypnosis may lead to "dissociation" of experience (Hilgard 1977), or "dissociated control" (Bowers 1992; Kumar, Pekala, & Cummings 1996). Understanding the nature of such changes during hypnosis, especially as they related to individual differences, may also have relevance to other altered states of consciousness (Tart 1975, 1977) and further illuminate the mystery of consciousness itself (Chalmers 1996).

Psychological Approaches to Understanding Consciousness and Its Various States

For Mandler (1985), consciousness is a construction. Drawing upon Marcel's (1983) work on perceptual processes, Mandler views consciousness as "a construction of phenomenological experience out of one or more of the available preconscious events, schemas, and structures" (Mandler 1985, p. 92). This is done by abstracting relevant information from the "preconscious state-of-the-world knowledge" to construct the conscious state. Our resulting phenomenological experience is then a constructed conscious experience dependent upon activated schemas that are set in motion in response to the requirements of the moment.

According to Mandler, attention is "the process whereby a specific part of the space-time continuum is automatically made available for further processing" (Mandler 1985, p. 83). Attention partakes of both "top down" and "bottom up" processing using both parallel and serial processing modes. Because of limited attentional capacity, consciousness is also of limited capacity and only particular schemas or structures can be activated at any particular time to occupy the attentional field.

As a first approximation, Mandler defines a state of consciousness as "constructed out of the most general structures currently being activated by current concerns and environmental requirements" (Mandler 1985, p. 60). States of consciousness change "whenever there is a change in the state of the world, defined as any change in the sensory evidence or in intentions, instructions, content, or situation" (p. 61).

Izard (1977), a theorist who has spent much time in trying to understand affect and emotions, defines consciousness as "the total array of sensations, perceptions, cognitions, and affects that characterize the individual" (Izard 1977, p. 137). Special or altered states of consciousness result when an individual "breaks" the affective-cognitive bonds that couple affect and cognitive structures, since they "provide the principal structures of ordinary consciousness" (Izard 1977, p. 158). For Izard, altered states of consciousness are usually the result of a radical shift in interest and attention and a breakdown of very stable and well-learned affective-cognitive processing patterns.

Tart (1975, 1977) has probably spent more time theorizing how to understand various states of consciousness than any other theorist. Like Mandler, he views states of consciousness as active constructions. According to Tart (1975), states of consciousness are a function of various subsystems or structures of mind that combine in particular patterns to form a specific or discrete state of consciousness. A state of consciousness is "a unique configuration or system of psychological structures or subsystems, a configuration that maintains its integrity or identity as a recognizable system in spite of variations in input from the environment and in spite of various (small) changes in subsystems." (Tart 1975, p. 62)

For Tart (1975, 1977), it is the pattern or organization between these different elements that determine the particular state of consciousness experienced. An altered state of consciousness occurs when there is a significantly different pattern of organization among structures/elements of consciousness in comparison to ordinary, waking consciousness, and the phenomenological perception of being in a radically different state of awareness. This perception of being in a radically different state has previously been defined as SSAS — the subjective sense of being in an altered state (Pekala & Wenger 1983).

Pekala (1991a) has built upon the theorizing of Tart. He also defines altered states of consciousness as states with both a change in pattern among subsystems and the perception of being in an altered state of awareness. A discrete state of consciousness, on the other hand, is a state of consciousness that is distinguished from other states by a significantly different patterning among dimensions (in comparison to ordinary, waking consciousness or other states). There is not, however, the perception of being in an altered state of consciousness. Thus, discrete states are nonaltered states of consciousness characterized by a significant pattern change among dimensions in reference to other states, but no SSAS. In contrast to the above, Singer (in Zinberg 1977) has suggested that it is primarily intensity, and not pattern, parameters that determine a particular state of consciousness.

Although changes in intensity of the various subsystems of consciousness are no doubt important, we believe the it is primarily the changes in pattern, as enumerated by Tart (1975, 1977), Mandler (1985), Izard (1977), and Pekala (1991a) that define states and altered states of consciousness. The psychological theorizing of Tart, Izard, and Mandler concerning the importance of the patterning of information flow among various subsystems of consciousness is remarkably similar to burgeoning research in parallel distributed processing models of cognition (Matlin 1998; McClelland & Rumelhart 1985, 1988; McClelland et al. 1986; Rumelhart et al. 1986; Tryon 1993a, 1993b).

Parallel Distributed Processing (PDP) Models of Cognition

In a review of the work of Mountcastle (1978), Arbib (1980), and Geschwind (1979), Baars (1988) noted that the human brain has been conceptualized as a "gigantic mosaic of different modules and processors" (Baars 1988, p. 219) that are thought to be in parallel communication with one another via a "global workspace" (Baars 1996). Since such processors are thought to be distributed throughout the brain and to be in constant communication with other processors or subsystems, the nature of such processing can be conceptualized as parallel, as opposed to the sequential processing of modern digital computers (McClelland, Rumelhart et al. 1986; Rumelhart, McClelland et al. 1986). These multiple specialized processors can be quite active and yet can be quite independent of one another. Through interconnections with each other they allow information of various contents to be processed. These processors, sometimes referred to as "parallel distributed processors" (PDPs) (McClelland & Rumelhart 1985) "create a 'society' of specialized systems; each able to handle some predetermined type of problem" (Baars 1987, p. 215).

Somewhat similar to Mandler (1985), Izard (1977), and Tart's (1977) pattern approach to understanding consciousness, the parallel distributed processing (PDP) models postulate a pattern approach to understanding cognition. This approach postulates a set of processing units or processors that define cognition and a pattern of connectivity among units that define and constitute what the system "knows." The PDP approach to cognition is neural-based and is a function of the organization of parallel processing units. With PDP approaches to cognition "almost all knowledge is implicit in the structures of the device that carry out the task rather than explicit in the states" (Rumelhart et al. 1986, p. 75) of the processors:

> Representation occurs through the pattern of connection weights across the network. Learning entails changes in these weights. New memories are written nondestructively on top of other memories up to a finite system limit, yet each memory can be fully and separately recalled. (Tryon 1993, p. 344)

Hence, it is the weights, associations, or correlations amongst the processors that determine the thoughts, percepts, emotions, and stimuli that are experienced, learned, and recalled (Baars 1997). The data suggest that PDP models appear to have robust ability to generalize automatically to new situations and are especially "tunable" to changing environments.

Although the PDP approach to cognition is relatively new, it is also quite complicated in its attempt to understand the brain at a neural level, and makes certain assumptions too numerous to enumerate in this short chapter (Matlin 1998). Suffice it to say, however, that the theorizing of Tart, Mandler, and Izard for understanding states of consciousness appears consistent with this new approach for understanding cognition in the fundamental sense of looking at the patterns or associations amongst processors/subsystems of consciousness.

A Phenomenological Pattern Approach to Consciousness

Pekala and Kumar (1986, 1989) have phenomenologically operationalized a pattern approach to consciousness that is based upon the psychological theorizing of Tart (1977), Mandler (1986), Izard (1977), and Baars (1987, 1996). It is also consistent on a very general level with current PDP models of human cognition, that is, a network of interconnected units that use parallel processing which varies with the degree of association among them (Matlin 1998). With Pekala and Kumar's approach, phenomenological experience is retrospectively assessed by a self-report inventory such as the Phenomenology of Consciousness Inventory (PCI) (Pekala 1982, 1991b). The PCI provides phenomenological intensity scores on 12 major subsystems of consciousness. These include: internal dialogue, self-awareness, altered state of awareness, imagery, positive affect, negative affect, altered experience, attention, memory, rationality, volitional control, and arousal (See Appendix, Figures 1–8).

The PCI and its predecessor instruments have been found to be reliable and valid state instruments (Kumar & Pekala 1989; Pekala, Forbes, & Contrisciani 1988/89; Pekala & Levine 1981, 1982; Pekala, Steinberg, & Kumar 1986) for assessing subjective effects not only with hypnosis, but also with progressive relaxation and deep abdominal breathing (Pekala & Forbes 1988), an out-of-the-body experience (Maitz & Pekala 1990/91), and firewalking (Pekala & Ersek 1992/93).

The PCI allows for the phenomenological quantification of the aforementioned subsystems of consciousness in terms of intensity variations within these subsystems; that is, little or much imagery, complete or no volitional control, little or great alteration in state of awareness, etc. In addition, the construction of correlation matrices composed of the PCI subsystems allows for associations among differing subsystems to be quantified, which can then be used for inferring the nature of the information processing occurring among the subsystems of consciousness. High correlations among the subsystems suggest that these subsystems are processing information in relation to each other (positively or negatively); whereas low or statistically nonsignificant correlations suggest subsystems of consciousness that are processing information independently from one another.

Whereas correlations provide a measure of the relationship among subsystems, the squared correlation, or the coefficient of determination, provides a measure of the variance in common between two subsystems of consciousness. Whereas a coefficient of determination of zero between two processors indicates no variance in common, or complete independence, a coefficient of determination of 1.00 indicates 100% of the variance in common, or a complete identity; that is, knowing the parameters of one system allows for the parameters of the other system to be perfectly predicted.

The relationships or degrees of association among various subsystems of consciousness can be also diagramed via a device called a psygram (Pekala

1985; 1991a) and statistically assessed via Jennrich's (1970) test (Pekala & Kumar 1985). This graphic device positions the various subsystems of consciousness mapped by the PCI on the circumference of a circle and uses lines (each line represents approximately 5% of the variance in common) running between subsystems to denote the percentage of variance (squared correlation coefficient or coefficient of determination) in common among two subsystems. Numbers next to the lines represent the exact percentages of variance (with negative numbers used to depict negative correlations). So as not to "clutter" the graph, only variance percentages associated with significant correlations are depicted.

The psygram represents a "snapshot" or graph (across a group of individuals) of the psychophenomenological state (Pekala 1985; Pekala 1991a) associated with the stimulus condition assessed. In a sense, the psygram represents the "state of mind" (Baars 1988, 1997) or "state of consciousness" (Tart 1975) associated with the particular stimulus condition (e.g., hypnosis, meditation, eyes-closed-sitting-quietly) for which it was assessed.

There is no intention to reify the PCI dimensions. Rather, the PCI dimensions are putative subsystems of consciousness that have been found to be empirically reliable and valid when assessed in reference to specific stimulus conditions (Kumar & Pekala 1988, 1989; Pekala 1991a; Pekala & Levine 1981, 1982; Pekala & Wenger 1983; Pekala, Steinberg, & Kumar 1986; Pekala & Kumar 1984, 1987, 1989).

By illuminating the differences in patterns of consciousness across individuals of low or high hypnotic susceptibility, researchers can use this methodology to determine how hypnosis may differentially affect low or high hypnotizables. Such information may have important theoretical or clinical implications. The following section will summarize prior research on the use of this approach for looking at such differences across low and high susceptible subjects.

Patterns of Consciousness During Hypnosis and A Baseline Comparison Condition

Pekala and Kumar (1986) assessed the pattern of relationships among phenomenological dimensions or subsystems of consciousness across low and high hypnotically susceptible individuals by means of the PCI. Participants (n = 163) experienced a baseline condition of eyes-closed-sitting-quietly for 4 minutes and then retrospectively completed the PCI in reference to that condition. They then experienced the induction procedure of the Harvard Group Scale of Hypnotic Susceptibility, Form A (Shor & Orne 1962) and retrospectively completed the

PCI in reference to a four minute sitting quietly period embedded in that induction during which they were told: "to continue to experience the state you are in right now. For the next several minutes I'm going to stop talking and I want you to continue to experience the state you are in right now."

Pekala and Kumar (1989) completed a replication of the above study in which 324 participants experienced a 3 minute eyes closed sitting quietly period and afterwards completed the PCI in reference to that condition. As with the first study, upon completion of the first stimulus condition, all subjects experienced the induction procedure of the Harvard Scale and a 3 minute period embedded in the Harvard scale. After the end of the hypnosis participants completed the PCI in reference to the sitting quietly period embedded in the hypnotic intervention.

To increase sample size data from the studies were combined. Because the subjects represent two different studies and the time intervals (during baseline and hypnosis) were slightly different, that is, 3 and 4 minutes, preliminary analyses were conducted assessing the feasibility of combining data from the two studies. Multivariate analyses of variance with the PCI major dimensions as the dependent variables, and Susceptibility Groups and Study as the independent variables, revealed neither a significant main effect for Study nor a significant interaction between Study and Group for either the baseline or the hypnosis conditions. This suggested no contraindications for combining the two data sets (Table 1).

Participants were divided into 4 Susceptibility Groups: lows (scores of 0 to 4, n = 111, M =2.40), low-mediums (scores of 5–6, n = 88, M = 5.49), high-mediums (scores of 7–8, n=99, M=7.50), and highs (scores of 9–12, n=106, M = 10.18).

Table 1. *Chi-Square Values for the Comparison of Intercorrelation Matrices for the Hypnosis Condition*

	Susceptibility Groups[a]		
Susceptibility Groups	Low-Mediums	High-Mediums	Highs
Lows	93.08*	92.86*	115.23***
Low-Mediums		95.65**	117.77***
High-Mediums			84.98

[a] *df* for 12 PCI dimensions = 66
* = $p < .05$; ** = $p < .01$; *** = $p < .001$

Pattern Comparisons as a Function of Hypnotic Susceptibility and Between the Eyes-Closed and the Hypnotic Induction Conditions

Correlation matrices were constructed for the four Susceptibility Groups using the 12 major PCI dimensions for both the eyes-closed and the hypnotic induction conditions. These matrices were compared with Jennrich's (1970) test (Pekala & Kumar 1985). Although none of the comparisons for the eyes-closed condition were significant, all comparisons for the hypnotic induction condition were significant except for that between highs and high-mediums. Table 1 lists the chi-square values for these comparisons for the hypnotic induction condition.

The intercorrelation matrices of the four Susceptibility Groups also were compared across the eyes-closed versus hypnosis conditions. Comparisons for lows (chi-square = 150.9, $p < .001$), low-mediums (chi-square = 133.7, $p < .001$), high-mediums (chi-square = 115.7, $p < .001$), and highs (chi-square = 88.59, $p < .05$) were all significant.

Psygram Visual Analysis

Psygrams were constructed using the intercorrelation matrices for the low and high susceptible participants for the baseline eyes-closed and the hypnosis conditions. To be conservative, only those correlations significant at the .001 level ($r > .33$) were used in the psygram construction.

A perusal of the psygram for low susceptibles during eyes closed (Figure 1) and high susceptibles during eyes closed (Figure 3) shows a much higher degree of association amongst subsystems of consciousness for lows. Whereas the high susceptibility group during eyes closed has only 10 associations that are significant ($p < .001$), low susceptibles have 17. The average coefficient of determination for low susceptibles was 19.3% versus 19.7% for the high susceptibles. Hence, although the level of association averaged across the significant correlations was nearly identical, low susceptibles had almost double the number of significant associations as high susceptibles.

For low susceptibles, hypnosis appears to have potentiated the magnitude of the associations amongst the subsystems. Although the number of significant associations increased from 17 to 21, the average percentage of variance in common now increased from 19.3% (during eyes-closed) to 36.6% (during hypnosis). This suggests that hypnosis, for low susceptibles, was associated with the subsystems of consciousness that became more highly associated in comparison to the baseline eyes closed condition. (Jennrich's test comparing hypnosis with the baseline condition for low susceptibles was significant.) A different effect occurs for highs as they move from eyes closed to hypnosis. Not only does the number of significant associations remain about the same (10 for eyes-closed versus 9 for hypnosis), but the intensity of association also remains almost identical, that is, 19.7% to 19.8% (see Figures 3 and 4).

A visual examination of the psygram for low susceptibles shows a higher degree of association as they move from baseline to hypnosis. In contrast, the high susceptibles show a pattern shift from strong associations among rationality, memory, and attention during eyes closed, to strong associations only between imagery and positive affect, and imagery and rationality. As with the low susceptibles, the Jennrich test yielded a statistically significant pattern difference for hypnosis in comparison to eyes closed for high susceptibles.

In conclusion, what appears interesting is the very different (and statistically significant) phenomenological shifts in patterns of association among PCI dimensions that occur as these susceptibility groups move from baseline into hypnosis.

Pattern Analyses Concerning Very-Low and Very-High Susceptibles

To determine if the shift observed above would intensify when looking at very-low, versus very-high, hypnotically susceptible individuals, subjects who scored very low or very high on the Harvard were selected for additional analysis; that is, those subjects who scored either 0 or 1 on the Harvard Scale ($n = 36$, $M = 0.64$) and those subjects who scored either 11 or 12 ($n = 39$, $M = 11.41$) on the Harvard. (These analyses were first reported in Pekala & Bieber 1989/90.) Because of the small n's used, pattern comparisons using Jennrich's test are not reported. (Approximately 60 subjects per group are needed, Pekala 1991a, for the Jennrich test to have adequate power.)

To determine if the specific nature of the pattern differences between conditions for very-low versus very-high susceptibles paralleled those obtained between the lows and highs, psygrams were constructed for both groups for both conditions using the same .33 cutoff for the Pearson r (but now $p =$ about .05 due to the small n for these analyses).

Figures 5 and 6 depict the psygrams of very-low susceptible participants during eyes-closed and hypnosis, respectively. Whereas very-lows have 27 significant correlations depicted during eyes-closed, there are 20 significant associations depicted in reference to hypnosis, with average coefficients of determinations of 24% and 51%, respectively (i.e., the associations during hypnosis are approximately twice as large as during eyes-closed).

Figures 5 and 6 are contrasted with Figures 7 and 8, depicting psygrams for very-high susceptibles during eyes-closed and hypnosis, respectively. Very-highs demonstrated the same number of significant associations during the eyes-closed and hypnosis conditions, that is, 12 and 12, although the average coefficients of determinations are slightly different (21% versus 17%). The overall pattern of association during hypnosis for very-highs seems quite different, however, from that of the eyes-closed condition.

Concerning very-highs versus very-lows, most of the associations among PCI dimensions for very-highs during eyes-closed are also evident with very-lows during eyes-closed (see Figures 5 and 7). There are, however, more associations among PCI dimensions for very-lows than very-highs and other major differences. Not only are there fewer and less intense associations among the PCI dimensions for very-highs versus very-lows, but the patterns of associations among dimensions are also quite different. Besides strong associations between memory and attention, rationality and memory, altered state and altered experience, and self-awareness and volitional control, most PCI dimensions for very-highs during eyes closed are weakly associated.

When comparing Figures 1 and 2 with Figures 5 and 6 respectively, one sees an increase in the frequency of associations between Figure 1 (17 significant associations) and Figure 5 (27 significant associations) and an increase in the magnitude of the associations between Figure 2 (37% of the variance in common) and Figure 6 (51% of the variance in common).

Although there is a slight increase in the frequency of associations between Figures 3 and 4 and 7 and 8 (the number of significant associations goes from 10 and 9, respectively, for Figures 3 and 4, to 12 and 12 for Figures 7 and 8), the magnitude of the associations remain about the same, that is, from 19 to 20%. This suggests that the patterns of associations for very-high hypnotizables (Harvard scores of 11 or 12) are of similar magnitude for this group as for highs (individuals with Harvard scores of 11 to 12 and also 9 to 10). In contrast, the differences for lows versus very-lows are much more striking.

Pattern Effects Among Susceptibility Groups: Understanding How Hypnosis May "Work"

Pattern Differences Among Low and High Susceptibles

Pattern differences among low, low-medium, high-medium, and high susceptible individuals during eyes-closed were not found significant. This suggests that all four groups are processing information rather similarly during the baseline condition of sitting-quietly-with-eyes-closed. Yet a hypnotic induction procedure appears to have had rather dramatic effects upon the different susceptibility groups. Pattern differences between lows and highs, lows and low-mediums, lows and high-mediums, and low-mediums and highs were all significant during hypnosis.

Hypnosis appears to have almost doubled the average variance in common among PCI subsystems when comparing eyes-closed (average $r^2 = .19$) against hypnosis (average $r^2 = .37$) for lows, while the effect for highs moving from eyes-closed (average $r^2 = .20$) to hypnosis (average $r^2 = .20$) for the PCI dimensions was negligible. These observations, coupled with the significant differences among the matrices (Jennrich test) for both groups (lows and highs) as they moved from baseline to hypnosis, suggests that hypnosis had a significant quantitative change in both the frequency and magnitude of the associations amongst PCI processors for lows, while it had a significant qualitative, rather than quantitative, change for highs.

Thus, although the pattern among dimensions shifted somewhat among PCI dimensions for highs, the average association among all PCI dimension-pairs was not appreciably affected. In contrast, not only did the pattern change rather dramatically for lows, but so did the degree of association, with hypnosis being characterized by a much more highly associated organization among PCI dimensions than eyes-closed.

The data suggest that it appears to be not what a hypnotic induction does for highs, but rather what it appears to do for lows, that may be related to low susceptibles' inability to experience hypnotic effects. Hypnosis appears to result in a higher degree (both frequency and magnitude) of association among PCI subsystems of consciousness for lows, as reflected not only in almost doubling of the average coefficient of determination, but especially in a much greater coupling among selected subsystems, such as rationality, volitional control, memory, self-awareness, altered state and altered experience.

Increased magnitude and frequency of associations among subsystems may make it much more difficult for lows to experience a hallucinated fly or to dissociate the perceptual experience of one's arm, since a change in one particular subsystem appears to lead to changes in associated subsystems. This would make it quite difficult for lows to modify the phenomenological contents of a particular subsystem of consciousness without affecting many other subsystems concurrently (as shown in the more highly coupled psygram of Figure 2).

Research by Kumar, Pekala, and Cummings (1996) suggested the factor of "dissociated control" as a major state factor underlying hypnotic experience. (See also Kumar, Pekala, and McCloskey 1997.) The higher frequency and increased magnitude of associations among PCI dimensions for low susceptibles during hypnosis, vis-a-vis high susceptibles, supports this factor as demonstrated in the psygram visual analysis. How can low susceptibles dissociate or relinquish control of one particular subsystem of consciousness during hypnosis, if this subsystem of consciousness is highly associated with other subsystems of consciousness?

More concretely, because of the high degree of association and the number of significant associations between subsystems of consciousness for low susceptibles, the clinician or researcher will have a difficult time manipulating one particular subsystem of consciousness, be it anesthetizing a hand, creating anosmia, or suggesting a visual hallucination, if an intervention in this particular subsystem, causes corresponding changes in other systems. On the other hand, the decreased associations among subsystems for highs (in comparison to lows) will make it much easier for the clinician/researcher to affect one particular subsystem with hypnosis without affecting other subsystems concurrently.

As an example, a high susceptible during hypnosis is able to dissociate pain in, let us say, the hand from the rest of the body as if the hand were completely separated from it. Somewhat similarly, thoughts or feelings of a traumatic memory can become functionally divorced from the memory, or the whole memory itself separated from other memories, leading to amnestic experiences or even multiple personality (Kluft 1984) for high susceptibles that is not possible for lows.

Pattern Differences among the Very-Low and the Very-High Susceptibles

When taking the top and bottom 9% of the distribution, one has at one's disposal what most hypnosis researchers would call the somnambulistic and the refractory hypnotic subjects (Hilgard 1977). The coefficient of determination results obtained with participants scoring 0 to 4 on the Harvard were intensified in magnitude with the very-low (0 to 1 Harvard score) participants (as evinced in psygrams 5 and 6). Whereas lows had an average coefficient of determination among PCI dimensions of 19% during eyes-closed, the very-lows have an average coefficient of determination of 24% during eyes-closed. Additionally, whereas lows had 17 coefficients of determination based on correlations that were significant, very-lows had 27 such significant correlations. Both the number of significant correlations and the magnitude of those correlations increased when looking at those subjects who scored 0 to 4 on the Harvard in comparison to those subjects who scored only 0 or 1 on the Harvard.

Hypnosis further increased the magnitude of the associations amongst PCI subdimensions for very-lows, vis-a-vis lows, as they moved from the baseline condition into hypnosis. Although the number of significant associations remained almost identical, that is 21 and 20, the magnitude of the coefficients of determination increased from 37% with the lows, to 51% with the very-lows. This contrasts with an average coefficient of determination of 21% for eyes-closed for the very-highs, and 17% for hypnosis for very-highs. Visual comparison of the eyes-closed psygram for very-lows and very-highs supports major differences in pattern structure, and also illustrates that although very-lows have many of the same associations as do very-highs during eyes-closed, they also have many more significant associations.

Conclusions: Individual Differences in Patterns of Hypnotic Experience

By retrospectively assessing subjective experience during a baseline condition and hypnosis across groups of subjects differing in hypnotizability level the psygram results represent a "snapshot" of the degree of association amongst phenomenological subsystems of consciousness across individuals of differing susceptibility. Hypnosis appears to be doing very different things phenomenologically to individuals who are not that hypnotizable, in comparison to those individuals who are highly hypnotizable. With low (and very-low) susceptibles, hypnosis actually increases the significant associations amongst various phenomenological subsystems of consciousness, probably making it more difficult to affect a particular subsystem, without concurrently affecting many other subsystems.

Consequently, given the increased frequency and magnitude of association amongst subsystems evident in Figure 2 (and Figure 6), it is probably no wonder that one cannot usually attempt to establish anesthesia in the arm of a low susceptible. Rather, every thought, feeling, and sensation in a low susceptible is strongly "linked" or associated with other thoughts, feelings, and sensations, that such an intervention cannot occur. In other words, low susceptibles during hypnosis cannot "let go" and just accept and experience the anesthesia, since the high associations among the various processors of consciousness trigger evaluations, feelings, and interpretations about the intervention, making "dissociated control" (Kumar, Pekala, & Cummings 1996) impossible.

Researchers have failed to find consistent physiological "markers" of the hypnotic state (Dixon & Laurence 1992; Kirsch & Lynn 1995). Although this may partially relate to the tremendous variety of suggestions that can be given during hypnosis (with different suggestions possibly activating different brain functions), it may also relate to the fact that the "secret" of hypnosis is not to be found in the processors themselves. That is, the neurophysiological "secret" of hypnosis may not be found in the different modular "parts" of the brain, including but not limited to speculations concerning right versus left brain (Crawford 1994), or the limbic system (De Benedittis & Sironi 1986, 1988), but rather in the "connections" or associations amongst those parts; something that an EEG, brain scan, or PET scan cannot easily monitor.

Just as knowledge in a PDP network will not be found in the processors themselves, but rather in the weights or connections, the aforementioned phenomenological pattern approach to hypnosis and consciousness suggests important differences in the phenomenology of the hypnotic experience across low and high susceptible subjects that resides not necessarily in the intensities of the various PCI processors themselves, but rather in the nature or degree of their association or disassociation.

Do the psygrams of high/very-high susceptibles during hypnosis represent "dissociated control" vis-a-vis low/very-low susceptibles? Correlational studies like that reported in this chapter cannot prove causality. However, the results, we believe, do support a different type of pattern organization of subsystems of consciousness for high (very-high), vis-a-vis low (very-low), susceptibles that is consistent with dissociation (Hilgard 1977) or "dissociated control" (Kumar, Pekala, & Cummings 1996; Kumar, Pekala, & McCloskey 1997).

Appendix

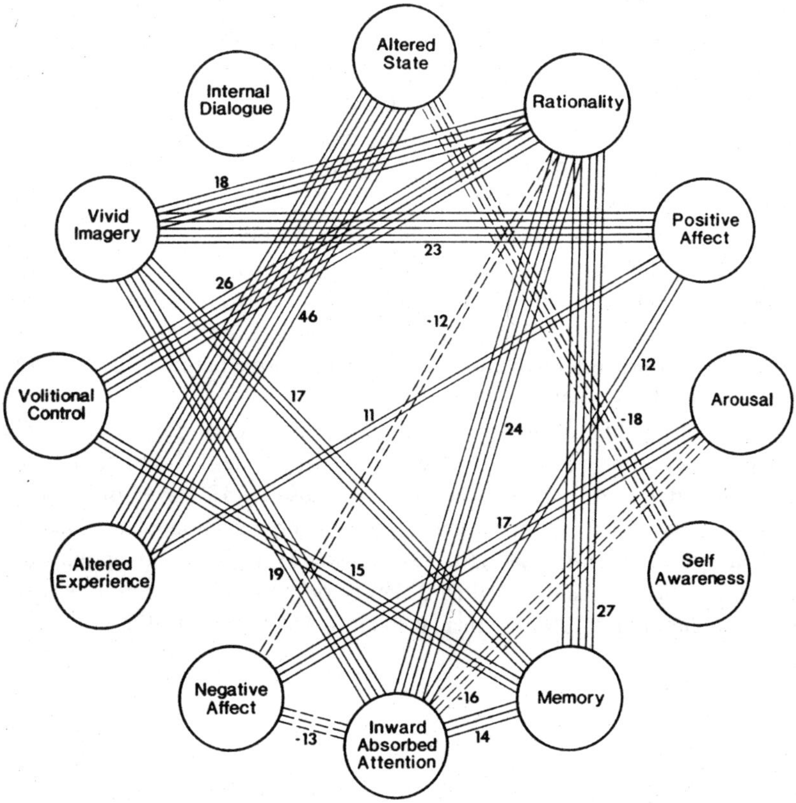

KEY

Each line represents approximately 5% of the variance in common.
(All variance percentages represent correlations significant at alpha less than approximately .001.)

n = 111

Figure 1. *Low Susceptible Individuals: Eyes Closed*

[From: Pekala, R. J., & Bieber, S. L., 1990. Operationalizing pattern approaches to consciousness: An analysis of phenomenological patterns of consciousness among individuals of differing susceptibility. Imagination, Cognition, and Personality, *9, 303–320; © 1990, Baywood Publishing Co., Inc.]*

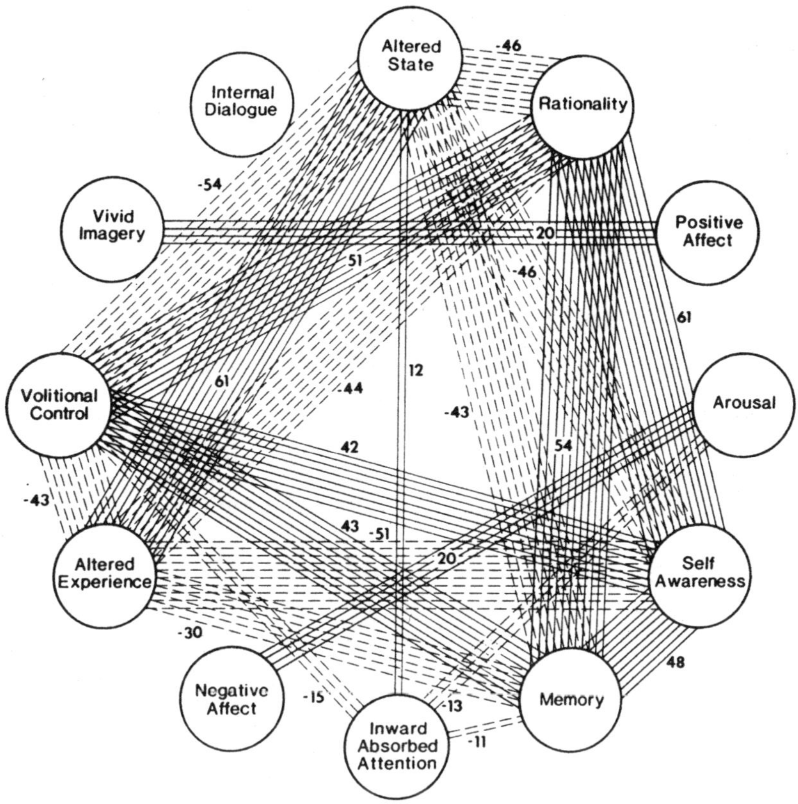

KEY

Each line represents approximately 5% of the variance in common.
(All variance percentages represent correlations significant at alpha less than approximately .001.)

$\underline{n} = 111$

Figure 2. *Low Susceptible Individuals: Hypnotic Induction*

[From: Pekala, R. J., & Bieber, S. L., 1990. Operationalizing pattern approaches to consciousness: An analysis of phenomenological patterns of consciousness among individuals of differing susceptibility. Imagination, Cognition, and Personality, *9, 303–320; © 1990, Baywood Publishing Co., Inc.]*

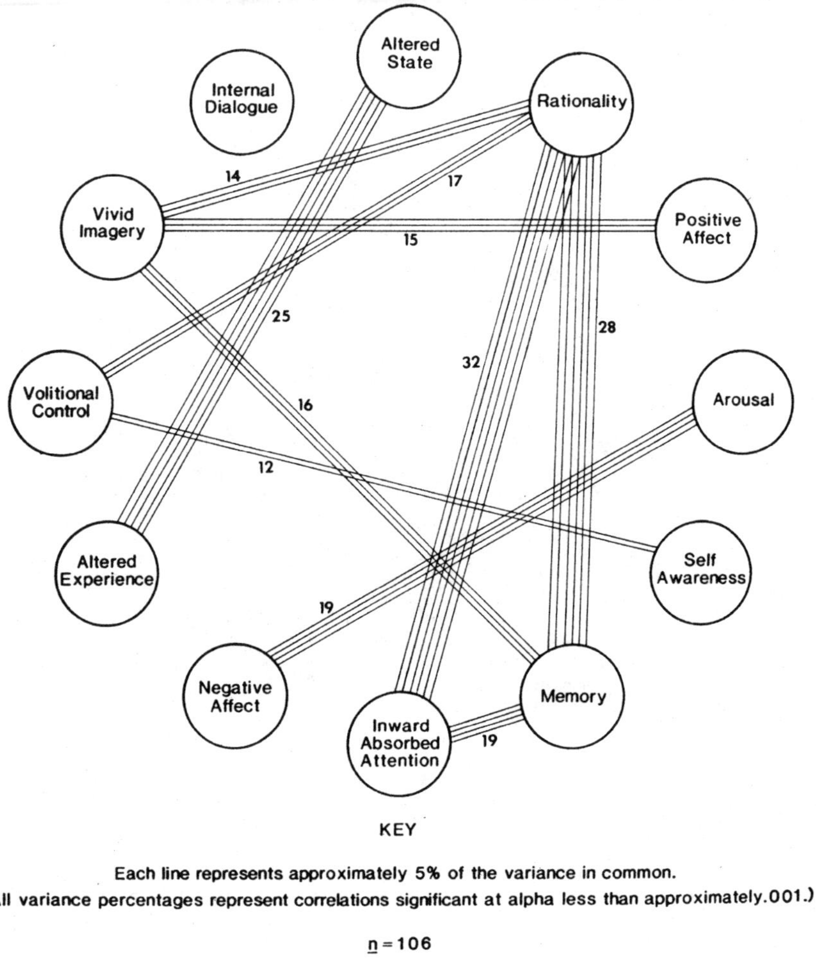

Figure 3. *High Susceptible Individuals: Eyes Closed*

[From: Pekala, R. J., & Bieber, S. L., 1990. Operationalizing pattern approaches to consciousness: An analysis of phenomenological patterns of consciousness among individuals of differing susceptibility. Imagination, Cognition, and Personality, *9, 303–320; © 1990, Baywood Publishing Co., Inc.]*

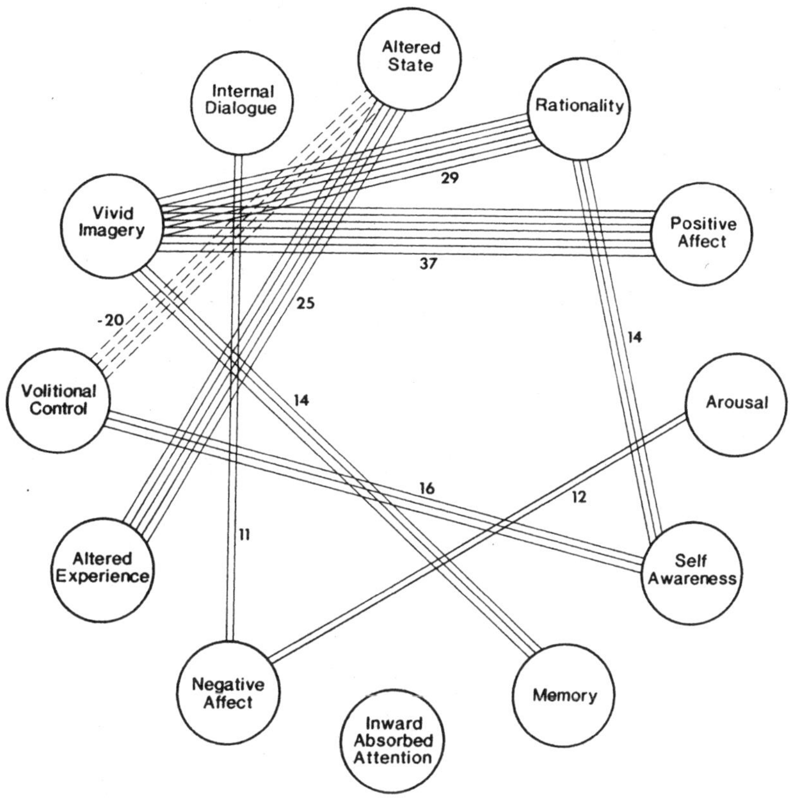

KEY

Each line represents approximately 5% of the variance in common.
(All variance percentages represent correlations significant at alpha less than approximately.001.)

n = 106

Figure 4. *High Susceptible Individuals: Hypnotic Induction*

[From: Pekala, R. J., & Bieber, S. L., 1990. Operationalizing pattern approaches to consciousness: An analysis of phenomenological patterns of consciousness among individuals of differing susceptibility. Imagination, Cognition, and Personality, *9, 303–320; © 1990, Baywood Publishing Co., Inc.]*

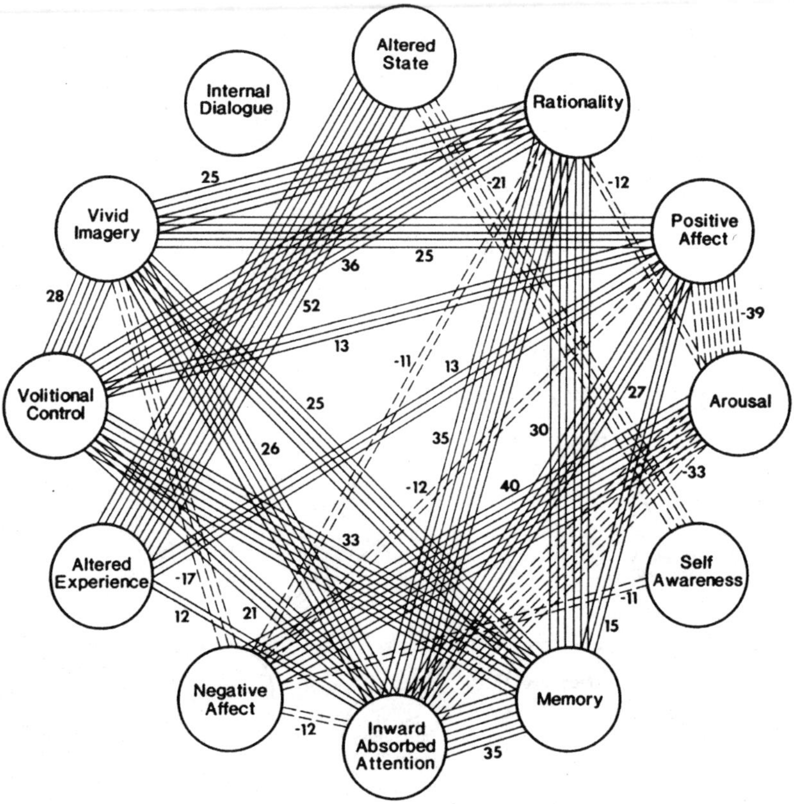

KEY

Each line represents approximately 5% of the variance in common.
(All variance percentages represent correlations significant at alpha less than approximately .05.)

$\underline{n} = 36$

Figure 5. *Very-Low Susceptible Individuals: Eyes Closed*

[From: Pekala, R. J., & Kumar, V. K. (1989). Phenomenological patterns of consciousness during hypnosis: Relevance to cognition and individual differences. Australian Journal of Clinical and Experimental Hypnosis, *17, 1–20.]*

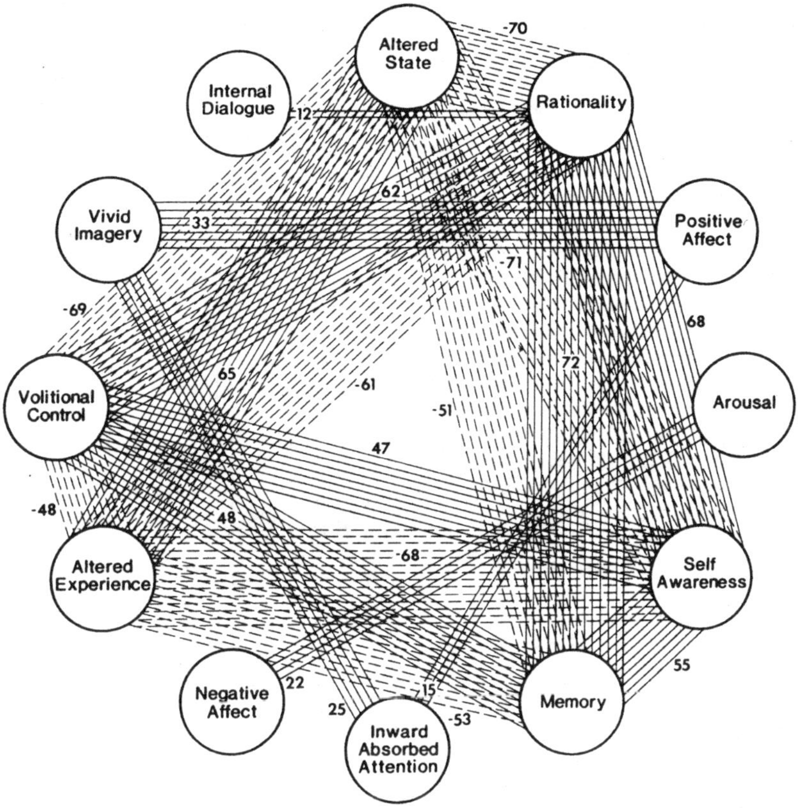

KEY

Each line represents approximately 5% of the variance in common.
(All variance percentages represent correlations significant at alpha less than approximately .05.)

n = 36

Figure 6. *Very-Low Susceptible Individuals: Hypnotic Induction*

[From: Pekala, R. J., & Kumar, V. K. (1989). Phenomenological patterns of consciousness during hypnosis: Relevance to cognition and individual differences. Australian Journal of Clinical and Experimental Hypnosis, *17, 1–20.]*

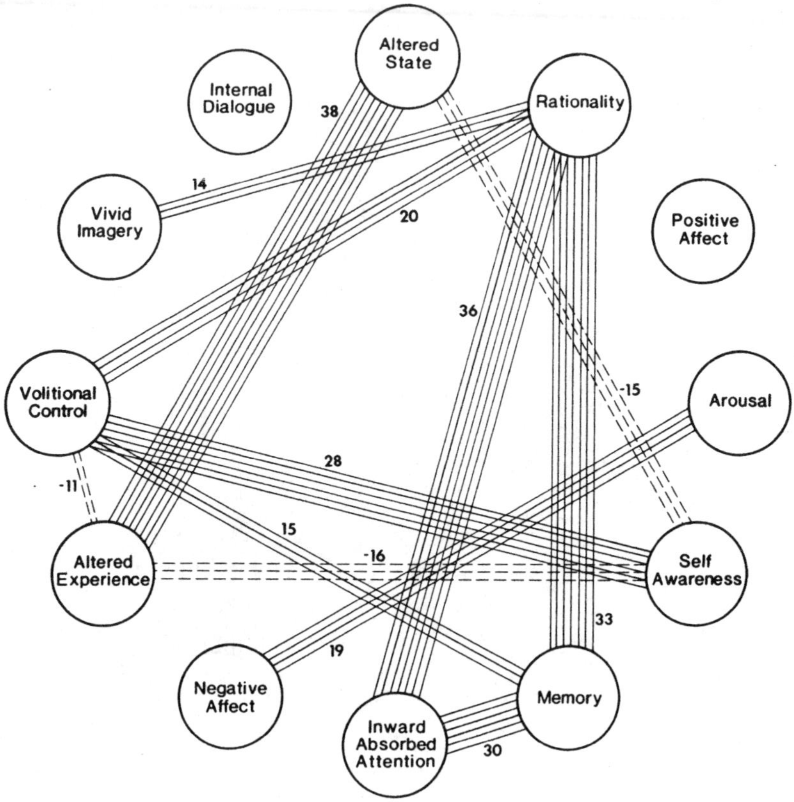

KEY

Each line represents approximately 5% of the variance in common.
(All variance percentages represent correlations significant at alpha less than approximately .05.)

n = 39

Figure 7. *Very-High Susceptible Individuals: Eyes Closed*

[From: Pekala, R. J., & Kumar, V. K. (1989). Phenomenological patterns of consciousness during hypnosis: Relevance to cognition and individual differences. Australian Journal of Clinical and Experimental Hypnosis, *17, 1–20.]*

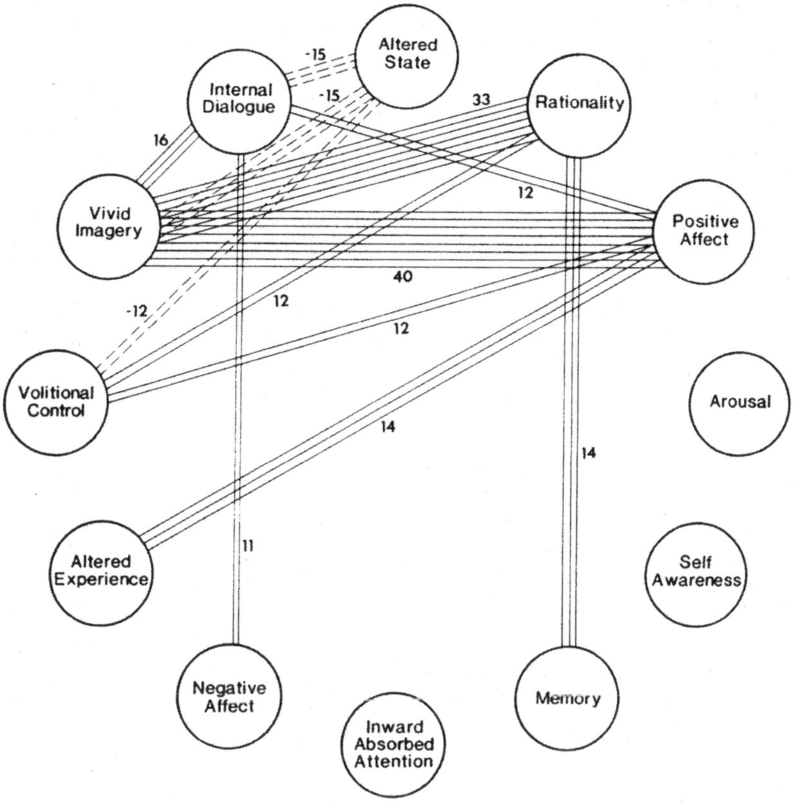

KEY

Each line represents approximately 5% of the variance in common.
(All variance percentages represent correlations significant at alpha less than approximately .05.)

$\underline{n} = 39$

Figure 8. *Very-High Susceptible Individuals: Hypnotic Induction*

[From: Pekala, R. J., & Kumar, V. K. (1989). Phenomenological patterns of consciousness during hypnosis: Relevance to cognition and individual differences. Australian Journal of Clinical and Experimental Hypnosis, *17, 1–20.]*

References

Arbib, M. A. 1980. “Perceptual structures and distributed motor control”. In V. B. Brooks (ed), *Handbook of Physiology (Vol III)*, 321–345. Bethesda, MD: The American Physiological Society.

Baars, B. J. 1988. *A Cognitive Theory of Consciousness*. Cambridge, Ma.: Cambridge University Press.

Baars, B. J. 1997. *In the Theater of Consciousness*. Oxford: Oxford University Press.

Barber, T. X. and Calverly, D. S. 1962. “‘Hypnotic behavior’ as a function of task—motivation”. *Journal of Psychology* 54: 363–389.

Barber, T. X., Spanos, N. P. and Chaves, J. F. 1974. *Hypnosis, Imagination, and Human Potentialities*. New York: Pergamon Press.

Bowers, K. S. 1992. “Imaginative and dissociative control in hypnotic responding”. *International Journal of Clinical and Experimental Hypnosis* 40: 253–275.

Chalmers, D. J. 1996. *The Conscious Mind: In Search of a Fundamental Theory*. Oxford: Oxford University Press.

Crawford, H. J. 1994. “Brain dynamics and hypnosis: Attentional and disattentional processes”. *International Journal of Clinical and Experimental Hypnosis* 42: 204–231.

De Benedittis, G. and Sironi, V. A. 1986. “Deep cerebral electrical activity in man during hypnosis”. *International Journal of Clinical and Experimental Hypnosis* 34: 63–70.

De Benedittis, G. and Sironi, V. A. 1988. “Arousal effects of electrical deep brain stimulation in hypnosis”. *International Journal of Clinical and Experimental Hypnosis* 36: 96–101.

Dixon, M. and Laurence, J. 1992. “Two hundred years of hypnosis research: Questions resolved? Questions answered!” In E. Fromm and M. Nash (eds). *Contemporary Hypnosis Research*, 34–66. New York: Guilford.

Geschwind, N. 1979. “Specializations of the human brain”. *Scientific American* 241: 180—201.

Hilgard, E. R. 1977. *Divided Consciousness: Multiple Controls in Human Thought and Action* (2nd ed.). New York: John Wiley & Sons.

Hilgard, E. R. and Tart, C. T. 1966. “Responsiveness to suggestions following waking and imagination instructions and following induction of hypnosis”. *Journal of Abnormal Psychology* 71: 196—208.

Izard, C. E. 1977. *Human Emotions*. New York: Plenum Press.

Jennrich, R. J. 1970. “An asymptotic Chi^2 test for the equality of two correlation matrices”. *Journal of the American Statistical Association* 65: 904—912.

Kirsch, I. and Lynn, S. J. 1995. “The altered state of hypnosis: Changes in theoretical landscape”. *American Psychologist* 50: 846–858.

Kluft R. P. 1984. “An introduction to multiple personality disorder”. *American Journal of Clinical Hypnosis* 14: 19–24.

Kumar, V. K. and Pekala, R. J. 1988. "Hypnotizability, absorption, and individual differences in phenomenological experience". *International Journal of Clinical and Experimental Hypnosis* 36: 80—88.

Kumar, V. K. and Pekala, R. J. 1989. "Variations in phenomenological experience as a function of hypnosis and hypnotic susceptibility". *British Journal of Experimental and Clinical Hypnosis* 6: 17—22.

Kumar, V. K., Pekala, R. J. and Cummings, J. 1996. "Trait factors, state effects, and hypnotizability". *International Journal of Clinical and Experimental Hypnosis* 44: 232–249.

Kumar, V. K., Pekala, R. J. and McCloskey, M. 1997. Phenomenological State Effects During Hypnosis: A Cross-Validation of Findings. Paper presented at the Conference "Toward a Science of Consciousness" sponsored by the University of Arizona, Danish Medical Association, and "Year of the Brain," Elsimore, Denmark.

Laukes, J. 1997. *Consciousness Research Abstracts: The Brain and Self Workshop: Toward a Science of Consciousness*. Tucson, AR: University of Arizona Extended University.

Maitz, E. A. and Pekala, R. J. 1990/91. "Phenomenological quantification of an out-of-the-body experience associated with a near-death event". *Omega*, 22: 199–214.

Mandler, G. 1985. *Consciousness: An Essay in Cognitive Psychology*. Hillsdale, N. J.: Lawrence Erlbaum Associates.

Marcel, A. J. 1983. "Conscious and unconscious perception: An approach to the relations between phenomenal experience and perceptual processes". *Cognitive Psychology* 15: 238—300.

Matlin, M. W. 1998. *Cognition* (4th ed.). New York: Harcourt Brace College Publishers.

McClelland, J. L. and Rumelhart, D. E. (eds). 1985. "Distributed memory and the representation of general and specific information". *Journal of Experimental Psychology: General* 114: 159—188.

McClelland, J. L. and Rumelhart, D. E. 1986. *Explorations in Parallel Distributed Processing: A Handbook of Models, Programs, and Exercises*. Cambridge, MA: MIT Press.

McClelland, J. L., Rumelhart, D. E. and the PDP Research Group. 1986. *Parallel Distributed Processing, Vol. 2: Psychological and Behavioral Models*. Cambridge, MA: MIT Press.

Mountcastle, V. B. 1978. "An organizing principle for cerebral function: The unit module and the distributed system". In G. M. Edelman and V. B. Mountcastle (eds), *The Mindful Brain*, 7–50. Cambridge, MA: The MIT Press.

Orne, M. T. 1977. "The construct of hypnosis: Implications of the definition for research and practice". *Annals of the New York Academy of Sciences* 296: 14—33.

Pekala, R. J. 1982. *The Phenomenology of Consciousness Inventory (PCI)*. Thorndale, Pa.: Psychophenomenological Concepts. (Now published by Mid-Atlantic; see Pekala, 1991b)

Pekala, R. J. 1985. "A psychophenomenological approach to mapping and diagraming states ot consciousness". *Journal of Religion and Psychical Research* 8: 199—214.

Pekala, R. J. 1991a. *Quantifying Consciousness: An Empirical Approach.* New York: Plenum Press.

Pekala, R. J. 1991b. *The Phenomenology of Consciousness Inventory (PCI).* West Chester, PA: Mid-Atlantic Educational Institute.

Pekala, R. J. and Bieber, S. L. 1989/90. "Operationalizing pattern approaches to consciousness: An analysis of the phenomenological patterns of consciousness among individuals of differing susceptibility". *Imagination, Cognition, and Personality* 9: 303–320.

Pekala, R. J. and Ersek, B. 1992/93. "Firewalking versus hypnosis: A preliminary study concerning consciousness, attention, and fire immunity". *Imagination, Cognition, and Personality* 12: 207–229.

Pekala, R. J. and Forbes, E. 1988. "Hypnoidal effects associated with several stress management techniques". *Australian Journal of Clinical and Experimental Hypnosis* 16: 121–132.

Pekala, R. J., Forbes, E. and Contrisciani, P. A. 1988/89. "Assessing the phenomenological effects of several stress management strategies". *Imagination, Cognition, and Personality* 8: 265–281.

Pekala, R. J. and Kumar, V. K. 1984. "Predicting hypnotic susceptibility by a self—report phenomenological state instrument". *American Journal of Clinical Hypnosis* 27: 114—121.

Pekala, R. J. and Kumar, V. K. 1985. "A short program for assessing the equality of two independent correlation matrices". *Educational and Psychological Measurement* 45: 175—177.

Pekala, R. J. and Kumar, V. K. 1986. "The differential organization of the structures of consciousness during hypnosis and a baseline condition". *Journal of Mind and Behavior* 7: 515—539.

Pekala, R. J. and Kumar, V. K. 1987. "Predicting hypnotic susceptibility via a self—report instrument: A replication". *American Journal of Clinical Hypnosis* 30: 57—65.

Pekala, R. J. and Kumar, V. K. 1989. "Phenomenological patterns of consciousness during hypnosis: Relevance to cognition and individual differences". *Australian Journal of Clinical and Experimental Hypnosis* 17: 1–20.

Pekala, R. J. and Levine, R. L. 1981. "Mapping consciousness: Development of an empirical—phenomenological approach." *Imagination, Cognition, and Personality* 1: 29—47.

Pekala, R. J. and Levine, R. L. 1982. "Quantifying states of consciousness via an empirical—phenomenological approach." *Imagination, Cognition, and Personality* 2: 51—71.

Pekala, R. J., Steinberg, J. and Kumar, V. K. 1986. "Measurement of phenomenological experience: Phenomenology of Consciousness Inventory." *Perceptual and Motor Skills* 63: 983—989.

Pekala, R. J. and Wenger, C. F. 1983. "Retrospective phenomenological assessment: Mapping consciousness in reference to specific stimulus conditions". *Journal of Mind and Behavior* 4: 247—274.

Rumelhart, D. E., McClelland, J. L. and the PDP Research Group. 1986. *Parallel Distributed Processing: Explorations in the Microstructure of Cognition: Volume 1: Foundations*. Cambridge, MA: The MIT Press.

Sheehan, P. W. and McConkey, K. M. 1996. *Hypnosis and Experience: The Exploration of Phenomena and Process*. Hillsdale, NJ: Erlbaum.

Sheehan, P. W. and Perry, C. W. 1976. *Methodologies of Hypnosis: A Critical Appraisal of Contemporary Paradigms of Hypnosis*. Hillsdale, N. J.: Lawrence Erlbaum.

Shor, R. E. and Orne, E. C. 1962. *The Harvard Group Scale of Hypnotic Susceptibility*. Palo Alto, Ca.: Consulting Psychologists Press.

Tart, C. T. 1975. *States of Consciousness*. New York: Dutton.

Tart, C. T. 1977. "Discrete states of consciousness". In P. R. Lee, R. E. Ornstein, D. Galin, A. Deikman, and C. T. Tart (eds), *Symposium on Consciousness*, 89–176. New York: Penguin.

Tryon, W. W. 1993a. "Neural networks: I. Theoretical unification through connectionism". *Clinical Psychology Review* 13: 341–352.

Tryon, W. W. 1993b. "Neural networks: II. Unified learning theory and behavioral psychotherapy". *Clinical Psychology Review* 13: 353–371.

Wilson, S. C. and Barber, T. X. 1983. "The fantasy—prone personality: Implications for understanding imagery, hypnosis, and parapsychological phenomena". In A. A. Sheikh (ed), *Imagery: Current Theory, Research, and Application*, 340–387. New York: John Wiley.

Zinberg, N. E. 1977. "The study of consciousness states: Problems and progress". In N. E. Zinberg (ed), *Alternate States of Consciousness*, 1–36. New York: Free Press.

Biological Rhythms and Individual Differences in Consciousness

Benjamin Wallace
Cleveland State University

Leslie E. Fisher
Cleveland State University

All of the chapters in this volume are concerned with individual differences in consciousness, or between-subject variability. This chapter is concerned not only with between-subject variability but also with within-subject variability. More specifically, we are concerned with consciousness as it is experienced at different times within a 24-hour cycle. In essence, this chapter is concerned with those individuals who are most alert during daylight hours versus those individuals who are most alert during hours of darkness. The former group is usually referred to as *larks* while the latter group is referred to as *owls*.

A Brief History of Biological Rhythms

Before examining the science of consciousness as a function of daylight versus nighttime periods, we present a brief overview of the study of biological rhythms. For example, Androsthenes, a scribe for Alexander the Great, noted that the tamarind tree (Tamarindus indicus) opened its leaves during the day and closed them at night. A close reading of this journal entry, however, does not suggest that these leaf movements were interpreted as being anything more than passive responses to a cyclic environment (Bretzl 1903).

Based on his observations that the petals of many flower species open and close at regular times, the famous Sixteenth Century taxonomist, Carolus Linnaeus (1751) created a garden with flowers that opened at various times so that he could tell the time of day by simply looking at his garden. Again, however, these petal movements were seen as nothing more than passive responses to environmental cues.

A more experimental approach to chronobiology (the study of biological rhythms) was employed by the Dutch astronomer, Jean Jacques d'Ortous deMairan. In 1724, deMairan observed that his heliotrope plant (Mimosa pudica) leaves opened during the day and folded at night. When deMairan moved his plant to a place where the sunlight would not reach it, he found that the plant still opened its leaves during the day and folded them for the entire night. This manipulation demonstrated that even in the absence of the normal environmental time cues, the observed biorhythms still occurred. DeMairan believed that these biorhythms were similar to the sleeping patterns of bedridden patients. These sleeping patterns appeared to follow a circadian schedule even when the patient was not cognizant of day and night.

Certainly deMairan's interest in the study of biorhythms had been peeked by his findings. However, he was also aware that his work as an astronomer would not permit him the time to continue his experiment. This did not prevent deMairan from making suggestions concerning possible follow-up studies. He proposed that other plants should be studied to determine whether they evidenced the same rhythm. He also proposed that the role of environmental temperature in the determination of these patterns should be explored. Finally, he suggested that future researchers should reverse light and dark periods and examine the response of the plant to such manipulations (Moore-Ede, Sulzman, & Fuller 1982).

DeMairan had thrown out an invitation to all interested investigators to pursue his research suggestions. Nevertheless, some thirty years passed before J. G. Zinn (1759) and Duhamel DuMonceau (1759), working independently, repeated the earlier experiments and demonstrated that the variations in environmental temperature did not cause the rhythm of the leaf movements.

Eliminating the light-dark cycle by keeping his heliotrope plant in a constant state of darkness, Augustin de Candolle (1832) observed that the daily leaf movements not only persisted but they also opened an hour or two earlier each day. In doing so, they eventually displayed a cycle of 22 to 23 hours in duration. The importance of de Candolle's demonstration was that it showed that circadian clocks would "free-run" on their own wired-in period once they were no longer synchronized to a 24-hour light-dark cycle.

Despite these findings, the scientific community was very slow to accept the idea that the circadian leaf movements were endogenously produced. For example, in his book *Physiologische Untersuchungen*, Wilhelm Pfeffer (1873) suggested that the persistence of rhythms reported in earlier studies was simply the result of poor controls such that ambient light was permitted to leak into the dark rooms employed by the investigators (Moore-Ede, Sulzman, & Fuller 1982).

Following the publication of his book, Pfeffer performed a series of experiments designed to provide further support for his position. His results, however, were far from what he predicted. As a result, he was finally forced to accept the notion of endogenous circadian leaf movements. Unfortunately, this change of mind together with the results of his research were published in an obscure German journal titled, *Abhandlungen der Mathematish-Physischen Klasse der Koeniglich Saechsischen Akadamie der Wissenschaften*. As a result, everyone remembers Pfeffer's initial position as set forth in his text, but not his later findings (Bunning & Chandrashekeran 1975).

It was also about this time that the first studies focusing on the discovery of endogenous circadian rhythms in mammals were undertaken. In 1842, Gierce, using himself as his only subject, recorded his oral temperature over a 24-hour period for several days and noted that there was a rhythmicity in this physiological variable that did not appear to be simply a reaction to activity changes (Wever 1979). William Ogle (1866) also observed that there were rhythmic changes in body temperature such that it increased in the early morning hours while his subjects were still asleep and then dropped in the evening while they were still awake. Based on these observations he concluded that these changes could not be attributed to either variations in light or activity. They were most likely related to cyclic variations in the activity of organic functions. Ogle had demonstrated that body temperature rhythm in humans was not directly dependent on either obvious environmental influences or on the sleep-wake cycle.

It remained, however, for Simpson and Galbraith (1906) to demonstrate that mammalian body temperature rhythmicity was endogenous. These researchers measured the rectal and axillary temperature of five monkeys every two hours, night and day, over a 60-day period. Not only did they find a body temperature rhythm but discovered that it persisted in both constant darkness and in constant light with a periodicity that was endogenous.

Toward the end of the 19th Century the research focus broadened to include not only the characteristics of the biorhythms but also on how these circadian rhythms might affect human performance. Thus, Ebbinghaus (1885) observed a consistent tendency for the learning of nonsense syllables to be most rapid in the morning. He explained this finding in terms of a decrease in "mental vigor" and "receptivity."

Bechterew (1893) challenged these findings as he maintained that his research clearly demonstrated that psyche processes were retarded in the morning, became even slower during the afternoon, and then accelerated to reach their peak during the evening hours. Kraepelin (1892), conducting extensive research on the "work curve", also observed this decreased performance level during the afternoon and attributed it to the midday meal. He also reported a "warm-up" period in the morning.

Despite all of these observations and research, however, the circadian rhythm was still viewed more as a scientific curiosity than anything of great biological importance. It required the careful observation of the Swiss physician, August Forel (1910) to change the attitude of the scientific community. One morning, while at breakfast on the terrace of his summer home in the Alps, Forel noticed that a few worker bees from a nearby hive had come to sample the breakfast fare that was left on the table. Several days later, Forel observed that the bees appeared at the table just a few minutes before breakfast was served. It seemed that the bees somehow knew that it was time for the food to be served. Now it became almost impossible for the family to enjoy their morning meal on the terrace. So they decided to move inside and away from their unwanted guests. Even though the family had moved indoors for breakfast and had taken the tasty morsels with them, the bees continued to arrive on the terrace exactly at breakfast time. At this time the bees would walk around the table looking for the food they obviously expected to find. Noting that the bees came only at that time of day, and at no other, Forel (1910) concluded that the bees actually possessed a memory for time.

Forel was successful in focusing the attention of the scientific community on circadian systems as time-measuring devices rather than as a biological curiosity. However, it remained for Karl von Frisch and his research assistant, Ingeborg Beling, to demonstrate that organisms are capable of measuring the passage of time. To accomplish this, Beling (1929) individually marked bees and then, at the same time each day, offered the bees sugar water at an artificial feeding station for several days. These training days were followed by a test day when no food was available at the feeding station. During such days, time of arrival of each bee was observed and recorded.

With few exceptions the bees arrived at the feeding cite within the training time. Also, to demonstrate that an internal circadian rhythm was responsible for this behavior, Beling had to slightly modify his research technique. During the training period, groups of bees were offered the sugar water at 19, 24, or 48-hour periods. In agreement with earlier findings, the bees that had been trained using the 24-hour period were observed arriving at the feeding cite within the training time on the test day. However, both the 19-hour nd the 48-hour interval bees were unable to recognize the pattern and entrain to it.

Kramer (1952) added to the growing body of supporting literature which suggested the existence of an endogenous circadian timekeeping system in animals by demonstrating that starlings, migratory birds, were able to use the sun as a compass even though the sun itself moves across the daytime sky. The birds compensate for the changing position of the sun during the day by using their circadian clocks to adjust their flight with respect to the sun.

But what if Forel's or Beling's bees had been responding to some environmental stimulus which the experiments had missed rather than an endogenous timekeeping system? Renner (1955) conducted a definitive experiment in an attempt to eliminate this possibility. In his laboratory in France, he trained 40 bees to collect sugar water during a two-hour period each evening in a closed room. Renner then transported his trained bees overnight to New York City where they were housed in a laboratory room similar to the one they had left in France. The next day, the bees arrived at the feeding table to obtain their sugar water during the same two-hour period, but on French time not New York City time.

Loci for Regulating Biological Rhythms

The Society for Biological Rhythms was organized in 1937, but it was not until the 1960s that research in the area reached both the qualitative and quantitative levels befitting a scientific discipline. Time and space do not afford us the opportunity to develop a comprehensive discussion of this period. However, a brief discussion of the development of an understanding of the anatomy of these endogenous timekeeping systems does seem to be in order.

Researchers interested in the anatomical location of the circadian system obtained their first clues as early as 1918 from a number of human neuropathological studies. These studies suggested that an area in the anterior hypothalamus was important in the regulation of sleep (see von Economo 1929). Nauta's (1946) lesioning studies in rodents further localized this sleep center in the suprachiasmatic-preoptic area of the hypothalamus. These findings provided Richter (1965, 1967) with the research background necessary to undertake the first direct search for a circadian pacemaker in mammals.

Richter lesioned a variety of areas within the central nervous system of a number of rats. Additionally, he removed many of the endocrine glands in an attempt to disrupt the circadian rhythmicity of wheel-running activity. Richter discovered that the only surgical location that produced such disruption was in the anterio-ventral hypothalamus.

Finally, researchers working independently in two laboratories (Moore & Eichler 1972; Stephan & Zucker 1972) discovered that the primary biological clock of the rat is located in the suprachiasmatic nucleus (SCN) of the hypothalamus. These investigators found that lesions in this area of the hypothalamus disrupted circadian rhythms in wheel running, in drinking, and in hormonal secretions.

The SCN, however, is only one part of the mechanism by which biological time is kept. Light is the primary *zeitgeber* (an environmental stimulus that usually helps reset the biological clock to a 24-hour day) for most mammals' activity cycles. It is obvious, therefore, that the SCN should receive input from the visual system. Anatomical studies have revealed a direct projection of fibers, the retinohypothalamic pathway, from the retina to the SCN (Hendrickson, Wagoner, & Cowan 1972). This pathway provides a mechanism by which the circadian sleep-waking rhythm may be entrained by the light-dark cycle of the natural environment.

Additional visual information is made available to the SCN by projections from the lateral geniculate nucleus which is the thalamic relay for the primary visual system. Consistent with a role as the primary pacemaker for the circadian sleep-waking and related bodily rhythms, the SCN project to a wide variety of brain areas including other regions of the hypothalamus, the brain stem, the pineal gland, and the pituitary gland (Moore-Ede, Sulzman, & Fuller 1982). Thus, the SCN is in an anatomical position to orchestrate, both directly and indirectly, the activity of the sleep and waking systems of the brain stem.

More on Larks and Owls

As was previously mentioned, a lark is an individual who is most alert during daylight hours. An owl is most alert during hours of darkness. And it so happens that the two authors of this chapter are prime examples of these categories. The senior author has always been a lark. That is, he has always (as far back as can be remembered) been most active and most alert during daylight hours. On the other hand, the junior author has always been an owl.

The first author of this chapter still remembers when the two of us were engaged in writing a textbook. I would write my chapters during daylight hours; he would write very late at night. Needless to say, this sometimes presented some difficulty, especially if I wanted to discuss a portion of a chapter while it was being produced. I soon learned not to phone him in the early morning hours. Similarly, he learned not to phone me in the late evening hours. A compromise was reached such that when we needed to work together, it was during the late morning or early afternoon hours.

Beyond textbook writing, the senior author has always preferred to teach university courses during daylight hours; the junior author prefers late afternoon and evening hours for instruction. The two of us are also distinguishable by when we eat meals, when we go to sleep, and when we engage in other daily and life activities and events.

A similar disparity exists between the first author and his spouse. The spouse is an owl and the author is a lark. While this sometimes presents some difficulties with respect to socializing and other activities, it is still possible to find periods of compromise. Also, the first author's son is a lark and his daughter is an owl.

As is evident from my few examples, the population seems to be separated into larks and owls. Given this situation, can we predict early in life who will become a lark and who will become an owl? Can we presently measure who is an owl and who is a lark? If owls and larks vary on levels of consciousness or alertness throughout the day and night, can such levels be measured? Do levels of alertness change throughout the day for both owls and larks? And, finally, what if any implications exist for being an owl versus a lark? These questions will be addressed in the remainder of this chapter.

Determining Larks and Owls

Aserinsky and Kleitman (1953) and Kleitman (1961, 1963) have provided evidence that there exists a fragment of a 24-hour basic rest-activity cycle (BRAC) that they believe is a waking counterpart of the sleep rapid eye movement-nonrapid eye movement (REM-NREM) cycle. These investigators believe that some behaviors and skills may be affected by peaks and valleys in activity during the wakeful hours of the day and night. During peak periods, performance appears to be optimal while during valley periods performance appears reduced. This apparent, spontaneous cycle of peaks and valleys in activity or arousal is referred to as an *ultradian rhythm* (Lavie 1989).

There have been a number of published studies that support the existence of ultradian rhythms. In essence, these studies report cycles of activity that appear to have an average duration of approximately 90 minutes (Kleitman 1983). These rhythms have been reported for many physiological responses including gastric motility (Hiatt & Kripke 1975), eating, drinking, and smoking (Friedman & Fisher 1967), urinary flow (Lavie & Kripke 1981), and the ability to fall asleep throughout the day (Lavie & Scherson 1981).

The aforementioned cycles have also been shown to exist for such diverse behavioral activities as vigilance (Okawa, Matousek, Nueth, & Peterson 1981; Orr, Hoffman, & Hegge 1974), response to apparent motion such as beta movement (Lavie & Sutter 1973), perception of the spiral aftereffect (Lavie, Levy, & Coolidge 1975; Lavie, Lord, & Frank 1974), and reports of fantasy (Kripke & Sonnenschein 1978).

While the typical ultradian cycle appears to be about 90 minutes in duration, other researchers have reported either shorter or longer cycles. As an example, Horne and Whitehead (1976) reported 30- to 60-minute cycles in human respiration. Longer cycles, lasting up to 6.5 hours, have been reported in alpha brain wave activity associated with variations in mood (Tsuki, Fukida, Okuno, & Kobayashi 1981).

Since there appears to be variability in the length and frequency of an ultradian cycle (Horne & Ostberg), some researchers have speculated that such rhythms cannot be represented by the activity of a single oscillator but rather by a number of oscillators (Lavie 1985). Thus, ultradian rhythms may vary in length as a function of activity being monitored and/or as a result of possible variability or individual differences in the type of task performed.

In addition to the existence of ultradian cycles for the previously-discussed activities, Rossi (1982) suggested that hypnotizability is rhythmic. That is, he proposed that there are best times and worst times to use hypnosis in a therapy session. And, in fact, Aldrich and Bernstein (1987) reported rhythmic influences on hypnotic susceptibility with a bimodal distribution of peak periods around noon and between 4 p.m. and 6 p.m. Also, Aldrich and Bernstein suggested that these peak periods appeared to be related to the rhythmic nature of body temperature. In essence, peak hypnotic susceptibility was related to peak times in body temperature.

In an attempt to replicate the findings reported by Aldrich and Bernstein, Wallace (1993) assessed hypnotic susceptibility using both the Harvard Group Scale of Hypnotic Susceptibility, Form A (Shor & Orne 1962) and the Stanford Hypnotic Susceptibility Scale, Form C (Weitzenhoffer & Hilgard 1962). Wallace also administered his Alertness Questionnaire (see Wallace 1993) which asks subjects to indicate "day" or "night" in response to 10 items or activities. Basically, as in Aldrich and Bernstein's study, peak periods in hypnotic susceptibility were found. However, the times of these peaks differed. This is probably due to Aldrich and Bernstein's use of a between-subjects design and to their failure to consider the variability inherent in the performance of day persons (larks) and night persons (owls).

When larks (those responding "day" to 8 of 10 items on the Alertness Questionnaire) are distinguished from owls (those responding "night" to 8 of 10 items on the questionnaire) in an analysis of rhythms, the former group showed peak hypnotic susceptibility at 10 a.m. and 2 p.m. The latter group showed peak susceptibility at 1 p.m. and between 6 p.m. and 9 p.m. Also, with respect to body temperature, a speculated correlate of susceptibility by Aldrich and Bernstein, two peaks of temperature increase (1 p.m. and 6 p.m.) appeared to be associated with peaks in hypnotic susceptibility. However, such was shown to be associated with periods of food intake rather than with increases in hypnotic susceptibility.

The findings reported by Wallace were replicated in a study on different subjects by Wallace and Kokoszka (1995). As in the Wallace study, larks exhibited greatest hypnotic susceptibility at 10 a.m. and at 2 p.m. Owls exhibited greatest susceptibility at 1 p.m. and between 6 p.m. and 9 p.m. In addition, Wallace and Kokoszka administered the Vividness of Visual Imagery Questionnaire (VVIQ; Marks 1973) to participants. Like hypnotic susceptibility, imaging ability varied as a function of time of administration. However, these peak periods occurred before and after hypnotic susceptibility peaks. This sinusoidal-like pattern of imaging ability was interpreted as indicating the possible existence of an ultradian cycle for imaging ability.

Given the aforementioned results on hypnotic susceptibility and imaging ability as a function of whether one is judged to be a lark or an owl, an important question emerges. What contributes to becoming a lark or an owl? Has one learned to be a lark or an owl? Or was one born to be most active during the day or the night?

If we are born larks or owls, perhaps there is a relationship between this variable and time-of-birth. This is possible because first exposure to light upon birth may start the biological clock for alertness (see Crosthwaite, Loros, & Dunlap 1995; Ding, Chen Weber, Faiman, Rea, & Gillette 1994). If this is the case, then individuals born during daylight hours and exposed to light should eventually become day persons or larks. Similarly, those born during hours of darkness should eventually become night persons or owls, given that this is when they were first exposed to light. Also, if a relationship exists between time-of-birth and being a lark or an owl, then these variables may also relate to other factors such as when one eats meals, engages in entertainment, does chores, etc. These possibilities were examined by Wallace and Fisher (1998).

Wallace and Fisher conducted two experiments, one with high school students and one with college students. In both experiments, time-of-birth was significantly related to being a lark or an owl. However, with college students, this relationship did not hold for those over the age of 21. The investigators believed that this latter finding was due to the fact that as individuals have to adapt to the world of the day person, even owls must become larks or they cannot acclimate to typical, daytime work hours.

Conclusions

In summary, biological rhythms play a major role in consciousness. These rhythms seem to begin their effects upon first exposure to light following birth. After that, consciousness and/or alertness is, to a great degree, dictated by hours of light (for larks) and hours of darkness (for owls). Thus, larks tend to eat their meals earlier than owls. They also choose to work during morning and early afternoon hours; owls prefer to work in the late afternoon and evening. In essence, time-of-birth with its accompanying exposure to first light sets the clock for alertness.

Unfortunately for owls, the world revolves around the hours of the lark. The typical work day begins around 8 a.m. and ends around 5 p.m. Needless to say, the owl does not care to begin the work day that early. Thus, the owl will tend to be more tired than the lark in the morning. The implications of such for work activity and productivity are not known. However, it is possible that school children who are owls will have a more difficult time with early morning classes than with those later in the day. This might also be true for the typical worker whose alertness and productivity might be adversely affected in the morning if he/she is an owl. Similarly, the lark will probably be less alert and productive during late afternoon and evening hours.

While the study of larks and owls is in its infancy, it is clear that each of us is one of these types. And the type will affect alertness throughout the day and evening. It is also clear that consciousness, in general, and its potential altered states, should more closely be examined in light of the findings that differences exist as a function of whether one is classified as being an owl or a lark. Alertness as a function of time-of- birth would appear to be a very important variable in the study of consciousness. Future research should take this into account.

References

Aldrich, K. J. and Bernstein, D. A. 1987. The effect of time of day on hypnotizability: A brief communication. *International Journal of Clinical and Experimental Hypnosis* 35: 141–145.

Aserinsky, E. and Kleitman, N. 1953. Regularly occurring periods of eye motility and concomitant phenomena during sleep. *Science* 118: 273–274.

Bechterew, W. 1893. Über den Einfluss der traumatischen Entzundung der Hirnrinde auf die Enegbarheit derselben. *Neurologische Centralblatt* 14: 2.

Beling, I. 1929. Uber das zeitgedachtnis der bienen. Cited in M. C. Moore-Ede, F. M. Sulzman, and C. A. Fuller 1982. *The clocks that time us*. Cambridge: Harvard University Press.

Bretzel, H. 1903. *Botanische Forschungen das Alexanderzuges*. Leipzig: B. G. Teubner.

Bunning, E. and Chandrashekeran, M. K. 1975. Pfeffer's views on rhythms. *Chronobiologia* 2: 160–167.

Crosthwaite, S. K., Loros, J. J. and Dunlap, J. C. 1995. Light-induced resetting of a circadian clock is mediated by a rapid increase in frequency transcript. *Cell* 81: 1003–1012.

De Candolle, A. P. 1832. *Physiologie Vegetale* 2. Paris: Bechet Jeune.

Ding, J. M., Chen, D., Weber, E. T., Fraiman, L. E., Rea, M. A. and Gillette, M. U. 1994. Resetting the biological clock: Mediation of nocturnal circadian shifts by glutamate and NO. *Science* 266: 1713–1717.

Duhamel DuMonceau, H. L. 1759. *La Physique des Arbres*. Paris: Guerin and Delatour.

Ebbinghaus, H. 1885. *Über das Gedächtnis*. Leipzig.

Forel, A. H. 1910. *Das Sinnesleben der Insekten*. Munich: Ernst Reinhardt Verlag.

Friedman, S. and Fisher, C. 1967. On the presence of a rhythmic, diurnal, oral instinctual drive cycle in man. *Journal of the American Psychoanalytic Association* 15: 317–351.

Hendrickson, A. E., Wagoner, N. and Cowan, W. M. 1972. Autoradiographic and electron microscope study of retino-hypothalamic connections. *Zeitschrift fur Zellforschung und Mikroskopische Anatomie* 125: 1–26.

Hiatt, J. F. and Kripke, D. F. 1975. Ultradian rhythms in waking gastric activity. *Psychosomatic Medicine* 37: 320–325.

Horne, J. A. and Ostberg, O. 1976. A self-assessment questionnaire to determine morningness-eveningness in human circadian rhythms. *International Journal of Chronobiology* 4: 97–110.

Horne, J. A. and Whitehead, M. 1976. Ultradian and other rhythms in human respiration. *Experientia* 32: 1165–1167.

Kleitman, N. 1961. The nature of dreaming. In G. E. W. Wolstenholme and M. O'Connor (eds), *The nature of sleep*, 349. London: Churchill Press.

Kleitman, N. 1963. *Sleep and wakefulness* (2nd Ed.). Chicago: University of Chicago Press.

Kleitman, N. 1983. Basic rest-activity cycle: 22 years later. *Sleep* 5: 311–317.

Kramer, G. 1952. Experiments on bird orientation. *Naturwissenschaften* 92: 265–285.

Kripke, D. F. and Sonnenschein, D. 1978. A biologic rhythm in waking fantasy. In K. S. Pope and J. L. Singer (eds), *The stream of consciousness* 321–334. New York: Plenum Press.

Lavie, P. 1980. The search for cycles in mental performance from Lombard to Kleitman. *Chronobiologia* 7: 247–255.

Lavie, P. 1985. Ultradian rhythms: Gates of sleep and wakefulness. *Experimental Brain Research* 12: 148–164.

Lavie, P. 1989. Ultradian rhythms in arousal: The problem of masking. *Chronobiology International* 6: 21–28.

Lavie, P. and Kripke, D.F. 1981. Ultradian circa 1 1/2 hour rhythms: A multioscillatory system. *Life Sciences* 29: 2445–2454.

Lavie, P., Levy, C.M. and Coolidge, F.L. 1975. Ultradian rhythms in the perception of the spiral after-effect. *Physiological Psychology* 3: 144–146.

Lavie, P., Lord, J.W. and Frank, R.A. 1974. Basic rest-activity cycles in the perception of the spiral after-effect: A sensitive detector of a basic biological rhythm. *Behavioral Biology* 11: 373–379.

Lavie, P. and Scherson, A. 1981. Ultrashort sleep-waking schedule. I. Evidence of ultradian rhythmicity in "sleepability." *Electroencephalography and Clinical Neurophysiology* 52: 163–174.

Lavie, P. and Sutter, D. 1973. Differential responding to the beta movement after waking from REM and NONREM sleep. *American Journal of Psychology* 88: 595–604.

Linnaeus, C. 1751. *Philosophia Botanica*. Stockholm: Godofried Kiesewetter.

Marks, D F. 1973. Visual imagery differences in the recall of pictures. *British Journal of Psychology* 64: 17–24.

Moore, R.Y. and Eichler, V.B. 1972. Loss of circadian adrenal corticoseterone rhythm following suprachiasmatic lesions in the rat. *Brain Research* 42: 201–206.

Moore-Ede, M.C., Sulzman, F.M. and Fuller, C.A. 1982. *The clocks that time us*. Cambridge, MA: Harvard University Press.

Nauta, W.J.H. 1946. Hypothalamic regulation of sleep in rats: An experimental study. *Journal of Neurophysiology* 9: 285–315.

Ogle, J.W. 1866. On the diurnal variations in the temperature of the human body in health. *St. George's Hospital Report* 1: 220–245.

Okawa, M., Matousek, M., Nueth, A.L. and Peterson, I. 1981. Changes of daytime vigilance in normal humans. *Electroencephalography and Clinical Neurophysiology* 52: S17.

Orr, W.C., Hoffman, H.J. and Hegge, F.W. 1974. Ultradian rhythms in extended performance. *Aerospace Medicine* 45: 995–1000.

Pfeffer, W. 1873. *Physiologische Untersuchungen*. Leipzig: Wilhelm Engelmann.

Renner, M. 1955. Ein transozeanversuch zum zeitsinn der honigbiene. *Naturwissenschaften* 94: 540–541.

Richter, C.P. 1965. *Biological clocks in medicine and psychiatry*. Springfield, IL: C.C. Thomas.

Richter, C.P. 1967. Sleep and activity: Their relation to the 24-hour clock. *Proceedings of the Association for Research of Nervous and Mental Disorders* 45: 8–27.

Rossi, E. L. 1982. Hypnosis and ultradian cycles: A new state(s) theory of hypnosis? *American Journal of Clinical Hypnosis* 25: 21–32.

Shor, R. E. and Orne, E. C. 1962. *The Harvard Group Scale of Hypnotic Susceptibility, Form A*. Palo Alto, CA: Consulting Psychologists Press.

Simpson, S. and Galbraith, J. J. 1906. Observations on the normal temperature of the monkey and its diurnal variation, and on the effect of changes in the daily routine on this variation. *Transactions of the Royal Society of Edinburgh* 45: 65–106.

Stephan, F. K. and Zucker, I. 1972. Circadian rhythms in drinking behavior and locomotor activity of rats are eliminated by hypothalamic lesion. *Proceedings of the National Academy of Science* 69: 1583–1586.

Tsuki, Y., Fukida, H., Okuno, H. and Kobayashi, T. 1981. Diurnal rhythm of alpha wave activity. *Electroencephalography and Clinical Neurophysiology* 52: S43.

von Economo, C. 1929. Schlaftheorie. As cited by W. B. Webb 1982, *Biological rhythms, sleep, and performance*. Chichester: John Wiley.

Wallace, B. 1993. Day persons, night persons, and variability in hypnotic susceptibility. *Journal of Personality and Social Psychology* 64: 827–833.

Wallace, B. and Fisher, L. E. 1998. Day persons, night persons, and time-of-birth. Unpublished manuscript.

Wallace, B. and Kokoszka, A. 1995. Fluctuations in hypnotic susceptibility and imaging ability over a 16-hour period. *International Journal of Clinical and Experimental Hypnosis* 43: 20–33.

Weitzenhoffer, A. M. and Hilgard, E. R. 1962. *Stanford Hypnotic Susceptibility Scale, Form C*. Palo Alto, CA: Consulting Psychologists Press.

Wever, R. A. 1979. *The circadian system of man: Results of experiments under temporal isolation*. New York: Springer-Verlag.

Zinn, J. G. 1759. On the sleep of plants. *Hamburgisches Magazin* 22: 40–50.

Personality Variations in Autobiographical Memories, Self-Representations, and Daydreaming

Jefferson A. Singer, Jerome L. Singer
Connecticut College, Yale University

Carolyn Zittel
University of Massachusetts, Boston

The nature of conscious experience described first from a scientific perspective in the exquisite analysis of William James's chapter, "The Stream of Thought" (James 1890/1983) has had to wait almost a century to become a central topic of empirical research inquiry in psychology. After years of exile to epiphenomenal status by both "objective" behaviorism and psychoanalysis with its concern for the "deeper" mysteries of the unconscious, consciousness can now be recognized in Bernard Baars' phrase as the "private arena in which we live our lives. Many of us maintain a coherent narrative, some framework in which growing up, adulthood, and old age make up parts of a meaningful tale" (Baars 1997, p. 40). This arena or stage, to use Baars' preferred analogy, is narrow in its immediate coverage, like a spotlighted region of a stage encircled by "audience, actors, stagehands, spotlight operators," an "invisible direction," all "guided by an unknown script" (Baars 1997, p. 41). While the psychoanalysts have kept alive the importance of the *unconscious* and cognitive psychologists have increasingly been acknowledging and studying unconscious processes (Westen 1998), the special human function of that narrow spotlighted region of consciousness has not received the attention it deserves (Baars 1997; J. L. Singer 1998). This volume represents an excellent effort to redress the scientific and clinical community's comparative neglect of this important topic. Our chapter will especially call attention to the importance for personality research of three major features of the ongoing stream of consciousness: autobiographical memories, representations of possible selves, and daydreams about a variety of possible futures.

We wish in this chapter to emphasize in particular the significance of human imagination and its critical role as a reflection of personal privacy, autonomy, a sense of control and coherence and as an explorer of the subjunctive realm of human experience, "the mights, woulds, or coulds." As Edward Casey, a philosophic pioneer of "imagining" put it:

1. The autonomy of imagining consists in its strict independence from other mental acts, from its surroundings, and from all pressing human concerns.
2. The autonomy of imagining consists in the freedom of mind of which imagination is uniquely capable. (Casey 1976, p. 191)

This freedom of mind is wide-ranging and multi-shaded. Consciousness can range from contemplation of immediate sensory stimuli to rotation of mental images to abstract argument and mathematical calculation. Its shades can vary in intensity from hypnotic states to semi-waking reveries to intense focus on a conversation or problem at hand. We propose to discuss those moments of consciousness in which the spotlight of attention turns to the self and one's efforts to construct a meaningful narrative out of past, present, and future events from one's life.

Contemporary personality theorists (Emmons 1990; McAdams 1988, 1993; J. A. Singer 1997; J. A. Singer & Salovey 1993; Thorne 1995b) have argued that individuals are engaged from adolescence onward in an effort to construct a meaningful life narrative that will provide a sense of unity and purpose to their lives. As McAdams (1988), drawing upon Erikson's seminal work on identity development, first proposed, individuals fashion a "life story" that consists of archetypal characters, ongoing ideological assumptions about the fairness and security of their surroundings, significant self-defining episodes, and expectations about the outcome of the story's chapters and of the story as a whole. Each of these components contributes to a complex and evolving answer in narrative form to the question of "Who am I?" and "Who might I become?"

Researchers working to describe the empirical units of this life story model of identity and personality have identified several important operationalized features. McAdams and his colleagues (McAdams, Hoffman, Mansfield, & Day 1996) have demonstrated how significant life episodes can be coded for overarching themes of relationship (Communion) and personal autonomy and accomplishment (Agency). Ed de St. Aubin and McAdams have collected T.A.T. stories, self-report inventories, and behavioral checklists to demonstrate how individuals' concern with their story's legacy (Generativity) is reflected in their daily thoughts and behaviors (McAdams, Diamond, de St. Aubin, & Mansfield 1997). Emmons (1986; Emmons & King 1988) has examined how individuals' most desired "personal strivings" play a role in their current sense of well-being and in the overall of coherence of their personality. McAdams (1993), drawing upon a healthy middle class sample and J. A. Singer (1997), extending this research to a chronically-addicted population, have demonstrated the role that archetypal characters play in the recurring themes of life narratives.

All of these findings persuasively argue that narrative structures like autobiographical episodes, motivational strivings, and archetypal characters play a pivotal role in self-definition and identity formation. Yet this research needs to be considered from the standpoint of its relationship to consciousness and conscious experience. Returning to the metaphor of consciousness as a theater, personality may be considered the play to be performed — the overarching text that ties all the activities of the players and the crew together into a coherent whole and gives them both a sense of meaning and value. When the spotlignt of consciousness comes on to a given actor, the self (as conceptualized through a narrative framework) is also lit. This self, which is more than sensory awareness of immediate stimuli, may contemplate its story by turning back in time, evaluating its current status, or contemplating its future prospects. What are the mechanisms and dynamics of consciousness that account for these activities that link the personality's narrative and that give it an imaginative autonomy from the rest of thought and from the world itself? In the next three sections of this chapter, we will in turn consider how consciousness interweaves with narrative with regard to memory, self-evaluation, and future imaginings.

Autobiographical Memories

In considering the relationships among memory, consciousness, and personality, we need to distinguish between two different modes of thought that play a role in how information is expressed to the observing self. Four thousand years ago in Egyptian hieroglyphics and Sumerian cuneiform, some of the earliest known written material, we can find dream interpretation guides that imply a distinction between the manifest imagery of sleep mentation and the predictive latent meanings and messages. The great biblical story of Joseph as both a dreamer and interpreter of his own and others' dreams, dating back almost three thousand years, continues this notion of two systems of thought, a realistic and perceptual mode and a meaning-oriented and analytic form. In his poetic, speculative, but also scholarly and insightful, *The Origin of Consciousness in the Breakdown of the*

Bicameral Mind, Julian Jaynes (1976) has argued that consciousness in the form of self-reflective cognition is an evolutionary brain development of only about three thousand years, perhaps still underway. Our brains may retain a proneness to unconscious hallucination that characterized the ancient Egyptians, Babylonians, Greeks, or Hebrews before about 1,500 B.C.E. This may account for recurrent tendencies for quasi-hallucinatory mystical, superstitious or irrational private experiences and beliefs.

In the *Zohar*, a segment of the medieval period Jewish mystical text, the *Kabala*, one finds a distinction between two kinds of cognition, *hokmah* or wisdom and *binah* or intelligence (Bakan 1978). The former emphasizes holistic thought or *synthesis*, the latter *analytic* thought. Amazingly, *hokmah* is specifically associated with the right brain hemisphere while *binah* reflects the left hemisphere (Bakan 1978). Further examples of the distinction between a form of analytic, logical or rational thought and a kind of synthetic, holistic, imaginative narrative thought have been reviewed elsewhere as they emerge in the writings of early Enlightenment thinkers like Hobbes and Leibniz as well as the poetry of the Romantic movement of the Nineteenth century (J. L. Singer 1981–82).

More systematic scientific approaches that reflect some sense of the two modes of thought can be found in the writings of the mid-Nineteenth century neurologist, J. Hughlings Jackson (1958), who distinguished *propositional* from *representational* thought. Sigmund Freud, influenced to some extent by Jackson, introduced a more "dynamic" notion of primary and secondary thought processes as early as 1900 in his *The Interpretation of Dreams* and in his much respected article, "Formulations concerning the two principles of mental functioning" (Freud 1900/1962, 1911/1962). In these writings, Freud contrasted a primitive and impulse-driven illogical form of thought (primary) with a more calculating, goal-directed, and logical mode (secondary). Jackson's and Freud's influence can be detected in the subsequent neurological perspectives of Henry Head (1926) with his concept of *vigilance* and Kurt Goldstein (1940) with his distinction between *abstract* and *concrete* mental processes.

More recently, Jerome Bruner (1986) has proposed two distinct modes of thought, the *paradigmatic* or logical-sequential and the narrative. The former mode reflects our capacity for "truth-seeking," the kind of precise, orderly analytic and abstract thinking that we use for science, for effective scholarly communication, or for careful organizational planning. Narrative thought, our ability to create stories out of event-sequences or to project "possible" against "actual" worlds, seeks versimilitude rather than reality. It relies on imagistic rather than quantitative expression and remains anchored in the sensorial world of sight, sound, smell, taste, and touch. In language similar to Bruner, Epstein (1990) has elaborated a Cognitive-Experiential Self Theory that distinguishes between a Rational system and an Experiential system, the former system based in abstract reasoning, language, and analytic responses and the latter system based in metaphor, imagery, integration, and connections to the sensory world.

Parallel to these more recent theoretical depictions of mode of thought, the memory researcher Endel Tulving has over the last twenty-five years refined a model of autobiographical memory that distinguishes between two major long-term memory systems, the semantic and the episodic (Tulving 1983, 1989, 1993).

> Semantic memory enables individuals to represent and mentally operate on situations, objects, and relations in the world that are not present to the senses...Episodic memory enables a person to remember personally experiences as such. That is, it makes it possible for a person to be consciously aware of an earlier experience in a certain situation at a certain time. Thus, the information of episodic memory could be said to concern the self's experiences in subjective time and space. In contrast, the information of semantic memory processes concerns subjects and their relations in the world at large. (Tulving 1993, p. 67)

Semantic memory consists of the abstracted knowledge of physical principles, definitions of words, names of people and places, and any other example of context-less information the brain accumulates. Episodic memory encompasses memories in which we can say that this event happened to me and is traceable (albeit with more or less difficulty) to a distinct time and location in my life.

Katherine Nelson (1993), a researcher who studies the development of memory in children, makes the additional demarcation of three types of episodic memory. She identifies the "generic event memory" (p. 7) in which a familiar event from an individual's life is depicted in schematic terms that suggest a blending of many instances of the same event into a single generic narrative. The "generic event memory" has been researched and coded as a "generic summary memory narrative" by J. A. Singer and Moffitt (1991–92). As Nelson correctly points out, though this memory refers to a specific type of event in an individual's life and may date this event to a broad time period, its summarized nature possesses properties of semantic as well as episodic processing.

The second type of episodic memory is simply that — an episodic memory from one's life that has no particular personal significance. If asked what I had for breakfast four days ago, I could retrieve a specific memory of that breakfast and perhaps even recall one or more events that transpired during that particular breakfast. Assuming that this was a breakfast of no great import in my life, I would eventually lose any recollection of that meal or the events that accompanied it.

The third type of episodic memory, autobiographical memory, consists of memories that matter and endure in long-term memory due to their affective intensity and personal significance.

> Autobiographical memory, as used here is specific, personal, long-lasting, and (usually) of significance to the self-system. Phenomenonally, it forms one's personal life history. (Nelson 1993, p. 8)

Nelson and her colleagues' research suggests that this type of autobiographical episodic memory develops through children's interaction with parents and other adults who, through dialogue and questions, encourage them to organize their memories into narrative structures that reflect upon the self and its social interactions. Parents in our culture ask children, "How was your day at school?," "What happened next?," "How did things end up?" As children gain language in our culture, they gain the capacity to engage in these social dialogues with adults and slowly begin to develop a narrative memory system that will eventually situate them as pivotal figures of the narrative. This socialization works in tandem with cognitive changes in the late pre-school child's thought process that facilitate representation, imagery, and perspective-taking (Nelson 1993, p. 12). The child's ability to draw connections between new and previous experiences illustrates a capacity to sustain an image of a prior event and to "reinstate" this remembered event for the sake of comparison, even when immediate sensory cues that might activate the memory are not salient. The child's increasing competence with language and the capacity to activate recollected and shared narratives in consciousness reflects the workings of a fledgling system of autobiographical memory (Nelson 1993, pp. 12–13).

As children enter the early elementary school years, they gradually embark on the steps of defining themselves with regard to siblings, relatives, children who live near-by, and increasingly their peer group from school. McGuire in a series of studies (McGuire & McGuire 1988) has emphasized that much of children's nascent sense of identity depends upon their sense of distinctiveness from the most common or normative characteristics. Children of color are more likely to list their ethnicity or race in response to the question, "Describe yourself" than white children; left-handed children will be much more likely to record their handedness as a characteristic than right-handed children; children with red hair will note their hair color more often than children who are brunette or blond (See also Dutton, J. A. Singer, & Devlin 1997).

Still another way that children can draw distinctions between others and themselves is to recount memories of incidents that clearly identify an attribute with a particular child (e.g., "Garth is so loud that one time he was telling Matt about this show he had watched and a teacher from the class next door had to come in and tell him to be quiet"). Although at first these accounts of incidents may indicate simple physical attributes or preferences of activities, games, foods, or playmates, children begin to draw upon autobiographical memories to provide justifications and attributions for attitudes and behaviors (e.g., "I don't see why I should go to day camp this summer, I remember last summer that Katie and Sandra were together all the time and I didn't know a single other kid in my group. I had to eat my lunch alone just about every day. Don't you remember that time we drove home at the end of day with me crying?"). Similarly by the fourth grade, children begin to associate the stories they read or the memories they are told by others with particular themes and underlying motives (McAdams 1993; McAdams & Losoff 1984).

With the advent of adolescence and its accompanying acceleration of formal thought processes of abstraction, hypothetical thinking, and metaphoric reasoning, individuals can increasingly recruit autobiographical memories to be a vital source of information about their burgeoning sense of identity. As McAdams (1993) details,

> Life becomes mythic in our teenage years. The formation and reformation of identity remains thereafter the central psychosocial task of the adult years. From adolescence onward we face this task of creating an integrative life story through which we are able to understand who we are and how we fit into the adult world. As our views of ourselves and our worlds change over time, we revise the story. (p. 91)

J. A. Singer (1995; Singer & Salovey 1993) introduced the concept of the "self-defining" memory to conceptualize how individuals might translate important aspects of their life story into conscious experience. As we have seen, narrative structures of the kind that McAdams postulates to be important for identity include information about self and others (cognitive categorizations), affective states (positive, negative, and mixtures), and motives (e.g., agency and communion). Self-defining memories are autobiographical memories that are particularly vivid, affectively-charged, repetitive, linked to other similar memories and related to important unresolved themes or enduring concerns in individuals' lives (Singer & Salovey 1993). Through a series of studies, we have been able to demonstrate that the affective intensity of self-defining memories may be predicted from their relevance to the attainment or non-attainment of individuals' most important *current* life goals (Moffitt & Singer 1994; Singer 1990). We have also demonstrated that self-defining memories are linked to one's personal values and sense of racial/ethnic identity (Sadler 1994) and that individuals will rate their self-defining memories as more important than other types of autobiographical memories (Moffitt & J. A. Singer 1991–92). Self-defining memories through repetitive and vivid reviews in conscious thought become easier and easier to see within the internal visual world. In situations that are relevant to the self-defining memory's content and themes, individuals are likely to "reinstate" these important episodes and use them as a frame of reference for interpretation of the cueing event. Indeed, clinical case studies suggest that transference, which has traditionally been considered an unconscious process, may also be activated by conscious recall of self-defining memories that are linked to current interactions with the therapist (J.A. Singer & J.L. Singer 1992; J.A. Singer & Salovey 1995). Although not discounting the importance of unconscious themes within the therapy, we have found that clients can identify the driving memories of their lives and then perceive the repetitive resurfacing of these memories' themes in the central conflicts of their interpersonal relationships.

In research closely linked to the study of self-defining memories, Thorne (1995a) has shown that individuals memories of problematic interpersonal episodes in their lives can be associated with their particular stage of identity concerns (e.g. identity formation vs. intimacy) and that these kinds of memories retain a thematic stability over time (Thorne, Cutting, & Skaw 1998). She has pointed out that the use of memory episodes allows for a more dynamic and complex portrayal of "juxtaposed" or competing motives that might exist simultaneously within the same individual. Content analysis of memories may allow for the scoring of these multiple motives in a way that forced-choice personality or trait inventories may not reveal.

Offering additional support for the thematic stability underlying narrative memories, Demorest and Alexander (1991) found that the scripted patterns of affect and event sequences contained within important memories (see Tomkins 1979) are actually repeated by participants when asked at a later date to generate imagined scenarios. In a separate line of research, this finding was also obtained when Buchanan, Kern, and Bell-Dumas (1991) asked participants to recall three actual early memories and then to create an additional three that might have happened to someone else. Raters blind to the identity of each memory coded them and found a significant degree of thematic similarity in the actual vs. created early memories.

These findings suggest that consciously-recalled autobiographical memories, far from being protective screens, as Freud and the psychoanalytic tradition characterized them (see J. A. Singer and Salovey 1993 for an historical discussion of this issue), can indeed be vital sources of information about individual difference in personality. The early memory researcher, A. R. Bruhn (1990, 1995) goes further to make the point that specific recalled memories may be more revealing in personality assessment than more extensive personal histories and autobiographies. Factual and generalized information about an individual, even if presented in narrative form, may not convey what holds particular significance and affective intensity in a given life. An account of a specific and extremely vivid recollection, such as an early memory or self-defining memory, provides a more dynamic insight into the on-going concerns and strivings of individuals. Bruhn (1995) writes,

> The "facts" in the traditional autobiography can be likened to the bones of our personality. These facts provide a framework and context for the individual's memories, which reveal the detailing of who the writer was as an individual. If I say to you that I know a man who was the eldest of four brothers born to his physician father, he may have subsequently evolved into a mass murderer or a Nobel prize winner. If I tell you that his first memory celebrated his feeling of triumph at learning to ride his bicycle for the first time after taking several spills, you may feel you know him better than with the biographical facts alone. (p. 206)

Finally, individual differences in the tendency to employ self-defining memories as a source of information for personality are likely to be a function of cultural variation in the content and structure of self and identity (Markus & Kitayama 1991) and in the acquisition of certain cognitive skills including narrative construction (Cole 1985; Fivush 1991). Aside from cultural differences, some individuals may have defensive personality styles that block access to negative memories that might be useful sources of information (Davis 1990), while depressed individuals may be less able to access specific positive memories that would repair their negative mood states (Josephson, J. A. Singer, & Salovey 1996; Moffitt, J. A. Singer, Carlson, Nelligan, & Vyse 1994).

What all of these variations make clear is that autobiographical memories are indeed a fertile ground for the study of personality and in particular its narrative aspects. Individuals draw upon a narrative mode of thought to review and re-experience salient and affectively significant episodes from the past. Through cultural influence and parental socialization they gradually organize these memories into the narrative conventions that reflect the themes and priorities of a given culture. Their particular personal variation on these themes evolves into a meaningful set of self-defining memories that informs individuals of what has mattered to them and what may continue to be important in the future. Having stated this in theory, we now have scientific methods to code the affect, theme, motive, and structure of these conscious memories. Through these techniques, we can create a more precise mapping of how the recollected past is linked to the forms of self-representation and evaluation that are active in the current consciousness of individuals. It is to these current thoughts and understandings of the self that we now turn.

Self-Representation, Consciousness, and Personality

Although it is true that most people don't actually "picture" themselves, since we "see" ourselves ordinarily only in mirrors, we usually actively participate in the plots of our fantasies and dreams (Domhoff 1996). It is also likely that we do not picture a unitary coherent self in every situation. As William James (1890/1950) long ago suggested, we are more prone to an awareness of multiple self-representations rather than a single, "core" self. The experimental research of Markus and Nurius (1986) on possible selves has shown how some of James's conceptions can be translated into operational forms suitable for experimental and clinical study within a social cognitive framework.

One important feature of our thoughts that emerges from the concept of multiple selves is the opportunity they afford for self-evaluation. Dating back to James's original writings about an actual vs. ideal self and Freud's conception of the superego as the internalized voice of our parents, researchers have postulated that individuals often measure their current selves against an imagined ideal drawn from parental and societal influences (Rogers 1959; J.L. Singer & McCraven 1961; J.L. Singer & Schonbar 1961). In the most extensive contemporary research program, Higgins (1987), working within a social cognitive framework, has operationalized some key elements of what might have been called Freud's superego into the so-called self-guides of actual self, ideal self, ought self, and their relationships. Thus, the actual self-ideal self discrepancy (measured by scoring respondents' descriptions of each self-representation) identifies the degree of gap between a currently perceived functioning self and an ideally-desired personal representation. This work has been especially effective in demonstrating how discrepancies between actual and ideal self-representations are linked to depression and saddened moods, while discrepancies between actual and ought selves are linked to agitation and social anxiety (Strauman 1992, 1994; Strauman & Higgins 1988). Even more remarkable are the dramatic findings linking these discrepancies between actual and ideal or ought selves to the functioning of the "psychologically silent" immune system of the individual (Strauman, Lemieux, & Coe 1993).

All of this research suggests that one aspect of the theater of consciousness is to compare various representations of the current self to past expectations and future aspirations as a way of evaluating the quality of one's life story. In a crude sense, consciousness allows individuals to answer the question, "How am I doing?," thereby providing feedback about the success, meaning, enjoyment, and interest generated by the narrative they have constructed thus far. Consciousness, by making possible active self-evaluation, introduces a critic into the theater, which means that revision and redirection of the narrative are rendered possible.

As individuals register various kinds of pleasing and displeasing self-evaluations, one should expect to see corresponding variations in self-esteem and mood. Recent research by Hart, Field, Garfinkle, and J. L. Singer (1997) and Garfinkle (1994) have demonstrated how self-discrepancies may be linked to the on-going thought of the individual over a week's time as measured through thought sampling procedures.

In the Hart et al. study, student participants created adjective lists that depicted their actual, ideal, ought, and undesired selves. The discrepancy between the actual and each of the latter three self-representations was calculated, leading to three separate quantitative scores. Participants also responded to a series of other inventories that examined their "Big Five" personality traits — Neuroticism, Extroversion, Agreeableness, Conscientiousness, and Openness (Costa & McCrae 1985, 1989). To examine mood and interpersonal functioning, we also included standardized questionnaires to evaluate anxiety, depression, self-esteem, and interpersonal problems.

In addition to these more typical sit-down pencil and paper surveys, we also required participants to carry paging devices for seven days. They were paged randomly during the day and had to record the following information at the point of interruption — what they were doing, what their current thoughts were, and what their immediate mood state was. Through the combination of self-report inventories and the thought sampling procedure, we sought to test out the ability of the self-discrepancy measures to predict ongoing thought over a week's time.

Building on Higgins' and Strauman's findings, we first examined whether discrepancies in actual and ideal self-representations would be correlated with depressive and anxious mood states. Discrepancy in actual vs. ideal selves was indeed linked to Neuroticism, anxiety, and depression. Self-esteem, as measured by the Rosenberg Scale, was also negatively linked to discrepancy; the closer one's actual and ideal selves were matched, the more positively one felt about oneself. But what meaning do these relationships hold for ongoing thoughts about the self? How do they fit into the story we weave of our lives as we move through the daily events of a typical week?

Our thought sampling data revealed a clear significant correlation between these daily reports (which also contained positive fantasies about the self) and the size of the discrepancy between the actual and ideal self-ratings as recorded weeks earlier. With regard to mood as sampled over the week's time, self-discrepancy correlated with positive emotion, calmness, and in a negative direction with melancholic mood. The relationship of mood to self-discrepancy emerged even when we controlled for the relationship of mood to the Big Five trait characteristics. In other words, self-representations are uniquely related to daily mood above and beyond the underlying and enduring variations in personality and temperament.

The Hart et al. study suggests that individuals' ratings of self-discrepancies are indeed correlated with self-esteem, personality traits, and ongoing mood. Yet one could argue that these self-discrepancies are operating below the surface of consciousness. Though they influence the personality, they might play only a marginal role in the conscious narrative the individual constructs and by which identity is defined. They may be important information for the psychodynamic therapist, but not for individuals as they consciously register the events of their lives and assign meaning to these experiences. To address this question, we shall review Garfinkle's (1994) study in which he observed how conscious registration of a self-discrepancy in an experimental session does indeed have an enduring effect on ongoing thought over a subsequent week's sampling.

We proposed that individuals with more pronounced discrepancies between their actual and ideal or ought selves would be more sensitive in their daily lives to negative mood states of dejection and agitation respectively. We further surmised that if we could experimentally activate these discrepancies and make them salient in consciousness, subsequent mood states would be clearly affected. To achieve this end, we matched individuals with differing degrees of actual/ideal and actual/ought discrepancies with yoked controls and then exposed them to an experimental intervention. Employing the conflict imagery techniques of Klos and J. L. Singer (1981), we presented the high discrepancy groups with scenarios of a "coercive confrontation" that was shaped around a trait they had indicated as highly important to them and one that they felt they had not fully attained in their lives. In the actual/ought discrepancy groups, the confrontation consisted of the participant imagining not living up to a parent's desire that they possess this trait (the experimenter would pose the following question asked by a parent, "Why aren't you more ______?"). In the actual/ideal discrepancy groups, the participant would be asked to imagine an "inner voice" asking, "Why is it so important for you to be _______?" where the trait would again be one the participant had listed as an important ideal that they had not yet attained. In contrast, the yoked controls would receive the same confrontations in both the ought and ideal conditions, but with trait words that did not hold any particular discrepant significance for them. Once these priming conditions were established, participants were encouraged to simulate their responses to both their parental and inner inquisitors and actively engage in role-played confrontations. On the very next day after the experimental sessions, participants commenced their seven days of carrying paging devices and filling out rating scales of their mood states. Some participants also kept dream logs to examine the possibility that the discrepancy concerns might slip into dream imagery as well as daytime rumination.

The results of the daily thought sampling showed cleared differences between the ideal and ought discrepancy groups compared with controls. Participants who had had their discrepancies in actual vs. ought or ideal selves primed in the experimental sessions displayed decreased positive affect reports and increased negative lethargic (depressed) moods, as well as decreases in calm (less agitated) mood states. We found a particularly strong effect for individuals with the largest ideal vs. actual discrepancies. These individuals showed a sustained increase in negative and agitated mood over the week's sampling. The ought vs. actual discrepancy group was close behind, also significantly different in negative mood from the control groups. Though the ideal and ought groups differed from controls, they did not differ in distinctive ways from each other, as Higgins' model would have predicted. It would appear that any kind of discrepancy evoked a global negative mood in this sample, but we could not show a specificity of negative mood such that anxiety would be more linked to ought-actual discrepancies and sadness to ideal-actual discrepancies.

The overall findings indicate that self-representations do play a role in ongoing conscious rumination and can indeed have an active influence over mood state. They contribute to the fundamental way in which we experience a sense of "personhood" and unique identity as we respond to external and internal stimuli throughout our waking hours. When a person responds to a particular stimulus in a given situation, part of who is responding is an individual with a sense of "who I am and how I measure up to what I would like to be and what I ought to be." Subsequent responses from this individual may be affectively-tinged by a recognition of the discrepancies between ideal/ought and actual self-standards. In the theater of consciousness, the critic does not always sit in anonymity in the back of theater, but can in fact take a more conspicuous and active role in how the actor/self proceeds.

In the next section of this chapter, we turn to research evidence for how daydreams and fantasies reflect a concern with the real and imagined future in the individual's personality. This work demonstrates that personality variations in the content and structure of consciousness find their way not only into our constructions of the past and our affective responses to the present, but into our visions of the possible as well.

Questionnaire Studies of Daydreaming and Related Imaginal Processes

To begin, we need to review how waking fantasies and daydreams can be measured quantitatively. Although it is true that self-reported tendencies for daydreaming are correlated with the Human Movement or M response on the Rorschach ink blots (J.L. Singer 1966; J.L. Singer 1975; J.L. Singer & Brown 1977) too many layers of inference remained necessary to generalize from such responses to the naturally-occurring waking fantasies of the daily stream of thought. It seemed reasonable therefore to attempt to study daydreaming more directly by simply interviewing people about their daydreams and eventually accumulating much larger samples and more normative data through questionnaires. This has led to considerable evidence that documents the apparent universality of daydreaming and the acknowledgment by large numbers of people from different walks of life that such activity is a general phenomenon in their daily lives.

We developed fairly precise measures of individual variations in styles of daydreaming that characterize the genders, cultural groups or age groups (J. L. Singer 1974, 1975; Huba, J. L. Singer, Aneshensel & Antrobus 1982; Segal, Huba & J. L. Singer 1980). A factor analytically derived instrument called the Imaginal Processes Inventory (IPI) in longer and shorter questionnaire forms has been developed and has been widely used. Review of the extensive range of correlates of self-reported fantasies and fantasy styles emerging from this direct form of questioning about individual's awareness of their daydreams are reported elsewhere (J. L. Singer & Bonanno 1990; J. L. Singer & Kolligian 1987). For our purposes here it seems enough to state that daydreaming is a normal, widespread, human phenomenon that many people are aware of quite consciously and can describe reliably in response to the direct inquiry that is possible through questionnaires. It can also be shown that these self-reports have reasonable degrees of construct validity. Persons who score as showing more daydreaming tendencies are also more likely to show such patterns when they are examined systematically under laboratory conditions (Antrobus, Coleman & J. L. Singer 1967). Similarly, people are also willing and able to attest to a considerable range of sexual fantasies of a kind ordinarily thought to be mentioned only in clinical sessions (Hariton & J. L. Singer 1974; Campagna 1985–1986; Smith & Over 1991).

Of special importance for this chapter is the linkage between daydreaming patterns and more general personality dimensions. Early work in this area had shown that one can delineate three major forms of self-reported daydreaming from the Imaginal Processes Inventory: Positive-Constructive Daydreaming, Guilty-Dysphoric Daydreaming and Poor Attentional Control (Segal, Huba, & J.L. Singer 1980; Huba, J.L. Singer, Aneshensel & Antrobus 1982). The first factor seems to characterize a wide range of normal, future-oriented positive and wishful fantasy. The second dimension, somewhat more characteristic of males' fantasy than females' involves guilty or fear of failure future scenarios or ruminations while the third dimension is characterized by relative fragmented, fearful fantasies associated with distractibility and boredom. Earlier studies exploring personality correlates of these dimensions have been reviewed elsewhere (J.L. Singer & Bonanno 1990; J.L. Singer & Kolligian 1987). Recent work has reflected the relative consistency of the Positive Daydreaming subscales across the adult age span for more than two thousand participants between 17 and 92 years of age (Giambra, Camp & Grodsky 1992; see also Chapter by Giambra in this volume). Similar results for a younger sample have also emerged (Gold, Jarvinen, & Teague 1982). A study which identified "worriers", individuals prone to distressing rumination at least 50% or more of conscious awareness in a given day, scored significantly higher than low "worriers" on the Guilty-Dysphoric and Poor Attentional Control factors of the IPI, but no differences emerged on the more normative Positive Daydreaming factor (Pruzinsky & Borkovec 1990).

Having established that daydreaming and fantasy patterns exist for different individuals, how might we connect these patterns to variations in personality? Though the ultimate goal of our research program is to determine how these patterns become integrated into the narrative structure of personality, we have thus far only taken the first step of linking these daydreaming characteristics to trait measures of personality.

The recent important research on personality traits has converged in the identification of the so-called Big 5 dimensions, Extraversion, Neuroticism, Emotional Stability, Agreeableness, Conscientiousness and Openness to Experience (Costa & McCrae 1992; McCrae & Costa 1997). There is at this time strong psychometric and cross-cultural research support for the stability and convergent validity of these major traits. Zhiyan and J. L. Singer (1997) examined the relationships between the short from of the Imaginal Processes Inventory and the Big 5 traits as well as two dimensions of emotionality. As predicted, the Positive Daydreaming scale was related significantly to the Openness factor of the Neo-FFM, while the other two daydream patterns related to Neuroticism, with Poor Attentional control also somewhat linked negatively to Conscientiousness. It should be stressed that the very few actually overlapping items in the tests were omitted without seriously affecting results. In effect, then, Positive future-oriented daydreams, self-imaginings such as winning a lottery, engaging in a variety of a happy experiences socially or at work or school, finding adventure, planning for achievement were part of a general human trait of Openness. Since Openness is associated with imagination, creativity, and originality, these findings suggest that individuals high in this trait may also be more flexible in allowing their narrative identities to shift and find new directions over time. It is possible that their tendency toward positive fantasy and productive planning reflects a continual preparedness for new experience and challenge in their lives. As McCrae and Costa (1997, p. 826) write, Openness involves "breadth, depth, and permeability of consciousness, and the recurrent need to enlarge and examine experience" (McCrae & Costa 1997, p. 826).

One may also mention some other measures that seem to be linked to Openness. Hartmann (1991) developed a Boundaries questionnaire which includes awareness of and fluidity of dreams, aesthetic experiences, acceptance of ambiguities in art and gender roles and inclinations for thoughts and feelings to blend. McCrae (1994) demonstrated the association of this measure with Openness. There is a clinically-developed notion of Alexithymia, a personality trait characterized by a lack of psychological-mindedness, a restricted discussion of personal or subjective experiences, and the absence of a vocabulary for defining emotions. A measure of this trait, the Toronto Alexithymia Scale (Bagby, Taylor & Atkinson 1988) was correlated for a sample of 117 male and female undergraduates with the Short IPI. As one might expect the Positive Daydreaming factor correlated significantly and negatively with this trait while significant positive correlations emerged between Alexithymia and Guilty-Dysphoric Daydreaming and Poor Attentional Control. Alexithymia was also negatively correlated with an Ego Strength scale and a tendency to inhibit expression of anger.

Still another measure of daydreaming which has emerged is the Fantasy-Prone scale studies by Lynn and Rhue (1986). Although originally this instrument's rationale led it to be compared to measures of hypnotizability, multiple personality and to possible psychopathology, it soon became clear in several studies that many high fantasizers were likely to be within the normal range. These high fantasizers were also more creative and imaginative than low fantasizers, but no more likely to have genuine dissociative experiences.

In summary, a growing body of evidence suggests that positive awareness and acceptance of daydreams that are future-oriented and vivid is a feature of personality associated with a general openness to novelty, tolerance for ambiguity, and exploratory tendencies. At the same time we need more extensive research systematically linking a variety of measures such as Boundary tendencies, Alexithymia and Fantasy-Proneness to the Imaginal Processes Inventory and to the Big-5 Openness scales within a common factor analytic structure.

Once such firm relationships between stable traits of the personality and daydreaming styles are established, we will be in a strong scientific position to extend the relationship of daydreaming styles to the narrative features of personality. For example, we could explore the possibility that individuals who are characterized by openness and optimism might tend to focus on "commitment stories" in their life histories (experiences in which a negative affective experience is invariably turned around into a positive growth-oriented experience, see McAdams, in press; McAdams et al. 1997). Empirical studies might also show that these commitment stories are not just the way individuals understand their past history, but how they think and fantasize about the future. In the previous sections in this chapter, personality researchers interested in narrative have demonstrated how conscious memories and current affective responses can be linked to the on-going narrative of the individual. Applying this work to the anticipatory dimension of personality would allow researchers to show that the conscious daydreams and fantasies of individuals arc also reflections of the salient themes of their life stories.

Moffitt and Singer (1994) have been able to show the connection of memory narratives to a measure of future goals ("personal strivings," Emmons 1986), but it is unlikely that individuals' on-going thought is focused on abstract conceptualizations of the future (such as, "I strive to be successful" or "I strive to be attractive"). It is more likely that these strivings are depicted in thought through visualized images of the individual sitting in an large office taking an important phone call or being noticed by an equally attractive partner in a social situation. Future research on daydreaming content and style will seek to confirm these linkages between the imagistic products of desired goals and the overall narrative themes of the individual's personality.

Conclusion

To conclude this summary of personality and consciousness research, we return to Baars' image of the "theater of consciousness" that began this chapter. Baars depicted consciousness as the lighted stage that gives us brief insight into the "unknown script" that is written into each individual's life. We have suggested that this script, far from being unknown, has a narrative content and structure that defines an on-going sense of identity for a given person. Individuals craft this narrative identity over a lifetime and the products of consciousness — memories, current affective responses, and future-oriented daydreams and fantasies — are reflections of the important themes and conflicts that comprise the core concerns of this narrative. Personality researchers have already had success in demonstrating that conscious thoughts are related to abstract features of personality, such as judgments of self-discrepancy, personal strivings, and self-evaluations on personality inventories. This chapter reviews the beginning efforts of researchers to show that consciousness reflects not just Bruner's (1986) "paradigmatic" aspects of personality, but the "narrative" ones as well. What we may discover is that memories and daydreams are not just the imagistic renderings of semantic categories of self-definition, but rather they are continuous with a larger story of the self. This story is known to and embellished by the individual, and the moment to moment shifts in waking thought are often simply commentaries upon or interpolations of this overarching narrative. In turn, this narrative can guide conscious thought, not unlike how stage directions may influence the lighting and positioning of the set. Together, the expression of the self through consciousness and its underlying narrative that is less frequently illuminated account for major variations in personality. Our story can be told by no one else, and consciousness gives that story its unique voice.

References

Antrobus, J. S., Coleman, R. and Singer, J. L. 1967. Signal detection performance by subjects differing in predisposition to daydreaming. *Journal of Consulting Psychology* 31: 487–491.

Baars, B. J. 1997. *In the theater of consciousness: The workspace of the mind.* New York: Basic Books.

Bagby, R. M., Taylor, G. T. and Atkinson, L. 1988. Alexithymia: A comparative study of three self-report measures. *Journal of Psychosomatic Research* 32: 107–116.

Bakan, P. 1978. Two streams of consciousness: A typological approach. In K. S. Pope & J. L. Singer (eds.). *The stream of consciousness.* 159–184 New York: Plenum.

Bruhn, A.R. 1990. *Earliest childhood memories: Theory and application to clinical practice, Vol. 1*. New York: Praeger.

Bruhn, A.R. 1995. Ideographic aspects of injury memories: Applying contextual theory to the comprehensive early memory scoring system — revised. *Journal of Personality Assessment* 65: 195–236.

Bruner, J.S. 1986. *Actual minds, possible worlds*. Cambridge, MA: Harvard University Press.

Buchanan, L.P., Kern, R. and Bell-Dumas, J. 1991. Comparison and content in created versus actual early recollections. *Individual Psychology* 47: 348–355.

Campagna, A.F. 1985–1986. Fantasy and sexual arousal in college men: Normative and functional aspects. *Imagination, Cognition, and Personality* 5: 3–20.

Casey, E.S. 1976. *Imagining: A phenomenological study*. Bloomington, IN: Indiana University Press.

Cole, M. 1985. The zone of proximal development: Where culture and cognition create each other. In J.V. Wertsch (ed.), *Culture, communication and cognition: Vygotskian perspectives*, 146–161. New York: Cambridge University Press.

Costa, P.T. and McCrae, R.R. 1985. *The NEO personality inventory manual*. Odessa, FL: Psychological Assessment Resources.

Costa, P.T. and McCrae, R.R. 1989. *NEO PI/FFI: Manual supplement*. Odessa, FL: Psychological Assessment Resources.

Costa, P.T. and McCrae, R.R. 1992. *Revised NDO Personality Inventory and NEO Five-Factor Inventory, Professional Manual* Psychological Assessment Resources, Inc., PO Box 998, Odessa, FL 33556.

Davis, P.J. 1990. Repression and the inaccessibility of emotional memories. In J.L. Singer (ed.), *Repression and dissociation*, 387–403. Chicago: University of Chicago Press.

Demorest, A.P. and Alexander, I.E. 1991. Affective scripts as organizers of personal experience. *Journal of Personality* 60: 645–663.

Domhoff, G. 1996. *Finding meaning in dreams*. New York: Plenum.

Dutton, S.E., Singer, J.A., and Devlin, A.S. 1998. Racial identity of children in integrated, predominately White, and Black schools. *Journal of Social Psychology*, 138: 41–53.

Emmons, R.A. and King, L.A. 1988. Conflict among personal strivings: Immediate and long-term implications for psychological and physical well-being. *Journal of Personality and Social Psychology* 54: 1040–1048.

Emmons, R.A. and King, L.A. 1989. Personal striving differentiation and affective reactivity. *Journal of Personality and Social Psychology* 56: 478–484.

Emmons, R.A. 1986. Personal strivings: An approach to personality and subjective well-being. *Journal of Personality and Social Psychology* 51: 1058–1068.

Emmons, R.A. 1990. Motives and life goals. In S. Briggs, R. Hogan, and W. Jones (eds), *Handbook of personality psychology*. Orlando, FL. Academic Press.

Epstein, S. 1990. Cognitive-experiential self-theory. In L. A. Pervin (Ed). *Handbook of personality: Theory and research*, 165–192. New York: Guilford Press.

Fivush, R. 1991. The social construction of personal narratives. *Merrill-Palmer Quarterly* 37: 59–82.

Freud, A. 1937–1959. *The ego and the mechanisms of defense*. London: Hogarth.

Freud, S. 1900/1962. The interpretation of dreams. In the *Complete Psychological Works of Sigmund Freud*, vol. 4 and 5. London Hogarth Press.

Freud, S. 1911/1962. Formulations regarding the two principles of mental functioning. In *The Complete Psychological Works of Sigmund Freud*, vol. 12. London: Hogarth Press.

Garfinkle, J. R. 1994. *Discrepant representations of self: Relations to personality, emotion and continuous mood*. Unpublished doctoral dissertation, Yale University.

Giambra, L. M., Camp, C. J. and Grodsky, A. 1992. Curiosity and stimulus seeking across the adult life span: Cross-sectional and 6- to 8-year longitudinal findings. *Psychology and Aging* 7: 150–157.

Gold, S. R., Jarvinen, P. J. and Teague, R. G. 1982. Imagery elaboration and clarity in modifying college students' depression. *Journal of Clinical Psychology* 38: 312–314.

Goldstein, K. 1940. *Human nature in the light of psychopathology*. Cambridge, MA: Harvard University Press.

Hariton, E. B. and Singer, J. L. 1974. Women's fantasies during sexual intercourse: Normative and theoretical implications. *Journal of Consulting and Clinical Psychology* 42: 313–322.

Hart, D., Field, N., Garfinkle, J. and Singer, J. L. 1997. Representations of self and others: A semantic space model. *Journal of Personality* 65: 77–105.

Hartmann, E. 1991. *Boundaries of the Mind*. New York: Basic Books.

Head, H. 1926. *Aphasia and kindred disorders of speech*. London: Macmillan.

Higgins, E. T. 1987. Self-discrepancy: A theory relating self and affect. *Psychological Review* 94: 319–340.

Huba, G. J., Singer, J. L., Aneshensel, C. S. and Antrobus, J. S. 1982. *The short imaginal processes inventory*. Port Hurson, MI: Research Psychologists' Press.

Jackson, J. H. 1878. On affections of speech from diseases of the brain. Brain 1:304.

James, W., 1890/1950. *The principles of psychology*. New York: Holt. (Original work published 1890.

Jaynes, J. 1976. *The origin of consciousness* in the breakdown of the bicameral mind. Boston: Houghton Mifflin.

Josephson, B. R., Singer, J. A. and Salovey, P. 1996. Mood regulation and memory: Repairing sad moods with happy memories. *Cognition and Emotion* 10: 437–444.

Klos, D. S. and Singer, J. L. 1981. Determinants of the adolescent's ongoing thought following simulated parental confrontations. *Journal of Personality and Social Psychology* 41: 975–987.

Lynn, S. and Rhue, J. W. 1986. The fantasy-prone person. Hypnosis, imagination and creativity. *Journal of Personality and Social Psychology* 51: 404–408.

Markus, H. and Nurius, P. 1986. Possible selves. *American Psychologist* 41: 954–969.

Markus, H. R. and Kitayama, S. 1991. Culture and the self: Implications for cognition, emotion, and motivation. *Psychological Review* 98: 224–253.

McAdams, D. P. 1987. A life-story model of identity. In R. Hogan and W. H. Jones (eds), *Perspectives in personality* 2: 15–50. Greenwich, CT: JAI Press.

McAdams, D. P. 1988. *Power, intimacy, and the life story: Personological inquiries into identity*. New York: The Guilford Press.

McAdams, D. P. 1993. *The stories we live by: Personal myths and the making of the self.* New York: Morrow.

McAdams, D. P. (in press). Personal narratives and the life story. In L. Pervin, and O. John (eds), *Handbook of personality (2/e)*. New York: Guilford Press.

McAdams, D. P. and Losoff, M. 1994. Friendship motivation in fourth and sixth graders: A thematic analysis. *Journal of Social and Personal Relationships* 1: 11–27.

McAdams, D. P., Diamond, A., de St. Aubin, E. and Mansfield, E. 1997. Stories of Commitment: The psychosocial construction of generative lives. *Journal of Personality and Social Psychology* 72: 678–694.

McAdams, D. P., Hoffman, B. J., Mansfield, E. D. and Day, R. 1996. Themes of agency and communion in significant autobiographical scenes. *Journal of Personality* 64: 339–377.

McCrae, R. R. 1993–94. Openness to experience as a basic dimension of personality. *Imagination, Cognition and Personality* 13: 39–55.

McCrae, R. R. and Costa, P. T. 1997. Personality trait structure as a human universal. *American Psychologist* 52: 509–516.

McGuire, W. J. and McGuire, C. V. 1988. Content and process in the experience of self. In L. Berkowitz (ed.), *Advances in experimental social psychology* 21: 97–144. New York: Academic Press.

Moffitt, K. H. and Singer, J. A. 1994. Continuity in the life story: Self-defining memories, affect, and approach/avoidance personal strivings. *Journal of Personality* 62: 21–43.

Moffitt, K. H., Singer, J. A., Nelligan, D. W., Carlson, M. A. and Vyse, S. A. 1994. Depression and memory narrative type. *Journal of Abnormal Psychology* 103: 581–583.

Nelson, K. 1993. The psychological and social origins of autobiographical memory. *Psychological Science* 4: 7–13.

Pruzinsky, T. and Borkovec, T. D. 1990. Cognitive and personality characteristics of worriers. *Behaviour Research and Therapy* 28:507–512.

Rogers, C. R. 1959. A theory of therapy, personality, and interpersonal relationships, as developed in the client-centered framework. In S.Koch (ed.), *Psychology: A study of a science* 3: 184–256. New York: McGraw-Hill.

Sadler, I. 1994. *Earliest memory of racial identity and prejudice*. Unpublished master's thesis, Connecticut College, London.

Segal, B., Huba, G. J. and Singer, J. L. 1980. *Drugs, daydreaming and personality: A study of college youth*. Hillsdale, NJ: Erlbaum.

Singer, J. A. 1990. Affective responses to autobiographical memories and their relationship to long-term goals. *Journal of Personality* 58: 535–563.

Singer, J. A. 1995. Seeing one's self: Locating narrative memory in a framework of personality. *Journal of Personality* 63: 429–457.

Singer, J. A. 1997. *Message in a bottle: Stories of men and addiction*. New York: The Free Press.

Singer, J. A. and Moffitt, K. H. 1991–1992. An experimental investigation of specificity and generality in memory narratives. *Imagination, Cognition, and Personality* 11: 233–257.

Singer, J. A. and Salovey, P. 1993. *The remembered self: Emotion and memory in personality*. New York: Free Press.

Singer, J. A. and Salovey, P. 1995. Motivated memory: Self-defining memories, goals, and affect regulation. In L. Martin and A. Tesser (eds*), Striving and feeling: Perspectives on the interplay of goals and affect.*. New York: Earlbaum.

Singer, J. A. and Singer, J. L. 1992. Transference in psychotherapy and daily life: Implications of current memory and social cognition research. In J. W. Barron, M. N. eagle, and D. L. Wolitzky (eds) *Interface of psychoanalysis and psychology* 516–538. Washington DC: American Psychological Association.

Singer, J. L. 1966. *Daydreaming*. New York: Random House.

Singer, J. L. 1974. Daydreaming and the stream of thought. *American Scientist* 62: 417–425.

Singer, J. L. 1975. Navigating the stream of consciousness: Research in daydreaming and related inner experience. *American Psychologist* 30: 727–738.

Singer, J. L. 1981–82. Towards the scientific study of imagination. *Imagination, Cognition, and Personality* 1: 1–5.

Singer, J. L. 1985. Transference and the human condition: A cognitive-affective perspective. *Psychoanalytic Psychology* 2: 189–219.

Singer, J. L. and Bonnano, G. A. 1990. Personality and private experience: Individual variations in consciousness and in attention to subjective phenomena. In L. Pervin (ed.), *Handbook of personality* 419–444. New York: Guilford Press.

Singer, J. L. and Brown, S. L. 1977. The experience-type: Some behavioral correlates and theoretical implications. In M. A. Rickers-Orsiankina (ed.). *Rorschach psychology* 325–374. Huntington, NY: Krieger.

Singer, J. L. and Kolligian, J. 1987. Personality: Developments in the study of private experience. *Annual Review of Psychology* 38: 533–574.

Singer, J. L. and McCraven, V. 1961. Some characteristics of adult daydreaming. *Journal of Psychology* 51: 151–164.

Singer, J. L. and Salovey, P. 1991. Organized knowledge structures in personality: Schemas, self-schemas, prototypes, and scripts. In M. Horowitz (ed.), *Person schemas* 33–79. Chicago: University of Chicago Press.

Singer, J. L. and Schonbar, R. 1961. Correlates of daydreaming: Dimensions of self-awareness. *Journal of Consulting Psychology* 25: 1–17.

Smith, D. and Over, R. 1991. Male sexual fantasy: Multidimensionality in content. *Behaviour Research and Therapy* 29: 267–275.

Strauman, T. J. 1992. Self-guides, autobiographical memory, and anxiety and dysphoria: Toward a cognitive model of vulnerability to emotional distress. *Journal of Abnormal Psychology* 101: 87–95.

Strauman, T. J. 1994. Introduction: Social cognition, psychodynamic psychology, and the representation and processing of emotionally significant information. *Journal of Personality* 62: 451–458.

Strauman, T. J. and Higgins, E. T. 1988. Self-discrepancies as predictors of vulnerability to distinct syndromes of chronic emotional distress. *Journal of Personality* 56: 685–707.

Strauman, T. J. and Lemieux, A. and Coe, C. 1993. Self-discrepancy and natural killer cell activity: Immunological consequences of negative self-evaluation. *Journal of Personality and Social Psychology* 64: 1042–1052.

Tang, Zhiyan, and Singer, J. L. 1997. Daydreaming Styles, Emotionality and the Big Five Personality Dimensions. *Imagination, Cognition and Personality* 16(4) 399–414.

Thorne, A. 1995a. Developmental truths in memories of childhood and adolescence. *Journal of Personality* 63: 139–163.

Thorne, A. 1995b. Juxtaposed scripts, traits, and the dynamics of personality. *Journal of Personality* 63: 593–616.

Thorne, A., Cutting, L. and Skaw, D. (in press). Young adults' relationship memories and the life story: Examples or essential landmarks? *Narrative Inquiry*.

Tomkins, S. S. 1979. Script theory: Differential magnification of affects. In H. E. Howe and R. A. Dienstbier (eds), *Nebraska symposium on motivation* 26: 201–236. Lincoln: University of Nebraska Press.

Tulving, E. 1972. Episodic and semantic memory. In E. Tulving and W. Donaldson (eds) *Organization of memory*. New York: Academic Press.

Tulving, E. 1983. *Elements of episodic memory*. New York: Oxford University Press.

Tulving, E. 1989. Memory: Performance, knowledge, and experience. *European Journal of Cognitive Psychology* 1: 3–26.

Tulving, E. 1993. What is episodic memory. *Current Directions in Psychological Science* 2: 67–70.

Westen, D. 1998. Unconscious thought, feeling, and motivation: The end of a century-long debate. In R. F. Bornstein and J. M. Masling (eds) *Empirical Studies of Psychoanalytic Theories* 7: 1–43.

Individual Differences in Self-Conscious Source Monitoring

Theoretical, Experimental, and Clinical Considerations

Robert G. Kunzendorf
University of Massachusetts Lowell

Theoretical Considerations

Any theoretical understanding of self-consciousness must begin with Gustav Fechner (1860/1966), William James (1890), and Morton Prince (1910, 1921, 1925) — all of whom grounded their theoretical frameworks on Leibniz's psychophysical parallelism. Unlike Descartes (1650/1892), who reduced the mind to an immaterial 'subject of consciousness' and the body to a physical 'object of consciousness', Leibniz (1765/1896) reduced the mind to a 'stream of conscious sensations' paralleling the dynamics of neural activity. Accordingly, whereas Descartes assumed that unconscious stimulation becomes an 'object of consciousness' only during perception by a self-conscious 'subject of consciousness', Leibniz posited that weak stimulation can yield 'subliminal sensation' (i.e., conscious sensation below the limen for self-consciousness *that one is perceiving the sensation*).

Fechner's Theoretical Position

Following Leibniz's lead, Fechner (1860/1966) developed both a scientific procedure for measuring supraliminal sensations and a psychophysical equation for extrapolating subliminal sensations. Fechner also theorized, in general, that parallelism should be construed as double-aspect materialism and, in particular, that supraliminal sensations and subliminal sensations should be deemed 'subjective aspects' of the same neural activity. James and Prince picked up on one of the most important implications of this: that *the experience of self as a subject* "which in some sense *has*, not *is*, its different [objects of consciousness]" (Campbell 1957, p. 81) is *just an illusory experience paralleling a neural function which, sometimes, accompanies sensations and, othertimes, does not*. The particular neural function paralleled by such illusory self-consciousness is a critical issue, however, on which James and Prince and the current author have developed different theoretical positions.

James' Theoretical Position

James (1890) noted that many students of consciousness mistake self-concept (the representation of self as an 'object of consciousness') for self-consciousness (the illusory experience of self as 'subject of consciousness').[1] Focusing on self-consciousness, James sought to explain why constantly changing sensations are accompanied by the illusion of an unchanging 'subject of consciousness', to which the sensations seemingly "belong". His explanation was that the process of remembering these changing sensations produces an unchanging 'raw feel' of familiarity, creating the illusion of a Cartesian subject to which the sensations previously belonged.

James' equation of self-consciousness with this 'raw feel', this subjective aspect of working memory, stands in contrast to Baars' (1988) attempt to turn working memory into a *physical* 'subject of consciousness'. Specifically, Baars has suggested that nonconscious representations from low-level processors throughout the nervous system become "conscious events [which] are *objectlike*" (p. 187) whenever such representations "gain access to the global workspace" or working memory (p. 43). Baars' (personal communications, February 12 and April 10, 1996) notion of a physical 'subject of consciousness' begs the question, however, of how any physical entity can be "conscious of" another physical entity (and why any entity other than the Global Workspace cannot be). Memory-based theories of consciousness should be framed in terms of Leibniz's parallelism and James' feeling of familiarity, not in terms of Descartes' subject/object dualism, if theoretical understanding is to be advanced.

Indeed, at the beginning of this century, James' equation of self-consciousness with raw familiarity advanced the hypothesis that various manifestations of plural selfhood — from multiple personality disorder (MPD) at one extreme, to normally forgotten dreaming at the other extreme — are attributable to dissociated memory systems. According to James' *1896 Lowell lectures* (Taylor 1984), some MPD patients have dissociated memory systems that are totally nonoverlapping, and alternating personalities that are totally amnestic for each other, whereas other MPD patients have memory systems that are hierarchically dissociated, and alternating personalities that are unidirectionally amnestic. Furthermore, according to James, some dissociatively disordered patients have dissociated memory systems which coexist rather than alternate — when, for example, one personality orally denies feeling a prick during hysterical anesthesia and, at the same time, a secondary personality "automatically writes" a description of the pain. In mentally healthy people, normally integrated personality is only dissociated from secondary personalities which arise in dream life.

Prince's Theoretical Position

Prince (1925) took issue with James' suggestion that the contemporaneous operation of dissociated memory systems gives rise to a plurality of independently self-conscious entities:

> A plurality of coexisting selves is theoretically possible, particularly as we know that in the complex conditions of so-called multiple personality, dual (or more) selves occur, but....the empirical evidence entirely denies self-awareness to such coconscious experiences. The introspective testimony of my dissociated subjects, who in [the hypnotic] condition recalled vividly and precisely these subconscious experiences, has been unanimous that these experiences were without self-consciousness....The conscious events were just sensations. (p. 182)

Thus, in cases where automatic writing about pain coexists with oral reporting of no pain, Prince interpreted the pain as a subliminal sensation accompanied by the feeling of familiarity, but not by the illusion of self-consciousness. Applying this interpretation to case after case of multiple personality, Prince (1921) described how a secondary personality with conscious emotion but no self-consciousness emerges into coexistence with the dominant personality, immediately before the secondary personality takes over self-consciousness from the dominant personality. No alternating of multiple personalities would occur without this coexistence and the emotional conflict it engenders, and no duplication of self-consciousness can occur while the conflicting personalities coexist. Moreover, from Prince's standpoint, the restrictive focus of self-consciousness in automatic writing and multiple personality stands in contrast to the lack of self-consciousness in dreaming. Throughout normal dreaming, many conscious sensations come and go alongside many feelings of familiarity, some based on wakefully encoded memories, but self-consciousness never makes an appearance until the dawn of wakefulness itself.

Even as Prince's position undercuts James equation of self-consciousness with raw familiarity, it has two weaknesses of its own. First, it fails to account for lucid dreaming or "the attainment of self-reflective consciousness during dreaming" (Kahan & LaBerge 1994, p. 254). Second, it fails to specify any functional underpinnings for self-consciousness. Both of these weaknesses are remedied by Kunzendorf's theoretical refinement of Prince's position.

Kunzendorf's Theoretical Position

According to Kunzendorf (1987–1988), the illusory experience of a self-conscious subject 'having' sensations is subjectively manifested as either the tacit knowledge *that one is 'imaging' sensations* or the sensationless knowledge *that one is 'perceiving' them*. Furthermore, the tacit knowledge *that one is imaging* is the subjective aspect of a neural mechanism monitoring the central innervation of sensations, and the tacit knowledge *that one is perceiving* is the subjective quality of the same mechanism monitoring the peripheral excitation of sensations. It is important to note that the source-monitoring mechanism itself is not 'conscious of' sensations or their source of innervation. Rather, this neural mechanism physically monitors the source of particular sensations, and such physical monitoring is paralleled subjectively by a sensationless disposition to treat those sensations as either 'imaginally generated by the self' or 'perceptually given to the self'. Present in either instance of source monitoring is the generic self-awareness *that one is 'having' sensations*–in the absence of any Cartesian subject actually 'having' sensations or being 'conscious of' them. This generic self-consciousness, when it accompanies varying sensations, is both sensationless and invariant. Hence, "I am not aware of my *self* as a content of consciousness along with other contents…but of my thoughts as mine" (Cavell 1987, p. 60).

Without recourse to Descartes' subject/object dualism, then, Kunzendorf's source-monitoring theory of self-consciousness allows one to experience oneself from both a mental perspective and a physical perspective. Accordingly, if one is self-consciously perceiving some of the gray hair ontop one's head or some of the gray matter inside one's brain, then one is self-consciously aware that the experience of gray fibers is generated perceptually, externally, *physically*. On the other hand, if one is self-consciously imaging a Cartesian soul inside a brain, then one is self-consciously aware that the experience of a soul inside a brain can only be generated imaginally, internally, *mentally*.

Like Prince's theoretical position, Kunzendorf's source-monitoring theory allows one to experience sensations with self-consciousness, or without self-consciousness. For example, if one images a blue sky during normal wakefulness, the sensations of blueness are accompanied by self-consciousness *that one is imaging*. In contrast, if one dreams of a blue sky during normal sleep, the blue sensations are accompanied by no self-consciousness. Moreover, Kunzendorf's theory allows for the possibility that lucid dreams are not self-consciously monitored and are not directly experienced as imaginary but, rather, are indirectly inferred to be imaginary. For example, while riding in the backseat of a car full of strangers, one of my students dreamed that she was being strangled by a monster, became aware that she "must be dreaming" of this monster, then nonlucidly dreamed that she had awoken and was really being strangled by the girl riding in the backseat with her. Most likely, the bizarreness of the monster enabled her indirectly to infer that she "must be dreaming", but she was not sufficiently self-conscious to monitor the central innervation directly or to know *that she was dreaming* all the time.

Also like Prince's position, Kunzendorf's source-monitoring theory has a variety of clinical implications — extending not only to dissociative phenomena, such as multiple personality disorder, but also to psychotic phenomena. However, before considering clinical issues per se, let us consider the experimental evidence in support of the source-monitoring theory of self-consciousness.

Experimental Considerations

An experimental paradigm for measuring self-conscious source monitoring has evolved from Kunzendorf's (1979) finding that, during normal self-consciousness, percepts are distinguished more quickly from vivid images than from faint images — notwithstanding the fact that percepts appear to be more similar to vivid images. Kunzendorf's explanation for this paradoxical finding is that the neural mechanism for monitoring the 'source of innervation' of sensations, when given more vividly imaged sensations, registers a greater amount of 'central innervation' and more quickly produces self-consciousness *that one is imaging*. Experimental and clinical conditions under which such self-conscious monitoring ceases, or attenuates, have been explored in some of Kunzendorf's more recent studies, which will be reviewed after details of the paradigm are described.

On each trial in the computerized version of this paradigm, then, participants fixate on a dot, perceive a visual stimulus to one side, image an identical stimulus on the other side and rate its vividness while continuing to image. Immediately thereafter, either the dot becomes an *I* and subjects press a button on the side of the *i*mage, as quickly as possible, or the dot becomes a *P* and subjects press a button on the side of the *p*ercept. After 28 such trials, each participant's image/percept discrimination times are plotted over his or her image vividness ratings, and the *within-subject slope* or regression coefficient is computed. As Figure 1 illustrates, a negative slope indicates that percepts are more quickly discriminated from vivid images than from faint images — *as if the brain is able to monitor a greater amount of 'central innervation' behind any image which, subjectively, is more vivid and more percept-like*. In contrast, a positive slope indicates that percepts are more slowly discriminated from more vivid images — as if the brain is no longer *self-consciously monitoring* the 'central innervation' of images and, instead, is more slowly *inferring* the nonperceptual character of vivid images.

In one study based on this paradigm, Kunzendorf (1985/1986) predicted that positive within-subject slope, reflecting the attenuation of self-conscious source monitoring, would manifest in the sleeplike state of hypnosis. An earlier study by Kunzendorf, Brown, and McGee (1983) revealed that highly hypnotizable persons get very little sleep, and a recent study by Rader, Kunzendorf, and Carrabino (1996) showed that attenuated source-monitoring during nonhypnotic wakefulness is associated with getting too little sleep. The induction of hypnotic sleep, therefore, seems like an appropriate method to employ in the experimental study of self-conscious source monitoring.

In the 1985/1986 study employing hypnosis, 30 randomly sampled participants were administered the source-monitoring paradigm twice: once, prior to the induction of hypnosis and, once again, under the influence of hypnosis. Prior to hypnotic induction, the 30 participants exhibited significantly *negative* within-subject *slope* ($M = -.03$, $SD = .05$, $t = 2.78$, $p < .01$), which did not correlate significantly with greater hypnotizability ($r = -.03$). Under the influence of hypnosis, the 30 participants no longer exhibited negative within-subject slope ($M = .01$, $SD = .05$), and the change from their prehypnotic slopes to their hypnotic slopes was a significant change in the direction of greater positivity ($M = .04$, $SD = .06$, $t = 3.70$, $p < .001$). Moreover, greater hypnotizability correlated positively both with higher within-subject slope during hypnosis ($r = .47$, $p < .01$) and with greater change between prehypnotic and hypnotic slopes ($r = .40$, $p < .01$).

In other words, hypnosis attenuates source monitoring in those individuals who are highly hypnotizable, and yields dreamlike sensations which are unaccompanied by waking self-consciousness *that one is imaging* or *that one is perceiving*. During hypnotic imaging, these dreamlike sensations constitute positive hallucinations whenever they are incorrectly inferred to be perceptual in origin, and constitute pseudohallucinations whenever they are lucidly inferred to be imaginal in source. Even a *faint* hypnotic image of a deceased pet would be a positive hallucination if it were inferred to be the ghost of the deceased animal, whereas this hypnotically 'unmonitored' image would be a pseudohallucination if it were inferred to be imaginary on account of its transparency.

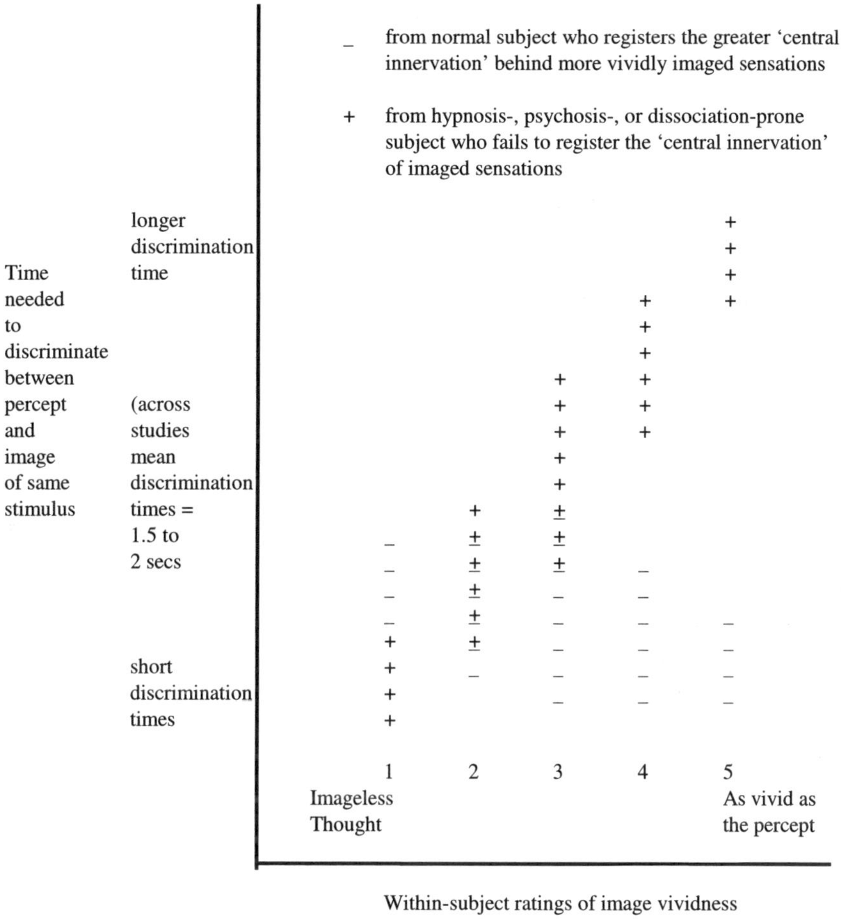

Figure 1. *Hypothetical 28-trial scattergram from a normal subject during wakeful self-consciousness and from a hypnotized, psychosis-prone, or dissociation-prone subject during the attenuation of self-conscious source monitoring*

During hypnotic perceiving, however, 'unmonitored' dreamlike sensations would constitute *dissociated percepts*, as experimental research by Kunzendorf, Beltz, and Tymowicz (1991–1992) has confirmed. In the latter research, 9 deeply hypnotized college students, 9 autistic adolescents, and 18 control subjects participated in two experimental procedures — one testing for deficiencies in self-concept, and one testing for deficiencies in self-consciousness.

The test of self-concept was a variation of Gallup's (1979) test of mirrored self-recognition, in which the participants could not directly see a white line inside a box on their lap, but could view the line in a televised mirror image. When instructed to touch the line, the deeply hypnotized students and the control subjects reached toward the actual line occluded inside the box, whereas the autistic adolescents reached towards the televised line. Thus, autistic adolescents' concepts of self, as spatially related to the mirror image and the occluded line, were deficient in Kunzendorf, Beltz, and Tymowicz's first test.

In the second test, a newly developed test of self-consciousness, the participants were instructed to use a televised mirror-image to move their hands together until touching, but were not told that they were actually seeing a pre-recorded tape of their hands struggling unsuccessfully to touch. When their hands made contact tactually but not visually, the autistic adolescents and control subjects confirmed that their fingertips were actually touching, whereas the deeply hypnotized students denied that their tactually joined hands were touching. Thus, hypnotized students' hand-touching sensations were dissociated, neurally, from the source-monitoring mechanism and, subjectively, from the incontrovertible self-awareness *that one is perceiving the hands touching (and not imaging them touching).*

Kunzendorf, Beltz, and Tymowicz's experimental distinction between self-concept and self-consciousness has important implications for normal and abnormal development, in light of experimental research with human children. Anderson's (1984) and Hart and Fegley's (1994) review articles suggest that the normal child does not exhibit mirrored self-recognition until 18–24 months of age, by which time he or she has developed a visually and spatially sophisticated concept of self. Freudian psychology erroneously equates such ego development with the differentiation of self from outside sources. However, Watson's (1994) experimental findings suggest that self-consciousness of source does not develop at all, but is prewired into the infant's brain: Watson found that the human infant at 3–5 months of age is capable of discriminating televised mirror-images of self-generated movements from televised images of another infant's movements. By implication, the deficient self-concept of the autistic child is unconnected to the deficient self-consciousness of the schizophrenic, despite misleading connections suggested by Freudians like Mahler (1952). Let us now consider schizophrenic psychosis and other clinical manifestations of deficient self-consciousness.

Clinical Considerations

From the standpoint of source-monitoring theory, psychotic hallucinations and delusions, dissociative percepts and amnesias, and even phobic images reflect an underlying deficiency in self-consciousness. The differences among these disorders and other individual differences in self-consciousness stem from the fact that source monitoring is a two-stage process — in which self-conscious monitoring, if not fully functional, is succeeded by less direct efforts to infer the source of sensations. The following subsections demonstrate how these inferences differ qualitatively from one disorder to the next, while the underlying deficiency in self-conscious source monitoring remains the same.

Psychotic Hallucinations and Delusions

The notion that psychotic hallucinations are dreamlike images devoid of self-consciousness is evident in the work of Freud (1924). And as Johnson (1988) and Kunzendorf (1992–1993) point out, psychotic delusions tend to be 'unmonitored' images about past or future happenings, whereas hallucinations are almost always 'unmonitored' images of present happenings.

In an empirical study of both individual differences in psychoticism and individual differences in self-conscious source monitoring, Kunzendorf, Moran, and Gray (1995–1996) administered Overall and Gomez-Mont's (1974) MMPI-168 and Kunzendorf's (1979) source-monitoring paradigm to 149 college students. As results across the MMPI psychoticism scales in Table 1 show, the students who scored higher on either the Paranoia scale or the Mania scale had more positive within-subject slopes: In other words, these psychosis-prone students took longer to discriminate percepts from vivid images than from faint images, as if they failed neurally to monitor the greater 'central innervation' behind more vivid images (as in Fig. 1) and failed subjectively to experience the normal self-awareness *that one is imaging sensations.*

It is important to note that the psychosis-prone students in the rightmost columns of Table 1 were not psychotic. Most of them were able correctly to *infer* that fainter sensations were imaged sensations, even though they were not immediately self-conscious *that they were imaging*. However, a subset of the students did exhibit psychotic inferences during the source-monitoring paradigm, as well as during a query regarding religious fantasy. Specifically, the 9 subjects who reportedly "have heard God speak to [them]" were deficient in self-conscious source monitoring (as the positive slope of 33.3 in Table 2 indicates), and were at chance levels in inferring the correct sources (as the .55 proportion of correctness in Table 2 indicates).

Table 1. *Results from Kunzendorf, Moran, and Gray (1995–1996): Mean Within-S Slope (Mean Regression Coefficient for Discrimination-Time over Image-Vividness as in Fig. 1), broken down by MMPI-168 Psychoticism Scales (Pa = paranoia, Sc = schizophrenia, Ma = mania) and by T-scores*

Psychoticism Scale		T-scores (higher = greater psychoticism)				
		T<50	50≤T<60	60≤T<70	70≤T<80	80≤T
Pa	***Slope******	**-9.8**[<]	**-1.8**	**1.5**	**1.1**	**27.4**[>>]
	[*S*]	[40.7]	[53.5]	[55.5]	[42.1]	[31.7]
	[*n*]	[48]	[44]	[25]	[20]	[12]
Sc	***Slope***	**-5.0**	**-3.2**	**-6.9**	**11.2**	**11.1**
	[*S*]	[63.9]	[37.6]	[35.7]	[68.5]	[36.9]
	[*n*]	[33]	[51]	[31]	[14]	[20]
Ma	***Slope******	**-13.2**[<]	**-1.5**	**5.4**	**11.2**	
	[*S*]	[39.8]	[50.9]	[53.0]	[32.2]	
	[*n*]	[36]	[58]	[38]	[17]	[0]

[*] linear increase of slope across higher T-score groups, two-tailed $p < .05$
[<] less than zero slope, 1–tailed $p < .05$
[<<] less than zero slope, 1–tailed $p < .01$
[>] greater than zero slope, 1–tailed $p < .05$
[>>] greater than zero slope, 1–tailed $p < .01$

Kunzendorf, Moran, and Gray (1995–1996) argue that people with deficient source monitoring only generate psychotic inferences for defensive purposes. For example, a depressed person with an 'unmonitored' image of a recently deceased relative talking about heaven might infer that he or she is being visited by the relative's ghost, in order to defend against the correct inference that such heavenly visits are purely imaginary. Or in a culture hostile to gay people, a young person with 'unmonitored' homoerotic imagery might infer that it is being beamed into his or her head by the C.I.A. or the devil, in order to defend against the correct inference that such imagery is self-generated. It is noteworthy that, in either of these two cases, if the person's imagery were self-consciously monitored rather than 'unmonitored', then the person would probably be depressed by his or her self-conscious knowledge. Indeed, Nietzsche (1892/1954) described certain depressed persons as "over-awake" (p. 43) — consistent with Kunzendorf, Moran, and Gray's finding that existentially depressed persons exhibit higher levels of self-conscious source monitoring (i.e., negative slope) rather than proneness to psychosis.

Table 2. *Results from Kunzendorf, Moran, and Gray (1995–1996): Image/Percept Discrimination and Mean Within-S Slope, broken down by Reports of Religious Hallucinating, Religious Imaging, or Neither*

	Proportion of image-percept pairings that were discriminated correctly*	Within-S slope (within-S regression coefficient) for discrimination-time over vividness, as in Figure 1
Subjects who reportedly "have heard God speak to [them]"	***M*=.55** [*S*=.21] [*n*=9]	***M*=33.3**> [*S*=50.1] [*n*=9]
Subjects who reportedly "have imagined hearing God speak to [them]"	***M*=.72**# [*S*=.23] [*n*=61]	***M*=-6.2** [*S*=56.5] [*n*=61]
Subjects who reportedly "have neither heard nor imagined hearing God"	***M*=.72**# [*S*=.24] [*n*=79]	***M*=-1.1** [*S*=37.4] [*n*=79]

*The proportion of correct discriminations did not correlate significantly with scores on scale Pa ($r = .04$) or scale Sc ($r = .07$) or scale Ma ($r = .07$) from Table 1, or any other basic clinical scale of the MMPI-168.

#significantly different from .5 or chance level of correctness, $t > 7.33$, $p < .05$.

>significantly greater than zero slope, $t(8) = 1.99$, one-tailed $p < .05$, and significantly different from mean slope of the other 140 subjects, $F(1,146) = 5.29$, $p < .05$.

Dissociative Percepts and Amnesias

The view that dissociative percepts are experienced as dreamlike sensations and are recalled as dreamlike memories, if they are recalled at all, has been revived by Bliss (1986). Reframed into the terms of monitoring theory, then, dissociative percepts are sensations which, neurally, are not monitored for source and, subjectively, are not paralleled by self-consciousness *that one is perceiving*.

In a study measuring individual differences in dissociation, as well as differences in self-conscious source monitoring, Kunzendorf and Karpen (1996–1997) found monitoring deficiencies (i.e., positive slopes as in Fig. 1) in students who scored higher on Bernstein and Putnam's (1986) Dissociative Experiences Scale. In addition, Kunzendorf (1989–1990) and Kunzendorf and Moran (1993–1994) showed that dissociative amnesia stems from source amnesia — wherein dissociative percepts can be remembered as 'familiar' if familiarity is the only memory criterion, but cannot be remembered as 'perceived' if source criteria are invoked.

Thus theoretically, psychosis and dissociation reflect the same underlying deficiency in self-conscious source monitoring. Psychosis emerges from this deficiency when imaginal sensations are 'unmonitored' and are defensively inferred to be percepts, whereas dissociation emerges when perceptual sensations are 'unmonitored' and are defensively inferred to be images. For example, in the latter case, a person with 'unmonitored' percepts of sexual abuse might defensively infer that the abuse is not really happening, and might subsequently remember it as part of a bad dream or, if source criteria prevail, not remember it at all. And by implication, there is nothing to prevent this same person from having 'unmonitored' images which, if traumatic, should lead to psychotic inferences. Indeed, consistent with this important implication of monitoring theory, Kluft (1987) observed 'first rank' psychotic symptoms in 30 out of 30 patients with multiple personality disorder, the most severe of the dissociative disorders.

Phobic Images

From the cognitive perspective of Beck (1976), people with cynophobia do not fear dogs per se, but imagine and fear being bitten; people with acrophobia do not fear heights per se, but imagine and fear falling from such heights; and people with claustrophobia do not fear tight spaces per se, but imagine and fear being suffocated. And yet, images of suffocating or falling or being bitten by a dog do not elicit strong emotional responses in all people.

Kunzendorf, Francis, Ward, Cohen, Cutler, Walsh, and Berenson (1996–1997) discovered that the person who is most strongly responsive to such imagery is the one who is not self-conscious of its imaginal source. In their study of 60 students, Kunzendorf et al. (1996–1997, Experiment 2) administered Kunzendorf's (1979) source-monitoring paradigm and, then, measured each student's blood pressure before and after he or she imagined "being held at gunpoint inside a hijacked airplane…hearing a crazed terrorist shout at you again and again in a language that you do not understand…seeing him wave his gun repeatedly in your face…[and] feeling the barrel of the gun bump into your forehead and your cheek". Across all 60 students, the image-induced increase in diastolic blood pressure was 3.5 mm on average. However, for the 13 students with source-monitoring deficiencies (i.e., both a positive slope, as in Fig. 1, and a below-median proportion of correct image/percept discriminations), the image-induced increase in diastolic blood pressure was 8.0 mm on average — significantly higher than the pooled mean for the other 47 students. Moreover, for the 5 students with above-median vividness of imagery, as well as the source-monitoring deficiencies above, the image-induced increase in diastolic blood pressure was 15.0 mm on average--significantly higher than the pooled mean for the other 55 students.

Thus, the college students who were most affected physiologically by an imaginary hijacking were those who were not self-conscious of its imaginal source. But despite this deficiency in self-conscious source monitoring, the affected students were surely not psychotic, just as patients with simple phobias are not psychotic. When phobic patients imagine and fear being bitten by a dog or a spider, one part of them fails to monitor the "central innervation" of their sensations of being bitten, but another part of them infers and discriminates the imaginal nature of these sensations. In contrast, when psychotically paranoid patients hallucinate being bitten by a blasphemy-inducing spider or being hijacked by a sexually perverted alien, they not only fail to monitor the "central innervation" behind such imaging, but also fail to discriminate any of the phenomenally inferable differences between imaged and perceived sensations — presumably because they are motivated to infer that the blasphemy or perversion is not self-generated.

Final Considerations

During normal wakefulness, one's sensations are subjectively accompanied by the tacit quality *that one is 'having' sensations*. This self-consciousness *that one is 'having' sensations* is the generic manifestation of either the tacit quality *that one is imaging sensations* or the tacit quality *that one is perceiving sensations*. Moreover, the tacit quality *that one is imaging* is the subjective aspect of a neural mechanism monitoring the central innervation of sensations, and the tacit quality *that one is perceiving* is the subjective quality of the same mechanism monitoring the peripheral excitation of sensations.

Paradoxically, because this neural mechanism monitors a greater amount of "central innervation" during more vivid imaging, percepts are self-consciously discriminated more quickly from vivid percept-like images than from faint images. But for some individuals, the neural mechanism behind self-conscious source monitoring is not fully functional and, as a result, percepts are inferentially discriminated more quickly from faint images than from vivid percept like images. In particular, hypnotized individuals, psychosis-prone individuals, dissociation-prone individuals, and phobic individuals are demonstratively not self-conscious of the self-generated nature of their imagery, although they can still infer that their imagery is too faint or too bizarre to be real.

Ultimately, the fact that most individuals' imaginal sensations occur *with* the self-conscious quality *that one is imaging them*, but some individuals' imaginal sensations occur *without* this self-conscious quality, requires us to return either to the psychophysical parallelism of Leibniz (1765/1896) or to the double-aspect materialism of Fechner (1860/1966). The theory of self-conscious source monitoring represents a return to double-aspect materialism.

Notes

1. For instance, Kihlstrom (1987) made this mistake when he asserted that "in order for ongoing experience, thought, and action to become conscious, a link must be made between its mental representation and some mental representation of the self" (p. 1451). In contrast with Kihlstrom and in accordance with William James (1890), Kunzendorf, Beltz, and Tymowicz (1991–1992) empirically distinguished self-concept or self-representation from self-consciousness, through an experiment detailed in this chapter.

References

Anderson, J.R. 1984. "The development of self-recognition: A Review". *Developmental Psychobiology* 17: 35–49.

Baars, B.J. 1988. *A Cognitive Theory of Consciousness*. New York: Cambridge University Press.

Beck, A.T. 1976. *Cognitive Therapy and the Emotional Disorders*. New York: International Universities.

Bernstein, E.M. and Putnam, F. 1986. "Development, reliability, and validity of a dissociation scale". *Journal of Nervous and Mental Disease* 174: 727–735.

Bliss, E.L. 1986. *Multiple Personality, Allied Disorders, and Hypnosis*. New York: Oxford University Press.

Campbell, C.A. 1957. *On Selfhood and Godhood*. New York: Macmillan.

Cavell, M. 1987. "A response to Otto Kernberg's 'The dynamic unconscious and the self'". In R. Stern (ed.), *Theories of the Unconscious and Theories of the Self*. London: Analytic Press, 58–63.

Descartes, R. 1892. *Passions of the Soul* (H.A.P. Torrey, trans.). New York: Henry Holt. (Original work published 1650)

Fechner, G.T. 1966. *Elements of Psychophysics* (H.E. Adler, trans.). New York: Holt, Rinehard, and Winston. (Original work published 1860)

Freud, S. 1924. "The loss of reality in neurosis and psychosis". In A. Richards (ed.), *Penguin Freud Library* 10: 219–226.

Gallup, G. G. 1979. "Self-recognition in primates". *American Scientist* 67: 417–421.

Hart, D. and Fegley, S. 1994. "Social imitation and the emergence of a mental model of self". In S. T. Parker, R. W. Mitchell, and M. L. Boccia (eds.), *Self-Awareness in Animals and Humans*. Cambridge: Cambridge University Press, 149–165.

James, W. 1890. *The Principles of Psychology*. New York: Henry Holt.

Johnson, M. K. 1988. "Discriminating the origin of information". In T. F. Oltmanns and B. Maher (eds.), *Delusional beliefs*. New York: Wiley, 34–65.

Kahan, T. L. and LaBerge, S. 1994. "Lucid dreaming as metacognition: Implications for cognitive science". *Consciousness and Cognition* 3: 246–264.

Kihlstrom, J. F. 1987. "The cognitive unconscious". *Science* 237: 1445–1452.

Kluft, R. P. 1987. "First-rank symptoms as a diagnostic clue to Multiple Personality Disorder." *American Journal of Psychology* 144: 293–298.

Kunzendorf, R. G. 1985–1986. "Hypnotic hallucinations as 'unmonitored' images: An empirical study". *Imagination, Cognition, and Personality* 5: 255–270.

Kunzendorf, R. G. 1987–1988. "Self-consciousness as the monitoring of cognitive states: A theoretical perspective". *Imagination, Cognition, and Personality* 7: 3–22.

Kunzendorf, R. G. 1989–1990. "Posthypnotic amnesia: Dissociation of self-concept or self-consciousness?". *Imagination, Cognition, and Personality* 9: 321–334.

Kunzendorf, R. G. 1992–1993. "The effect of image vividness on reality monitoring". *Imagination, Cognition, and Personality* 12: 197–205.

Kunzendorf, R. G., Beltz, S. M. and Tymowicz, G. 1991–1992. "Self-awareness in autistic subjects and deeply hypnotized subjects: Dissociation of self-concept versus self-consciousness". *Imagination, Cognition, and Personality* 11: 129–141.

Kunzendorf, R. G., Brown, C. and McGee, D. 1983. "Hypnotizability: Correlations with daydreaming and Sleeping". *Psychological Reports* 53: 406.

Kunzendorf, R. G., Francis, L., Ward, J., Cohen, R., Cutler, J., Walsh, J. and Berenson, S. 1996–1997. "Effect of negative imaging on heart rate and blood pressure, as a function of image vividness and image 'realness'". *Imagination, Cognition, and Personality* 16: 139–159.

Kunzendorf, R. G. and Karpen, J. 1996–1997. "Dissociative experiences and reality-testing deficits in college students". *Imagination, Cognition, and Personality* 16: 227–238.

Kunzendorf, R. G. and Moran, C. 1993–1994. "Repression: Active censorship of stressful memories *versus* source amnesia for self-consciously dissociated memories". *Imagination, Cognition, and Personality* 13: 291–302.

Kunzendorf, R. G., Moran, C. and Gray, R. 1995–1996. "Personality traits and reality-testing abilities, controlling for vividness of imagery". *Imagination, Cognition, and Personality* 15: 113–131.

Leibniz, G. W. 1896. *New Essays Concerning the Understanding* (A. G. Langley, trans.). New York: Macmillan. (Original work published 1765)

Mahler, M. 1952. "On childhood psychosis and schizophrenia: Autistic and symbiotic infantile psychosis". *Psychoanalytic Study of the Child* 7: 286–305.

Nietzsche, F. 1954. *Thus Spoke Zarathustra* (W. Kaufmann, trans.). New York: Penguin Books. (Originally published 1892)

Overall, J. E. and Gomez-Mont, F. 1974. "The MMPI-168 for psychiatric screening". *Educational and Psychological Measurement* 34: 315–319.

Prince, M. 1910. "Chapter Five". In H. Münsterberg, T. Ribot, P. Janet, J. Jastrow, B. Hart, and M. Prince (eds.), *Subconscious Phenomena*. Boston: Gorham Press, 71–101.

Prince, M. 1921. *The Unconscious: The Fundamentals of Human Personality Normal and Abnormal* (2nd ed.). New York: Macmillan.

Prince, M. 1925. "Awareness, consciousness, co-consciousness and animal intelligence from the point of View of the data of abnormal psychology: A biological theory of consciousness". *Pedagogical Seminary* 32: 166–188.

Rader, C. M., Kunzendorf, R. G. and Carrabino, C. 1996. "The relation of imagery vividness, absorption, reality boundaries and synesthesia to hypnotic states and traits". In R. G. Kunzendorf, N. P. Spanos, and B. Wallace (eds.), *Hypnosis and Imagination*. Amityville, NY: Baywood, 99–121.

Taylor, E. 1984. *William James on Exceptional Mental States: The 1896 Lowell Lectures*. Amherst: University of Massachusetts Press.

Watson, J. S. 1994. "Detection of self: The perfect algorithm". In S. T. Parker, R. W. Mitchell, and M. L. Boccia (eds.), *Self-Awareness in Animals and Humans*. Cambridge: Cambridge University Press, 131–148.

Author Index

Z

Subject Index

In the series ADVANCES IN CONSCIOUSNESS RESEARCH (AiCR) the following titles have been published thus far or are scheduled for publication:

1. GLOBUS, Gordon G.: *The Postmodern Brain.* 1995.
2. ELLIS, Ralph D.: *Questioning Consciousness. The interplay of imagery, cognition, and emotion in the human brain.* 1995.
3. JIBU, Mari and Kunio YASUE: *Quantum Brain Dynamics and Consciousness. An introduction.* 1995.
4. HARDCASTLE, Valerie Gray: *Locating Consciousness.* 1995.
5. STUBENBERG, Leopold: *Consciousness and Qualia.* 1998.
6. GENNARO, Rocco J.: *Consciousness and Self-Consciousness. A defense of the higher-order thought theory of consciousness.* 1996.
7. MAC CORMAC, Earl and Maxim I. STAMENOV (eds): *Fractals of Brain, Fractals of Mind. In search of a symmetry bond.* 1996.
8. GROSSENBACHER, Peter G. (ed.): *Finding Consciousness in the Brain. A neuro-cognitive approach.* n.y.p.
9. Ó NUALLÁIN, Seán, Paul MC KEVITT and Eoghan MAC AOGÁIN (eds): *Two Sciences of Mind. Readings in cognitive science and consciousness.* 1997.
10. NEWTON, Natika: *Foundations of Understanding.* 1996.
11. PYLKKÖ, Pauli: *The Aconceptual Mind. Heideggerian themes in holistic naturalism.* 1998.
12. STAMENOV, Maxim I. (ed.): *Language Structure, Discourse and the Access to Consciousness.* 1997.
13. VELMANS, Max (ed.): *Investigating Phenomenal Consciousness. Methodologies and Maps.* n.y.p.
14. SHEETS-JOHNSTONE, Maxine: *The Primacy of Movement.* 1999.
15. CHALLIS, Bradford H. and Boris M. VELICHKOVSKY (eds.): *Stratification in Cognition and Consciousness.* 1999.
16. ELLIS, Ralph D. and Natika NEWTON (eds.): *The Caldron of Consciousness. Motivation, affect and self-organization - An anthology.* n.y.p.
17. HUTTO, Daniel D.: *The Presence of Mind.* 1999.
18. PALMER, Gary B. and Debra J. OCCHI (eds.): *Languages of Sentiment. Cultural constructions of emotional substrates.* 1999.
19. DAUTENHAHN, Kerstin (ed.): *Human Cognition and Social Agent Technology.* n.y.p.
20. KUNZENDORF, Robert G. and Benjamin WALLACE (eds.): *Individual Differences in Conscious Experience.* 2000.
21. HUTTO, Daniel D.: *Beyond Physicalism.* n.y.p.